The English Lyric
Tradition

The English Lyric Tradition

*Reading Poetic Masterpieces
of the Middle Ages
and Renaissance*

R. JAMES GOLDSTEIN

McFarland & Company, Inc., Publishers
Jefferson, North Carolina

LIBRARY OF CONGRESS CATALOGUING-IN-PUBLICATION DATA

Names: Goldstein, R. James, 1955– author.
Title: The English lyric tradition : reading poetic masterpieces of the Middle Ages and Renaissance / R. James Goldstein.
Description: Jefferson, North Carolina : McFarland & Company, Inc., Publishers, 2017. | Includes bibliographical references and index.
Identifiers: LCCN 2017006171 | ISBN 9781476664750 (softcover : acid free paper) ∞
Subjects: LCSH: English poetry—Middle English, 1100–1500. | English poetry—Early modern, 1500–1700. | Lyric poetry.
Classification: LCC PN691 .G66 2017 | DDC 809.1/4—dc23
LC record available at https://lccn.loc.gov/2017006171

BRITISH LIBRARY CATALOGUING DATA ARE AVAILABLE

ISBN (print) 978-1-4766-6475-0
ISBN (ebook) 978-1-4766-2756-4

© 2017 R. James Goldstein. All rights reserved

No part of this book may be reproduced or transmitted in any form or by any means, electronic or mechanical, including photocopying or recording, or by any information storage and retrieval system, without permission in writing from the publisher.

Front cover images:
Medieval illustration © 2016 Duncan Walker/iStock;
feather pen © 2017 Big_Ryan/iStock

Printed in the United States of America

McFarland & Company, Inc., Publishers
Box 611, Jefferson, North Carolina 28640
www.mcfarlandpub.com

For Barbara

Table of Contents

Acknowledgments	ix
Introduction—Canonical Forms	1
1. Vernacular Eloquence: Reading Older Poetry Rhetorically	11
2. What Was a Lyric Poem?	41
3. Anonymous Middle English Lyrics on the Virgin Mary	59
4. The Love Complaint Ballade: Chaucer and Wyatt	72
5. The Love Sonnet from Wyatt to Shakespeare	90
6. The Country House Poem: Lanyer and Jonson	132
7. The Pastoral Elegy: Milton's "Lycidas"	152
Coda—The Irish Dancer	183
Appendix—A Modified Version of Attridge's Scansion Symbols	185
Chapter Notes	187
Bibliography	207
Index	217

Acknowledgments

This book has been long in the making, and it is my pleasure to acknowledge the many people and institutions who helped make it possible. My oldest debt in matters poetical is to the late Anthony Hecht, whose course on the Lyric in English at the University of Rochester in 1974 first introduced me to many of the poems discussed in this book, and whose resonant voice helped teach me to listen to the sound of poetry. I am indebted to Alastair Fowler, who first introduced me to the theory of historical genres and expanded my poetic horizons in a graduate seminar on Renaissance poetry at the University of Virginia in 1979.

I am grateful to my department chair, Jeremy Downes, for his continued support, and to George Crandell, my former department head at Auburn University, for making possible a research leave in Spring 2009, when I began work on the book in earnest. I am also grateful to present and former colleagues in the Department of English for awarding me the privilege of holding the Hargis Professorship in English Literature from 2008 to 2013; without the reduced teaching load that came with this honor, my progress would have been slower. I wish to thank Anne Gramberg and Joseph Aistrup, the former and current dean of the College of Liberal Arts, for their support of the department's research mission. I also wish to thank the staff of the Ralph B. Draughon Library, Auburn University, especially Jaena Alabi, for help in obtaining materials. Three M.A. students served as my research assistants at the earlier stages of the project: Katharine Brown, Eric Anderson, and Christina Hildebrand; to each, my thanks.

I should thank the intrepid undergraduate students in my special topics course on the History of Lyric in Fall 2006, especially Douglas Anderson and Tawnysha Lynch Greene; I first conceived the idea of writing a book on early lyric poetry while teaching them. I am especially grateful to Caitlin Anderson, Paige Busby, Will Palmer, and Jeb Sharp, students in my graduate seminar on the Lyric in History and Theory in Spring 2015, for their many insights and for allowing me to try out some of my ideas on them.

For their support through the years, and especially for believing in this project, yet once more I owe a debt of gratitude to my former teachers and lifelong friends, Del Kolve and Tony Spearing. I also thank Paula Backscheider for her encouragement and advice. Friends and colleagues who read and commented on earlier drafts of one or more chapters of the book deserve to be mentioned here: Anya Riehl Bertolet, Bill Calin, Alex Dunlop, Steve Fallon, Kelly Jolley, Bobby Meyer-Lee, and Don Wehrs. I am also grateful to the two external readers for McFarland.

But my greatest debt of all is to Barbara Brumbaugh, who not only advised me on the manuscript at various stages of composition and generously shared her expertise in Renaissance literature, but also provided the emotional support I needed at every stage of the project. I dedicate this book to her: *Who will in fairest book of nature know / How virtue may best lodged in beauty be, / Let him but learn of love to read in thee.*

Introduction: Canonical Forms

It is no secret that of all the forms of creative writing, poetry finds the smallest audience. Although robust data for earlier periods are lacking, the number of adults who report that they read poetry seems to be in decline.[1] Even among the small percentage of adults who continue to read or listen to poetry as adults, relatively few seem to be interested in reading poetry that is not contemporary.[2] Outside the classroom, the number of readers of poetry from the Renaissance or earlier, with the possible exception of Shakespeare's sonnets, is very small indeed. Yet such readers do exist.

The following book is primarily addressed to students, teachers, creative writers, and educated general readers who wish to develop their ability to read early canonical forms of English poetry with greater understanding and appreciation, though I hope that professional scholars will find something of value in the book as well. For a very long time it was a central tenet of humanistic scholarship that the study of poetic masterpieces—an important part of what used to be called the literary canon—is an intrinsically valuable activity.[3] I propose to enlist poetry in precisely that humanistic cause, focusing on poems composed in English roughly between the years 1200 to 1645. I shall confine my attention to earlier *lyric* poetry, which for the time being may be defined as relatively short poetic compositions typically, though not invariably, voiced in the grammatical first person.

Learning to read earlier poetry in English is uniquely valuable, I suggest, in no small part because of its temporal and cultural distance from us on the one hand and the relative familiarity of its forms of linguistic invention on the other. Crafted with recognizable meter and usually with rhyme, older canonical lyric poetry has much to offer to speakers of the language, regardless of gender, ethnicity, race, nationality, class, religion, or any other markers of our social identities, although there is no denying that such differences serve as additional markers of interest and value.

It is often lamented, especially outside the academy, that the forces driving scholarly inquiry in the modern research university have led to increasingly narrow specializations. This circling of the wagons makes it difficult for scholars to communicate with others outside their own fields of expertise, much less with non-academics. Scholars in the humanities often hear complaints from the general public about the inaccessibility of their writing and the arcane nature of their research topics. The tendency toward specialization has meant that in recent decades relatively few literary scholars work across several historical periods. Although there are many books about early lyric poetry that cover much narrower periods of literary history, none devotes attention to more than a couple of centuries at most. Much more common are specialist studies that map out smaller pieces of the poetic field. By contrast, I wish to track important continuities and transformations taking place over many centuries, before the Romantic period began at the end of the eighteenth century. With Romanticism, the literary system was reorganized in ways that continue to reverberate to this day. (That so many aspiring poets today think that their chief task is to express their personal feelings is a legacy of the Romantics.)

Instead of focusing on a single lyric form like the sonnet, I include a representative range of different kinds (subgenres) of lyric poetry that are not usually placed alongside one another. My selection is designed to demonstrate how various lyric subgenres cast light on distinct areas of human concern. I believe that our lives may be further enriched by reading poetry on such topics as love, sexual desire, marriage, family, same-sex friendship, labor and employment, religious vocation, and grieving the dead. In discussing poems on these significant themes, the following study pays close attention to the craft of poetry. My focus on the historical development of poetic technique aims to help the non-specialist reader to recognize and appreciate the artistry of poems that have stood up well to the test of time.

Yet the story of lyric poetry can never be fully told, even if we limit ourselves to widely recognized masterpieces from the centuries that concern us here. The need for a highly selective narrative inevitably leads to difficult choices about what to exclude. Although all the poems I have selected are generally admired for their poetic excellence, at the end of the day my selection may seem somewhat arbitrary. I have allowed myself to be guided by generations of critics and teachers and by my own personal taste and interests. Other poems and lyric subgenres certainly could have been included instead. It would be foolish to claim that my selection is based on some absolute standard.

Regrettably, no space has been devoted to *carpe diem* poems like Andrew Marvell's "To His Coy Mistress" in the mid-seventeenth century, or to lyrics set to music like those of the Elizabethan poet and composer Thomas Campion. Nor has space been found for the intense devotional lyrics by the two greatest early seventeenth-century metaphysical poets, John Donne and George Herbert, or for English translations of the Psalms (especially by Mary Sidney). We must pass over poems written for public occasions, like Andrew Marvell's great Horatian ode on Oliver Cromwell or John Dryden's magnificent "Alexander's Feast," an ode in honor of the patron saint of music, St. Cecilia, to name just a few. To be sure, any of these poems or lyric kinds, had they been included, would also cast valuable light on significant human themes.

I certainly do not intend my selection to be mistaken for a definitive list of the best individual poems or subgenres of lyric poetry. Any effort to create such a list of canonical works would be deeply misguided.[4] At the same time, I am confident that my poetic tastes and interests are not merely arbitrary or idiosyncratic. In all but one case (Aemilia Lanyer) my selections include poets and poems that have been valued by many generations of readers over a long period of time, sometimes almost without interruption.

The book does more than introduce new readers to rich traditions of lyric poetry from about five centuries of English literature. It also differs from more narrowly specialized studies by offering non-specialist readers guidance in the appreciation of poetic value or excellence. Such issues were debated by Western philosophers and critics in the ancient, medieval, and early modern eras long before the modern terms *aesthetic*, *literary*, or *poetic value* became part of the mental landscape during the last few centuries of criticism and theory. However, non-academic readers should be aware that for the last several decades professional literary scholars have generally avoided discussing poetry in terms of its literary value. If many contemporary scholars have turned away from reading poetry for its aesthetic value and universal themes, other readers still turn to poetry because they find it meaningfully addressing common human concerns.[5]

The primary method I will follow involves reading the poetic text closely, alert to specific artistic choices made more or less consciously by skilled poets. At the same time, my close reading practice seeks to cultivate forms of historical awareness. The act of reading will proceed slowly, often only a few lines at a time, to assist relatively inexperienced readers of older poetry grappling with unfamiliar rhetorical and grammatical strategies. However, just as my selection of representative poems and poetic kinds cannot claim any absolute justification, I cannot pretend that my selection of poetic features to analyze is beyond challenge. Different readers (or sometimes the same reader at different times) may notice or find interesting different features of a poem. No reader, no matter how skilled, can pay attention to everything worth noticing in a good poem. But it is possible to become a better, more perceptive reader of poetry through dedicated practice and a sharpened awareness of historical change.

To help readers appreciate poetic craft during the Middle Ages and Renaissance, my discussions of individual poems analyze formal patterns of versification to a greater extent than is typically the case in specialized academic studies. However, I will not try the patience of readers by engaging in prolonged discussions of meter. The system of analysis that I employ is not the traditional system of versification or prosody still taught in schools and colleges. The traditional system borrows its terminology from classical meter and divides the poetic line into *feet*. It labels different combinations of syllables with Greek-derived terms such as *iambic*, *trochaic*, *anapestic*, and *dactylic*. Counting the number of feet in a line determines its measure as *tetrameter*, *pentameter*, *hexameter*, etc. Besides the disadvantage of its off-putting jargon, this classically derived system has long been recognized as creating serious problems when applied to English versification. But old habits die hard.

Rather than use the traditional system, I draw on the theory of poetic rhythm and meter first developed by Derek Attridge in *The Rhythm of English Poetry* (1982).[6] To my mind, Attridge demonstrates the fatal flaws in the "classical" approach to English meter, especially with its assumption that English verse is based on metrical *feet*.[7] The most important features of his theory may be explained briefly. His account of poetic rhythm is based on our perception of **beats**, similar to tapping our feet or clapping our hands to music. When you tap your foot down to the ground, you mark a beat. When you lift your foot up so that you can tap it down at the next beat, you mark an **offbeat**. The mechanics of tapping your foot confirm that you cannot put two beats immediately next to each other. You have to lift your foot in between. So at least one offbeat will always separate two beats. (As we will see later, an offbeat can be *implied* rather than actually contained in a syllable.)

Of course, few people find themselves moved to tap their feet when reading or hearing poetry, unlike they do when listening to a piece of rhythmically compelling music. But it can be done if you want to pay closer attention to the underlying poetic rhythm of metrically regular poetry. We can always exaggerate a poetic rhythm by chanting it, and this may induce listeners to clap their hands or tap their feet. Small children love that sort of thing: *Hickory, dickory, dock, / The mouse ran up the clock*.

Attridge's system of **beat prosody** eliminates the need to speak of stressed or accented words or syllables. Although he concedes that a more technical, linguistics-based approach to meter may be more scientific than his own account, he suggests that such theories tend to appeal only to specialists and are less useful for literary criticism that might have a broader appeal. By contrast, he offers a rigorous but not excessively technical system for analyzing versification. I join a growing number of critics who share his conviction that more traditional accounts of English meter are less useful than his approach.[8]

We are now ready for the next basic point. Attridge distinguishes between the underlying *rhythmic structure* of regular English verse and its *metrical pattern*. The underlying rhythmic structure of most metrical poetry in English is either a four- or a five-beat line. The metrical pattern, on the other hand, determines how the beats and offbeats organize the underlying rhythm. For example, when each syllable that takes a beat alternates with one syllable that marks an offbeat, we call that a *duple meter*. (*De dum de dum de dum.*) Since the twelfth century, duple meters have always been the most common variety in English. On the other hand, if each beat alternates with *two* consecutive syllables to mark the offbeat, we have a *triple meter*. If you tap your foot, these two syllables would be spoken in the time it takes you to lift up your foot before you set it down on the next beat.

Attridge has devised his own notation for his system of analyzing poetic meter. As we have seen, he dispenses with the traditional notion of dividing a line into feet. We need only to mark beats and offbeats. The most basic symbols are a big **B** written below the line to mark a metrical beat and small **o** to mark an offbeat. Here is a regular four-beat line in duple meter that I have made up (try tapping your foot to the beats):

    The beagle is a regal beast
    o   B o   B o   B o   B

The next example offers a three-beat line of triple meter. I modify Attridge's notation system to mark a **double offbeat** by joining the two syllables like this: **o-o**, where each **o** represents a syllable:

    I will sleep at the end of the day
    o-o   B   o-o   B   o-o   B

Attridge's system also accounts for a syllable that is *promoted* to a beat (marked with small **b**) and a syllable that is *demoted* to an offbeat (marked with a large **O**). I will explain these and other refinements at the appropriate time. (See Appendix for further details and my modification of his revised notation.)

The key to understanding Attridge's system is that it attempts to describe our *perceptions*—how we perceive rhythm in poetic language. As my appeal to foot-tapping suggests, poetic rhythm involves our bodies. The bodily experience of rhythm and meter is only one aspect of the sonic qualities of poetry, though poetic meter is especially important historically. But I will also have much to say about the sound of poetry beyond rhythm, analyzing patterns of individual vowels and consonants. We will thus explore patterns of rhyme and other features of the linguistic sound units known as *phonemes*, though technical analyses using the International Phonetic Alphabet (IPA) will be relegated to the notes. The close attention to sound patterns will help the reader gain a greater appreciation of the characteristics of lyric poetry that have traditionally been associated with the musicality of verse.

Traditional defenses of poetry from the Greeks down to at least the eighteenth century argued that poetry not only delights but instructs, presenting a wholesome content in an attractive form. The didactic value of poetry was widely thought to derive from its relation to moral philosophy. Few scholars in the twenty-first century are interested in poetry because it teaches moral lessons. Yet poetry still seems to serve as a repository of wisdom in the eyes of many people, as the findings in *Poetry in America* (cited above) suggests. Further confirmation of the reasons why poetry is valued by people from many walks of life is available in the often moving video testimonials assembled for the Favorite Poem Project by Robert Pinsky, the former poet laureate of the United States.[9] To this day, many readers who are not professional critics turn to poetry because they believe it offers inspiring or moving accounts of such universal themes as love, friendship, spiritual longing, loss and mourning, and mortality—in short, the meaning of life.

To conclude this introduction, a brief summary of the chapters that follow will provide a convenient roadmap for the journey ahead. Chapter 1, "Vernacular Eloquence: Reading Older Poetry Rhetorically," introduces readers to the specialized ways of thinking about poetry provided by the rhetorical tradition. The teaching of rhetoric began in ancient Greece, was adapted by the Romans, and continued to dominate formal education until at least the late eighteenth century. To understand and appreciate earlier lyric poetry, it is helpful to have a basic understanding of the classical tradition of rhetorical poetics that dominated Western culture in these earlier centuries. The chapter includes a brief discussion of the rise of poetry in vernacular languages during the Middle Ages before concluding with an overview of the earliest writings on poetic technique in English. After briefly reviewing the influence of Italian humanist ideas of rhetorical education on early sixteenth-century English humanists, the chapter analyzes George Gascoigne's *Certayne notes of Instruction concerning the making of verse or ryme in English* (1575), the earliest work of literary criticism in English and the first discussion of accentual-syllabic meter that grasps its basic principles (even if it struggles to articulate them clearly). In this context, further details of Attridge's theory of poetic rhythm are introduced. His theory helps demonstrate how a native sense of English rhythms depends on an embodied experience of language in ways that have proved enduring. After Gascoigne, the critical writings briefly discussed include those of Sir Philip Sidney, Thomas Campion, Samuel Daniel, and George Puttenham.

Chapter 2, "What Was a Lyric Poem?," provides a brief discussion of theories of lyric poetry and explains the critical notion of subgenre that will structure the organization of the following chapters. As we shall see, the history of attempts to define lyric poetry demonstrates tensions between universalizing and particularizing understandings of lyric. Universalizing critics view lyrics as sharing common features or essences, across ancient, medieval, and modern poetic traditions. By contrast, some recent historicist critics insist that "lyric" as a category of poetry first shows up in the modern era, at about the same time as the age of Romanticism.[10] Definitions of lyric have depended on which theory of literature is presupposed, whether mimetic, expressive, rhetorical/didactic, or objective/formalist theories, or more recent rejections of all traditional theories of literature. Drawing on the theory of literary kinds (historical genres) developed by the Renaissance literary scholar Alastair Fowler, I seek a middle ground between defining lyric in terms of universal essences and historical particulars.

The rest of the book is organized by chapters devoted to representative lyric subgenres. No effort to provide equal coverage between medieval and Renaissance poetry is attempted. Despite being trained as a medieval scholar, I have deliberately limited the number of medieval lyrics selected for discussion. One reason has to do with language. Even allowing for a somewhat modernized spelling and punctuation, Middle English (usually dated from about 1100 to 1500) poses significant barriers to comprehension by untrained readers. The other reason is that Middle English lyrics do not always lend themselves especially well to an appreciation of their poetic craft. Their interest often lies elsewhere. Old English lyric poetry from before the Norman Conquest, on the other hand, does repay the effort to study its aesthetic design, but it requires specialized training to read in the original language.

Chapter 3, "Anonymous Middle English Lyrics on the Virgin Mary," discusses three frequently anthologized and widely taught lyrics honoring the Virgin Mary. These Marian lyric poems should be read in the context of the devotional practices of medieval Europe and the manuscript environments of Middle English poetry. The earliest is one of the finest brief poems in the language, "Now goth sonne under wode." In addition, we examine two fifteenth-century Marian lyrics: "In a tabernacle of a toure" and "I sing of a maiden that is makeles." The chapter tests the value of Attridge's theory of poetic meter, using it to help account for some of the striking poetic effects of the lyrics. The linguistic concept of deixis is introduced to help readers appreciate how these older lyrics play upon spatial and temporal distance, near and far, in ways that continue to animate the poems.

Chapter 4, "The Love Complaint Ballade: Chaucer and Wyatt," looks at three examples of a courtly poetic subgenre that was equally popular in the later medieval and early Tudor periods. This subgenre combines a distinctive thematic concern (disillusion in love) and a regular metrical form (rhyme royal stanzas). The combination seems to have been introduced to English poetry by Geoffrey Chaucer, whose continuing prestige among fifteenth- and sixteenth-century poets and readers doubtless contributed to the longevity of the form. Not all ballades are love complaints or even about love. In fact, the most frequently read ballades of Chaucer are on philosophical themes, like the nature of true nobility ("Gentilesse"). But the thematic and metrical form of the love complaint ballade deserves to be understood as a lyric subgenre of a distinctive kind.

"Madame, for your newefangelnesse," the first example of love complaint discussed in the chapter, is presumed by many scholars to have been composed by Chaucer though it remains undeservedly neglected. The second example, "The Complaint of Chaucer to His Purse," is certainly his work, and perhaps the last poem he composed. This comic poem pretends to be a love complaint but is actually a begging poem asking his newly installed king to remember to pay his annual pension. The chapter ends with a widely anthologized lyric by Sir Thomas Wyatt, a pivotal figure in the history of English lyric. This early Tudor poet-courtier stands with one foot on late-medieval practices of court poetry and the other on new literary fashions that he discovered on the Continent. With its vivid and passionate language, "They flee from me that sometime did me seek" stands as the culmination of the late-medieval tradition of rhyme royal love complaint, though it provides metrical puzzles that may be unsolvable.

Chapter 5, "The Love Sonnet from Wyatt to Shakespeare," selects some of the best Renaissance sonnets from the sixteenth-century English sonnet tradition, including works by Wyatt, Sir Philip Sidney, and Edmund Spenser, before going on to examine a selection of Shakespeare's sonnets, including some of his most famous. Wyatt wrote at a time before metrical smoothness was sought or expected by poets and readers. However, Sidney and Spenser are the poets most responsible for establishing the system of accentual-syllabic meter (especially the iambic pentameter line) that remained canonical into the twentieth century. They were also remarkably inventive in how they adapted the sonnet to English poetry. Finally, the chapter concludes with several outstanding examples from Shakespeare's *Sonnets*, first published in 1609. Shakespeare's sequence is the only one that seems to divide its attention between two love-objects, one male and one female, though the homoerotic nature of the first subsequence did not attract much attention until relatively recently. For technical mastery and the dramatic intensity of its various moods, Shakespeare's sequence represents one of the highpoints of canonical English lyric poetry.

Chapter 6, "The Country House Poem: Lanyer and Jonson," looks at two "estate" poems from the early seventeenth century. The only known volume of poetry by Aemilia Lanyer, rediscovered only a few decades ago, was one of the first books of original poetry published by an English woman. The recovery of her work is one of the triumphs of recent feminist scholarship. The "Description of Cookham" is a remarkable meditation on her experience of living briefly in a country house with her aristocratic patron, Margaret Clifford, Countess of Cumberland, and her daughter Anne. The poet is socially insecure but remarkably confident in her art as she imagines an idealized feminine social space in which women's lives might flourish. The second half of the chapter turns to Ben Jonson, focusing on his great ode "To Penshurst," written in honor of Philip Sidney's younger brother, Robert, and his wife. First published in 1616, this celebration of the Sidney family is also an elegant study of the relationship between a poet and his patron.

The final chapter, "The Pastoral Elegy: Milton's 'Lycidas,'" introduces readers to pastoral elegies from classical Greek and Roman poets, including Theocritus and Vergil, whose work Milton imitates and supersedes in his elegy on the untimely death of Edward King, a young scholar-poet he knew from his days at Cambridge University. "Lycidas" used to be frequently described by critics as the greatest lyric in English, not only for its technical virtuosity but also because of its profound meditation on the meaning of life and death. The poem has often been read as being concerned as much with the poet's anxieties about his own mortality and the meaning of his life's project as with the elegy's ostensible subject. Because Milton's great elegy is generally viewed by critics to be the best of its kind and because it is concerned with last things, it provides a fitting end to this study of canonical forms of early lyric poetry.

A brief coda concludes the book, offering an appreciation of a haunting fragment of Middle English poetry. Sometimes anthologized as "The Irish Dancer," this charming work serves as a reminder of the close relations among the ancient sister arts of music, dance, and the art of lyric song.

1

Vernacular Eloquence: Reading Older Poetry Rhetorically

Many readers nowadays tend to think of poetry as a form of self-expression—a way to convey thoughts and feelings that are pent up inside of us. But what might happen to our reading of older poetry if we were to find out that this common assumption is, historically speaking, relatively recent?

In fact, thinking of poetry as the expression of a poet's unique inner life is a legacy of cultural shifts that began to take place in the West during the period of Romanticism starting around the last decades of the eighteenth century. By contrast, during earlier centuries poets and their audiences did not automatically assume that the main purpose of poetry was to express the feelings of a unique individual. Instead, they lived in a culture that valued the skillful use of language because of its potential effects on an audience. Educated readers and writers shared the assumption that the function of poetry is to delight, teach, and move us. If we are stuck with the post–Romantic expectation that all poetry is about the self-expression of a unique individual, we will miss out on much of what remains valuable and interesting in earlier lyric masterpieces. Our understanding and enjoyment of older poetry will be greatly increased if we try to orient ourselves to the rhetorical culture that helped shape it.

Rhetoric, the study and practice of persuasive speech, first arose in fifth-century Athens. Developed by later Greek and Roman writers and teachers, a rhetorical framework for thinking about poetry viewed it as a *pragmatic* activity, a verbal technique or craft intended to affect an audience. The rhetorical approach, though it hardly remained static through the ages, influenced most thinking about poetry until the end of the eighteenth century. This chapter introduces the earlier rhetorical orientation for understanding and evaluating poetry that began with the Greeks, was borrowed by the Romans, and was partially transmitted to the Latin West during the Middle Ages until it was more fully recovered during the Renaissance.

In addition to a rhetorical theory of poetry, the chapter also introduces the *mimetic* theory of poetry, which often held equal sway, thanks to the influence of Plato and Aristotle. According to a classic study by M. H. Abrams, the mimetic theory offered the most important way of thinking about literature from the ancient world through the eighteenth century, when it was replaced by the *expressive* theory, which assumes that poets express their thoughts and feelings.[1] According to the mimetic theory, the function of poetry is to *imitate* reality. Although some medieval writers certainly thought in such terms, the mimetic theory was most influential during classical antiquity and the Renaissance, after the rediscovery of previously forgotten works by the Greeks. Our story, therefore, begins with the Greeks during the fifth century BCE.

The teachings of Socrates and his student Plato were opposed to the sophists, the first professional teachers of rhetoric. The sophists taught paying clients in the Athenian governing class how to succeed in politics and public affairs through instruction in a variety of useful subjects, including the skillful use of verbal arts. Poetry was at the center of a traditional Athenian education during the classical period when the sophists were active. Many of the techniques used for persuasive orations could be illustrated with examples drawn from poets, especially Homer.[2]

Plato opposed the rhetoricians because he believed that they were more interested in winning over an audience than in pursuing the truth, the proper goal of philosophy. Plato's *Republic* is famous among literary critics for its attack on the dangers of poetry. His challenge remained a force to contend with long after poetry lost its claim to cultural centrality. Though it was far from his intention, Plato's discussion of poetry thus inaugurated literary criticism in the West.

In the first rehearsal of his argument against poetry, Plato objects to the harm that would be caused by poetry if it formed the basis of the guardians' education in his hypothetical ideal state. Plato has Socrates introduce the earliest known distinction among three different kinds of poetry. Plato explains that in the first kind of poetry (tragedy and comedy), the poet "imitates" the speech of other persons by having actors speak the lines. In another kind of poetry, rather than imitating another person's speech the poet gives his "own report." Finally, the epic is a mixed genre. Sometimes the poet imitates the speech of another person by directly quoting it; sometimes the poet speaks in his own voice as narrator.[3] (Drawing on Plato's classification, Aristotle was to refer to different *modes of presentation* based on who is represented as speaking.)

Plato objects to poetry for two reasons: it consists of false fables that make the gods look ridiculous, and it is detrimental to the practice of virtue.

The guardians of the republic should be discouraged from practicing poetic imitations (*mimētica*) unless "the subject of their imitation" is "what is appropriate to them" so that it does not lead to bad habits (*ALC* 63). Plato was as cautious about the style (*lexis*) of poetry (roughly speaking, its form) as he was of the matter or content of what was said (*logoi*). Instead of a mixture in the kinds of expression, which would draw on a variety of harmonies and rhythms that gave "the most pleasure" to the multitude, only an "unmixed" style would be appropriate for the limited kinds of imitation appropriate to the well-being of the republic (*ALC* 65).

By the time he returns to the topic of poetic imitation in Book 10 of *The Republic*, he has introduced his theory of Forms. The theory of Forms assigns the ultimate basis of reality to the unchanging realm of Forms that lend intelligibility to the sensible things of this world. If a bed made by a craftsman imitates or participates in the form or idea of a bed, the bed described by a poet stands at one further remove from the ultimate reality that underlies all beds. A bed encountered in poetry, in other words, is an inferior imitation (*mimēsis*) of an imitation of reality. For the education of the guardians of his ideal republic, therefore, poetry is worse than useless—it is positively misleading. Homer and his followers are "imitators of images of virtue and of all their other subjects, without any contact with the truth" (*ALC* 69). Only the philosopher can aspire to know the truth.

Before resuming his attack on poetry in Book 10, Plato has also analyzed the soul by breaking it into different components, giving primacy to the rational portion that must govern the lower spirited and desiring faculties. Poetry appeals to baser emotions instead of reason in ways that corrupt morality because (he thought) poetry "produces a bad government in the individual mind" (*ALC* 72). We indulge in morally suspect emotions when, for example, Homer imitates a hero's lamentations in mourning. The problem for Plato is not the emotion of grief *per se* but the hero's allowing himself to express it, and our being moved by that expression in poetry.[4] Aside from pleasurable patterns of rhythm, such imitations provide distinctively enjoyable experiences: "we feel pleasure and give ourselves up to it" when "we follow in sympathy and praise the excellence of the poet who does this to us most effectively" (*ALC* 73). Because poetry stimulates what ought to be suppressed, Plato concludes that, with the exception of hymns to gods and praise songs for good men, poetry should not be admitted to the ideal republic. He sums up by referring to "the old quarrel between poetry and philosophy" (*ALC* 74).

In this foundational moment in the history of literary criticism, Plato throws down the gauntlet by identifying poetic pleasure as deeply problematic and corrupting. Yet Plato does not deny poetry's power to charm its audience. Indeed, in admitting that well-crafted language has the ability to charm the listener, Plato concedes a crucial point made by the sophist Gorgias of Leontini (c. 483–c. 376) in *A Defense of Helen*, who argued: "Inspired charms which use speech are summoners of pleasure and banishers of pain. The force of charm meets the conviction of the mind and bewitches, persuades, and changes it by sorcery."[5]

Exemplified by the highly poetic prose of Gorgias, the power of artfully patterned language to move its audience is precisely what Plato reviles and condemns. In the *Phaedrus* (261a) Plato specifically denounces rhetoric for its incantatory power to use words to mislead the soul, calling it the "art of influencing the mind" (*tekhnē psychagōgia*). The bodily nature of poetic rhythm was thus recognized early on as a key component of the pleasures of poetry.[6] Those who would defend poetry against Plato's attack in the succeeding centuries needed strategies for justifying poetic pleasure.

The next contribution to the debate concerning poetry was Aristotle's *Poetics*, which implicitly responds to his teacher's concerns.[7] Unlike Plato, Aristotle accepts that poetry, and above all, tragedy, has useful functions for the individual and society. Since Aristotle bases his theory on the idea of imitation, he too offers a mimetic theory of art. But the *Poetics* also contains elements of what Abrams classifies as a *pragmatic* or rhetorical theory, which emphasizes the effect of the work on the audience; and an *objective* theory, which concentrates on formal features of the work itself.

Aristotle (like Plato before him) accepts the Greek belief that poetry consists of imitation or representation, though he differs from his teacher in having a much more positive evaluation of it. He also has a more positive view of poetic meter, since the language of poetry is "speech pleasurably enhanced" through "rhythm and song" (*ALC* 97). Aristotle argues that poetry offers imitations of what human are like—convincing images of what they might do or say in a given situation. For this reason Aristotle suggests that "poetry is at once more like philosophy and more worthwhile than history, since poetry tends to make general statements, while those of history are particular" (*ALC* 102). Rather than seeing poetry as antithetical to the interests of philosophy, in other words, Aristotle assumes that they are complementary, working in concert *to help us understand what human beings are like*.

Poetics forms a discrete body of knowledge for Aristotle owing to the specificity of its object, though the closely related verbal arts of poetics and rhetoric are in the final analysis inseparable from ethics and politics. For him, each discipline is implicated in the others. Aristotle believes that poetic imitations both provide pleasure and fine-tune our understanding of human beings. He may not provide a complete account of poetry, but he advances a reasonably coherent theory that has served as the most influential foundation of all.

One of the most remarkable aspects of Aristotle's *Poetics* is its pioneering attention to matters of literary form. Especially important is his assumption that the skillful craft or artistry (*tekhnē*) of making poetry is what leads to its excellence (*aretē*). "Excellence" is the closest Greek equivalent to the modern notion of poetic value. Aristotle is keenly interested in the evaluative criteria for good poetry considered *as poetry*. He assumes that we cannot judge poetic excellence without understanding the formal elements of poetry. In this assumption, Aristotle stands apart from other ancient literary theorists. He insists that poems must be judged by poetic criteria, rather than measured by "external standards of truthfulness and of morality," as one scholar observes.[8] We may hear a distant echo of this approach in T. S. Eliot's well-known dictum: "when we are considering poetry we must consider it primarily as poetry and not another thing."[9] To this day, creative writers for the most part remain committed to the notion of excelling at their *craft*.

Aristotle's scant attention to lyric poetry has been frequently observed. Lacking the cultural prestige of tragedy or epic, lyric tends to escape his notice. One scholar suggests that Aristotle ignored lyric poetry because he failed to recognize how its imitation of inner emotional life provides an understanding of human character.[10] Because Aristotle judged tragedy to be the highest form of poetry, much of his pioneering analysis of literary form relates to the construction of plot or the imitation of an action. But his prolonged attention to the crafting of poetic language would in the fullness of time prove relevant to the study of lyric. He is the first literary critic to offer a theory of stylistic excellence in the making of poetry, setting the stage for later assessments of lyric poetry when shorter poetic kinds could no longer be ignored.

Aristotle never mentions Plato by name, though he is his obvious opponent. Plato banished nearly all forms of poetry from his ideal republic on the grounds that it is morally dangerous and confuses the mind about the nature of reality. By contrast, Aristotle defends poetry because it offers a rationally based form of craft that provides morally intelligible instruction. Moreover, he avoids Plato's suspicion of the kinds of pleasure distinctive of poetry by observing that human beings derive pleasure from the way imitation (*mimēsis*) induces understanding of the way things are or should be.

Aristotle had noted the connection between *mimēsis* and cognitive pleasure in his *Rhetoric*: "Since to learn and to admire is pleasurable, other things are necessarily pleasurable, such as, for example, a work of imitation, as in painting and sculpture and poetry, and anything that is well imitated, even if the object of imitation is not in itself pleasant...."[11] Even imitations of unpleasant experiences (for example, the representation of extreme violence in Shakespeare's *King Lear* or a slasher film) can give pleasure. Surely Aristotle is right that we respond to a convincing representation of how people might act when faced with extremity because we recognize that *this is what people are like*.

Although a mimetic theory of art may not provide a fully adequate explanation of what art may be or do, such a theory does point to something vital and important. Indeed, a mimetic theory of art remains alive today with many readers and moviegoers, who often report dislike of novels or films that they feel are unrealistic. In any case, reading early poetry rhetorically also requires us to understand that poets and their audiences chiefly thought in terms of mimetic theories of literature until the Romantic period.

Aristotle's discussion of style in the *Poetics* as one of the qualitative criteria of poetic excellence is closely related to his discussion of prose style (*lexis*) in book three of the *Rhetoric*, where he identifies clarity as the chief virtue of style in prose, whether oral or in writing. The style of prose should be "appropriate" to the subject (221). Thus Aristotle introduces the principle of stylistic decorum (*to prepon*), which was to reappear in various guises in the history of ancient and neoclassical criticism. Poetry allows more deviations from the prevailing meanings of words than prose, according to what would later be described as poetic license. As always, Aristotle recommends that diction should seek the mean and avoid excess. Indeed, diction provides a source of "verbal beauty," which consists "in the sound or in the sense." After the pioneering work of Aristotle, reading poetry rhetorically meant reading with an awareness of the stylistic choices made by poets. Such an awareness could be cultivated through formal education.

One other major contribution by Aristotle needs to be mentioned at this stage because, for better or worse, it was to prove highly influential in later rhetorically based understandings of poetry. In his *Rhetoric* (1.3), Aristotle introduces a classification scheme that divides rhetoric into three distinct kinds, depending on the kind of audience an orator was trying to persuade. According to his classification, forensic rhetoric is employed by advocates hoping to persuade judges in the courtroom. Deliberative rhetoric is used by members of a democratic assembly hoping to persuade fellow citizens to take a specific course of action. Epideictic or demonstrative rhetoric is used by orators to persuade an audience about the ethical status of a person or thing that the speaker praises or condemns. However, epideictic rhetoric does not call on the audience directly to perform an action. "The definition of epideictic has remained a problem in rhetorical theory," writes George Kennedy, "since it becomes the category for all forms of discourse that are not specifically deliberative or judicial." Although Aristotle did not apply the label *epideixis* to poetry himself, "later ancient rhetoricians regarded it as including poetry and prose literature."[12] The catch-all nature of the category has allowed Jonathan Culler, a distinguished literary theorist, to advocate for a revival of the ancient notion of lyric poetry as epideictic. However, he expands the definition almost beyond recognition when he defines it as "public poetic discourse about values in this world rather than a fictional world."[13]

The project of a poetics that Aristotle had begun was continued by later Greek masters of rhetoric, whose doctrines were eventually to be taken up by the Romans. One writer who draws on Aristotle was Demetrius, author of *On Style*, the earliest surviving treatise on that topic.[14] Demetrius is the first rhetorician to distinguish figures of speech from figures of thought, and who provides technical terms for figures.[15] Unlike Aristotle, Demetrius does not neglect lyric poetry, praising "the divine Sappho" for her mastery of the "elegant style" (*ALC* 196). Some of the charm of lyric comes "from the content" (*ALC* 197). But charm also derives from stylistic choices such as refined diction: "Sappho uses beautiful, melodious words when she speaks of beauty or loves, spring and the halcyon" (*ALC* 203). Demetrius draws on the lost work *On Style* by Aristotle's student Theophrastus, who defined beautiful words thus: "There is beauty in a word if it is attractive to the ear or eye or has inherent nobility from its meaning" (*ALC* 204). Demetrius elaborates on this point to suggest that both beautiful sights and delightful sound patterns contribute to beautiful diction.

It has been rightly observed that the rhetorical orientation of ancient literary criticism, "though undoubtedly useful in suggesting principles of judgment and helping to elucidate authors' intentions, is fundamentally not equal to the task of appraising classical literature."[16] The same may be said of the rhetorical criticism produced during the medieval and early modern periods and the poetry it purports to explain. Yet we cannot read such poetry with understanding and appreciation if we ignore the rhetorical culture that gave rise to such poetry.

Roman letters had already begun to assimilate Greek models of literary kinds and canons of rhetoric when the Augustan poet Horace composed his verse epistle known as *The Art of Poetry* (*Ars poetica*) around 20 BCE.[17] Like the Greeks, Horace recognized that poetic composition is a demanding craft, one requiring great discipline, and that the appreciation of good poetry is a cultivated skill. In matters of metrical skill, as he notes in the *Ars poetica*, "not all critics notice when a poem fails to keep to a measure" (263). Horace offers evaluative criteria for judging good poems. For example, he describes "excellent arrangement" of material as the ability to "say now what needs to be said now" (42–43). In matters of diction, Horace displays an understanding of how linguistic usage is subject to historical change and custom: "Many words that have fallen out of use will find new life, and many words that are esteemed now will be dropped if usage would have it so, which is the guiding spirit of judgment in the rules and norms of speech" (lines 70–72).

In what are perhaps his most frequently quoted lines, Horace observes: "Poets wish to be beneficial or give delight (*prodesse ... delectare*), to say things that are both pleasing and useful for living" (lines 333–34). Poets earn the favor of readers when they "mix the useful with the delightful" (*miscuit utile dulci* [343–44]). By claiming that poetry is both useful and delightful, Horace modifies what historians of rhetoric call the "affective triad." Rhetorical theorists like Cicero taught that oratory has three proper ends: to teach, delight, and move the emotions in a way that induces action (*docere, delectare, movere*).[18] Although the poet's ability to move the audience seems implicit in Horace's formulation, he stresses that poetry teaches useful lessons in a pleasurable form.

The rhetorical orientation of ancient literary criticism would continue to influence medieval thinking about poetry, despite the cultural transformations that followed the advent of Christianity. Although some of the Latin rhetorical handbooks were well known throughout the medieval period, Horace gave scholars a distinctive vocabulary for thinking about poetry even after the rediscovery of Aristotle.[19] Ancient doctrines would be taken up and expanded in the Renaissance, as humanist scholars gained access to previously lost or neglected texts such as Aristotle's *Poetics* in the original Greek, Cicero's mature rhetorical works, Quintilian's *Education of the Orator* (*Institutio oratoria*), and Longinus's *On the Sublime*.[20] In the sixteenth century, a number of Italian humanists attempted to harmonize Aristotle's *Poetics* and Horace's *Ars poetica*, despite significant differences in their poetic theories.[21] The adaptation of classical literary theory to new cultural conditions led to an impressive body of thought during the Renaissance.

Before we turn our attention to post-classical developments in reading poetry rhetorically, however, it is worth pausing briefly with Quintilian, the first-century CE Roman teacher of rhetoric and author of the *Institutio oratoria*, the most extensive rhetorical handbook from the Roman world. The system of education in ancient Rome required young students to be exposed to canonical Greek and Latin poets early in their careers because such reading enabled students to master grammar and vocabulary, and studying the verbal polish of poets was believed to be of practical use for training in rhetoric.

Quintilian follows tradition in recommending that young pupils begin by reading Homer and Vergil. Although beginners do not yet possess the critical judgment fully to appreciate their excellence (*virtutes*), that may come in due time since these authors will be reread later.[22] He also recommends tragedy and selected lyric poetry in elementary education but warns against exposing pupils to erotic verse at too impressionable an age (1.8.6). Quintilian's passing remarks about poetry presuppose that it provides pleasure, nourishes the soul, and possesses distinctive forms of excellence that are subject to evaluative judgment by the discerning critic. In short, studying good poetry would help the student achieve eloquence in speaking.

Quintilian either does not recall or is not convinced by Aristotle's defense of poetry as offering general philosophical knowledge of what people are like, nor does he seem to accept Horace's claim that poetry is useful as well as pleasing. Quintilian discusses the value of refining the student's eloquence through the practice of literary imitation—not in the Aristotelian sense of *mimēsis* but in the sense of copying models from the best writers (10.2.21–22). His account of imitation implies that a parallel project of a poetics could have been contemplated. A systematic art of poetry would need to respect the distinctive forms of eloquence in metrical composition.

However, no systematic theoretical work appears to have been attempted after Aristotle until the Italian Renaissance.[23] Because poetics and rhetoric were so inextricably interwoven in the ancient world, there was evidently no perceived need to create a separate discipline for studying poetic composition, though it was widely accepted that the virtues of oratory could often be understood against the background of comparable poetic skills. Literary criticism as distinct from the teaching of rhetoric did not yet exist as a separate branch of learning in the classical world.

Yet a theoretical space for poetics was potentially available. Poetry was a distinctive form of discourse, and its value was inseparable from the pleasure it induced in listeners and readers. As metrical composition that used figures of speech more liberally than did prose, poetry was subject to its own rules of art. *Eloquence* was the general name assigned to the excellence shared by poetry and oratory. Eloquence could both be viewed as a means of persuasion and appreciated and admired in its own right as an effect of artistic technique.

Although many ancient grammatical and rhetorical teaching handbooks remained available during the Middle Ages, much of the rich classical heritage of thinking about poetry was generally lost in the medieval West.[24] One reason for this loss was that knowledge of Greek was a rare commodity in Western Europe during the Middle Ages. In addition, the advent of Christianity greatly determined how poetry, especially by pagan authors, was viewed during the next millennium and more of cultural transformation.[25] Certainly the church was often hostile to secular poetry and to fiction in general, and highly suspicious of the pleasure induced by poetry. Church Fathers like Jerome and Augustine were frequently cited on the moral dangers of poetry. After his conversion to Christianity, for example, St. Augustine wrote in his *Confessions* about the spiritual dangers of reading Vergil's *Aeneid*, though he had loved the poem as a student.[26]

On the other hand, when medieval arts of poetry were eventually created for classroom use, they drew on and refined the classical rhetorical inheritance.[27] Answering the criticism by moral rigorists that poetry was a frivolous or even dangerous enterprise, some medieval scholars adapted methods for the allegorical exegesis of pagan poetry first developed in later antiquity. These allegorical habits of reading, often influenced by Neoplatonic doctrine, enlisted poetic fiction for the cause of truth. In recent decades, the rediscovery of medieval commentaries to classical texts has been important for dispelling old myths about the neglect of literary theory during the millennium between the fall of Rome and the revival of classical learning in the Renaissance. Academic introductions to classical authors that were produced for medieval schools (*accessus ad auctores*) provide invaluable sources for understanding how educated readers were trained to think about literature.[28] For example, even potentially immoral texts like Ovid's collection of fictional letters between mythical lovers (*Heroides*) could be reinterpreted as "pertain[ing] to ethics, which inculcates good morality and eradicates evil behavior."[29]

Although pagan Roman literature could no longer be understood in its original cultural context during the Middle Ages, Latin was by no means a dead language but a living one used for oral and written communication throughout medieval Europe. With the dissolution of the Roman Empire, however, Latin came to enjoy a unique status. It could now be acquired only as a second language by those sufficiently privileged to receive such an education. It was therefore an elite language, almost entirely restricted to males. For most of the Middle Ages, to be literate (*literatus*) was synonymous with the ability to read and write Latin. Until lay literacy began to become more common in the fourteenth century, nearly all those who learned the language were clerics. Most vernacular poets had some form of clerical education (even if they were not destined for the Church) and thus knew at least some Latin.

Among the educated few, knowledge of the Latin system of quantitative poetic meter remained available throughout the Middle Ages. Classical Latin versification (adapted from the Greek system) is based on meters constructed according to syllable length. A long syllable, which contains either a long vowel or diphthong, takes twice as long to pronounce as a short one. Although the classical pronunciation of Latin was not completely understood during the Middle Ages, the medieval arts curriculum inherited the Roman classification of meter under the art of grammar.[30] In grammar school medieval students learned the traditional rules for determining syllabic quantity as well as the classification of the different kinds of poetic feet.[31]

Adopting the practice from the Roman education system, medieval grammar schools continued to teach schoolboys how to compose Latin verse, often by translating a passage of prose into poetry.[32] Such efforts would be assisted by handbooks for composing poetry (*ars poetriae*) written by medieval teachers of grammar. No fewer than six major poetic handbooks were written between the years of 1175 and 1280. Some of these included extensive discussions of classical meter for the benefit of students who wished to compose Latin verse (or were forced to do so by their teachers).[33] The earliest of these handbooks, *The Art of Versification* by Matthew of Vendôme (1175), offers instruction in composing elegiac distiches. This was the classical meter used, for example, by Ovid in the *Art of Love* and the *Heroides*.[34] Matthew's influential guide offers a modest contribution to poetics, generally along the lines suggested by Horace's *Art of Poetry*. The second book is devoted to verbal "elegance," while the third focuses on rhetorical figures. The practice of composing Latin poetry in quantitative meters during the Middle Ages thus remained strictly academic, most at home in the classroom.

During the later Roman Empire, the language of everyday spoken Latin, or what is known as Vulgar Latin (from *vulgus* "common people"), became ever more remote from the literate and artificial language of Classical Latin taught in Roman schools. During the early centuries of Christianity, speakers of Latin gradually began to lose distinctions between long and short vowels and syllables. The inevitable result was the gradual breakdown of quantitative meters. Systematic linguistic changes that had begun in Vulgar Latin eventually led to the development of the Romance languages and their regional dialects. Some of the greatest lyrics and most complex poetic forms ever devised were eventually composed in various medieval Romance vernaculars.

Historians of medieval poetry trace the introduction of accentually based meter, rhyme, and strophic or stanzaic patterns back to early Christian liturgy and hymns.[35] In the Western church, Latin hymnody dates back to at least the fourth century. *The Book of Hymns* compiled by Hilarius, bishop of Poitier, employs classical meters. More crucial for later developments were the hymns composed by his younger contemporary, Ambrose, bishop of Milan. Ambrose appears to have invented the so-called Ambrosian quatrain, the most common strophic form in later hymns.

The historical importance of the new quatrain form cannot be overstated. Before long, this meter became accentual and eventually led to "the octosyllabic *abab* quatrain, the great staple stanza meter of all modern vernacular song."[36] Accentual meters began to emerge as early as the third and fourth centuries CE. During the following centuries, as stress patterns became more regular, syllabic quantity ceased to be measured, and rhyme becomes more important.

By the twelfth century, lyric poetry in Latin had travelled quite a distance from its classical forebears. At about the same time, however, vernacular poets were already beginning to explore the resources of their various mother tongues. Poets experimented with syllabic and accentual meters, devising new strophic patterns and creating rich new lyric subgenres. Above all, we have the troubadours and *trobairitz* (the female equivalent) to thank for much of the excitement generated among European poets and their audiences by the discovery of intricate new lyric forms. These innovations in form could be translated across linguistic and national boundaries.

The troubadours and *trobairitz* composed their lyric poems in Old Occitan (Provençal) from the late eleventh through the thirteenth century. They were not, we now know, the first vernacular poets to use rhyme or to write of love in Europe. In medieval Spain, where Muslim, Christian (Mozarabic) and Jewish communities interacted, love poetry in the form of *kharjas* was written as early as the tenth century in a Romance language that shows many borrowings from Arabic.[37] But the wider European influence of troubadour poetry was without parallel, and the roughly 2,500 lyric poems that survive stand as one of the glories of medieval or indeed any poetry.

The largest portion of this body of work takes the form of *cansos* or love songs, about a thousand of which survive in manuscript. Although transcriptions of melodies survive for only about ten percent of the surviving troubadour lyrics, some kind of musical setting, perhaps improvised in performance, was probably the general rule.[38] In many cases little is known about their creators. Some survive as no more than names of doubtful attribution. One curious feature of troubadour poetry is the existence of brief pseudo-biographical introductions to lives (*vidas*) and commentaries on poems (*razos*) for about a hundred troubadours contained in some manuscripts. These introductions are generally not contemporary with the poets and most date from about 1220–50 or later.[39] Often these accounts simply invent information about the poets' lives based on the poems themselves. The vivid sense of individual personality that emerges from many of the lyrics helped create in later audiences a craving to know more about their authors than the poems themselves revealed, even if readers had to settle for fiction. The *vidas* also mark the early stages of an erosion in the ancient mimetic theory of poetry and the tentative first steps toward the modern expressive theory.

Standard accounts of the history of medieval love lyric trace the influence exerted by the Occitan poets on other European vernacular traditions in northern France, Germany, the Iberian peninsula, and Italy.[40] Conspicuously absent from this list is medieval England. To be sure, twelfth-century literary fashions such as courtly love (*fin'amor*) were imported to England from the Continent. Poetry and the attitudes it embodied crossed the Channel from northern France, and in such circumstances Middle English poets began to employ strophic forms of some complexity for the first time.

At roughly the same time, however, something much more culturally significant was taking place in Sicily at the cosmopolitan court of Frederick II. The so-called Sicilian school flourished in the mid-thirteenth century. The earliest known adaptations of the troubadours' formal innovations to a dialect of Italian is the work of Giacomo da Lentini (active c. 1230–40), a notary in the imperial court in Palermo. He is generally believed to have invented the sonnet.[41] The Sicilian school also developed the complex structure of the *canzone* from Occitan, French, and Middle High German models.

As these innovations in lyric poetry quickly travelled north, a generation later Guittone d'Arezzo (c. 1235–94) became the foremost poet in Tuscany. An even more seminal figure in the history of lyric poetry is Guido Guinizelli (c. 1240–76). His great innovation was to turn the courtly love lyric into a vehicle for exploring serious philosophical themes. Guido Cavalcanti took these experiments even further, combining complex lyric forms with intellectually ambitious ideas. Preeminent among the Tuscan poets of the "sweet new style" (*dolce stil nuovo*) was Dante Alighieri. Compiled c. 1294, Dante's memorial on the life and death of his great love, Beatrice, is called *Vita nova* (*The New Life*). For the first time since the Romans, we find a poet with the confidence to collect his own lyrics into a single volume.[42]

And so, by the time of the Italian *stilnovisti* poets of the 1290s, vernacular poetry in various European centers had been conducting experiments in style, form, and theme for about two centuries, always with a keen awareness of rhetorical doctrine. Lyric poetry and song had reached its greatest heights since classical antiquity. What was now urgently needed was a work of critical appraisal that could begin to take stock of these achievements in vernacular poetry.

Dante's forced exile from Florence in 1302 provided both the motivation and opportunity to begin this task in his unfinished Latin treatise, *On Vernacular Eloquence* (*De vulgari eloquentia*), written about 1303–05.[43] This landmark in the history of literary criticism it is not as widely known as it deserves to be. Yet it deserves our attention because Dante wrote with the unique advantage of being the foremost practitioner of lyric poetry of his age, as well as its most innovative literary theorist.

At the heart of his project lies his fundamental distinction between Latin and the vernacular. He defines vernacular language as that "which infants acquire from those around them," the speech "which we learn without any formal instruction, by imitating our nurses" (*DVE* 1.1.2). The most striking feature of his linguistic theory is his refusal to speak of Latin, substituting instead the more abstract notion of *gramatica*. After introducing this fundamental distinction, he makes this radical pronouncement: "Of these two kinds of language, the more noble is the vernacular" (1.1.4).

Overturning centuries of received knowledge about the superiority of Latin, Dante begins the project of reversing the linguistic hierarchy that had long placed Latin above the vernacular in the minds of medieval scholars. This upending of tradition would take centuries to complete. Yet as he surveys the number local dialects of Italy, if we expect him to select his own Tuscan variety as the best available vernacular, we are in for a surprise. Despite the notable achievements of Florentine poets (including Dante), neither Tuscan speech nor any of the other varieties of spoken Italian qualifies for the honorific title of "illustrious vernacular," though each one offers traces of it, like a panther "whose scent is left everywhere but which is nowhere to be seen" (1.16.1).

In its close analysis of the *canzone* form, the unfinished second book of Dante's treatise combines evaluative and prescriptive criticism in ways that were without precedent. His account is startlingly different from what classical and medieval rhetorical tradition might lead us to expect. Scholars point out that Dante does not follow the handbooks in discussing ornamentation. Instead, he "sets out to establish an authoritative tradition of his own by illustrating and analyzing the great examples identified by him in the field of Romance lyric, while at the same time urging his readers to study the Latin tradition."[44] Like the episode of Dante's encounter with medieval lyric poets in *Purgatorio* 24–26 composed some years later, the earlier project is driven by an idea of a poetic canon that places the lyric at its very center.

Lyric poetry had never occupied such a place of honor before, and Dante needed to invent a theoretical justification for breaking with critical tradition. In evaluating lyric poetry, he applies the standards of "worth" (*dignitas*) and "appropriateness" (*convenientia*), the medieval equivalent of the classical idea of decorum. Dante was the first critic since Aristotle to see that the poetic object should be understood in terms of the intrinsic formal structure required by the specific function it serves, and that such functions necessarily involve social relations.

At the time he was writing *On Vernacular Eloquence*, Dante believed the *canzone* was the noblest form of lyric poetry. Dante bases his theoretical knowledge on his practical know-how of poetic technique: "only in *canzoni* are the technical possibilities of the art fully exploited" (2.3.8). Dante's pioneering discussion of lyric form stresses the principle of harmony (which for Dante includes the relation of sound and sense) while discarding the Aristotelian idea of *mimēsis* or imitation (see 2.8.5–7). His discussion of the harmonious sound of lyric poetry may lack the precision of modern linguistics. But it demonstrates that he intuitively grasped what modern scholars, borrowing from the Greek, have called the "melic" aspect of the lyric.[45]

Dante explains that the term *stanza* "was coined solely for the purpose of discussing poetic technique." Stanza structure deserves close analysis because it is "the object in which the whole art of the *canzone* was enshrined" (2.9.1–2). He outlines a plan for analyzing the *canzone*, "beginning with its melody, moving on to its organization, and finally discussing its lines and syllables" (2.10.1). Unfortunately, the treatise abruptly ends before completing this plan. Dante views the stanza as the fundamental unit of composition for the *canzone*. Although he does not say so explicitly, evidently the reason why the smaller unit of the poetic line is not viewed as the basic building block of the preeminent early lyric form in Italian is because *all* poetry (ancient and modern) is measured in lines. The stanza, however, is distinctive of the *canzone*.

The first stanza type he analyzes is one composed to be "accompanied by an uninterrupted melody" (2.10.2). Dante discusses the "organization" of the *canzone*, which he considers "the most important aspect as far as technique is concerned" (2.11.1). He examines how different stanza patterns "weave lines together," sometimes using different line lengths to create subdivisions. Another important structural device that he notes, one that would remain central to European poetry for centuries to come, is the poet's ability "to create an effect of echo between rhymes" (2.12.8). For us the observation that rhyme creates sound echoes may seem too obvious to require stating. Yet for his readers this would not have been the case. Because classical quantitative verse did not employ rhyme, Dante had to modify the vocabulary of the medieval *poetriae*, which were written to help students compose Latin verse.

Unfortunately, most of what Dante intended to say about rhyme is postponed to the (unwritten) portion of the treatise dealing with the middle style, or what earlier he refers to as "comic" style (2.13.1). Fortunately, however, he anticipates some of those points here. In discussing how many rhymes to employ within a single stanza, he observes once again that "all poets grant themselves a considerable degree of license in this matter, and this is mostly what they aim at to achieve the sweetness of the overall harmony" (2.13.4).

Dante's *De vulgari eloquentia* may have marked a turning point in the history of literary criticism, but judging from the small number of surviving manuscripts, it seems to have found few readers at first. Indeed, it exerted no discernable influence on the theory or practice of vernacular poetry in Italy until its rediscovery by sixteenth-century Italian humanists. With the benefit of hindsight, however, we can see that Dante initiated the project of a literary criticism of the modern vernacular languages by his insistence that poetry in the mother tongue is worth our serious attention. Nothing like his theoretical clarion call was even remotely conceivable in England until well into the sixteenth century.

But the defense of poetry in the vernacular could only take root in England after the intellectual movement known as humanism began to flourish in Italy before spreading to northern Europe. The earliest Italian humanists were active in the generation immediately after Dante. One of the earliest, Giovanni Boccaccio, compiled a defense of poetry in the last two books of his encyclopedic work on pagan mythology, *The Genealogy of the Pagan Gods* (*Genealogia deorum gentilium*).[46] This pivotal work stands as the culmination of much serious medieval thought about poetry and looks forward to later trends of Renaissance humanism. Boccaccio shared many of the same interests in classical poetry as his fellow early humanist, the scholar-poet Francis Petrarch. Both these early humanists responded to attacks on the value of poetry. Theologians and clergy viewed poetry as morally dangerous; secular professionals in law and medicine dismissed it as a waste of time. Boccaccio and Petrarch defended classical poetry by insisting that it contained hidden truths under an allegorical covering. The purpose of allegory, Boccaccio explained, was to preserve hidden truths from the vulgar and to afford pleasure to those who were able to decipher its mysteries. Petrarch's and Boccaccio's views exerted an enormous influence on Italian humanists until the end of the fifteenth century, when Florentine Neoplatonists like Marsilio Ficino and Cristoforo Landino began to read serious poetry as allegorical versions of Platonic philosophical doctrines.[47]

However, even though Boccaccio and Petrarch were vernacular poets themselves, they and their immediate followers made little effort to defend vernacular poetry on theoretical grounds. When Boccaccio reviews modern authors in his *Genealogy* (15.6), he mentions few vernacular poets. Given the enormous influence of Petrarch's *Canzoniere* or *Rime sparse* on European love poetry for two centuries, it is ironic that Petrarch did so much to shift learned opinion away from the use of the vernacular in favor of the far more prestigious Latin. Under Petrarch's influence, Boccaccio "was forced into a series of recantations regarding his sympathy for the vernacular in general and his admiration for Dante in particular."[48] When Boccaccio reaches the name of Petrarch in his survey of illustrious modern Italian authors, it is telling that he makes no mention of his vernacular poetry, including the *Rime*. Poetic practice, as usual, was in the vanguard, with critical theory lagging far behind, sometimes even for the same author.

The debate over the value of the vernacular for poetry and other scholarly purposes continued in the fifteenth century. Leonardo Bruni (1374–1444) defended the use of the vernacular in his *Lives of Dante and Petrarch* (1436), "observing that whether a work is written in Latin or the *volgare* is immaterial…. [E]very language … has its own perfection, its own sound, and its own polished and learned style."[49] Leon Battista Alberti (1404–72) offered in the same decade "the most forceful theoretical defense of the vernacular articulated thus far," and he did so "by adopting rigorously humanist criteria" such as grammatical precision.[50] Momentum towards accepting the vernacular for both scholarly and poetic purposes continued to grow in the fifteenth century when the Florentine Neoplatonist Cristoforo Landino (1424–1504) observed that the *volgare* "is in a state of continuous, dynamic improvement, is already 'copious and elegant, and will become even more so every day, if scholars apply themselves to using it.'"[51]

The defense of poetic fiction by early humanists, based on allegorical readings of Vergil or Homer, may appear quaint or even risible to our eyes. Nonetheless, other grounds of defense were beginning to emerge in the fifteenth century. Coluccio Salutati (1331–1406) continued to defend poetry on the basis of allegorical interpretation, but unlike earlier humanists, he made the study of poetry an important part of a theory of education.[52] Unlike Salutati, Pier Paolo Vergerio does not rely on allegorical interpretation to defend poetry. In his humanist treatise on education, *On Liberal Manners* (*De ingenuis moribus*) from 1402 to 1403, Vergerio praises poetry and links it to rhetoric. Though he acknowledges that "[poetry] can contribute much to our lives and to our powers of eloquence," he suggests that "it seems more suited to purposes of enjoyment."[53] Pleasure thus emerges as a strongly positive value in its own right as the tide begins to turn away from centuries of suspicion beginning with Plato. Moreover, Guarino da Verona and Leonardo Bruni, two contemporaries of Vergerio's, shift their emphasis away from the traditional allegorical defense of poetry towards an "aesthetic appreciation of the poet's art."[54] With Italian humanism, the formal defense of poetry reaches a historical turning point. It was now possible to read poetry rhetorically as a distinctive and enjoyable form of eloquence without feeling the need to apply Platonic strictures to its appreciation.

To Renaissance humanism we owe the recovery of much of the literature and criticism of classical antiquity, especially in Greek. Without a knowledge of Greek, educated medieval poets and readers had long been shut out from access to such writings. To the humanists we also owe the advancement of new programs of education, including many of the habits of scholarship and reading that we now take for granted.[55] The humanists were thus responsible for what they tendentiously described as the "rebirth" of classical learning signaled by the term "Renaissance."

Given their devotion to Greco-Roman civilization, not all humanist scholars were sympathetic to vernacular learning. Latin remained at the cultural epicenter of Renaissance thought. However, fifteenth-century Italian humanists started to think of language as "a socio-historical product" created by a living "speech community."[56] Although early humanists like Lorenzo Valla continued to cling to the notion that Latin was innately superior to modern languages, during the sixteenth century succeeding generations of scholars began to recognize the radical implications of this newer understanding of language.

It now became possible for humanists to argue that the modern vernaculars not only could perform all the functions of Latin equally well but in some case might even surpass it. Perhaps the most important of these sixteenth-century attempts to challenge the supremacy of Latin was Sperone Speroni's *Dialogue on Languages* (*Dialogo delle lingue*), published in 1542. Speroni's work "virtually set the agenda for the quarrel between the ancients and moderns that would continue into the eighteenth century."[57] Speroni and his followers stressed a point that Dante had only begun to grasp, that "the language we learn 'della bocca'" (orally, instead of from books) possesses far greater "emotional power and cognitive accuracy" than the Latin artificially acquired as a second language.[58] Among those who picked up such ideas from Speroni was Joachim du Bellay, the French poet-critic, in his *Defense and Illustration of the French Language* (*Deffence et illustration de la langue françoyse*) of 1549.[59]

The growing self-consciousness among humanists on the Continent about the dignity and worth of the vernacular tongue eventually was eventually taken up by English writers. In many ways, Geoffrey Chaucer, a foundational figure for English poetry, anticipated these new ways of thinking about vernacular poetry. Chaucer absorbed many of the lessons of early Italian humanism as a result of his travels to Italy. Although his poetry itself frequently discusses his art (often with his characteristic touch of humor), Chaucer never composed a separate theoretical work defending his poetic practice. Such efforts were left to sixteenth-century English scholars.

One of the most influential English humanists was the early Tudor author and statesman, Sir Thomas Elyot (1490?–1546), a pioneer in bringing Italian humanism to England. In *The Boke named the Governour* (first published in 1531), Elyot outlined an ambitious program for the education of the governing classes. The study of classical poetry, as we might expect, was a central plank in his platform for a humanist education. He therefore adapts into Early Modern English the values and terminology found in the classical rhetorical authorities.

Elyot's definition of *eloquence*, for example, "runs together Quintilian's list of the four virtues of style: correctness, lucidity, elegance, and appropriateness (*Inst.* 1.5.1, 8.1.1), with Cicero's definition of the orator's three duties: *docere, movere, delectare*."[60] Elyot takes up the cause of defending poetry by responding to those moralists who object to Roman erotic verse, which he argues was intended as an instructive warning against vice. Here we can see a clear example of habits of reading that were inherited from ancient rhetorical poetics, which taught that poetry was a species of epideictic performance, praising virtue and blaming vice. Although composing his educational tract in English was historically unprecedented, like a good humanist, Elyot believes in a reading program of Greek and Roman authors.

The earliest book in English systematically to present classical rhetorical doctrine for the general reader unable to read Greek or Latin was *The Arte of Rhetorique* (1560) by Thomas Wilson (1523?–81). He repeats the traditional idea that the orator's three purposes are "to teach, to delight, and to persuade" (*ERLC* 77). Under the heading of elocution, he defines *exornation* as "a gorgeous beautifying of the tongue with borrowed words, and change of sentence [meaning] or speech with much variety."[61]

The next Tudor humanist whose educational program set the stage for the appreciation of poetic technique in England is the somewhat cranky figure of Roger Ascham (1515/16–68), who was tutor to Elizabeth I. His posthumously published *The Scholemaster* (1570) was intended to offer instruction in Latin for gentlemen and others who might need a refresher course or for anyone without access to a tutor. Although not entirely dismissive of vernacular language, Ascham is clearly biased toward classical learning. Yet rather than adopting the Aristotelian idea of mimesis, he recommends "imitation" that follows prestigious models: "if ye would speak as the best and wisest do, ye must be conversant where the best and wisest are" (*ERLC* 141). To the ancients, therefore, we must turn if we would study "the true pattern of eloquence" (*ERLC* 151). Reading the best classical poets attentively will train the reader to appreciate excellence until "he shall easily perceive what is fit and *decorum* in every one, to the true use of perfect imitation" (*ERLC* 151).

Ascham treats matters of poetics and prosody, unfavorably comparing modern English poetry to that of the ancients. With a prejudice against all things medieval that is typical of Renaissance humanism, he condemns rhyme altogether (*ERLC* 157). Thus he expresses disapproval at the English poets' use of "barbarous and rude rhyming," since men of learning must understand the poetic superiority of classical verse. Ascham wryly observes that those who "make Chaucer in English, and Petrarch in Italian, their gods in verses" will not like his book (*ERLC* 157–58). His prejudice against accentual meter—indeed his complete lack of understanding of how it actually works—was based on the belief that the only true meter was quantitative. This habit of mind was formed by the grammar school study of Latin.[62]

By the seventh decade of the sixteenth century, the battle lines were firmly drawn between culturally conservative classicists, who wished English could be more like Greek and Latin; and vernacular poets and their readers, who appreciated new experiments with the sound of English poetry. History, of course, was on the side of the poets of vernacular eloquence who felt no need to imitate classical prosody. Instead, poetic practice in the sixteenth century established the metrical rules of English versification, especially the iambic pentameter line.[63]

The earliest theoretical account of accentual meter in English is the short tract by the poet George Gascoigne (1542–77), *Certayne notes of Instruction concerning the making of verse or ryme in English* (1575), addressed to one Master Eduardo Donati.[64] Although modest in its proportions and scope (requiring under ten pages in a modern edition), this pragmatic short piece nonetheless carries the distinction of being the earliest work of English literary criticism. Gascoigne assumes that reading poetry well, no less than composing it, requires skills and competencies that are teachable and may be honed by experience.

As we have seen, Renaissance poetic theory was nearly unanimous in viewing poetry as a form of epideictic (demonstrative) or display rhetoric. Its object, in other words, is to praise virtue or blame vice.[65] "The most important innovation in epideictic theory after Aristotle," according to O. B. Hardison, "was the idea that praise and blame should didactic."[66] Gascoigne advises that poetic praise should be skillful: "If I should undertake to write in praise of a gentlewoman, I would neither praise her crystal eye, nor her cherry lips, etc. For these things are *trita et obvia* [trite and obvious]" (163).

Recalling the classical dictum that one of the purposes of poetry is to delight, Gascoigne advises that the poet's words must not undermine the invention of matter in a vain pursuit of pleasure: "take heed that neither pleasure of rhyme nor variety of device do carry you from [invention]: for as to use obscure and dark phrases in a pleasant sonnet is nothing delectable, so to intermingle jests in a serious matter is an *indecorum*" (164).

The largest portion of the tract is devoted to matters of prosody, and here Gascoigne's contribution shows some originality. Such an attempt to explain English metrical practice would have been unthinkable only a few decades earlier. The pentameter line used by Thomas Wyatt often appears to be highly irregular, as we shall see in a later chapter. A more stable metrical norm was evident by the time *Tottel's Miscellany* was published in 1557. In this collection Wyatt's poems were revised to make his meter more regular. Gascoigne's precepts concerning versification thus provide early evidence for a new appreciation of how poetry sounds when spoken aloud, especially the rhythmic patterns that speakers of English naturally grasp if it is their mother tongue.

Gascoigne advises the would-be poet to "remember to place every word in his natural *emphasis* or sound, that is to say, in such wise, and with such length or shortness, elevation or depression of syllables, as it is commonly pronounced or used" (164; italics in original). Poets, that is, must have an ear for the natural rhythms of English speech patterns. Because the only model for scansion available at this time was the classical quantitative system, Gascoigne assumes that he must speak in terms of syllable length. By "elevation or depression of syllables," on the other hand, he points to the syllabic *stress* (often described as *accent*), the perceived degree of relative prominence of syllables.[67] The qualifier *perceived* is crucial here because poetic rhythm and meter are more a matter of subjective perception than of objective patterns of physical, acoustic events that can be measured by machines in laboratories.[68]

In describing what we recognize as syllabic stress, however, Gascoigne further confuses matters when he "combines terms descriptive of pitch, stress, and length."[69] In this usage Gascoigne follows Latin grammarians, who distinguished among three types of "accents" (*gravis, levis, et circumflexa*), which he translates as "the long accent, the short accent, and that which is indifferent." Roman grammarians had adapted their system for describing Latin pronunciation from the Greeks, whose language originally employed three degrees of pitch accent (rising, falling, and rising-falling). Pitch accent is distinct from both syllabic stress and duration or length (long or short quantity).[70] Gascoigne proposes to use the grave accent / to mark the "drawn out or elevated" syllable that "maketh that syllable long whereupon it is placed." By contrast, "[t]he light accent is depressed or snatched up" and is marked \.[71]

As Gavin Alexander explains, "[i]n Gascoigne's system, the 'grave' accent equates with stress, length and a rise in pitch, and the 'light' accent with a lack of stress, shortness and a depression of pitch" (*SRLC* 407). Gascoigne illustrates his principle "of the emphasis or natural sound of words" with the example of the word *treasure*, which "has the grave accent upon the first syllable; whereas if it should be written in this sort *treasúre*, now were the second syllable long, and that were clean contrary to the common use wherewith it is pronounced" (164).

It is worth pausing for a moment to underline the historical significance of Gascoigne's unprecedented demonstration of the elementary principles of English scansion. Despite the many changes that the pronunciation of English has undergone since the mid-sixteenth century, to this day native speakers of English continue to perceive the stress pattern of the word *treasure* in the same way as Gascoigne. For the twenty-first century native speaker of English, Gascoigne's example still works just as he intended because we share the relevant background experience with language.

To clarify his meaning, Gascoigne offers a sample two-verse pairing (distich) in a regular accentual-syllabic meter. He provides two different notations to mark the basic stress pattern. The squiggly line above the first verse marks the rhythmic contour of the entire couplet. The high points on the scale correspond to stressed syllables, while the low points correspond to unstressed syllables, single or paired. The little points mark the juncture between two unstressed syllables. The notation above the second verse, on the other hand, uses an acute accent (/) to mark a stressed syllable, while a grave accent (\) marks a weak one:

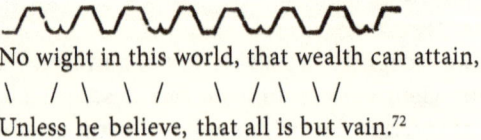
No wight in this world, that wealth can attain,
\ / \ \ / \ / \ /
Unless he believe, that all is but vain.[72]

Though the couplet is metrically regular, it is not by any measure especially good poetry.

Using Derek Attridge's system of scansion will help clarify Gascoigne's point.[73] The syllables that take *beats* are marked with a **B** under them. The syllables that do not take a beat are called *offbeats* and are marked with one **o** or two. Gascoigne's example employs a four-beat rhythm in a free triple meter. The meter is styled "free" because it can use either a single unstressed syllable (**o**) or two unstressed syllables (**o-o**) to realize an offbeat. The first verse of Gascoigne's couplet would be marked thus:

> No wight in this world, that wealth can attain
> o B   o-o   B   o   B   o-o   B

Without doubt, Gascoigne's unprecedented graphic method of indicating stress patterns with a squiggly line make metrical sense to us even now.

Gascoigne thus offers precious early evidence that confirms an essential point. Metrical patterns have remained relatively stable over long periods of time—from Early Modern English until the present day. Having a good "ear" for poetic rhythms is a durable skill transmitted down through the centuries. Gascoigne was writing at a time when the main tradition of regular accentual-syllabic verse had just begun to be firmly established. This metrical system survives to this day (though nowadays, relatively few poets still employ regular meter).

In the second half of the sixteenth century, poets and readers increasingly came to share an intuitive feel for a variety of rhythms and meters employed by accentual-syllabic verse, most often in four-beat or five-beat meters. When syllables alternate between beats and offbeats, we have a "duple" meter. In traditional terms, this gives us either iambic or trochaic verse. When syllables alternate between beats and two offbeats, we have a "triple" meter (in traditional terms, dactylic or anapestic verse). A feel for these rhythmic patterns constituted a shared sense that remained stable enough to be passed down through the centuries.[74]

Borrowing a term from the psychology of perception, Attridge describes the metrical framework shared by native speakers of English who are experienced readers of poetry as the "general 'set.'" This psychological "set" shapes patterns of expectation in the reader or listener. But sometimes the expectation of regularity over time is not fulfilled. This sense of broken expectation (not necessarily at a fully conscious level of awareness) creates a perception of metrical "tension."[75] Such moments of perceived *metrical tension* may function to express affective mental states, an important insight that I will illustrate in later chapters.[76]

Nonetheless, the sense of natural rhythms may be lost over long periods of time because languages inevitably change. This is precisely what happened to sixteenth-century readers of Chaucer. Gascoigne comments that "our father Chaucer" used "the same liberty in feet and measures that the Latinists do use." That is, "his lines are not always of one selfsame number of syllables" (165). Gascoigne's observation reflects an inability to grasp the finer points of Chaucerian meter owing to fifteenth-century sound changes, especially the loss of syllabic value for final *e*, which had become silent. Although Chaucer had effectively invented the iambic pentameter line in English, within a few generations his verse no longer seemed to scan regularly, and iambic pentameter had to be reinvented by sixteenth-century poets.

Gascoigne offers the earliest surviving explicit statement—however imprecisely formulated by our standards—that demonstrates an understanding of accentual-syllabic meter. His rules for composing verse with two-syllable feet assume a regular iambic norm of stress patterns. We should not be misled by his use of the inappropriate terminology of quantity and pitch to describe this norm. If we were to take him at his word, his rule that every even-numbered syllable in a line should be pronounced "long or elevated" would not permit any deviations from alternating unstressed-stressed.

In terms of Attridge's system, Gascoigne is claiming that in a duple meter (one which alternates offbeats and beats), only a single unstressed syllable can realize an offbeat and only a stressed syllable can realize a beat. Fortunately, Gascoigne's own verse generally does not suffer from quite so monotonous a rhythm as he appears to recommend. Yet his precept does not require poets to restrict themselves to choosing only disyllabic words, "for therein you may use discretion" (165). The proof of the metrical pudding is in the placement of the words.

Gascoigne illustrates this principle by using seven identical words arranged in both a regular iambic pentameter and a line that simply does not scan properly:

⌢⌣⌢⌣⌢⌣⌢⌣⌢⌣
I vnderſtand your meanyng by your eye,
\ / \ / \ / \ / \ /
Your meaning I vnderſtand by your eye.

(I understand your meaning by your eye.
Your meaning I understand by your eye.)

Gascoigne offers two different systems for marking scansion, I believe, because his attempt to convey the sense of English meter is unprecedented, and he does not wish to risk being misunderstood. Gascoigne's invents a graphic representation of English stress patterns using squiggly lines. This way he can demonstrate poetic meter in a printed text when his speaking voice is absent. Thus the rising and falling contours of his line supplement the use of standard diacritical marks to indicate "accent" (that is, what we think of as syllabic stress).

His uncontroversial evaluative comment on the poetic inferiority of the second version of the line drives home a crucial point. Metrical skill is in part a function of the poet and reader sharing the same sense of what it means to have a good ear. The shared psychological set establishes the difference between a line that works well metrically and one that simply does not feel right.

Gascoigne explains this principle thus: "In these two verses there seemeth no difference at all, since the one hath the very selfsame words that the other hath, and yet the latter verse is neither true nor pleasant, and the first verse may pass the musters. The fault of the latter verse is that this word 'understand' is therein so placed as the grave accent falleth upon 'der,' and thereby maketh 'der' in this word 'understand' to be elevated; which is contrary to the natural or usual pronunciation, for we say 'ùndèrstánd,' and not 'ùndérstànd'" (166). Native speakers of English even today will share Gascoigne's sense of the correct and pleasurable way to pronounce *understand*. This sense allows us to know how to place the word in a line of iambic pentameter to exploit its perceived rhythmic shape.

"When we read regular verse aloud," Attridge explains, "we participate directly in the muscular rhythmic activity that underlies metrical form, and when we listen to it we participate empathetically."[77] Poetic rhythm plays a powerful emotional function because regular meter mimetically imitates "the emotions, attitudes, and modes of thought that constitute mental experience (and the bodily experience that feeds and realizes it)."[78] In other words, just as the rhetorical tradition generally informs us, the sound-patterns of poetry *move* us. Obviously, Gascoigne or his sixteenth-century successors cannot draw on our more refined vocabulary. Yet because his examples still make good *sense* to modern native speakers of English, they provide strong evidence of a durable skill or knack passed down through the centuries.

Gascoigne turns briefly to word-choice (lexis) and its relation to poetic meter, warning against using too many rare polysyllabic words. Because so many English words are monosyllabic, "the truer Englishman you shall seem, and the less you shall smell of the inkhorn" if you avoid words of many syllables. But "words of one syllable will more easily fall to be short or long as occasion requireth" (166). Turning to word-choice leads Gascoigne to the topic of rhyme, with the exhortation "to beware of rhyme without reason." It is better to "hold your first determined invention, and … search the bottom of your brains for apt words than change good reason for rumbling rhyme" (166). He then gives some practical advice for going through the alphabet in search of a rhyme. If no suitable rhyme is available, it is better to change the "the last word of your former verse" than to "alter the meaning of your invention" (167).

Gascoigne offers brief advice on the use of rhetorical figures and tropes. In judging that "they serve more aptly and have greater grace in verse than they have in prose" (167), he agrees with Quintilian and other classical rhetoricians. He quotes "the old adage, *Ne quid nimis*" (nothing in excess). For example, moderate use of alliteration "lendeth a good grace to a verse," though its overuse can be deadly. Following a classical precept on the stylistic virtues, he advises the poet to maintain clarity, "for the haughty obscure verse doth not much delight" (167).

Gascoigne surveys some prominent stanza forms used in English, including rhyme royal (Gascoigne is the earliest writer to give this name to the seven-line stanza invented by Chaucer), ballad, sonnet, and a meter that alternates twelve- and fourteen-syllable verses, known as "poulter's measure." This last one he describes as "the commonest sort of verse which we use nowadays" (170). Although poulter's measure was extremely common in mid-sixteenth-century verse, it soon fell out of fashion. At the last minute he inserts a form he nearly forgot to include: Chaucer's rhymed pentameter couplets or "riding rhyme" (171). Thus Gascoigne hastily brings his small treatise to a close.

Less than a decade after Gascoigne's tract, Sir Philip Sidney wrote the greatest work of literary criticism of the English Renaissance, the posthumously published text known alternatively as *An Apology for Poetry* or *The Defence of Poesy*.[79] The treatise provides testimony to how the rhetorical poetics advanced by the Italian humanists were translated into Renaissance England at a time of increasing national self-confidence. Sidney's definition of poetry returns us to familiar ground, bringing together Aristotelian and Horatian principles: "Poesy ... is an art of imitation, for so Aristotle termeth it in his word *mimesis*, that is to say, a representing, counterfeiting, or figuring forth—to speak metaphorically, a speaking picture—with this end, to teach and delight" (86). Sidney follows the definition of poetry by Franco-Italian humanist Julius Caesar Scaliger, who writes: "What is called Poesy describes not only what exists, but also non-existent things as if they existed, showing how they could or should exist. For the whole matter is comprehended in imitation. But imitation is only the means to the ultimate end, which is to teach with delight.... Poetry and the other arts represent things as they are, as a picture to the ear."[80]

Sidney values poetry for its ability to improve readers morally by appealing to their better selves: "right [true] poets ... most properly do imitate to teach and delight, and to imitate borrow nothing of what is, hath been, or shall be; but range ... into the divine consideration of what may be and should be" (86–87). With such an aim, poetry is superior to history and moral philosophy because its delightful sensuous texture is ultimately more persuasive than those forms of writing. The historian only teaches by example, the philosopher by precept. The delights of poetry, however, lead men "to see the form of goodness (which seen they cannot but love) ere themselves be aware, as if they took a medicine of cherries" (96). And thus "the poet, with that same hand of delight, doth draw the mind more effectually than any other art doth" (97). Once again, we find ourselves inhabiting the world of epideictic poetry, which teaches readers to emulate virtue and avoid vice.

In a lengthy digression, Sidney reviews English poetry from the time of Chaucer in search of understanding why England is "so hard a stepmother to poets" (108). Sidney's list is an important document in the history of English evaluative criticism since it conceives of the possibility of a literary history, though one that (typically for the Renaissance) was highly prescriptive. The greater portion of his survey of English poetic history is devoted to drama, replicating Aristotle's emphasis on drama at the expense of other forms of poetry in the *Poetics*. However, he devotes pertinent attention to "that lyrical kind of songs and sonnets" (113). Yet he faults contemporary love poets on technical grounds for their lack of skill. Much of their poetry, he wryly observes, "if I were a mistress, would never persuade me that they were in love" because of a lack of "forcibleness" (113). Moreover, contemporary lyric poets fare worse in their use of diction. At times they employ "far-fetched words" or appear "to follow the method of a dictionary; another time with figures and flowers extremely winter-starved" (113).

Tellingly, as Sidney continues to rail against the majority of his unnamed contemporaries, he finds his discussion soon "straying from Poetry to Oratory" (115). Indeed, the movement of his mind reinforces our sense that the project of a poetics or literary aesthetics in the Renaissance remained a subcategory of rhetoric rather than developing into a fully independent branch of learning. From all this we may conclude that because Sidney took a traditional view of poetry as a distinctive form of eloquence and imitation, its excellence for him was not purely a matter of aesthetics. At the same time, however, his ethical and rhetorical understanding of the function of poetry is far from indifferent to considerations of poetic form and beauty.

As Sidney surveys English poetry from Chaucer until his own time, he considers the suitability of the English language as a vehicle for vernacular eloquence. Although not a professional scholar, Sidney knew how to read and speak Latin, French, and Italian fairly well and had a limited reading knowledge of classical Greek, modern Dutch and Spanish. His extensive linguistic experience stands behind his opinion that English is second to none "for the uttering sweetly and properly the conceits of the mind." In his judgment, English surpasses Latin and stands "near the Greek" in the formation of compound words, "which is one of the greatest beauties can be in a language" (115.20–25).

Sidney, who himself experimented with adapting quantitative measures to English verse, was remarkably open-minded about the comparative virtues of the two systems of versification. He suggests that it would be futile to debate which system of versification is "most excellent," since each one has its advantages: "the ancient [is] (no doubt) more fit for music, both words and [tune][81] observing quantity, and more fit lively to express divers passions, by the low or lofty sound of the well-weighed syllable. The latter likewise, with his rhyme, striketh a certain music to the ear; and, in fine, since it doth delight, though by another way, it obtains the same purpose: there being in either sweetness, and wanting in neither majesty" (115.31–37). If Dante's *De vulgari eloquentia* is the earliest defense of vernacular poetry in general, Sidney's *Defense* marks the same turning point for English by proclaiming that its dignity rivals that of the ancient tongues.

Sidney even claims that "truly the English, before any other vulgar language I know, is fit for both sorts" of versification. French and Spanish, he explains, have stress patterns that prevent words from accenting the syllable two back from the final position, "and therefore very gracelessly may they use dactyls. The English is subject to none of these defects." As for the suitability of English for composing *rhyme* (that is, accentual meter), English has linguistic resources that exceed those of the Romance languages, allowing English poets to "observe the accent very precisely" (116). At this point Sidney ends his digression and winds up the entire virtuoso performance.

Other discussions of vernacular poetry by Renaissance English writers took up the themes we have discussed in this chapter, though we have no space to consider them at any length. Readers who wish to pursue rhetorical poetics further should look at the longest and most interesting of the Elizabethan discussions of poetic technique, *The Art of English Poesy* by George Puttenham (1529/30–1591). First published anonymously in 1589, the book seems to have been composed mostly in the early 1580s, though some portions may date from as early as 1569. Until recently, Puttenham's fascinating treatise was unavailable in a form accessible to modern readers, though that is no longer the case.[82] His extensive analyses of poetic form and his evaluative precepts offer evidence for how one intelligent and well-educated Elizabethan read poetry rhetorically and what he valued in the experience.

Puttenham's first book, "Of Poets and Poesy," includes a definition of poetry and an overview of its early history. Much of its matter takes the form of a defense of poetry, before he outlines the different poetic genres developed by the ancients. The final chapter (1.31), which was added later, surveys the history of English poetry from Chaucer into the Elizabethan Age. Book 2, "Of Proportion Poetical," analyses poetic meter, rhyme, and stanzaic forms. Finally, Book 3, "Of Ornament," is devoted to rhetorical figures. One of the most charming aspects of the treatise is Puttenham's invention of English descriptive labels for the traditional Greek and Latin terms, such as *ironia* or "the Dry Mock" (273).

The only other known effort at composing a complete art of poetry in the Elizabethan period is the newly discovered *Model of Poesy* (c. 1599) by William Scott (c. 1571–c. 1617), which has only recently been printed for the first time.[83] A much better known discussion of poetic technique from the period is by Thomas Campion (1567–1620), who belatedly took up the cause of defending quantitative verse. In addition to some of the most successful experiments in quantitative verse, Campion wrote *Observations in the Art of English Poesy* (published 1602), urging English poets to abandon rhyme and accentual meter in favor of quantitative meters.[84]

Yet for all his fussy classicism, Campion's ear is remarkably acute. His grasp of syllabic quantification demonstrates a musician's sense of rhythm, accent, and pause. His theory of quantitative meter, though greatly influenced by Sidney's discussion, is even more concerned than the earlier treatise with ensuring that the rules of quantity be determined by normal pronunciation. Campion's last-ditched effort to renew the debate about quantitative meter in English was directly answered by another practicing poet, Samuel Daniel (1562–1619) in *A Defence of Ryme* (London c. 1603).[85] So persuasive was his refutation of Campion that it effectively ended the debate. For Daniel, the practice of accentual meter is natural to the English language as imitations of classical meter simply are not. His position has stood the test of time.

The habits created by the formal study of rhetoric led Renaissance English critics to an unprecedented level of self-consciousness about poetic technique. The sixteenth century thus marks an important cultural turning point. Because the language of poetry in Early Modern English maintains relatively close links to many of our own speech patterns, we may attune our ears and take pleasure in that early verbal music. For the untrained reader, the barriers to reading medieval poetry in the original are significantly greater than they are to reading sixteenth-century verse. Beginning around 1500, however, the language becomes sufficiently modern that without too much effort non-specialists may continue to enjoy this poetry in ways that have endured for centuries.

Like the Renaissance critic, we may respond to the charms and rhythms of poetry and be moved by a love of its beauty. Since time immemorial poetry has seemed to many a fundamental mode of understanding our humanity. The rhetorical approach to poetic excellence offers useable ways of thinking about how poetry can enrich one's life and why it might matter.

Our survey of over two millennia of rhetorical poetics has taught us that the surest grounds for defending poetry are both aesthetic and ethical in the broadest sense. The ancients were clearly on to something when they told us that poetry delights, teaches, and moves. To abandon that understanding is to risk impoverishing human possibilities.

2

What Was a Lyric Poem?

When readers encounter poetry in the early twenty-first century, it is almost exclusively in the form of short poems. From our earliest exposure to poetry in the nursery or elementary school we form the expectation that poems are relatively brief things. This expectation is reinforced as we grow older and encounter poetry in new venues. Many of the poems we are exposed to are only a few lines long, and few take up much more space than what can fit on a single printed page. We might hear them described as *lyric* poems, though we also are told that songs have *lyrics*. But it was not always thus. In earlier ages, a single poem could be the length of a hefty book (epic) or be written for the stage (drama). In the last century or so, fewer and fewer poets have attempted to write epic poems or dramas in verse as the audiences for such ambitious works have all but disappeared. Given these cultural shifts, how can knowing something about changing conceptions about lyric poetry help us read short poetic masterpieces of an earlier age?

Ever since the Greeks, it is often assumed, lyric poetry has naturally taken its place as one of three fundamental kinds of poetry, along with epic and drama. Yet the lack of a coherent theory of lyric poetry in Plato and Aristotle as discussed in Chapter 1 should alert us that it is misleading to assume a systematic three-part division of poetry in Greek thought. Indeed, it was not until the Renaissance that writers began to attribute this division to the Greeks. By the eighteenth century, however, the idea that lyric was one of the three fundamental kinds of poetry was firmly established as a kind of critical back-formation.[1]

All this suggests that the literary genre of lyric poetry is an important example of a *historical kind*, not a timeless essence. In the medieval and early modern periods, the generic category of lyric did not do the same cultural work that it later came to perform. In the rhetorical culture described in the previous chapter, the various forms of short poems that later critics would place under the umbrella category of lyric would not have been read under the guiding assumptions that characterize post–Enlightenment readers. The notion of lyric poetry that has been familiar for the last two centuries is thus a relatively recent invention, though it has roots in earlier traditions, ultimately going back to the Greeks.[2]

To speak of lyric as a historical kind or genre of poetry is to draw more generally on a theory of literary genre. Genre theory, like most other aspects of literary theory in the West, began with the Greeks. Many nonwestern cultures (such as Classical India) developed their own theory of genres, but these lie outside the scope of this book. As we saw in Chapter 1, Aristotle's *Poetics* adapted an idea from Plato to identify three different *modes of representation*, based on who is speaking. His distinction between tragedy and epic is fundamental to his theory of genre. During the Hellenistic age, scholars developed a more sophisticated theory of literary genres to help them catalogue literary works for the great library at Alexandria.

Before long, genre theory involved creating a system of classification for dividing literary works into different kinds. This historical tendency often led genre theory to end up becoming a dry, prescriptive exercise. Critics began to identify the characteristics that a literary work *ought* to have to be a good example of its distinctive kind (already we see this tendency in Aristotle). This prescriptive tendency led critics to formulate rules that literary works were expected to follow. Modern critics rightly reject the prescriptivism of neoclassical critics. But genre theory, when used flexibly, remains valuable for helping us understand how an individual literary work fits into the larger system of literature. In other words, genre theory can help us become better informed readers.

What, then, is lyric poetry? The question is deceptively simple. A frequent starting point in attempting to answer this question is to recall the term's historical link with verses composed to be sung to the accompaniment of the lyre (*lyra*) in ancient Greece. After noting the etymological connection with the ancient stringed instrument and the sung mode of presentation implied by the root meaning of *lyric*, the *Oxford English Dictionary* offers this definition: "Now used as the name for short poems (whether or not intended to be sung), usually divided into stanzas or strophes, and directly expressing the poet's own thoughts and sentiments."[3] A similar definition is offered by M. H. Abrams in his *Glossary of Literary Terms*, which defines lyric as "any fairly short poem, uttered by a single speaker, who expresses a state of mind or a process of perception, thought, and feeling."[4] Abrams thus introduces the crucial concept of a *speaker*, whose voice is not necessarily to be identified directly with that of the poet. In fact, the default mode in Anglo-American criticism and pedagogical practice for much of the twentieth century was to treat lyric poems as the *dramatic speeches of fictional personae.* It is an approach that has survived to this day, especially in the classroom.

This relatively recent conception of lyric poetry provides one of the two main targets of Jonathan Culler's recent book, *Theory of the Lyric*, the most substantial theory of lyric poetry to emerge in Anglo-American criticism in over fifty years. (His other target, as we shall see in a moment, is an older form of expressive theory associated with Romanticism). Culler is surely correct that although some lyrics invite us to read them as though they are voiced by a fictional speaker in a specific dramatic situation, many other poems commonly assumed to be lyrics gain nothing from being read as though they are dramatic monologues.[5]

Given the variety of poems that have been placed under the category of lyric, perhaps there is a problem in trying to arrive at a universal definition of "lyric." David Lindley suggests in his introductory text that "many lyrics are short, many speak of heightened feeling in a poetic present and are uttered by a voice in the first person, and a significant number are written for music or out of a musical impulse. But many other poems we might wish to call 'lyrics' have few or none of these qualities."[6] More recently, Scott Brewster comments that "[l]yric has proved a problematic case for genre theory" insofar as it is sometimes viewed "as a timeless, universal aesthetic disposition," but at other times "as a generic category clearly defined by its subject matter, formal features, and purposes."[7] Roland Greene, in a suggestive essay on Renaissance lyric, agrees that defining lyric is fraught with difficulty: "lyric is always—even today—the most fugitive of genres when it comes to a theory of its identity," and he properly notes the lack of a good fit between "what we now call by that name" and what the term was used to describe during the early modern period.[8] Heather Dubrow, another specialist in early modern lyric poetry, speaks of the "limitations of transhistorical definitions of lyric," lamenting that "generalizations about lyric rendered dubious by the absence of historical inflection continue to flourish."[9]

As the definitions from the *OED* and Abrams's *Glossary* quoted above make clear, the most crucial aspect of lyric poetry normally identified as essential to the genre is its putatively *subjective* nature. The idea that lyric poetry is subjective played a central role in G. W. F. Hegel's theory of art, which was inseparable from his philosophy of history as the progressive unfolding of Spirit. In his *Lectures on Aesthetics*, Hegel associates "the lyrical" with romantic art, the stage at which art transcends itself by focusing on "subjective inwardness…. It is this *inner* world that forms the content of the romantic…."[10] Culler succinctly restates the main idea of Hegel's romantic theory as hinging on "the centrality of subjectivity coming to consciousness of itself through experience and reflection. The lyric poet absorbs into himself the external world and stamps it with inner consciousness, and the unity of the poem is provided by this subjectivity."[11]

This romantic conception of the lyric is the other main target of Culler's critique. In fact, the idea of lyric as the subjective utterance or expression of a fictive speaker is a direct offshoot of the earlier romantic theory most fully developed in Hegel. Such ultimately philosophical notions lie behind the *OED* definition echoed by Abrams: the generic label *lyric* designates poems that express the feelings and thoughts of an individual, whether identified with the poet or with a more ambiguously defined speaker, who may be entirely fictional or else stand in an uncertain relation to the poet. (We shall return to the problem of the relation between the lyric "I" and the biographical poet in later chapters.)

This emphasis on expression, as we saw in Chapter 1, depends on what Abrams identifies as the *expressive theory* of poetry.[12] Although this theory has its roots in earlier periods, it is especially associated with Romanticism, an intellectual movement that made it the dominant theory of poetry. The eighteenth century proved to be a pivotal moment in the history of literary criticism. In 1747, Batteux's *Principles of Literature* (*Principes de la littérature*), as Culler observes, "reinserts the lyric within the Aristotelian framework of literature as mimesis and yet lays the groundwork for the romantic elevation of lyric to the very type of literature." Batteux insists, "lyric poetry is wholly devoted to feelings."[13]

We find a succinct formulation of this romantic view in Wordsworth's Preface to *Lyrical Ballads* (1800), which famously describes poetry as "the spontaneous overflow of powerful feeling: it takes its origin from emotion recollected in tranquility."[14] The romantic conception of poetry tended to make the subjectivity (or in more traditional terms the personality) of the poet or artist the central object of critical concern. Although Plato and Aristotle identify one kind of poetry as spoken in the poet's own voice, it would not have occurred to either thinker to describe what the poet was doing when speaking in the first person as *expressing* his or her private thoughts and feelings.

By the later eighteenth century, however, the newly dominant theory began to take for granted that the very purpose of lyric poetry was for poets to express their "emotion recollected in tranquility," to quote Wordsworth's Preface again. Under the influence of nineteenth-century dramatic monologues by Robert Browning, modernist poets like the early T. S. Eliot and Ezra Pound among others took to the creation of first-person utterances by fictional personae. The continuing force of the expressive theory is clear from Eliot's conclusion in his classic essay, "Tradition and the Individual

Poet" (1919): "Poetry is not a turning loose of emotion, but an escape from emotion; it is not the expression of personality, but an escape from personality. But, of course, only those who have personality and emotions know what it means to want to escape from those things."[15]

The older assumption that lyric is marked by the *presence of a speaking voice* whose origin is a fictive or historical person (the "sovereign subject," as poststructuralists like to say) is precisely what the theoretical project of "deconstruction" called into question.[16] The traditional link between lyric poetry and subjective expression has been greatly complicated by new theories of the "subject." These theories began with structuralist linguistics and were extended by deconstruction. Such theories approach subjectivity as a linguistic phenomenon, the effect of using first-person grammatical forms and other instances of language whose variable meaning depends on the context of who is speaking, where, and when. Linguists refer to these aspects of language as *deixis* or linguistic "shifters" like *here, now,* etc.[17]

The play of near and far in time and space that occurs through deixis contributes to the "presence effects" of poetry. These presence effects use language as "techniques that produce the impression (or, rather, the illusion) that worlds of the past can become tangible again."[18] The poet-critic Susan Stewart explains how deixis works: "Whenever we use the terms *now* or *here* or *I* or *you*, we find ourselves immersed in the 'now' of articulation, the 'here' of the space in which speech is spoken, the 'I' of the speaker, the 'you' of the listener.... Yet we also understand such terms across contexts—we carry over their meaning, but not their particular referents."[19]

For some observers, to associate lyric with subjectivity means that lyric is the kind of poetry made of first-person utterance, whether spoken or (more archaically) sung. However, critics differ on the question of whether these utterances are experienced as "real" or "fictive."[20] In traditional accounts not influenced by poststructuralist theories of the subject, this lyric "I" marks the place of a coherent individual speaker. But many theoretically up-to-date critics oppose lingering attempts to "read 'the lyric' as a genre defined in terms of subjective expression."[21]

Until recently the dominant theory of lyric was wedded to the notion that "the lyric is subjective; it is the expression of feeling, of experience, *Erlebnis*."[22] Indeed, as Abrams demonstrates, the shift from mimetic to expressive theories of poetry led to the lyric becoming "the essentially poetic form" and "the paradigm for poetic theory."[23] To be sure, Renaissance critics occasionally speak of poetry as an expression or utterance of personal passions, feelings, or moods, but this remained a minor feature of their rhetorical poetics.[24] However, by the nineteenth century, the lyric expression of the inner life was beginning to stand in for poetry itself.[25]

Edgar Allan Poe makes it clear how by the mid-nineteenth century the lyric had gobbled up other forms of poetry. Poe states in "The Poetic Principle" (1850) that a long poem is a contradiction in terms because true poetry excites and elevates the soul, which "cannot be sustained throughout a composition of any great length." Thus even Homer's *Iliad* should be understood as "a series of lyrics."[26] Especially influential in helping lyric take over poetry as a whole was an essay by John Stuart Mill in which he famously suggested that poets speak out to the world as though they are turning their backs to the audience: "Eloquence is *heard*, poetry is *overheard*."[27] Mill thus thinks of lyric poetry as analogous to a soliloquy in drama. Culler observes that Mill's "opposition between poetry and eloquence would have been unintelligible to the Greeks."[28] In fact, this opposition would have been just as unthinkable in the Middle Ages and Renaissance. It is no coincidence that Mill was writing shortly before the dramatic monologue was fully developed. A dramatic monologue is like a soliloquy for a fictional persona.[29]

One influential twentieth-century critic who more or less accepted Mill's dictum was Northrop Frye. His theory of genre distinguishes among the literary kinds by their dominant mode of delivery or "radical of presentation." Frye means that literary genres are rooted in a characteristic kind of situation. A work may be composed for the stage, for recitation before an audience (epic), or, like the novel, for reading in a printed book.[30] By this account, lyric poetry is marked by "the concealment of the audience from the poet," a notion that Frye explains by citing with approval Mill's insistence that lyric is "preeminently the utterance that is overheard. The lyric poet normally pretends to be talking to himself or to someone else.... The poet, so to speak, turns his back on his listeners" (249–50).

Frye's sense of the lyricist's implied relation to the poem's recipient, however, seems too narrowly based on an expressive theory of poetry. Indeed, Frye himself evidently believes that it does not provide a fully satisfying account because it leaves out mimesis. Thus Frye concludes that if drama is defined by "external mimesis, or outward representation," lyric is based on "an internal mimesis of sound and imagery" (250).

What this internal mimesis involves becomes clearer when Frye takes the liberty of reworking two of Aristotle's terms for analyzing different components of tragedy, *melos* and *opsis* (usually translated as "song" and "spectacle") and applies them to lyric.[31] With the term *melos* he draws attention to lyric's association with musical effects like rhythm and other forms of patterned sound, such as "rhyme, assonance, alliteration, and puns" (275).[32] He stretches Aristotle's original meaning of *opsis* (spectacle) beyond recognition to highlight the visual elements in lyric. For Frye *opsis* includes "the typographical appearance of a lyric on a printed page," including stanza patterns and variable line lengths visible on the page. He also includes "visual imagery" in the poem (274). Such a catch-all category seems to ignore some important distinctions, if everything from a writing system, a vivid figure of speech, or a verbal description equally appeals to the eye, not the ear. He whimsically translates the twin components of *melos* and *opsis* associated with lyric poetry as "babble and doodle" (275), though few critics have taken up his proposed terminology.[33]

Frye goes on to suggest that "the radical of *melos* is *charm*: the hypnotic incantation that, through its pulsing dance rhythm, appeals to involuntary physical response, and is hence not far from the sense of magic, or physically compelling power" (278). Whether Frye had the Greek sophists in mind here is not clear. But his description of the seductive sound quality of poetry as "charm" uses precisely the same term as Gorgias's *Encomium to Helen*, as we saw in Chapter 1. In any event, he goes on to suggest, "the radical of *opsis* in the lyric is *riddle*, which is characteristically a fusion of sensation and reflection, the use of an object of sense experience to stimulate a mental activity in connection with it" (280).

Along these lines, Frye suggests that the lyric more than other literary genres relies "for its main effect on the fresh or surprising image" (281). For all its quirkiness and limitations, Frye's theory of lyric enjoys the advantage of not being reducible to an expressive theory of emotion recollected in tranquility, whether real or fictional. By placing the enchantment of *melic* sound effects in the same conceptual frame as the fusion of the concrete and abstract, he offers one possible way to map in multiple dimensions the lyric poetry of many different historical periods. Jonathan Culler translates Frye's attention to *melos* as a non-mimetic feature of lyric into its *ritualistic* dimension, which Culler sees as lending memorability and repeatability.[34]

Frye wrote *The Anatomy of Criticism* at a time when the dominant form of literary criticism in North America was known as the New Criticism. Despite differences among the critics who are associated with New Criticism, the received understanding of their work suggests that New Critics shared an assumption that poems are individual or autonomous works of art that possess an organic unity. One of Frye's main ambitions was to offer a systematic alternative to that style of criticism.

Literary interpretations, New Critics believed, should focus on the internal form or structure of the "poem itself" rather than on its external relations to society or the biography of the poet. Accordingly, New Criticism is classified as a variety of *formalism*. The method of literary analysis most associated with the New Criticism is the technique of "close reading," the painstaking attention to minute verbal detail to uncover nuances of meaning and complexities of tone. New Critics were especially interested in finding ambiguity and irony in poems. If you are looking for it, you will generally find it.

The New Critical idea of the work of art as free-standing (autonomous) is often traced back to the aesthetic theory of Samuel Taylor Coleridge, which ultimately finds its roots in the philosophy of Kant. This orientation aligns New Criticism with what Abrams classifies as an "objective" theory of poetry. It is frequently observed that the New Critics tended to focus most of their attention on lyric poetry. Although Frye attempted to displace the dominant critical paradigm of his day, later commentators have observed that he shared the aesthetic assumptions of New Criticism. By viewing literature as a self-referential "order of words," he constructs one more variety of literary formalism, only on a much grander scale.[35]

For over forty years, professional literary scholars have warned us about the limitations of New Criticism, close reading, and formalist approaches to literary texts. The various schools of thought that began to draw on Continental literary theory in the 1960s and '70s share one principle in common. Individual literary texts are not autonomous but are part of larger textual systems.[36] By the time the influential essay collection *Lyric Poetry: After the New Criticism* was published in 1985, it seemed time to take stock of the potential results of bringing new literary theories to bear on the study of lyric poetry.[37]

Following Derrida's deconstruction of the primacy of speech over writing, many of the essays in the collection try to put the final nail in the coffin of Romantic expressive theory. For example, Paul de Man deconstructs the poetic text by unraveling the reader's sense that she is encountering a speaker's voice in a lyric. De Man calls this imagined encounter "the phenomenalization of the poetic voice."[38] By this he means that the presence of a voice is nothing but an effect of linguistic figures and tropes. Especially implicated in this deconstruction is the figure of speech often called personification. De Man uses the Greek term *prosopopoeia*, which literally means the "making of a face." He sees prosopopoeia as a radical play of signifiers: "Prosopopoeia undoes the distinction between reference and signification on which all semiotic systems ... depend."[39] Coherent meaning ultimately breaks down in his hands.

In addition, the figure of *allegory* looms large in de Man's deconstruction. For him allegory is more than just another rhetorical figure. It is no less than the figure of figuration as such. By this strange notion he means that allegory makes it impossible to tell whether a poetic statement should be taken literally or figuratively.[40] Although de Man remains a major figure in the recent theory of lyric, his career focused almost exclusively on the period of Romanticism and its successors.

Jonathan Culler's contribution to anti-new critical lyric theory in the 1985 collection returns to a deconstructive theme that he first proposed as early as 1977. In that year Culler began to notice the widespread use in lyric poetry of direct addresses to inanimate objects or listeners who are not present—the figure of *apostrophe*. Culler argues that apostrophe challenges the received view that lyrics should be understood as though they are the fictive utterances of speakers. After all, real people do not normally talk to birds or trees. "The figure of apostrophe is critical," Culler suggests, "because its empty 'O,' devoid of semantic reference, is the figure of voice, the sign of utterance." In other words, apostrophe makes it difficult "to treat the poem as fictive representation of personal utterance. Apostrophes trouble attempts to read poems as dramatic monologues."[41]

Culler certainly deserves credit for drawing attention to how earlier theorists of lyric poetry tended to ignore the frequent use of apostrophes. In *Theory of the Lyric* (2015), Culler continues to use apostrophe to highlight the limitations of a mimetic theory of the lyric. Once again he resists the theory that lyric poems should always to be interpreted as though they imitate an act of speech. He suggests that apostrophe addresses somebody else in addition to a "you." This other recipient creates an indirect or *triangulated* form of address—a kind of threesome.

Culler distinguishes between the *addressee* of a lyric (which may be anything from a historical or fictional person to a non-human entity) and the *audience*, "the presumed beneficiaries of lyric communication—most often listeners or readers."[42] (As we shall see in later chapters, historicist scholars try to find out as much as possible about the actual, not the presumed, historical audiences of lyric poetry.) He associates apostrophe with other extravagant or "hyperbolic" gestures of lyric poetry, seeing them as aspects of the ritualistic and performative dimension of lyric.[43]

In his earlier work on apostrophe, Culler's range of reference was almost entirely limited to nineteenth- and twentieth-century poetry. His book offers many earlier examples from Greek and Roman lyric tradition as well as some from the Renaissance, a welcome extension of his poetic archive. But as in his earlier work, Culler continues to insist that apostrophe contributes not to a sense of a voice but to *voicing* (note the active verb), even in lyrics that do not employ first-person discourse or seem to create the illusion of a coherent speaker.[44]

In the years since the publication of the landmark collection, *Lyric Poetry: After the New Criticism*, literary critics interested in lyric poetry have continued to distance themselves from the New Criticism and its associated literary and aesthetic values. As a result, close attention to the aesthetics of poetic form in older lyrics has often been pushed aside. An important reason for the shift of critical attention away from lyric form in recent decades is the dominance of historicist approaches to literature and culture, such as the so-called New Historicism.[45]

Recently, however, the so-called New Formalism has attempted to revive interest in poetic form while trying to avoid the deficiencies of New Criticism.[46] New Formalists (not everyone accepts this label) are typically interested in poetic form and the texture of history in equal measure. At the same time, much of the best recent work seeking to contribute to lyric theory has focused almost exclusively on poetry of the last two centuries, leaving unanswered questions about the relevance of such theories to lyrics from earlier periods. Culler's *Theory of the Lyric* seems to be a partial exception, though he does not discuss many poems in English from the early modern period and almost none from the Middle Ages.

We are now in a better position to answer the question "What was lyric?" The most fruitful approach when approaching older lyric poetry moves back and forth between a universal or general framework and a historical perspective. Neither approach seems adequate on its own. A robust awareness of historical difference generally seems to be missing in poststructuralist theories that make sweeping claims about lyric on the basis of a limited chronological sample. On the other hand, in attempting to be historically precise, critics run the risk of overstating their case. One critic of Renaissance literature, for example, claims that subjectivity per se was first invented c. 1600.[47] All-encompassing theories about the origin of the individual self or subjectivity are always vulnerable to challenge.

Culler wishes to avoid foundering on the Scylla of universal essences and the Charybdis of a historical specificity. His comparative approach seeks to discover continuities in literary history. He thus begins *Theory of the Lyric* using an inductive method, paying close attention to a selection of canonical lyric poems from Sappho to John Asberry. This inductive approach allows him to identify some recurrent features that help structure lyric poems in different times and places as available possibilities in many different lyric traditions.

Culler offers four recurrent features of lyric poems from different periods. First, he notices a variety of poetic strategies for voicing lyrics. He calls these strategies their "enunciative apparatus," which allows for "a range of possibilities of indirection." Here, we should recall his theory of apostrophe as triangulated address. Second, he finds that lyrics "attempt to be itself an event rather than the representation of an event." For this purpose he revives the category of epideixis as a kind of verbal performance. Third, he suggests that lyrics tend to have a "ritualistic" character. This ritualistic tendency ensures that lyrics are "not representations of speeches by fictional characters but memorable writing to be received, reactivated, and repeated by readers." Finally, lyrics usually demonstrate "an explicitly hyperbolic quality, which is especially striking because they are brief."[48]

Culler thus avoids traditional theories that read lyrics as representing either the poet's subjective experience or the speech acts of a fictive speaker. His approach often leads to impressive results. I will frequently draw on some of his ideas in later chapters. However, with such a broad theoretical approach, there is always the risk of missing opportunities for certain kinds of historical understanding. As we shall see, Culler's expansive definition of epideictic greatly underestimates the pressures exerted on medieval and Renaissance writers by historically specific rhetorical doctrines and classroom training.[49]

If we wish to think clearly about historical variety in poetry that we now tend reductively to call *lyric*, few genre theorists can match the historical awareness of Alastair Fowler, a scholar of Renaissance literature. His *Kinds of Literature* remains unsurpassed as an account of how historical genres work in literature.[50] Fowler is exceptionally sensitive to how literary genres change over time. His awareness of the rise and fall of literary genres allows him to avoid a rigid definition of a genre such as lyric. He uses the term *kind* as "equivalent to 'historical genre'" (56). Over time, he observes, critics tend to share broad agreement about the nature of historical kinds, thanks to the influence of traditional authorities and exemplars.

One of Fowler's most useful ideas for thinking about genre is the notion that a literary kind offers a "range of potential points of resemblance." He calls this range a *generic repertoire*. Often the bag of tricks that goes into making a literary genre only becomes clear retrospectively. "Every genre has a unique repertoire," Fowler suggests, "from which its representatives select characteristics." No work of literature needs to contain all of these possible characteristics, just enough to be recognizable as belonging to a distinctive genre. These points of resemblance "may be either formal or substantive." As Fowler observes, "the best of the older theories" (such as Aristotle's) "always kept external and internal forms together in discussing the historical kinds" (55).

Fowler's awareness of changes in genres over time leads him to insist that for any given period in history, the theorist needs to figure out what features may be selected from the generic repertoire (57). It is impossible to predict in advance what features will become associated with a genre. "Almost any feature," Fowler observes, "can become genre-linked and belong more or less regularly to a kind's repertoire. This applies equally to what used to be called content, as opposed to form. Images, motifs, and topics ... all form part of a repertoire."[51] For example, a poem on the topic of love may select flower imagery from the lyric repertoire.

Fowler offers this concise definition of a kind: it "is a type of literary work of a definite size, marked by a complex of substantive and formal features that always include a distinctive (though not usually unique) external structure" (74). In *De vulgari eloquentia*, for example, Dante defined the *canzone* in terms that easily may be mapped according to Fowler's list of distinctive features, such as its characteristic subject matter (sixth feature); metrical structure (third feature); size (fourth feature); attitude as a feature of style (tenth), and so on.

Fowler clarifies two additional genre-related terms that I will frequently employ in later chapters: *mode* and *subgenre*. Fowler explains mode this way: "kinds ... can always be put in noun form ('epigram'; 'epic'), whereas modal terms tend to be adjectival" (106). Moreover, modes are based on "an incomplete repertoire" selected from among "the corresponding kind's features, and one from which overall external structure is absent" (107). *Lyrical* is often used in this modal sense. When a film or a novel is described (not necessarily very precisely) as "lyrical," this label does not imply any relation to an external structure of stanzas composed in rhyme and meter.

When one kind is blended with features from another kind, Fowler describes such blending as "generic modulation." For example, the sonnet was taken over between the sixteenth and eighteenth century by "epigrammatic modulation." Epigrammatic features of concision and wit or "point" (especially evident in the final couplet of the English form) began to take over the sonnet. Soon the sonnet itself came close to extinction for over a century, having been replaced by epigram.[52]

The other genre-related term clarified by Fowler is *subgenre*. As the term implies, a subgenre is a subset within a genre. Subgenres therefore share "the same external characteristics with the corresponding kind" but are distinguished by the "additional specification of content" (56). Thus "subgenres have the common features of the kind—external forms and all," but they also add to the general kind some more specific content, in characteristic motifs or subject matter (112).

So far, Fowler's theory of subgenre may sound rather abstract, but he uses the example of the sonnet to illustrate the value of recognizing subgenres when reading poetry from an earlier period: "the Elizabethan love sonnet, itself a subgenre, might easily be divided into secondary subgenres, and even tertiary ones. Distinguishable types would include (a) liminal sonnets; (b) psychomachies; (c) symptomologies of love; (d) *blasons*; (e) *baisers*; (f) narratives of exploits of Cupid; (g) sonnets on the beloved's absence; (h) complaints of unkindness; and (i) renunciations of love—all of them with respectable Petrarchan, Petrarchist, or French genealogies."[53]

Getting to know old literature," Fowler insists, "is very largely a matter of learning the subgenres" (113). Learning to recognize subgenres requires the study of changes over time through a "process of imitation, variation, [and] innovation" (114). Although less talented poets slavishly imitate their predecessors' use of subgenres, much of the vitality of literary change and innovation takes place at the level of subgenre. We shall discuss some of the canonical forms of lyric subgenres in later chapters.

Fowler's theory of genre also helps us understand the historical problem of literary canons in some helpful ways. Many social forces, especially institutions of education, are at work in the selection of literary canons. Fowler points out how often chance and historical contingency work to limit the available canon. Such factors include the fortunes of patronage, printing history, or (especially for medieval literature) the survival of manuscripts (214–15).

Another force at work in the process of selective transmission is the traditional perception of generic hierarchy. "From the late sixteenth to the early eighteenth century," Fowler notes, "epic ruled as not only the highest but also the best of all genres.... At the other extreme, love poetry, and short poems generally, were rated low" (216–17). The placement of epic at the top of the generic heap in the early modern period has much to do with the hierarchy of social classes.[54]

Beginning with eclogue (about humble shepherds) and ending with epic (about the princely class), the example of Vergil's poetic career did much to reinforce normative ideas of stylistic height, generic hierarchy, and their relation to social class. Edmund Spenser imitated Vergil's normative poetic career in the sixteenth century in part because it was politically expedient (he was trying to impress Queen Elizabeth and her courtiers). One way to understand the tendency of lyric to stand in for poetry itself in the nineteenth century is to see the rise of "serious" poetic forms like the ode as a belated reversal of earlier systems of generic hierarchy.[55]

Another principle for sorting poetic genres hierarchically that was inherited from the ancient world and repeated in the Renaissance is *poetic meter*. In ancient Greece and Rome, each meter was closely associated with a distinctive subject matter. Epics in the ancient world, for example, always use dactylic hexameter to narrate heroic exploits. Cicero distinguishes between melic and dithyrambic poetry, while Horace includes elegiac, iambic, and lyric poetry as separate categories. Renaissance English critics like Sidney and Francis Meres (1598) continue to respect ancient authorities by including a long-fossilized category of "iambic" as a distinct poetic kind.[56] Sometimes the weight of tradition puts a heavy thumb on the scale.

In short, generic labels always refer to something that is subject to historical change or revision. "Lyric" can mean many different things in earlier periods, and these various meanings must be reconstructed in relation to other historically fluid genres, such as epigram or epic. If nowadays students of poetry automatically tend to think of lyric as including ode, elegy, and perhaps epigram, to John Dryden in the later seventeenth century these were all distinctly different kinds. We must avoid thinking about genres and modes as though they are stable entities over time. This caution will help us avoid the misunderstandings that arise from assuming that "lyric" refers to a universal kind of poetry.

Unfortunately, such historical caution is missing in the work of Helen Vendler, widely regarded as one of the finest critics of poetry of her generation (she was born in 1933). Like the New Critics, she has spent her career defending the aesthetic value of poetry. For Vender, the purpose of "aesthetic criticism ... is not primarily to reveal the *meaning* of an art work or disclose (or argue for or against) the ideological *values* of an art work." Instead, the point of aesthetic criticism is "to *describe* the art work in such a way that it cannot be confused with any other art work ... and to *infer* from its elements the aesthetic that might generate this unique configuration."[57]

Vendler's textbook *Poems, Poets, Poetry* casts valuable light on her theory of poetry.[58] She argues that poems originate from the concerns of life. Lyric poems are not identical to life, they are "about" life. To understand a poem we should try to imagine the circumstances under which we might find ourselves saying its words. "The poem is *written for you to say. You* are the speaker of every lyric poem you read. That is what a lyric poem is: it is a speech made for you to utter."[59]

This claim suggests that, at least in part, hers is a *mimetic* theory of poetry that assumes lyric poems are best read as imitations of a certain kind of speech that might occur under the pressure of specific circumstances. Yet she is too sophisticated a critic to assume that poems mirror life directly or serve as transparent windows through which portions of life may be viewed. "The poet discovers the emotional import of that life-moment by subjecting it to analysis," she suggests. The poet's "analysis then determines how the moment is described, and the invented organizational form that replicates it." In short, poems give us "*arranged* life," inviting us to examine how "they are formal constructions of life."[60]

We should notice how her account implicitly depends on the notion of lived experience (our old romantic friend *Erlebnis*) as it falls into the perceptual field of the individual poet. Specific choices about poetic form thus reflect the poet's *analysis* of her prior experience, which breaks it down into meaningful patterns.

Yet the result of this analytic shaping still implies an imitation of a kind of speech. "Though poetry has become a written art," she later observes, "it has never lost its roots in speech" (183). Her critical presuppositions become clearer when she suggests, "lyric poems are usually *inner meditations*, not dramatic or declaimed speeches; one can't be an orator or an actor in speaking a lyric aloud." Even in poems that represent a specific auditor as present, she suggests, "the lyric represents the *inner* speech or meditation of its utterer, and must sound inward and reflective rather than outer-directed and rhetorical" (185–86; her italics).

On the one hand, she views poems as *imitations* of the utterances we might ourselves wish to make (if we had the talent) in similar circumstances. On the other hand, her focus on lyric poetry as an inner, meditative speech of an individual "self" whose voice we can imaginatively echo suggests that Vendler views lyric primarily in terms of the expressive theory crystallized by Mill's famous suggestion: "Eloquence is *heard*, poetry is *overheard*." Her subtle approach may be well suited for understanding much of the lyric poetry of the last few centuries, given the aesthetic shifts that Romanticism and modernism entailed. However, for earlier poetry written at a time when formal training in rhetoric was part of the standard curriculum, the dismissal of the relevance of oratory to the art of poetry clearly will not do. (In Chapter 5 we shall see some of the distortions of her position when reading Shakespeare's sonnets.)

Yet not everything about her understanding of poetry may be comfortably placed within the framework of either a mimetic or an expressive theory. In the chapter devoted to formal considerations, she reviews what are traditionally described as "external" elements of poetic form (rhythm and meter, rhyme, stanzaic structure), as well as more "internal" elements of form (images, argument, poignancy, wisdom). Yet what is perhaps most significant about her discussion of poetic form is that she presents it in terms of *pleasure*. Her discussion deserves to be quoted at some length:

> Every artwork exists to evoke pleasures that are easier to feel than to describe.... We can say in general that all artworks appeal to our (apparently inborn) love of patterning, whether the rhythmic and melodic patterning we hear in music, or the visual patterning we see in a painting or a quilt, or the patterning of volume that we see in architecture.
>
> ....
>
> Since the base of all organic life is repetition (repeated motion in growth and form), and since human life, by its heartbeat and breathing, is innately rhythmic, we can suppose that there is a biological basis for our recognition of, and apparently instinctive pleasure in, repetition.... Babies learn by patterned repetition, and the pleasure of learning and recognizing new and old patterns is probably the source of our deepest pleasure in art [73].

Her account of the biological basis for babies' pleasure in learning by imitating and repeating patterns echoes Aristotle's observation that "*mimēsis* is innate in human beings from childhood" and human beings derive pleasure from it (*Poetics* 1448b). Her description also recalls Frye's playful rewriting of Aristotle's *melos* and *opsis* as "babble and doodle."

In short, Vendler's insistence that poetry produces pleasure and moves us returns us once more to "the old quarrel between poetry and philosophy" remarked by Plato in *The Republic* (607b). If sophists like Gorgias and Isocrates celebrated the incantatory power of poetic language, its "charms" were held in suspicion by Plato, who feared the harmful effects of rhetoric and poetry. Its pleasures could lead the rational mind astray in the pursuit of the truth. Although Vendler distances herself from rhetorical or pragmatic theories of poetry, in different critical hands her sensitivity to aesthetic pleasure could lead precisely in that direction.

Finally, in the chapter on "the play of language," Vendler shows clear signs of the so-called objective theory of poetry, which views the work of art as an organic unity or self-contained world. We have seen how this concern with the internal function of poetic form begins with Aristotle. However, not until the eighteenth century, especially with Kant's theory of disinterested aesthetic contemplation, does the objective theory of poetry begin to gain prestige. From German idealist philosophy it entered English criticism through Coleridge and eventually flourished in the New Critical insistence that the only proper object of attention is "the poem itself."

This lineage is evident when Vendler cites with approval Coleridge's observation that "poetry is the best words in the best order." She explains that the student's task "is to form hypotheses about why the poet arranged *these* words in *this* order till the poem seemed a satisfying whole" (157; her italics). My point in unraveling the various critical strands in Vendler's theory of poetry is not to fault her choices or to point out possible inconsistencies. Instead, I simply wish to suggest that no theory of poetry is powerful enough to enable an adequate description of all poetry, of every kind or from every time and place. Elements of mimetic, pragmatic, expressive, and objective theories, alone or in combination, remain of potential use. Each theory carries its own forms of blindness and insight.

We also need to be aware of how different theories of poetry tend to produce different kinds of evaluative judgment. As Culler reminds us, "in European literature up until the late eighteenth century, generic categories were essential to literary evaluation as well as to literary creation."[61] Definitions of lyric poetry that depend on one or more of these theories may or may not prove adequate to any given purpose. For example, Vendler points to the conventional distinction between narrative and lyric poems, explaining that the former "tells a story" whereas the latter "may contain the germ of a story—say, a man's regret that a love affair is ending—but the poem dwells less on the plot than on the man's feelings (despair, grief, resentment, and so on)" (107–08).

Vendler's emphasis on feelings points clearly toward an expressive theory of lyric poetry, which may indeed remain the most attractive theory to the lay reader, even when it remains unarticulated. Far be it from my intention to suggest that non-academic readers must be disabused of their naïve beliefs about poetry. A classicist might take a pragmatic approach to the representation of emotion in, say, one of Catullus's bitter poems about the unfaithful Lesbia. Such a reader might interpret Catullus as making an *argument* to persuade readers that certain forms of passion are undesirable. A rhetorical and a mimetic reading may be equally valid or instructive depending on the context.

Vendler's theory of lyric as the representation of inner, meditative speech creates problems for seventeenth-century epigram, which only with difficulty can be read as though a voice were speaking to itself to express emotion. For example, Robert Herrick addresses this amusing epigraph to his book *Hesperides*:

Who with thy leaves shall wipe, at need,	Whoever
The place where swelling piles do breed:	hemorrhoids
May every ill that bites or smarts	
Perplex him in his hinder-parts.[62]	

It does not seem especially helpful to describe this epigram as either an imitation of speech that the poet internally voices to himself or as an expression of his emotion. Although Herrick may well be expressing his impatience with potential critics, surely that is not the main purpose of his humorous inscription at the beginning of his volume.

It is not even clear that it helps to read the poem as an instance of *voicing*, as opposed to the representation of a *voice*, as Culler's theory suggests. Instead, the poem seems mainly designed to delight the reader for its pointed, concise wit. This is a good example of Fowler's general observation that Herrick's epigrams are often modulated by other genres (I would describe this epigram as modulated by satirical magic spell or curse).[63] The toilet humor also identifies this as an example of the frequently unrecognized subgenre of "fetid" epigram.[64] Before we can decide whether Herrick's "foul" epigram about hemorrhoids is good poetry, surely we have to understand the literary tradition he draws on to appreciate what he is aiming at.

To be fair to Vendler, in addressing her discussion to undergraduates with limited experience reading poetry, she no doubt has made a strategic choice about the kinds of lyric poetry most likely to appeal to twenty-first-century students. Yet she includes the better-known opening poem of *Hesperides* to illustrate the need to pay close attention to syntax as an element of inner form. Although we may certainly read the first epigram as the record of a speaker's rising emotion, it would be more helpful to notice its witty generic modulation, beginning with its playful rewriting of epic conventions. Vergil begins the *Aeneid*: "I sing of arms and the man." Herrick is less ambitious by far: "I sing of brooks, of blossoms, birds and bowers," etc.[65] In short, if we have not learned the subgenres of older poetry, we risk applying inappropriate criteria of evaluation.

Some confusion about lyric voice or utterance might be avoided if we recognize that a theory of poetry may need to accommodate both its oral and written possibilities. On the one hand, poetry may take its being in the human voice, whether as song in an entirely oral culture, as oral performance in a literate one, or even as silent reading from a printed text when the mind's ear "hears" rhyme and rhythm. On the other hand, at least after the technology of writing becomes available, we may focus on poems as exclusively *textual* objects rather than as representations of the human voice.[66]

At this point, we may be tempted to throw up our hands in exasperation at the never-ending prospect of theory. If so, it may come as some relief to recall William Empson's suggestion that "a critic ought to trust his own nose, like a hunting dog, and if he lets any kind of theory or principle distract him from that, he is not doing his work."[67] Empson's resistance to critical dogma seems an attractive quality. However, following your nose necessarily involves you in *some* kind of theory. Thus it may be fitting to end this chapter with the not entirely frivolous conjecture that if dogs made poetry, it would be likely to engage their sense of smell. The dog who marks territory by lifting his leg may perhaps be understood as a form of canine *poiēsis*.

3

Anonymous Middle English Lyrics on the Virgin Mary

The preceding chapters propose rhetorical frameworks for reading early lyric. The following chapters, arranged in roughly chronological order, offer glimpses into the early stages of a canonical tradition of lyric poetry in English. Literary canons are formed by generations of writers and readers. Without appreciative readers in successive generations, a poem that once was valued may be forgotten later. Sometimes what is forgotten is rediscovered and brought back to life. Literary canons are thus always subject to change and are never set in stone.

Each of the following chapters presents one or more short masterpieces to illustrate an identifiable historical lyric subgenre. Given my emphasis on poetic technique, the term *masterpiece* seems apt, since it originally comes from the world of early modern craft guilds.[1] After years of training to become a skilled artisan, an apprentice could only become certified as a master by producing a virtuoso work. Although poets did not literally belong to guilds, they had to hone their verbal technique to master the craft of making poetry.

In fact, the metaphor of the creative writing *workshop*, which persists in modern university writing programs, continues to serve as a ghostly reminder of the old craft guilds. Like writers and artists today, talented poets in earlier generations learned through imitation, experiment, and innovation, though originality was not as highly valued as it is now. If lyric poetry in earlier periods was not viewed as the self-expression of unique individuals, what other claims to our attention can we expect to find in the earliest masterpieces of English lyric poetry? If lyrics were not read as isolated or autonomous works of art during the Middle Ages, how do medieval religious lyrics derive rhetorical power by blending artistic and devotional practices? Finally, how might knowing something about the circulation of lyrics in a manuscript culture help us understand and value medieval lyrics from before the invention of the printing press?

To be honest, reading Middle English (traditionally dated from about 1100 to about 1500) presents stumbling blocks that might seem discouraging to some potential readers. But these linguistic barriers should not be overestimated. Many difficulties can be overcome by editions that regularize spelling and punctuation. Marginal glosses of words no longer in use or that have drastically changed their meaning also go a long way toward helping readers grapple with earlier texts.

Fortunately, rhyme and poetic rhythms remain intact even after making these concessions to modern readers. The same cannot be said of such lyric masterpieces in Old English as the "The Seafarer" or "The Dream of the Rood." Aside from the much more difficult language that makes Anglo-Saxon poetry unsuitable for inclusion here, its Germanic system of unrhymed alliterating verse makes Old English lyrics stand outside the tradition that gets underway after rhyme was introduced. If space is made for Old English poetry in the canon of English literature, it must be in translation for all but the most dedicated readers.

Within a century or two after the Norman Conquest (1066) the native system of versification began to be replaced by one adapted from French into English. Unlike poets in the Anglo-Saxon period, Middle English lyric poets used rhyme and a new kind of meter.[2] Frankly, only a small portion of the roughly two thousand surviving Middle English lyrics seem to offer the kind of poetic qualities that remain attractive to readers who are not professional scholars of medieval literature.

Like most surviving medieval literature, Middle English lyrics were written primarily for practical, not aesthetic, purposes. The most widely read Middle English poem was the long fourteenth-century didactic poem, *The Prick of Conscience*, which survives in over a hundred manuscripts. But the didactic purpose of most medieval literature does not imply that medieval poets were always indifferent to aesthetic considerations. Chaucer certainly found ways to combine *sentence* (serious meaning) and *solaas* (poetic delight), earning him the esteem of later generations and eventually securing his place as the first canonical author in English. On a much smaller scale, many Middle English lyrics, both secular and religious, remain effective as works of poetic art—well crafted, vividly imagined, and emotionally powerful. Yet before we can claim Middle English lyrics for inclusion in a medieval literary canon, we must come to terms with recent historicist scholarship, which typically resists such a notion.

Research in the last few decades has "concentrated almost exclusively on questions of manuscript context and compilation, patronage, and readership."[3] Because poetry circulated in manuscripts that were easily lost or destroyed, Middle English lyrics lived a fragile existence that owed much to chance. Before the arrival of the printing press, we can only speak of canon formation in a relatively weak sense. In addition to the inherent instability of texts copied by hand, there was little institutional support for selecting and preserving lyric poems in English. During the Middle Ages, nothing remotely resembled the work of scholars at the ancient library at Alexandria to collect, classify, and preserve lyric poetry—to create something recognizable as a literary canon.

However, we may be tempted to begin speaking loosely of a canon of Middle English lyrics when they are gathered together in manuscript anthologies or miscellanies. One such example is the early fourteenth-century Harley MS 2253, which contains some of the best religious and secular Middle English lyrics. Unfortunately, its difficult dialect rules out presenting any examples of its lyric poetry here.

In addition to lyrics selected for miscellanies, lyrics that survive in multiple manuscripts (a rough measure of popularity) may be considered as the medieval equivalent of a literary canon. But we must not imagine that such poems ever enjoyed a wide readership by modern standards. Indeed, there could be no truly national literary culture or vernacular canon before the advent of printing. Instead, "there are plural literary canons, dependent on a good many variables," including access to earlier manuscripts that scribes could copy.[4]

The process of selection behind a medieval manuscript miscellany is a very different matter from the modern selection of Old and Middle English lyric and other medieval poetry included in modern textbook anthologies or high school and university syllabi.[5] However, the selection and (largely chance) manuscript preservation of individual poems was necessary for Middle English poetry to be included in the canon later. Once such lyrics crossed the threshold of modernity and were committed to the printed page, it became more likely (though by no means inevitable) that they would survive to find new readers and admirers.

One of the mostly highly admired Middle English lyrics probably dates from the beginning of the thirteenth century. It is only four lines long:

    Now goth sonne under wode: *goes; sun; wood (i.e., sets behind a tree)*
      B   B   B   B

    Me reweth, Marye, thy faire rode.   *I pity; face*
      B   B   B   B

    Now goth sonne under tree:
      B   B   B   B

    Me reweth, Marye, thy sone and thee.[6]   *Son*
      B   B   B   B

This famous quatrain is perhaps the earliest surviving example in English of an internationally shared lyric form sometimes referred to as the *dolnik* (a word borrowed from Russian).[7] Using Derek Attridge's system, I have marked the beats under each line (see Appendix for my modified version of his symbols). With its roots in song, the dolnik uses four-beat lines with a variable number of syllables serving as offbeats, though usually only one or two.

Although this quatrain is possibly a fragment from a poem on the Hours of the Cross or an even longer Passion poem, it seems satisfyingly complete as it stands.[8] We owe its chance survival to the fact that it is quoted in manuscripts of the Anglo-Norman French translation of a Latin devotional treatise. The Latin work *The Mirror of the Church* (*Speculum Ecclesie*) by St. Edmund of Abingdon is now recognized as earlier than the French version.[9] The lyric is a rare thirteenth-century example of a subgenre that would become quite common in the fifteenth century, the Compassion of the Virgin.[10] Even though the lyric communicates its core meaning effectively in isolation, an understanding of the textual and institutional environment from which it emerged in the thirteenth century greatly enriches the modern experience of reading the poem.[11]

The *Speculum Ecclesie* was originally composed c. 1213–14 as a treatise on contemplation to assist monastic readers in meditation, prayer, and spiritual exercises. Many of the surviving manuscripts of Latin versions of the work were in fact owned by monasteries. The original Latin was adapted in different Anglo-Norman French translations during the thirteenth century. Different versions seem to have been aimed at different audiences, both professional religious and lay.[12]

The section of the treatise into which the lyric is inserted offers brief meditations on the life of Christ. This format shows that Edmund was familiar with spiritual exercises used by monks. The monastic meditative tradition used events in the life of Christ as subjects for contemplation and prayer, correlating them to the seven canonical hours. In the contemplative exercise for the hour of sext, Edmund invites the reader to visualize the moment recounted in the Gospel of John (19:26–27) when Jesus on the cross commends his mother to the care of his most beloved apostle, John. "Here you must think of the very sweet Mother of Jesus," writes Edmund, "and how much sorrow filled her as she stood by Son's right side and accepted the disciple as her master."[13]

Thanks to his training in traditional monastic meditation, Edmund recognized that the terse scriptural account could be elaborated to make its implied emotional impact more explicit. Unlike the biblical author, the religious in the later Middle Ages believed that stimulating an emotional involvement in the details of the Passion offered spiritual benefits. Modern scholars have given the name "affective piety" to this style of spirituality. Experiencing such emotions personally was thought to draw the communicant closer to God, who had experienced the horrific events of the Crucifixion as a human being in the person of Jesus.

"Now goth sonne under wode" provides a good test case of a theory of interpretation proposed by the German philosopher Hans-Georg Gadamer. He is perhaps best known for the idea of trying to meet a historical text halfway, or what he calls a "fusion of horizons." His metaphor suggests that we can see further than the confines of our own world if we combine our ways of seeing with those of the past to the extent possible. Of course, this process will always remain incomplete. But knowing how affective piety worked allows us imaginatively "to project a historical horizon that is different from the horizon of the present." At the same time, our own experience of sympathy and grief offers us a familiar standpoint in the present from which to understand the medieval poem. One does not need to be a Catholic or even a Christian to understand the emotional response the poem solicits from its reader. "Every encounter with tradition," Gadamer suggests, "involves the experience of a tension between the text and the present."[14]

The affective piety that was characteristic of late-medieval religion was first associated with the monastic forms of meditation described above.[15] Especially influential were St. Anselm, Abelard, and above all St. Bernard of Clairvaux, the most important Cistercian author and one of Edmund's major sources. A new chapter in the history of affective piety began when from the mid-thirteenth century the Franciscans began to popularize this new style of worship. The Franciscans encouraged lay men and women to experience sorrow when contemplating the suffering Jesus. Although Edmund died at a time when Franciscan spirituality was still at an early stage of its rapid growth, soon his work found itself in the company of the most influential Franciscan work of the Middle Ages. The early fourteenth-century *Meditations on the Life of Christ* (formerly attributed to St. Bonaventure) was eventually translated into the major European vernaculars.[16] For the professional religious and eventually the laity, visual images (iconography) or verbal representations elaborating the Passion scene were frequently used as tools to assist spiritual exercises.

In the terrible human scene recounted in Edmund's *Mirror* and other similar works, Mary exemplifies the universal grief that would be experienced by any mother forced to watch helplessly as her son died in agony before her eyes. She remains in silent dignity in the gospel version, but Edmund wished his monastic readers to imagine the kind of verbal expression Mary might have used to give voice to her unbearable grief.

Monastic traditions of the "ruminative" reading of scripture encouraged using one text to recall to memory other biblical passages on related themes or images.[17] This practice explains what may appear to be a puzzling digression when Edmund compares Mary's suffering to that of another grieving woman, Naomi (Noemi in the Vulgate) from the Book of Ruth (1:20). "Thus she could say about herself what Noemi had said: 'Do not say that I am very beautiful, but call me bitter, for the Almighty Lord has filled me with bitterness and great sorrow.'"[18] This recollection is soon joined by another, from what Edmund calls the "Song of Love" (Song of Songs 1:5), when the beloved—usually interpreted allegorically in the Middle Ages as the Church but also sometimes as Mary—says, "Do not consider me that I am brown, because the sun hath altered my color." Edmund's associative play of texts is typical of medieval meditative reading habits of monastic origin.

At this point in the French version, the translator observes: "And for this reason, an Englishman said in such a manner of pity," thus introducing the Middle English quatrain.[19] The *Speculum Ecclesie* introduces the lyric even more pointedly: "Thus said an Englishman *moved by pity*."[20] Framed in this way, the theme of the poem stands out clearly: it is primarily about the spiritual value of a sympathetic emotional response, first towards Mary, then her Son as the speaker intimately addresses the grieving mother.

The first-person pronoun in this and other medieval religious lyrics is not meant to represent a unique individual who expresses a subjective meaning, as post-romantic audiences may naturally assume. The "I" typically marks a placeholder that both the author and any reader can occupy in a shared orientation to the sacred story.

As we saw in the previous chapter, an important source of the presence effects of lyric poetry is the operation of linguistic "shifters" (deictics) that permit us to enter the past world in the time of *now*. The poem's temporal and spatial deictics allow us to enter the "now" of the poem and thus to be "present," at least during our meditation, at the Crucifixion. In a religious lyric about a biblical event, the deictic effect allows the believer to reap the additional reward of experiencing the sacred story firsthand.[21] The lyric thus offers a culturally specific instance of Jonathan Culler's general point: the "complexity of the enunciative apparatus ... makes the poem not the fictional representation of an experience or event so much as an attempt to be itself an event." Or to put the matter differently, what Culler calls the "lyric present" is folded into sacred time.[22]

Like most anonymous Middle English lyrics, this one achieves its effects by employing diction that is clear and direct, conveying its meaning without the density of description or complexities of rhythm prized by later lyric poetry. Here the diction, with the exception of the proper name, is entirely Old English in derivation, attesting to the great power of the plain style when skillfully used. The twilight setting, gentle rhythms, and songlike repetitions of this quietly evocative poem seem reminiscent of a lullaby.

Repetitions of significant vowel and consonant sounds contribute to its poetic effect. Knowledge of etymology allows us to see that the first verse in a reconstructed Middle English pronunciation uses a short *u*-sound in three syllables: *sun-*, *un-*, *wud-*.[23] Two of the syllables in the following verse repeat this vowel, but semantically the second line, with its expression of sympathy for a fellow human being, contrasts with the description of sunset in line one, a natural event almost universally recognized as beautiful. The symbolic link between sunset and death is traditional, and contributes much to poem's meaning.

Reading the lyric within the biblical frame that Edmund assigns it, moreover, directs attention to the disfiguration of Mary's fair face in grief.[24] The poet provides only the barest outline of the scene, allowing the reader to do the actual work of mentally visualizing it. That is the point of the contemplative tradition. The rhyming pairs create parallel meanings, since one word in each pair refers to the wood, one to Mary. Some commentators have further suggested that the poem uses multiple wordplay, *wode* referring to both woods and the wood of the cross, which seems likely. But a pun on *rode* as both face and rood (cross) may be doubted since the vowels are noticeably different.[25] Much more likely is a pun on *sun* and *son*. The word *tree* was also frequently used for the cross in early English. (The substitution of the material for something made from that material is the rhetorical figure of metonymy.)

I do not wish to suggest that all these details of sound and sense would have been within the perceptual horizon of any specific medieval reader. But such poetic effects are at least latent within the verse and provide one available means for a fusing of horizons. In its quietly understated way, the poem is skillfully crafted, capable of standing on its own to speak directly to us after over eight hundred years. Recovering its medieval textual horizon allows it to take on a much deeper resonance.

"In a tabernacle of a toure," the next Marian lyric I wish to discuss, was originally composed in northern England in the later fourteenth or early fifteenth century.[26] The poem was clearly esteemed by late-medieval readers because it survives in eight manuscripts.[27] In addition, one stanza is copied in another manuscript. The number of manuscripts is unusually large for a Middle English lyric. It is easy to underestimate the sophistication of this lyric because its language is deliberately plain in style to ensure its popular appeal. The language of such poetry is essentially public in nature.[28]

The lyric, though not without aesthetic appeal, primarily serves a pragmatic rhetorical function. Its earnest style of devotion is typical of the late-medieval cult of the Virgin Mary in pre–Reformation England, dramatizing her as an accessible human figure who is eager to serve as mediator between the sinner and Christ.

In the fullest version (Oxford, Bodleian Douce MS 322) the poem consists of twelve stanzas, each made up of seven lines in the vernacular and a repeated Latin refrain drawn from the Song of Songs (2:5, 5:8): *Quia amore langueo* (Because I languish with love).[29] The four-beat rhythm established by the English verses is maintained in the Latin refrain. The number of syllables in the offbeats varies, confirming that this poem is another dolnik. The insistent beats and the repeated refrain help convey the ritualistic dimension that Culler associates with lyric. The poem seeks to be an event for the reader, who is placed in the presence of Mary. Her heightened emotions support Culler's point that lyrics tend toward the hyperbolic.

The lyric begins by creating a mysterious dramatic setting, a riddle easily solved. At first the speaker (who is our representative, not a unique individual) appears to be located within the tower of a castle, standing before an architectural niche, perhaps gazing through a window at the moon:

In a tabernacle of a toure,	wall-niche; tower
As I stode musing on the mone,	moon
A comly quene, most of honoure,	
Apered in gostly sight full sone.	spiritual; soon
5 She made compleynt thus by hir one,	by herself
For mannes soule was wrapped in wo:	
"I may nat leve mankinde allone,	
Quia amore langueo."	

The image of the moon recalls Song of Songs 6:9 and Apocalypse 12:1 and was often interpreted typologically as the Virgin Mary.[30] The figure of Mary as the Queen of Heaven was long familiar from iconography and the liturgy.[31] Other manuscripts develop the image of queenship with an alternative line four: "I sawe syttynge on a trone" (throne), leaving the mystical nature of the vision implicit.[32] It would be a mistake to think of any one version of the poem as more authentic, since scribes in a manuscript culture felt free to rearrange, add, or omit stanzas or to substitute words or lines, especially for lyric poems meant for practical use.

The image accompanying the poem in a late-fifteenth-century Carthusian miscellany (Additional MS 37049, fol. 25v) depicts a turreted tower. Within, a monk kneels in prayer before a statue of the Virgin Mary in a recessed niche. Adorned with a huge golden crown, she stands holding the infant Jesus, who in turn holds a Eucharist wafer. Both mother and child smile serenely. But the static image cannot convey the shifting mood of the poem, which line five tells us begins as a *complaint*.

The complaint is filled with maternal love and longing for all humankind: "I longe for love of man my brother, / I am his vokete [*advocate*] to voide his vice; / I am his moder [*mother*]" (9–11). Although love-longing frequently appears in courtly love poetry, here it remains suitably chaste. No matter how often the sinner falls, Mary's love enables him to rise: "Through flesshes freelte fall me fro, / Yet must me rewe him till he rise" (If he falls from the frailty of flesh, yet I must pity him till he rises [14–15]). In this falling and rising movement, the line encapsulates both the salvation of the individual sinner and the fall and redemption of humankind as a whole.

Halfway through the third stanza, Mary unexpectedly shifts to address the reader directly in the second person:

> Wolde he aske mercy, he shuld it have.
> Say to me, soule, and I shall save;
> Bid me, my childe, and I shall go;
> Thou prayed me never but my son forgave [20–23].

Her complaint continues in this vein, addressing the reader directly throughout most of the poem. She constantly pleads with the sinner to heed her call to abandon sin and accept her loving maternal embrace: "Thou, man, beholde where thy moder is! / Why lovest thou me nat sith [*since*] I love thee?" (43–44). Even if it takes a hundred years to return to her (70), she will gladly welcome you: "I clippe [*embrace*], I kisse" (71).

In the Carthusian manuscript the poem continues on the next leaf, which provides two more images for contemplation. In the upper right stands a crudely drawn tree with the Latin name *Maria* written in the center. Halfway up the trunk two branches extend on either side, each captioned in English with a single word: *luf* (love)/*Mari*. Below the tree in the lower right corner appears Christ rising from the tomb, displaying his wounds. This is a familiar iconographic image known as the *Imago pietatis* (image of pity). For the Carthusian audience of this manuscript, the injunction to love Mary enacted by the kneeling monk leads to a remembrance of the Passion, which in turn leads to the Resurrection of Christ. At the beginning of stanza seven, as the poem crosses its exact center in Douce 322, Mary recalls the Crucifixion: "My childe is outlawed for thy sinne, / My barne [*child*] is bette [*beaten*] for thy trespasse" (49–50).[33]

Just as the shift from third- to second-person address in stanza three was unexpected, so is the shift in stanza seven when Mary directly speaks to her son for the first time:

> ... O Sone, allasse!
> Thou art his brother; his moder I was;
> Thou soked my pappe, thou loved man so;   *sucked; breast*
> Thou died for him; mine hert he has,
>   *Quia amore langueo*[34] [52–56].

The sweetness of the nativity and the bitterness of the Passion are the two scenes most integral to medieval practices of affective meditation. The presence effect reinforced by the linguistic shifters encourages the reader to travel in space and time to experience these emotions and draw closer to Mary and thus to God.

The final stanza reinforces these meanings while introducing some new elements:

> Nowe, man, have minde on me forever.
> Loke on thy love thus languisshing;
> Late us never fro other dissevere;   *Let; from; separate*
> Mine helpe is thine owne; crepe under my winge.
> Thy sister is a quene, thy brother a kinge,
> This heritage is tayled; sone come therto;   *inheritance; settled; soon*
> Take me for thy wife and lerne to singe,
>   *Quia amore langueo* [89–96].

The reference to using the *mind* and *looking* confirms that the poem exists to facilitate a spiritual exercise, available to lay and religious alike. The second line rewards the reader with delayed gratification, finally turning the Latin verb from the refrain into English. The wing alludes to the iconography of Mary as Mother of Mercy (*Maria Misericordia*), who shelters her followers beneath her outspread mantel.[35]

Boundaries become blurred as family relationships merge: Mary is our sister and mother as well as the mother of Christ, our brother and lord. The intimate sibling relations blend with the universal identities of the heavenly queen and king, with echoes in the feudal law of inheritance. By the poem's end, the (apparently) secular architecture of the tower in the opening line has been refashioned by the image of the Queen of Heaven to recall the description of the Heavenly Jerusalem in the Apocalypse.

The invitation to take Mary as spouse reminds us that the beloved (*sponsa*) in the Song of Songs, the speaker of the refrain, was sometimes interpreted allegorically as either the individual soul or Mary in the Middle Ages.[36] The idea of learning to sing raises the possibility that the lyric may have been literally sung to a tune now lost. However, the strong four-beat rhythm and the ritualistic repetition of the refrain may be all the music the poem ever possessed. The singing may also allude to the "new song" described in the Book of the Apocalypse (5:9, 14:3). If so, the total number of stanzas in Douce 322 may be symbolically linked with the number twelve (and its square) in the biblical text.

The final poem I have selected is one of the finest Marian lyrics and dates from the fifteenth century:

I sing of a maiden	
That is makeles,	*matchless/mateless*
King of alle kinges	
To here sone she chese.	*As her son she chose*
He cam also stille	*as quietly*
Ther his moder was	*Where; mother*
As dew in Aprille	
That falleth on the gras.	
He cam also stille	
To his moderes bowr	
As dew in Aprille	
That falleth on the flour.	*flower*
He cam also stille	
Ther his moder lay	
As dew in Aprille	
That falleth on the spray.	*branch*
Moder and maiden	*virgin*
Was never non but she:	
Well may swich a lady	*such*
Godes moder be.[37]	

This epideictic poem in praise of the Virgin (*laus Marie*) has been much admired by modern critics. The simplicity of its language and its effective use of nature imagery help its reader imagine the Incarnation, the central mystery of Christianity, in terms that may easily be understood by an unsophisticated popular audience.[38]

The poem offers what may be a unique case of a fifteenth-century lyric poet borrowing from a thirteenth-century predecessor.[39] Both this fifteenth-century poem and the first lyric examined above "combine the incremental repetition of the ballads, with verbal subtlety and an oblique, emotive, use of symbolism."[40] Such poetry offers an especially striking instance of how the aesthetic function of medieval religious verse was secondary to its devotional function. The primary purpose, like that of other medieval meditational verse, is to elicit an emotional response from the audience, to move the reader to greater love for Mary and her son.[41] With such poetry, we clearly find ourselves within the horizon of a pragmatic or rhetorical poetics, as discussed in Chapter 1.

The poet refrains from using a common typological symbol for the virgin birth, the dew falling on Gideon's fleece.[42] Instead, he or she draws on the conventional association of spring with creation and birth. A series of three parallel images of dew falling on grass, flower, and branch vividly re-imagines the quiet mystery of the Virgin's conception of the Son of God.[43]

The poem wears its learning lightly. The branch or *spray* recalls the prophecy in Isaiah 11:1: "And there shall come forth a rod (*virga*) out of the root of Jesse, and a flower shall rise up out of his root." (The Latin *virga* "rod" and *virgo* "virgin" was a common medieval pun.) The sequence of natural imagery progressively rises from the earth toward heaven. As our eyes are drawn upward from the familiar images of the visible creation, the mind begins to contemplate the invisible mystery of divine grace. This progression is balanced by the central stanzas' ever-sharpening focus on Mary's location as the Son of God quietly seeks her out, from an unspecified place, to a bower befitting a courtly lady, to the silent bed where she lay, as if at the still point of the turning world. Rhetorical balance is also achieved by symmetrical structure: with three central stanzas flanked by introductory and concluding stanzas, deliberate number symbolism seems likely. The number three represents the Trinity and the number five is associated with the Virgin.[44]

One sure sign of the poet's self-confidence in adapting traditional ideas is the subtle alteration of syntax in line four, reversing the earlier poem's relation between subject and object. Instead of emphasizing that the King of kings chose Mary for her unique honor, the poet tells us that *she* chose *him* as her Son. The effect is as brilliant as it is startling, conveying a more complex sense of the cooperative relation between human and divine agency than was imagined by the thirteenth-century poet.

How may we account for this bold move on the part of the later poet? The poet imagines freshly the scene of the Annunciation as recorded in the first chapter of the Gospel of Luke. In that account, the angel Gabriel initiates the divine action by greeting her: "Hail, full of grace, the Lord is with thee: blessed art though among women." The scriptural author probes her subjective experience, emphasizing her inner disturbance as she "was troubled at his saying, and thought with herself what manner of salutation this should be." As the angel explains the meaning of his greeting by informing her that she is to give birth to the Son of God, the shy young woman questions how such a thing is possible since she has never known a man. His reply is all about the force of divine agency: "The Holy Ghost shall come upon thee, and the power of the most High shall overshadow thee." Assured of God's ability to work miracle, she calmly submits to the divine will: "Behold the handmaid of the Lord; be it done to me according to thy word."

The poet re-imagines her acceptance of God's will as her act of deliberate choice, which initiates her son's act of seeking her out like the dew falling silently and gently from heaven.[45] The concluding stanza, with its sure and confident rhythms, affirms the rightness of God's singling out of Mary, which the audience has already grasped experientially from the progression of natural images. The lyric thus demonstrates how in the hands of a skillful poet the plain style normally employed in late-medieval didactic verse can achieve an elegant simplicity that is powerful in its emotional effect. Thus the poem persuades its reader.

As the Marian poems we have examined in this chapter are meant to demonstrate, the best Middle English lyric poets used poetic form as a vehicle for a highly sophisticated verbal art. By exploring public modes of language and shared feeling, such lyrics remain free of the post–Romantic assumption that lyric poetry expresses the thoughts and feelings of a unique individual. Learning about medieval styles of devotion within a manuscript culture helps us to widen our horizon to include past traditions. Without too great an effort, modern readers who love poetry can overcome the strangeness of the older language until we begin to feel at home in its rhythms and speech patterns.

4

The Love Complaint Ballade: Chaucer and Wyatt

Since the vast majority of surviving medieval lyrics are religious, we began by looking at three highly accomplished examples of the subgenre of Marian lyric. Although many other kinds of religious verse flourished, poetry inspired by devotion to the Virgin Mary represents a major branch of late-medieval religious lyric. The present chapter turns to an important secular subgenre, the love complaint ballade. Why was this peculiar fixed form of three rhyme royal stanzas used to explore the nearly universal theme of dissatisfaction with love? If love lyrics in earlier periods were not viewed as the self-expression of unique individuals, what other claims to our attention are presented by finely crafted poems on the game of love?

The ballade, first developed by Middle French court poets, was perfected by Guillaume de Machaut during the middle decades of the fourteenth century. Not all ballades in French were composed in seven-line stanzas, though in England rhyme royal remained the preferred form, in large part thanks to the influence of Geoffrey Chaucer. The rhyme royal ballade was perhaps the most important fixed form in secular lyrics of the later Middle Ages, and English poets continued to employ it in the sixteenth century.

The ballade was often used for love complaint. In this kind of lyric, a first-person speaker voices dissatisfaction with the pains of love, sometimes after his or her betrayal by the beloved. Once again, romantic assumptions that lyric poetry expresses the inner life of the individual poet swerve wide of the mark. The moods and emotions expressed in a love complaint are defined by poetic convention rather than personal experience.

Yet anyone who has personally experienced frustration, longing, and disappointment in love may find it easy to use the first-person pronoun as a placeholder for oneself. This transferable self is broadly similar to how the first-person pronoun works in devotional lyrics. In meditative poems the poetic "I" can be occupied by anyone who wishes to draw closer to God.

The main difference in love complaints, besides the secular form of love involved, is the tendency to use a gender-specific pronoun. As a result, love complaints were sometimes used as vehicles to express unflattering views of women, since the vast majority of poets in earlier periods were men, and men generally thought women were inferior beings. Such prejudices often came out in writing.

In the best love complaints, however, skilled poets could employ the form in surprisingly innovative ways. Poets and other readers clearly took notice. The continued use of the ballade form and lover's complaint in the early Tudor period helps illustrate how the traditional dividing line in literary history between the medieval and Renaissance periods is in many ways misleading. Accordingly, this chapter looks at two complaints by Chaucer and concludes with one by Sir Thomas Wyatt.

The love complaint and the ballade are fundamentally courtly in nature. To generalize about a complex matter, these lyric forms were originally developed by poets who wrote for aristocratic patrons. Sometimes members of the nobility and even royals themselves dabbled in making courtly verse. Reading and especially writing courtly verse was a mark of social distinction. The attitudes conveyed by courtly love lyrics thus open a window onto the social world of late-medieval aristocratic households. But we should never assume that the glass is transparent: it offers a distorted view at best. Sometimes poems that seem on their surface to be about love are also about ambition and power. As we shall see in the next chapter, this becomes especially true during the Elizabethan period.

The courtly love complaint entered English poetry by the early fourteenth century if not sooner. Some of the most accomplished pre–Chaucerian examples are collected in the important miscellany mentioned in the previous chapter, MS Harley 2253, though once again the difficult dialect makes them relatively inaccessible to modern readers. But the fusion of the rhyme royal ballade with the love complaint was introduced to English literature by Chaucer, who as a young poet was immersed in the world of Middle French court poetry.[1]

Some of Chaucer's best-known ballades are not love complaints at all but philosophical meditations based on ideas from *The Consolation of Philosophy* by Boethius. The ballades "Truth," "Lak of Stedfastnesse," and "Gentilesse" are frequently anthologized examples. The first two poems append an envoy (literally, a send-off) to the three-stanza structure. Chaucer also wrote love complaints that were not ballades. However, this chapter will concentrate on poems that fuse the rhyme royal ballade with the lover's complaint, representing a clearly defined branch of secular lyric in the emerging literary canon.

The first ballade I wish to discuss is relatively little known by non-specialists and rarely anthologized, even though it is probably by Chaucer. Like many of the Middle French court ballades, its theme is the pains of love:

Madame, for your newefangelnesse	*desire for novelty*
Many a servaunt have ye put out of grace.	
I take my leve of your unstedfastnesse,	
For wel I wot, whyl ye have lyves space,	*know; time to live*
5 Ye can not love ful half yeer in a place,	*one*
To newe thing your lust is ay so kene.	*pleasure/desire*
In stede of blew, thus may ye were al grene.	*blue; wear*
Right as a mirour nothing may impresse,	*mark permanently*
But, lightly as it cometh, so mot it pace,	*quickly/easily; may; pass*
10 So fareth your love, your werkes beren witnesse.	*bear*
Ther is no feith that may your herte enbrace,	
But as a wedercok, that turneth his face	*weathercock/wind vane*
With every wind, ye fare, and that is sene;	*seen*
In stede of blew, thus may ye were al grene.	
15 Ye might be shryned for your brotelnesse	*enshrined; instability*
Bet than Dalyda, Creseyde or Candace,	
For ever in chaunging stant your sikernesse;	*stands; sureness/security*
That tache may no wight fro your herte arace.	*stain/defect; person; remove*
If ye lese oon, ye can wel tweyn purchace;	*lose one; two; obtain*
20 Al light for somer (ye woot wel what I mene),	*lightly clothed (?); know*
In stede of blew, thus may ye were al grene.[2]	

The poem was first ascribed to Chaucer in the earliest printed edition, by John Stowe in 1561.[3] Although none of the three fifteenth-century manuscripts that record the poem attributes it to Chaucer, they include it in the company of other short poems known to be his. The Victorian editor W. W. Skeat (who believed the poem genuine) gave it the title "Against Women Unconstant," based on Stowe's heading. However, this description is misleading since the poem singles out one fickle lover and avoids attributing such behavior to women in general. Although we cannot be absolutely certain the poem is Chaucer's, its language, theme, and poetic technique make it more likely to be his than the work of another poet. Even so, the poem has not been much discussed by recent critics. Yet it is a highly accomplished piece of work that continues to have much to offer twenty-first century readers.

The early development of the ballade in France, as its generic name implies, associated the form with dance. To read late-medieval courtly lyric with imaginative power is thus to hear its verbal music. Many of Machaut's ballades were in fact composed for music, though even those that were not literally sung accentuated the sound qualities of language through rhyme, regular syllabic count, and other kinds of sound patterning. Chaucer's poem evidently borrows its refrain, with its traditional color symbolism, from the Machaut ballade "Se pour ce muir," where the proverbial refrain reads: "Qu'en lieu de bleu, dame, vous vestés vert" ("Instead of blue, lady, you wear green").[4] Blue symbolizes *trouthe* or constancy in love, green inconstancy, as is made clear in the *Squire's Tale*.[5]

Indeed, the arbitrary color-coding is only one instance of courtly artifice in both the French and English lyrics. Such poetry depends on the centuries-old conventions of courtly love, which playfully recodes feudal and religious faith as an important virtue for lovers. In the Chaucerian poem, the contrast between the lady's faith and works in lines ten and eleven playfully blurs the language of theology and courtly love. According to courtly love conventions, the lover was expected to perform his devout service to the lady regardless of whether she bestows "grace." Accordingly, the verb *shryned* in the third stanza carries a specifically religious connotation, since saints and their relics were provided shrines in the medieval period.

Rather than dutifully continuing in servile love as expected, here the poet adopts the persona of the bitterly disillusioned lover. Chaucer could find this conventional stance, for example, in Machaut's "Puis qu'Amours faut et Loyauté chancelle" ("Since Love deserts me and Loyalty wavers").[6] The poetic value of Chaucer's lyric is based less on its originality than on his skillful use of the poetic resources he inherited.

As a fixed form the Middle French ballade typically creates a "three-part logical chain."[7] The Middle English poem follows this pattern. The first stanza formally declares the lover's decision to renounce the lady because of her unfaithfulness. The two other stanzas provide additional analysis of her behavior while offering some vivid comparisons. The opening stanza uses the memorable word *newefangelnesse* to describe the lady's fickleness. Chaucer seems to have introduced this new word to the language of English poetry.[8] In Chaucer every other occurrence of this striking word and the related adjective *newfangle* is used to describe unfaithful men.[9] Here the word is used sarcastically in a poem meant to "stigmatize the lady."[10] In other words, this display of blame connects the poem with epideictic rhetoric.

The rhetorical orientation of this lyric prevents us from mistaking its expression of emotion as originating in the romantic history of the individual poet. Nonetheless, the poem captures the mood of what disillusionment in love is like. Although most people have probably felt this kind of emotion, the lyric lends a form and shape to that common feeling. Although the *addressee* of the poem is called "Madam," the *audience* or "presumed beneficiaries of [this] lyric communication" are readers who savor the bitter feeling of disillusionment in love. The poem's mode of address thus confirms Jonathan Culler's description of lyric as tending to use indirect address or triangulation to create a ritualistic dimension in the performance.[11]

The logic of the first stanza implies a background narrative. The woman's reputation was already questionable before the speaker became enamored, since he apparently knows that she has previously betrayed "many a servaunt." He is not the first man to be jilted by this particular woman. Yet unless he was actively seeking his own suffering, evidently he had hoped that this time might be different. His foolishness might be explained by the tendency of courtly lovers to be self-involved, impulsive, over-eager. But now he knows what he should have already known: her desire for novelty always ("ay") prevents her from settling her love in one "place" even for half a year.

That brief measure of time contrasts with the much fuller span of her life. His somewhat clumsy circumlocution, "whyl ye have lyves space," perhaps conceals a disguised wish for vengeance. The poem, after all, enacts a kind of poetic revenge by broadcasting her moral shortcomings. At the very least, the awkward phrase momentarily reminds us of her mortality, though this is not a *carpe diem* poem pretending to persuade a woman that life is too short to forego sexual pleasures. The relationship, however far it proceeded, is now over. The point of observing the passage of time is to suggest that the year's annual cycle cannot be completed even once before his unfaithful lover moves on to another partner. As the disappointed lover begins to take his leave, therefore, he recommends that she don the color green, an apt symbol for the spring-like freshness she seeks in her rage for the next "newe thing."

The second stanza offers two memorable images to describe her instability. The mirror and the weathercock are brought into the poem for their common moral symbolism. Her love is first compared to shapes in a mirror that "lightly" come and go without permanently etching ("impresse") their form into the glass. The adverb *lightly* conveys both the easy movement of reflections gliding on the mirror's surface, and the fact that mirrors depend on the play of light. Mirrors, of course, are traditional symbols of self-reflection, but also of vanity.

What would this woman see if she gazed at herself in the mirror that is the poem? Something or nothing? The syntax of lines eight and eleven contain mirror images of their own: *mirour* and *nothing* are reversible as grammatical subject and object. Likewise, *feith* and *herte* may be read as subject or object. The lover's true faith was unsuccessful in the effort to embrace her heart, while her heart in turn could not enclose any faith.[12] The mobility of her faithless heart is symbolized not only by the nothingness of the mirror's reflection, but by the proverbial weathercock that turns with every passing breeze. The second time the refrain is repeated its force seems sharper, now that the disillusioned lover has found the woman's proper measure in a familiar world of everyday symbolic objects.

The final stanza reaches a logical conclusion as the lover further distances himself from his fair-weather friend by turning her into an object of biting sarcasm. Like the brittleness of the mirror, her *brotelnesse* or instability surpasses that of three legendary faithless women from antiquity: Delilah, Creseyde, and Candace (the queen of India who tricked Alexander according to medieval legend). The outrageous comparison illustrates Culler's point that one of the salient features of lyric throughout its history is a tendency to extravagant, hyperbolic gestures.[13] More than any of these notoriously false women this one deserves a shrine. If the poem is Chaucer's, there is no way to know whether it was written before or after *Troilus and Criseyde*, or the *Legend of Good Women*, in which the god of Love assigns Chaucer the task of writing the later poem as penance for supposedly slandering women in his great romance.

Although most of the lines in the editorially reconstructed text fall into regular iambic pentameter rhythms or acceptable variations, the rhythm stumbles badly in the manuscripts when the lover recites the names of famously unfaithful women. Most modern editors emend the word *better* to *bet* for the sake of the meter, though no manuscript supports that reading. A possible scansion of the line as emended might appear thus:

Bet than Dalyda, Creseyde or Candace
B   o-o B o   B o b   o B(o)

No matter how we parse the line, however, it seems to stand out as if to emphasize their notoriety. After this extremely bitter comparison, the lover discovers a paradoxical consistency in her inconsistency. Constant in her mutability, she resembles the fickle goddess Fortune. By comparing her to these paradigmatic figures, the poet acknowledges that her behavior is hardly unprecedented.

However, he falls short of the common medieval antifeminist suggestion that this is how women are in general. Instead, the target remains individualized: "That tache may no wight fro your herte arace." If the embittered lover imagines her as the patron saint of a mock cult, he also implies that no one can remove the guilt of her original sin. She may be unredeemable, though in losing "one" (the faithful lover) she can always obtain two more—a bargain of sorts. She is thus appropriately clad in green, "al light for somer."

Ready to roam again, she is too *light* (inconstant) to be weighed down by the past. Despite all he has learned, evidently he still holds out the hope of successful communication with her.

Although "Madame, for your newefangelnesse" has all the hallmarks of a Chaucerian poem, its authorship remains uncertain. But there is no doubt that he wrote "The Complaint of Chaucer to His Purse." On its surface the poem imitates a love complaint but it is actually a poem asking his patron for money. The begging or petitionary poem is another late-medieval sub-genre of courtly lyric (some of the best were written by the Middle Scots court poet, William Dunbar around the turn of the sixteenth century). In the Chaucerian example, the poet reminds his new king not to forget his annuity, wittily translating a begging poem into a mock love complaint.

Dating from the first year of the reign of Henry IV, the "Complaint to His Purse" may be the last poem Chaucer ever wrote. Henry Bolingbroke, the eldest son of John of Gaunt, usurped the throne from Richard II and was accepted as the new king on 30 September 1399, thus establishing the Lancastrian dynasty. The abrupt transition of government meant that Chaucer did not receive payment toward his annuity on time. King Henry reconfirmed the grant, though Chaucer only received the first installment of his payment in February 1400 and another partial payment in June. He had still not received all the back pay he was owed when he died in October 1400.

The poem (or at least the envoy) must have been written while Chaucer found himself in difficult financial straits, during the narrow window between Henry's coronation and the poet's death. Given the assumed link to Chaucer's financial circumstances and his direct address to the king, the poem invites a brief summary of the life of Geoffrey Chaucer (c. 1342–1400).[14]

Chaucer was born around 1340 or shortly thereafter, the son of a prosperous wine merchant in London. His father John used his social connections to place Chaucer as a page in the household of the Elizabeth de Burgh, Countess of Ulster and wife to Edward III's second oldest son, Lionel, Duke of Clarence. (Both Lionel and his older brother, Richard the Black Prince, died later while Edward was still alive.) In these early years Chaucer became acquainted with the customs of courtly life, learning practical and social skills that made him useful to his superiors.

Chaucer served as a foot soldier under Lionel during a campaign in the Hundred Years' War. He was taken prisoner and ransomed by the king in 1360 for £16, a significant sum. By the end of the decade he became a member of the royal household of Edward III and was granted an annuity. Rising through the ranks he was eventually promoted to esquire, the lowest rank of gentry. He traveled to the Continent on various diplomatic missions, including journeys to France, Spain, and twice to Italy. As a result of his Italian travels he became the first English writer known to have been acquainted with Italian literature.

Chaucer spend most of his adult life working hard at various jobs that carried significant responsibilities in the royal bureaucracy. The post he held longest was Controller of Customs, in charge of making sure the export tax on wool was paid to the Crown. He was married to Philippa Roet, a French-speaking lady in waiting whose family was of higher social rank than his own. Her sister became the mistress and eventually the third wife of John of Gaunt. For much of their marriage, however, Chaucer and his wife lived in separate households, serving their respective masters.

As a reward for his loyal service, Chaucer received various forms of compensation from the royal coffers of Edward III and his successor, Richard II, son of the Black Prince. None of the roughly five hundred documentary records of Chaucer's life, however, refers to him as a poet. Although earlier generations assumed that he wrote under royal patronage and even performed his poetry orally as a court poet, this view no longer carries weight among scholars. Instead, his primary audience seems to have been men of similar rank within the civil service in London.

Despite having been loyal to Richard II for many years—he even supported the king by serving as a knight of the shire for Kent in the Parliament of 1386—Chaucer weathered the political storms successfully. When the conflict between Richard and his opponents turned deadly in 1387, Chaucer had already removed himself to the countryside of Kent and kept his head low. During his prolonged absence from London he wrote his unfinished masterpiece, *The Canterbury Tales*. He finally moved back to London at the end of 1399, taking up residence within the precincts of Westminster Abbey. He had survived these politically tumultuous times only to die in October 1400.[15]

Chaucer's witty "Complaint" is short enough to quote in full. Like a good courtly lover, the poet begs his lady for mercy:

```
    To yow, my purse, and to noon other wight      no other creature
    Complayne I, for ye be my lady dere.           dear
    I am so sory, now that ye been lyght;          are; light in weight/frivolous
    For certes but yf ye make me hevy chere,       surely unless you take me seriously
 5  Me were as leef be layd upon my bere;          I would be as pleased; bier
    For which unto your mercy thus I crye,
    Beth hevy ageyn, or elles mot I dye.           Be heavy; else must

    Now voucheth sauf this day or hyt be nyght     grant; before it is night
    That I of yow the blisful soun may here        sound; hear
```

10	Or see your colour lyk the sonne bryght	*sun*
	That of yelownesse hadde never pere.	*peer*
	Ye be my lyf, ye be myn hertes stere.	*heart's rudder*
	Quene of comfort and of good companye,	
	Beth hevy ageyn, or elles moot I dye.	
15	Now purse that ben to me my lyves lyght	*are*
	And saveour as doun in this world here,	
	Out of this toune helpe me thurgh your myght,	*through*
	Syn that ye wole nat ben my tresorere;	*Since; will; treasurer*
	For I am shave as nye as any frere.	*shaved clean as a friar*
20	But yet I pray unto your curtesye,	
	Beth hevy agen, or elles moot I dye.	

Lenvoy de Chaucer

	O conquerour of Brutes Albyon,	*(see below)*
	Which that by lyne and free eleccion	*line (of inheritance)*
	Been verray kyng, this song to yow I sende,	*true*
25	And ye, that mowen alle oure harmes amende,	*may*
	Have mynde upon my supplicacion.	

This amusing poem with the serious rhetorical purpose survives in twelve manuscripts and two early prints. Several copies lack the envoy, probably because some scribes did not recognize that it was part of the poem.[16] The large number of medieval and early modern copies make it a good candidate for inclusion in the early lyric canon.

The poem has all the hallmarks of lyric poetry identified by Culler as typical. The poem comically exaggerates the lover's desperate condition, using the typical courtly hyperbole of dying for love. It uses apostrophe to create a complex mode of address, triangulating among the speaker, the fictional addressee, and the real audience (King Henry or a member of his staff acting on his authority). It seeks to be an event rather than the representation of one. As a prayer or supplication for the purse to become full as if by magic, the lyric uses insistent rhythms and a repeated refrain to convey a ritualistic element to its "song."

The mock love complaint includes the obligatory plea for mercy from his "lady," who is praised as his heart's guiding rudder and his "queen of comfort and good company" because no one likes to hang out with a friend whose purse is empty. Chaucer had used "Queen of comfort" as a descriptive name or epithet for the Virgin Mary in his alphabetically arranged Marian lyric, "An ABC."[17] In the "Complaint," the lady's appearance is compared to the sun as the stereotypical color of the mistress's hair is transferred to the gold he desires. The clinking of gold coins would make a "blissful sound" indeed. Like every courtly love lyric worth its salt, the "Complaint" uses religious language to describe the lover's devotion. In addition to using the

Marian epithet he praises his lady as the "light" of his life and his "savior down in this world here," narrowly avoiding blasphemy by implying that another savior resides in heaven.

But his lady is no Virgin Mary. Chaucer's best joke of all is his ironic use of sexual innuendo. The adjective *light* implies both that the empty purse weighs little and that the lady is frivolous, unfaithful, or unchaste—in short, a woman of questionable morals.[18] We may compare the use of the word *light* as a complaint about her loose morals with its occurrence in the love complaint discussed above (see line 20). If the lover's prayers are answered and her purse is filled (an obvious metaphor for sexual activity) she will become *heavy*. Although the earliest use of the adjective to mean pregnant or heavy with child recorded by the *OED* is from about 1480, the metaphorical pattern of Chaucer's sexual innuendo clearly points in that direction.[19]

Finally, the envoy turns in all seriousness to address Henry IV directly as the conqueror of Brutus's Albion. Here Chaucer alludes to the well-known myth most famously told in Geoffrey of Monmouth's legendary *History of the Kings of Britain*. According to the old legend, the island once called Albion took the name *Britain* in honor of its Trojan conqueror Brutus, a descendent of Aeneas. As scholars have observed, Chaucer's three grounds for assigning legitimacy to Henry's kingship—conquest, lineage, and election—duplicate the justification given in Lancastrian propaganda.[20] Always the survivor, Chaucer evidently had transferred his allegiance to the new king, though whether out of conviction or political expediency we will never know. In any case, Chaucer closed out his poetic career with characteristic brilliance, comically transforming the genre of begging poem by recasting it as a love complaint.

Although the fifteenth century witnessed many further developments in an emerging lyric tradition, limits of space require us to fast-forward to the reign of Henry VIII. Medieval English lyric poems, including rhyme royal ballades, continued to be copied in manuscripts in the early sixteenth century, long after the advent of printing. In recirculating earlier lyrics, many Tudor readers evidently continued to value the sometimes misogynistic verses of their predecessors, though there is also evidence that women sometimes responded to the masculine tradition.[21]

The early Tudor poet, diplomat, and courtier Sir Thomas Wyatt (c. 1503–42) is a transitional figure.[22] His poetry continues the lyric tradition of late-medieval courtly "makers" while introducing new developments from the Italian Renaissance to English poetry (we shall examine his most famous sonnet in the next chapter).

Wyatt was active before English lyric poetry had gained the prestige necessary for it to flourish in a print environment.[23] Before such cultural shifts took place, Wyatt and other courtly makers used lyric and song for a variety of social purposes. Within a manuscript-based culture of performance, writers used poetry to communicate among fellow courtiers, poets, and their circles, advance semi-private erotic agendas, cement social bonds, mark one's distinction as a member of an elite social group, and so on. The famous Devonshire Manuscript (British Library MS Add. 17492), which includes many poems by Wyatt, is a collaborative project that circulated among an elite coterie of men and women associated with the court of Henry VIII.[24]

As one recent scholar suggests, the older tendency to focus critical attention on printed sources "creates a false sense of the separateness of literary texts from the social worlds in which they were so obviously immersed in the system of manuscript transmission."[25] Once a poem entered the manuscript system, the poet could not exercise control over his or her work. Anyone with access to a text could recopy it, alter it, imitate it, add it to a collection, and so on. To an even greater extent, print served to abstract such poetry from its original social contexts.

In Wyatt's case, the first edition of Richard Tottel's collection, *Songes and Sonettes*, better known as *Tottel's Miscellany* (1557), began to make his work available to a wider readership than the far more restricted audience that encountered it during or immediately after his lifetime. A large part of Wyatt's poetic canon remained hidden in obscure archives until the first modern edition appeared in the early nineteenth century. Tottel or his associates extensively edited and "improved" Wyatt's poems, making his meter more regular, adding more punctuation, removing archaisms, and otherwise smoothing out the style.[26]

As we saw in Chapter 1, the system of English versification was undergoing significant changes during these decades. This state of flux often leaves the intended rhythmic contours of Wyatt's poetry uncertain. Indeed, the idea of a regular system of meter was probably foreign to him. Because his verse gives the impression that we are witnessing a transitional stage before arriving at the canonical system of prosody established a few decades later, my discussion includes an extended discussion of his metrical practice.

Significantly, Tottel also included titles to many of the poems in his collection "to allow readers to perceive the poems' connection either to an actual social world or to the traditional fictional world of love experience."[27] The editorial practice inaugurated by Tottel of using titles to create a fictional literary context for lyric verse continued into the nineteenth century, in Francis T. Palgrave's influential collection of lyric verse, *The Golden Treasury*, often revised and never out print.[28]

First-person lyrics always potentially invite readers to consider how they might refer, however obliquely, to a personal life, whether real or fictional or somewhere in between. Certainly we should avoid assuming "stable, biographic identifications between the Wyatt who writes and the 'I' who speaks in his poems."[29] The same point, of course, applies to love poetry going all the way back to the troubadours, including Chaucer's love complaints. In short, the relationship between the lyric "I" and the author must always remain indeterminate.

Yet Wyatt's mastery of passionate, first-person utterance leads one critic to comment on how knowing the later history of English lyric may incline us to assume that the poet is opening his inner life to our inspection. Wyatt "is the first English poet whose work takes the form which since the Renaissance has come to seem normal—that of a large collection of short secular poems purporting to record isolated moments of personal emotional experience."[30] Although many of Wyatt's best poems are highly original and his voice often seems utterly distinctive, his work should not be judged by romantic-era standards of originality or sincerity.

Sixteenth-century printed collections of lyric poetry, of which *Tottel's Miscellany* is only the most famous, shared with contemporary manuscript collections conventional themes and genres. Print anthologies and manuscript collections record "courtly poems dealing with love, the vicissitudes of fortune, death and loss, ceremonial social occasions, the relationship of patronage and clientage," and so on.[31] However, in treating lyric poems more as socio-cultural documents than as works of poetic art, historicist scholars tend to ignore that these are precisely the themes of enduring human significance that help make older lyric poetry appealing to later generations—especially readers who are not scholars—long after the original social conditions and literary conventions have receded into the past.

The highly conventional nature of Tudor lyric poetry and the circulation of lyric poetry in manuscripts among restricted audiences make the ascription of individual poems to specific authors especially difficult. The canon of works attributed to Wyatt is thus uncertain around the edges.[32] Some of Wyatt's most powerful lyrics express an intense psychological suffering that at least *sounds* like he is drawing on his own experience, though to be sure, much of this impression may owe more to literary convention than to any personal revelation.

Nonetheless, reading through a collection of his verse, one may be struck by how often he draws on a vocabulary expressing psychological pain and loss. Although he works with inherited late-medieval stylistic conventions associated with the love complaint, few poets in the transition from medieval to Renaissance English verse rival the haunting quality Wyatt's use of such a vocabulary.

One of Wyatt's most widely admired love complaints is a three-stanza rhyme royal ballade, which introduces new rhymes in each stanza. Here is the poem in modern spelling:

> They flee from me that sometime did me seek
> With naked foot stalking in my chamber.   *walking softly/stalking game*
> I have seen them gentle, tame, and meek
> That now are wild and do not remember
> 5 That sometimes they put themselves in danger   *in my power/in peril*
> To take bread at my hand; and now they range
> Busily seeking with a continual change.
>
> Thanked be fortune it hath been otherwise
> Twenty times better, but once in special,   *more than twenty times*
> 10 In thin array after a pleasant guise,   *in a thin gown made pleasantly*
> When her loose gown from her shoulders did fall
> And she me caught in her arms long and small,
> Therewithal sweetly did me kiss
> And softly said, "Dear heart, how like you this?"
>
> 15 It was no dream: I lay broad waking.
> But all is turned thorough my gentleness   *through*
> Into a strange fashion of forsaking.
> And I have leave to go of her goodness   *as a result of her goodness to me*
> And she also to use newfangleness.   *i.e., seek a new lover*
> 20 But since that I so kindly am served   *with kindness/in a way natural to women*
> I would fain know what she hath deserved.[33]

Tottel's Miscellany gives this poem the descriptive title "The lover sheweth how he is forsaken of such as he sometimes enjoyed." But Tottel's description may be misleading. Alastair Fowler argues that the usual assumption, that *forsaking* in line 17 implies that the relationship has already ended, is not supported by the poem. He observes that it is more likely that *forsake* here is used in the older sense of "decline or refuse something offered."[34]

Although Tottel's fictional framing moves the poem further towards the category of "literature" by severing its social links to the manuscript system, such information does little to account for the poem's continuing power to move us. The poem's appeal depends on its keen analysis of what betrayal and the loss of love feels like, a pain made even sharper by memories of a happier time.

The lyric expresses disappointment with love by drawing on a familiar courtly theme—*newfangleness*. Wyatt found the word in Chaucer to describe an unexpected betrayal of affection. The lady falcon's lament in the *Squire's Tale*, a work more admired in the sixteenth century than in recent centuries, shows that inconstancy could also be the fault of the male lover.

It has also been claimed that some of the details of the amorous encounter in stanza two borrow from two of Ovid's *Amores*.[35] If so, the differences are far more striking than the similarities, and not only in style and attitude. In *Amores* III, 7, Ovid's lover embraces and kisses him. But Ovid has already taken the wind out of his own sails by making it clear that this night is an erotic disaster. He cannot achieve an erection, though he mentally surveys more successful past performances. The woman soon storms off in disgust. In *Amores* I, 5, on the other hand, we get a description of Ovid disrobing Corinna on a sultry afternoon, when his efforts prove more successful.

Wyatt begins the poem with the fleeting suggestion that the traditional metaphor of the hunt of love is reversed as former lovers are described as "stalking" him as though he is the prey. He longingly recalls past encounters when young women behaved like tame deer (or a similarly skittish animal), gently taking bread from his hand. But now they no longer remember former intimacies and keep their distance, reverting to their naturally "wild" state, restlessly seeking "continual change." In a sense, so did the speaker as long as he remained unsettled on one partner. The wistful stanza marvelously recaptures the delight of coaxing a fearful animal to accept an offer of food. Much of the first stanza's effectiveness comes from the fact that only a single detail asks us to see the gentle animal simultaneously in human terms by locating the recollected scene in the "chamber," hardly the natural place to encounter wildlife.

The metrical variations in stanza one also contribute to its expressive effects. Although a five-beat line seems to underlie the basic rhythmic pattern, in the first stanza only line one scans as a perfectly regular iambic pentameter.[36] However, line three can be read as an acceptable variation of iambic pentameter.[37] (Students of Chaucer's meter describe his occasional use of an iambic pentameter line that lacks the initial weak syllable as "headless.") Derek Attridge scans Wyatt's line thus:

> I have seen them gentle, tame, and meek
> B o B o B o B o B

Line two, according to Attridge, comes close to following "a five-beat duple rhythm, the only disturbance, perhaps appropriately, with the unpaired implied offbeat before 'stalking'":

> With naked foot stalking in my chamber
> o B o B ô B o b o B o[38]

Other lines in the first stanza seem easier to interpret as four-beat lines. Taking his cue from reading the lines according to their perceived natural rhythms, Attridge suggests scanning lines four and five thus:

> That now are wild, and do not remember
> o B o B   o B o-o B o
>
> That sometime they put themselves in danger
> o B   o-o   B o B o B o[39]

Speaking line two naturally, we might depart from Attridge's suggestion and scan it as a four-beat line with a triple offbeat:

> With naked foot stalking in my chamber
> o   B o B ô B   o-o-o   B o

No matter how we read the line, its rhythm refuses to settle into regularity. Yet it still avoids sounding like prose. The poem eases in and out of a stable metrical structure in ways that contribute to its expression of emotional tension.

Some lines seem ambiguously poised between five- and four-beat rhythms. The crucial line six seems rhythmically ambiguous, capable of being read as either a five-beat or, more probably in its immediate context, as a four-beat line. Attridge offers two different scansions by suppressing the first beat in the second realization:

> To take bread at my hand; and now they range
> o B ô B o-o   B   o B o   B
> o-o   B

The tentativeness of the animals' approach may perhaps be suggested by the tension created by the uncertainty of rhythm.

After thankfully recalling that the poet's fortunes in love used to be more favorable, the second stanza abandons the metaphor of the shy animal to recall one former lover, who momentarily becomes present in memory through the representation of her body, attire, voice, and erotic desire.

Again the flexible poetic rhythms contribute to the emotional effect. The first two lines of the stanza do not depart so far from iambic pentameter as to create a clashing rhythm:

> Thanked be fortune it hath been otherwise
> B   o B o-o b   o B o b
>
> Twenty times better, but once in special
> B o B ô B o-o   B   o B o-o[40]

The next line reinstates an acceptable variation of iambic pentameter (as scanned by Attridge):

> In thin array after a pleasant guise
> o B o B ô B o-o B o B

The greater regularity helps express the joyous mood of the occasion. But the next line seems to revert to a four-beat pattern. Three double offbeats lend lightness to the measure while an implied offbeat emphasizes the seductive item of clothing:

When her loose gown from her shoulders did fall
  o-o   B ô B   o-o   B   o-o   B

The next line describes her self-confident action with another regular variation of pentameter that uses an implied offbeat to pause after *arms*, an emphatic word (again using Attridge's scansion):

And she me caught in her arms long and small
  o   B   o   B   o-o   B ô B   o   B

This gesture is followed by an even more significant action, though the scansion is especially difficult:

Therewithal sweetly did me kiss
  B   o   B ô B   o   b   o   B

The lack of regularity and the short syllable count bothered Tottel, who smooths out the beginning of the line: "And therwithall so." In any case, the second half of the line clearly falls into a regular alternating pattern that suggests an emotional highpoint in the pleasant turn of events.

The buoyant mood is sustained in the concluding line of the stanza, which easily falls into a more regular pentameter:

And softly said, "Dear heart, how like you this?"
 o   B   o   B   O   B   o   B   o   B[41]

As Attridge comments, "there is no doubt that its rocking rhythm contributes to the satisfaction it expresses."[42] The stanza ending, of course, also expresses this sense of satisfaction through the strong closure created by the final rhyming couplet, especially pronounced because both lines are end-stopped.

After this recollection of erotic bliss, the next line implies that at some point the speaker has questioned its occurrence. The present reality is so dramatically different as to lend the earlier experience the quality of a dream. The jolting return to a more sober assessment is in part conveyed by the rhythmically ambiguous line fifteen, which begins the poem's final movement of thought. Attridge suggests that the line "hovers between a four-beat and a five-beat pattern" and offers two possible scansions:

It was no dream: I lay broad waking
 o-o   B ô   B   o B   O   B o
                  B ô B ô B o

The one thing that seems certain is the "slow, emphatic movement" of the line.[43] This rhythmic sense of deliberation helps convey his reawaking to the new reality.

Uncertainties about Wyatt's pronunciation certainly contribute to the modern reader's bafflement about his metrical intentions. In line sixteen the obsolete spelling of the preposition *thorough* may imply the poet pronounced it as two syllables. If we allow for the additional possibility that the past tense ending of the verb *turned* may not be realized as a syllable, once more we encounter a line that hovers between a five-beat and four-beat pattern: "But all is turned thorough my gentleness." Predictably, Tottel again imposes a clearer alternating pattern by reading "turnd now thorough."

However we realize the rhythm of the line, its ironic tone must not be ignored. Literally the speaker claims that his *gentle* behavior (in both the modern meaning and the older sense of noble and refined) caused the lady, originally conceived metaphorically as one of the *gentle* animals who used to take bread, to deny him in a strange manner. Yet clearly the real meaning is to blame the lady for her *ungentle* behavior. In displaying her faults, the poem engages in an act of epideictic rhetoric.

The poet conveys the alien quality of her changed demeanor through the rhythmically slow and deliberate progression of line seventeen: "Into a strange fashion of forsaking." Tottel's substitution of the adjective *bitter*, most modern readers would now agree, is less compelling, both rhythmically and semantically. Just as the metaphor of stanza one focused our attention on the strangeness of a wild animal tamely accepting his offering of bread, so we are now invited to pause and view the lady as strange in a different sense, one as disturbing as the other was thrilling.

After this emotional disruption, the next two lines nearly resolve themselves into acceptable variants of iambic pentameter:

> And I have leave to go of her goodness
> o B o B o B o-o   B ô b[44]

> And she also to use newfangleness
> o B ôB o-o B   o B o b[45]

Again, the ironic tone is unmistakable since he hardly reads her dismissal as a sign of her *goodness*, a point further emphasized not only by the alliteration but by drawing out the word just long enough for an implied offbeat to fall between the syllables, if the scansion above is accepted.

The final movement of the poem concludes with a couplet whose rhythms seem especially conjectural.[46] Both lines seem, when read according to a natural speech rhythm, to revert back to a four-beat pattern:

> But since that I so kindly am served
> o   B   o   B o   B   o-o   B (o)
>
> I would fain know what she hath deserved
> o-o   B ô B   o   B   o-o   B (o)

But it is possible that the Egerton MS spelling *kyndely* indicates a trisyllabic word, which is etymologically supported. That would then allow the promotion of *–ly* into a beat in a regular iambic pentameter. Moreover, it would be plausible to hear the final line edging toward triple meter to give it special emphasis:

> I would fain know what she hath deserved
> B   o-o   B   o   B   o-o   B (o)

The rhetorical question needs no answering by the poet because the reader makes a mental reservation.

Poetic closure is reached with the rhymed couplet and the repeated rhythmic contour of the ending of both lines. As for the understated suggestion of thoughts of revenge, what spurned lover has not entertained at least passing fancies of the other's suffering? Indeed, the rhythmic instability contributes to the ways in which "both the speaker and the reader are left lost and disorientated in a strangely altered land."[47]

The experience of love can be disorienting and painful. That is one reason the lover's complaint remains alive and well in popular song. Despite the initial unfamiliarity of the late-medieval lyric form of rhyme royal ballade, twenty-first century readers who pay close attention to the details of style and structure may rediscover how poetic technique helps make more persuasive the commonplace moods of the spurned lover in ways that continue to resonate.

5

The Love Sonnet from Wyatt to Shakespeare

How was it possible in the sixteenth century for a kind of poetry that deliberately imitated other poetry to leave room for individual poets to experiment and innovate? How could poets discover artistic freedom while following the strict rules of the sonnet, the most closed of lyric forms? How could the first-person pronoun in Renaissance sonnets be used to give concrete form to widely shared public moods?

Petrarch's *Canzoniere* or *Rime sparse* set in motion a European vogue for writing sonnets that lasted for well over two centuries, though England lagged behind Italy and France.[1] To read imitations of Petrarchan love poems is to be aware of reading not just the individual poem or sequence but one that is in dialogue with a well-defined tradition. Petrarchism was supremely imitable as a literary style, something translatable across linguistic, geographic, and generational boundaries. Even before reading the first line, the eye readily perceives in an instant what kind of poem is set out on the page. With its distinctive length, metrical patterns, and rhyme schemes, and with its conventional repertoire of conceits and poetic diction, Petrarchan sonnets offered a fashionable mode of turning inward, even if many examples appear stale and unimaginative in the hands of lesser poets.

The generic repertoire of the love sonnet, so memorably parodied in Shakespeare's Sonnet 130 ("My mistress' eyes are nothing like the sun"), created a shared literary space that placed poets and readers in the public world of the sonnet. Yet that shared world could seem to be an alienated and private one. Jonathan Culler describes Petrarchism as "a division of the world into the private space of unhappy passion and the public world in which the lover still moves." Yet the rhetorical commonplaces of the love sonnet, shaped by centuries of classroom training in epideictic, ensure that this private space is in fact a shared world, crowded with other people and other voices, some going back to the Middle Ages and beyond.[2] If Petrarch started something new, his collection of lyrics also marks the culmination of centuries of lyric tradition.

The love sonnet during the Renaissance seems to place on public display the minute inner workings of the self in relation to others, as Puttenham's rehearsal of "the many moods and pangs of lovers" confirms.[3] Indeed, the sonnet provided an especially fertile ground for sixteenth-century English poets to develop sophisticated means of exploring the inner workings of the heart at a time when the English language did not yet have our modern vocabulary for describing the inner life of what we are used to calling our true selves.[4]

The stylized drama of erotic passion was performed against a backdrop of other social involvements (friends, families, rivals, critics, patrons, mythical gods, etc.). In some cases, the scene includes geopolitical events, the widest possible public context for seemingly private passions confined to the small space of fourteen lines. Speaking about love provided a convenient vehicle for speaking in a coded way about such sociopolitical matters as personal ambition and the competition for social status and political favor. Indeed, this poetry not only used love as a metaphor for sociopolitical concerns but was in fact a way of participating in them.[5]

Yet if there is no doubt that the love sonnet indirectly addressed sociopolitical concerns, we should not forget that it was also a way of speaking about love, the affection "most general to all sorts and ages of men and women," as Puttenham observes.[6] To speak of love, he reminds us, amorous verse devises a variety of forms, "a thousand delicate devices ... moving one way and another to great compassion." Puttenham thus reminds us once again that we are witnessing a rhetorical poetics in action. Renaissance poets called on rhetorical techniques to heighten the effects of poetry on readers. To ignore the artistry of the sonnet's formal poetic devices, therefore, would be just as ahistorical as to treat poetry as autonomous aesthetic objects.

The clear structure of the sonnet and the weight given to the aural and visual patterns of words, syntax, poetic lines and groups of lines are put prominently on display. The verbal density and heft of language in a Renaissance sonnet draws writers and readers into a sharpened linguistic awareness. Responding to a sonnet intelligently calls for especially intensive reading practices. Accordingly, this chapter emphasizes metrical and rhetorical devices in selected masterpieces by sixteenth-century makers of sonnets: Wyatt, Sidney, Spenser, and Shakespeare.

Sir Thomas Wyatt's "They flee from me, who sometime did me seek" (examined in the previous chapter) stands near the end of a medieval lyric tradition. His Petrarchan sonnets, on the other hand, mark the beginning of a Renaissance poetic movement in England. Wyatt introduced the sonnet to English, though his younger contemporary, Henry Howard, Earl of Surrey, is credited with inventing the characteristically English form of three quatrains and a final couplet.

Wyatt's poetry circulated almost entirely in manuscript among an audience of friends and others connected with the court during his brief and often tumultuous life. Such relatively closed audiences are describe by scholars as a "coterie." Wyatt's gift for languages—he was fluent in Latin, French, and Italian—made him a useful ambassador. During his official travels he was introduced to a variety of Continental literary innovations.[7] Yet domestic and international court intrigues made working for Henry VIII a potentially hazardous occupation. He was twice imprisoned in the Tower, first in 1536 on unspecified charges, then on suspicion of treason in 1541.[8]

Wyatt's earlier troubles with Henry may have been linked to the fall of Anne Boleyn, whom the poet knew before the beginning of her tragic liaison with the ruthless king. Although the details of their relationship will never be known, Wyatt seems to have been enamored of her before the king began his courtship. Three different sixteenth-century accounts even claim that Wyatt and Anne had consummated their relationship, though it is impossible to know whether such rumors had any basis in fact.[9]

Wyatt's poetry is coded in ways that left his contemporaries in a better position than we are to understand the immediate social circumstances—if there were any—of his lyrics. This evasiveness makes it impossible to separate myth from reality in some of his poetry.[10] The following poem is a case in point:

> Whoso list to hunt, I know where is an hind,   *Whoever wishes; female deer*
> But as for me, helas, I may no more.   *alas*
> The vain travail hath wearied me so sore,   *futile effort*
> 4 I am of them that farthest cometh behind.
> Yet may I by no means my wearied mind
> Draw from the deer, but as she fleeth afore
> Fainting I follow. I leave off therefore
> 8 Sithens in a net I seek to hold the wind.   *Since*
> Who list her hunt, I put him out of doubt,
> As well as I may spend his time in vain.
> And graven with diamonds in letters plain
> 12 There is written her fair neck round about:
> "*Noli me tangere* for Caesar's I am,   *Do not touch me*
> And wild for to hold though I seem tame" [Rebholz XI].

This sonnet, which imitates Petrarch's *Rime* 190, is suspected by many modern critics of alluding to his relationship with Anne Boleyn and how Henry VIII interrupted it in 1526–27.[11]

In an English context the transparent allegory of royal power was unlikely to have been missed by early readers, even those who stood outside the inner circles of court and remained unaware of Wyatt's rumored love interest.[12] At the same time, the sonnet's calculated open-endedness easily lends itself to appropriation by any masculine reader—or indeed, any reader—who hopes to overcome social barriers and find success in love despite more powerful or attractive rivals.

Although the conventional courtly imagery of the hunt of love is not especially flattering to the real or fictional woman (or women in general), the first-person speaker's ironic self-deprecation places the metaphorical deer in a competitive advantage as a figure of greater energy and resourcefulness. In fact, the speaker's hunt of a single female deer would likely have seemed disturbing to Wyatt's readers since it violated the rules of hunting.[13] The dramatically unexpected inscription of the final couplet suggests, moreover, that even Caesar may overestimate his ability to tame her wildness or control her will.[14]

The poem's construction is artful in many ways. The opening octave is subdivided into quatrains that reveal different aspects of the lover's dilemma: he can neither attain the object of his pursuit nor can he give up pursuing her. As is often the case with later English sonnets, a structural tension develops between the alternate schemes of the Italian octave + sestet and the English form of three quatrains + couplet.

This tension is well suited to expressing the speaker's emotional conflict.[15] The rhyme scheme identifies the sestet as the second major sense unit and marks the turn by reiterating the opening clause with a significant variation that singles out "her" before advising potential rivals of the futility of this pursuit. The implied full stop at the end of line ten and the four-line sentence that completes the sonnet create a strong syntactical counter-structure to the rhyme scheme of the sestet.[16] The conjunction "And" at the beginning of line eleven, instead of the more causally explicit "For," leaves the reader to work out what the inscription on the collar implies about the poet's situation.[17]

Elsewhere in the poem the sentence boundaries are more open to interpretation. Lines one and three, for example, could easily end in full stops. The comma in the middle of line six could similarly be replaced by a period. Early modern poets like Wyatt in their own practice (as best determined when a manuscript in the author's own hand survives) typically punctuate more lightly than modern conventions require. Renaissance punctuation tends to mark rhetorical pauses rather than strict syntactic boundaries. A modern editor who wishes to assist readers with added punctuation must make choices that tend to close off different interpretations, though (like modernized spelling) this is a price worth paying if Renaissance poetry is to remain accessible to a non-specialist readership.

Even less certain in Wyatt's sonnets are his metrical intentions. As we saw in the previous chapter, we should not assume that his transitional verse was composed according to later expectations of more regular iambic pentameter, though the predominance of a five-beat line here seems unmistakable. Line endings are also an essential component of the underlying rhythmic structure. In poetry, lines that end with the completion of a clause or phrase are called *end-stopped*. Usually punctuation marks an end-stopped line, which is perceived to take a brief pause. Lines whose syntax and sense runs on to the next line, on the other hand, create *enjambment*. Run-on lines are perceived to have less of a pause at the end. In this poem end-stopped verse predominates, making the enjambments after lines five and six, combined with strong pauses (caesura) within lines six and seven, effective in expressing the lover's breathless dilemma.

Much early Tudor verse uses alliteration liberally and Wyatt's is no exception (the *f*s and *d*s being especially prominent here), though he employs the technique with moderation. Despite its courtly Petrarchan background, the poem for the most part employs a plain-style diction characteristic of Wyatt's best stylistic achievements.[18] Wyatt's mastery of the plain style and his use of a vocabulary that favors one-syllable native words helps recommend his verse to readers who may find more courtly idioms too "artificial" for their tastes.

Many mid–Tudor poets after Wyatt tried their hand at sonnets about love, but it was Sidney's *Astrophil and Stella* (*AS*) that inspired so many of his contemporaries, including Drayton, Daniel, Spenser, and Shakespeare, to follow his example and write entire sequences of sonnets.[19] Sir Philip Sidney (1554–86), courtier, diplomat, and soldier, was a prolific writer not only of poetry but also of prose fiction with his epic romance, *Arcadia*.[20] His literary works remained unpublished during his lifetime, circulating in manuscript only among a restricted coterie audience before he died tragically young on the Continent while engaged in a military campaign on behalf of the Protestant cause against the Spanish.[21] During a period in the early 1580s after falling out of Queen Elizabeth's favor, Sidney withdrew to Wilton House, the estate of his sister Mary, Countess of Pembroke, where he devoted time to writing the first version of *Arcadia*, as well as *The Defence of Poetry* and *Astrophil and Stella*. The sonnet sequence was in part inspired by his relationship with Penelope Devereux, daughter of the first Earl of Essex. She had married Robert, third Baron Rich, in November 1582.

Astrophil and Stella includes 108 sonnets and eleven songs. As a master craftsman in formal technique Sidney was endlessly inventive. By the time he wrote *Astrophil and Stella* he had already experimented with an unprecedented variety of metrical and stanzaic forms. His use of rhyme was exacting. He introduced to lyric stanzas the structural feature of using rhymes whose stress does not fall on the final syllable of the word (feminine rhyme).[22]

Sidney's technical innovations in *AS* are remarkable. He employs fourteen different rhyme schemes for the sonnets, and he tried his hand at using a longer six-beat (alexandrine) line in sonnets 1, 6, 8, 76, 77, and 102, a feat not previously attempted in English. In addition, he introduced to English the use of a falling pattern of beat-offbeat (trochaic) meter, perfecting it in six of the songs in *AS*. His finely tuned ear for the rhythms of polite conversation, his use of everyday vocabulary, and his preference for one-syllable words masks the careful craftsmanship that went into his poetry.[23]

The opening sonnet is among those most admired by critics, and it offers a characteristic example of Sidney's poetic excellence:

> Loving in truth, and fain in verse my love to show,
> That she (dear she) might take some pleasure of my pain;
> Pleasure might cause her read, reading might make her know;
> 4 Knowledge might pity win, and pity grace obtain;
>   I sought fit words to paint the blackest face of woe,
>   Studying inventions fine, her wits to entertain;
>   Oft turning others' leaves, to see if thence would flow
> 8 Some fresh and fruitful showers upon my sunburnt brain.
>   But words came halting forth, wanting invention's stay;   *support*
>   Invention, nature's child, fled step-dame study's blows;
>   And others' feet still seemed but strangers in my way.
> 12 Thus great with child to speak, and helpless in my throes,
>   Biting my truant pen, beating myself for spite,
>   "Fool," said my muse to me; "look in thy heart, and write" [*AS* 1].[24]

From the opening line of the sequence, the controlling voice belongs to a lover who is also a poet. Sidney follows Petrarch in using the figure of a poet-lover. Unlike Petrarch (the professional man of letters who plays off his laureate fame in the *Canzoniere*), the amateur English poet-lover Astrophil never promises anywhere in the sequence to make himself, or the object of his praise, immortal.[25]

The bold move of beginning his sequence with a poem in twelve-syllable lines has often been noted by critics. His control of syntax is pleasingly dramatic, with the subject of the graded series of present participles delayed until line five. In *The Aracadian Rhetoric* (1588), Abraham Fraunce, a member of the Sidney circle who read the sequence in manuscript, identified the opening rhetorical scheme, which takes the reader up a verbal ladder, as "climax" or *gradatio*.[26]

Structurally the poem is divided into octave and sestet, with the "turn" (*volta*) falling at the beginning of line 9 with the adversative conjunction *but*. The octave is made up of one syntactically complex and rhythmically supple sentence. The sestet, on the other hand, is syntactically divided into a structure of 3/2/1 lines, a technique that Sidney frequently employs "to explore ways in which syntactic or sense units might be counterpointed against the units created by rhyme."[27] After the careful control of syntax in the octet, the final tercet of the sestet surprises us with an unexpected dangling construction. We expect the grammatical subject of the sentence, whose present participles echo the construction of the opening lines, to be "I," not "my muse."

This syntactic jolt intensifies the dramatic force of the muse's scolding the poet and directing him to look not at the work of other poets' "leaves" but into his own *heart*. In the Renaissance the heart was identified as the seat of all the mental faculties or mind as a whole, including memory (we still speak of learning by heart). Astrophil stores the image of Stella in the book of his heart.[28] Moreover, by self-consciously beginning the sequence with a poem whose topic is the act of writing love poetry, the poet creates a distinction between the integrity of his "loving in truth" and his striving to compose poetry in such a way as to correspond with that inner truth.[29]

Yet the poem also describes the frustrating experience of writer's block. The failure to find a topic through rhetorical "invention" ironically becomes the topic. In lyric tradition (especially in Petrarchism) poetry "is frequently about poetry" and the making of poetry.[30] The self-referential function of the opening thus introduces an ongoing topic of the sequence. At the same time, the poem implies a rivalry with other poets, whose inventions lack a faithful correspondence of inner and outer truths. Poetic rivalry was well suited to serve as a metaphor for social ambition in the competitive public world of the Elizabethan court, yet it is also an ancient way of being a lyric poet.

Already in the opening poem the persona of the poet-lover revels in an exaggerated form of self-dramatization that is one of the hallmarks of the sequence. He appeals to Stella's "pity" by revealing "the blackest face of woe." His darkened face is paralleled by the witty description of his sterile brain as "sun-burnt." A humorous miniature personification allegory makes Nature the Mother of Invention, a metaphoric pupil who flees from the blows of Step-dame Study. Her blows are not entirely figurative since corporal punishment was the norm in Renaissance grammar schools.

With the poet's invention fleeing, he soon finds the (metrical) "feet" of other poets blocking his path of escape. The scene of classroom discipline extends the metaphor when his pen is refigured as truant. Instead of being punished by Dame Study, however, the poet now beats himself. He rapidly shifts the metaphor to a different form of pain and labor, comically comparing his struggle to find the right words to a difficult childbirth. Sidney is unsurpassed in the inventiveness of these rapid-fire turns of wit known as the Petrarchan conceit.

Although the first sonnet is not directly addressed to the lady, her presence as a potential reader is implied. The poet hopes to turn his pain into verse that will afford "pleasure" to that "dear she," enticing her to read the poems by which she will obtain "knowledge" of his love for her and thus to be moved to a "pity" that will result in her bestowing her "grace." In short, the first sonnet alludes to the classical rhetorical doctrine that the proper function of poetry is to teach, delight, and move the emotions, the "affective triad." *Astrophil and Stella* thus functions as epideictic rhetoric.

Many readers have asked themselves to what extent *AS* is merely a poetic fiction, or whether the passion it chronicles takes its source from Sidney's real emotional life.[31] On the one hand, its status as a well-shaped literary fiction is suggested by the comment of the contemporary writer Thomas Nashe, who in the preface to the 1591 edition of Newman describes the work as "the tragicommody of love ... performed by starlight.... The argument cruell chastitie, the Prologue hope, the Epilogue dispaire."[32]

On the other hand, the identity of Stella as a mask for Penelope Rich née Devereux was an open secret among Sidney's intimate circle, a secret that was eventually leaked. She was the eldest daughter of Walter Devereux, the first Earl of Essex, who expressed the wish shortly before he died in 1576 that Sidney (then twenty-two) might be matched with his thirteen-year-old daughter.[33] Sir John Harington may allude to her identity in the notes to his translation of Ariosto (1591), while a heading in his handwriting found in the Arundel-Harington manuscript refers to "Sonnetts of Sr Phillip Sydneys to ~~vppon~~ ye Lady Ritch" (note the sexual innuendo of Harington's cancelled preposition).[34]

It seems inevitable that readers both then and now must wonder what Sidney's "true" feelings were for the woman her father had hoped Sidney would marry. Scholars usually take pains to avoid the naïve assumption that first-person lyrics are autobiographical expressions of the poet's sincere feelings. That assumption was made by the Romantic critic Charles Lamb, who wrote of the sonnets: "They are full, material, and circumstantial ... an historical thread runs through them ... marks the when and where they were written."[35] Even as sophisticated a critic as Muriel Bradbook claims that "Sidney almost immediately fell in love with her" after the marriage to Lord Richard.[36]

Yet during the heyday of New Criticism, the imperative to avoid the "biographical fallacy" discouraged many critics from reading the sequence in terms of the poet's life at all, inducing them to focus instead on such matters as the delicate ironies created by the poet's construction of a fictional persona. As Duncan-Jones wisely observes, "[o]ur desire to know the truth behind *Astrophil and Stella* is ultimately a tribute to the *enargeia*, or forcefulness, of Sidney's rhetoric."[37] Indeed, we cannot rule out the possibility "that the whole Astrophil-Stella love affair was a kind of literary charade, in which both real-life participants knew exactly what was going on."[38] In short, we should avoid assuming that Renaissance lyric poetry offers anything remotely resembling straightforward autobiography. At the same time, viewing sixteenth-century lyric as a potential vehicle for poets to express their personal feelings, however fictionalized, is not in itself anachronistic, as we saw in Chapter 2. It may be more fruitful to leave aside questions of sincerity and read these sonnets as capturing a variety of public moods. Sidney helps readers understand what it would be like for a highly educated, socially advantaged young man to be in love with a charming, sophisticated, yet unattainable woman.

Sonnet 14 initiates a series of poems in which the lover addresses one or more friends who either criticize his present course or fail to understand the depth of his experience.[39] In response, the lover self-dramatizes his wound with a hyperbolic mythological comparison:

    Alas, have I not pain enough, my friend,
        Upon whose breast a fiercer gripe doth tire   *vulture*
        Than did on him who first stale down the fire,   *i.e., Prometheus; stole*
4 While Love on me doth all his quiver spend,
        But with your rhubarb words you must contend
           To grieve me worse, in saying that desire
           Doth plunge my well-formed soul even in the mire
8 Of sinful thoughts, which do in ruin end?
        If that be sin, which doth the manners frame,   *moral character*
    Well stayed with truth in word, and faith of deed,
    Ready of wit, and fearing nought but shame:
12 If that be sin, which in fixed hearts doth breed
        A loathing of all loose unchastity:
        Then love is sin, and let me sinful be [*AS* 14].

This sonnet offers a splendid example of Sidney's art-concealing art. As is typical of his diction, the great majority of his words are monosyllables (of the twelve words with more than one syllable, only *unchastity* contains more than two). Nearly all the words are drawn from everyday speech. None of the diction is especially learned, though the sonnet does contain an allusion to Prometheus's punishment for stealing fire for the benefit of humanity (the only public benefit of Astrophil's outrageous love, on the other hand, is that it inspires poetry that he shares with others).[40] The relatively uncommon word *rhubarb* refers to the medicinal root first imported from Asia for use as a purgative. First recorded in English around 1400, it was soon used figuratively to describe something bitter.[41]

Once again, Sidney shows an easy mastery of syntax, fitting one complex question with multiple dependent clauses into the octave. The sestet is also made up of a single sentence. The literariness of this description of pain makes it seem less raw than was the case in Wyatt. Yet for Astrophil the pangs of love are not as hurtful as his friend's effort at moral correction. The rhyme words themselves contain the core ideas of the argument: *friend, tire, fire, spend, contend, desire, mire, end, frame, deed, shame, breed, unchastity, be.*[42] If worms had eaten the rest of the page so that only these words on the edge remained, there would still be no doubt that they were drawn from a love sonnet, one in which some kind of moral struggle takes place.

The sonnet also uses a mastery of poet rhythm to capture a precise sequence of moods. The question posed by the octave gathers momentum in the second quatrain, with thoughts spilling across line-ends in three successive enjambments. How does the friend *contend*? *To grieve me worse than Cupid with his arrow.* What does his critic say about *desire*? It *doth plunge my well-formed soul.* Into what *mire*? *Of sinful thoughts.*

Deviations from regular iambic pentameter add rhythmic tension to this contest of perspectives. In line seven the pace slows near the end, hesitating slightly as if to teeter on a moral precipice at the word *soul* until the plunging action is speedily conveyed by the elision of a syllable in *even* followed by a double offbeat. A full scansion of the line verifies the expressive use of rhythm just described. When marking stress patterns above a line, Attridge distinguishes among different levels of linguistic stress. Syllables that take positive stress normally coincide with a beat. Syllables that are clearly unstressed normally realize an offbeat. Syllables that are indefinite can be used for either a promoted beat or a demoted offbeat. These three levels of stress are marked **+s, −s** and **s**. A syllable that is dropped (elided) is marked **(s)**. Here, then, is the full scansion of line seven:

```
 −s    +s   −s  +s   s     +s   s(s) −s  −s  +s
Doth plunge my well-formed soul even in the mire
  o    B    o   B    O     B ó b    o-o    B
```

In the closing couplet, Astrophil answers the friend's warning against unchastity by affirming his commitment to love—one perhaps hears an echo of the Wife of Bath's "Allas, allas! that evere love was synne." The first line deviates from a regular iambic pattern to create metrical tension (heightened by alliteration), only to resolve that tension by closing the couplet with a perfect iambic pentameter:

A loathing of all loose unchastity:
o B   o-o B ô B   o   B o b

Then love is sin, and let me sinful be.
o   B oB   o   B   oBo B

Astrophil's sense of social isolation reaches a new extreme in one of Sidney's most frequently anthologized sonnets. In this moving love complaint he imagines appealing to the sympathy of a distant, otherworldly companion:

> With how sad steps, O moon, thou climbs't the skies;
>   How silently, and with how wan a face.
>   What, may it be that even in heav'nly place
> 4 That busy archer his sharp arrows tries?
>   Sure, if that long-with-love-acquainted eyes
>   Can judge of love, thou feel'st a lover's case;
>   I read it in thy looks; thy languished grace
> 8 To me, that feel the like, thy state descries.
>   Then even of fellowship, O moon, tell me,
>   Is constant love deemed there but want of wit?
>   Are beauties there as proud as here they be?
> 12 Do they above love to be loved, and yet
>   Those lovers scorn whom that love doth possess?
>   Do they call virtue there ungratefulness? [*AS* 31].

It would be difficult to overstate the grace and elegance of this carefully controlled rhetorical performance. Yet its vocabulary remains accessible to twenty-first-century readers. None of words in the sonnet is far-fetched or new to the language. Even the Latinate *languishing* had been naturalized in English and habitually joined with the word *love* by 1300 at the latest, thanks to translations from the Song of Songs 2:5 (*OED*). We saw the Latin word and its translation appear in Chapter 3 ("In the tabernacle of a toure").

The complaint depends on the figure of apostrophe. Apostrophes to inanimate objects, as Jonathan Culler suggests, are "resistant to attempts to treat the poem as fictive representation of personal utterance."[43] Sane people do not normally speak to the moon (nor do they normally speak in rhyme and meter). Indeed, as figures of voicing rather than a voice, "apostrophes give us a ritualistic, hortatory act, a special sort of linguistic event in a lyric present."[44] The poem also serves as an example of what the Victorian critic John Ruskin famously termed the pathetic fallacy, the attribution of human emotions to nature.

Sidney's control of the rhythmic contour of words is masterly. Although one-syllable words predominate, only the first line relies exclusively on them, in imitation of the slow, step-like progress of the rising moon. The daring of the four-word adjectival modifier in line five (*long-with-love-acquainted eyes*) is somewhat tamed by Duncan-Jones's convenient hyphenation. The climax of multi-syllable words occurs in the very last word of the poem, four syllables long: *ungratefulness*. The final word sums up the general complaint against women motivated by one woman's cold-heartedness.

How the syntax of the final line should be taken has been debated since Charles Lamb first proposed reading it as inverted.[45] Katherine Duncan-Jones wonders whether the line questions, "'Do ladies in heaven call their lovers' virtue 'ungratefulness,' i.e., 'unpleasingness,' or 'Do ladies in heaven call their own ungratefulness virtue'?"[46] But surely Sidney knew the line reads equally well in both directions.

The relation between syntax and sonnet structure is also carefully designed. One mark of his deliberate care is the way Sidney exploits the grammatical ambiguity of the word *how*, an adverb used primarily in interrogative statements, but also in exclamations. Modern editors must make choices of punctuation, and such decisions necessarily shut down possibilities. Duncan-Jones makes the two *how*-clauses in lines 1–2 into direct exclamations and ends the sentence there. William Ringler, on the other hand, punctuates the first four lines as one continuous question.

The rhyme scheme of the octave creates two quatrains that mirror each other, each formed by a crossing (chiastic) pattern: *abba abba*. The syntax of both quatrains, on the other hand, is divided 2:2, where the second pair of lines forms a syntactically independent unit that responds to the first pair of lines. The sestet uses a 4:2 rhyme scheme (*cdcdee*) while the syntax forms "a counterpointing pattern of two triplets each in turn subdivided into a question taking up two lines followed by one occupying a single line."[47]

Furthermore, Sidney uses enjambment to create an interlocking pattern between syntax and verse shape. Although the lines are mostly end-stopped, the enjambments at lines 3, 5, 7, 9, and 12 help convey the sense of urgency to his observations and questions. Yet this urgency is part of a deliberate poetic design. All but the last enjambment occurs in alternating odd-numbered lines, creating a pattern of expectation that is broken in line 11. Finally, the rising emotional pitch of the sestet is reinforced by placing four grammatically distinct forms of the root *love* in quick succession in lines 12–13 (the rhetorical figure *polyptoton*). Such verbal artifice was greatly admired by Elizabethans. It was sure to be noticed by readers who had studied grammar, rhetoric, and logic (the old trivium) in school.

One such reader was the poet Edmund Spenser (c. 1552–99), the foremost English poet of the sixteenth century and indisputably the greatest English poet since Chaucer.[48] Although best known for *The Faerie Queene*, Spenser was a consummate craftsman who experimented with poetic form throughout his career. A boy of humble origins, he had attended the newly founded Merchant Taylors' School in London as a "poor scholar." His headmaster was the humanist educator Richard Mulcaster. Spenser's training in the liberal arts prepared him for higher education at Cambridge University. During the Renaissance, a humanist education, with its strong foundation in Latin, could be a means of professional advancement. Spenser made connections at court and spent most of his adult life as a civil servant in Ireland, the first English settler colony. He eventually rose to the rank of gentleman and possessed significant landed wealth in Ireland until native resistance forced him to abandon his estate.

Although lyric poetry represents only a small portion of Spenser's prodigious poetic output, *Amoretti and Epithalamion* (published in 1595) repays close attention. *Amoretti* (*Am*) is unique among Elizabethan sonnet sequences because it celebrates the poet's courtship and marriage to his second wife, Elizabeth Boyle. The *Epithalamion* is a wedding song celebrating their marriage in June of the previous year. The sonnet cycle is also unique because the poet makes no effort to mask his identity or that of his mistress.

Spenser breaks the fictional frame of the sequence in Sonnet 33, and he later identifies his lady as Elizabeth (*Am* 74). He allowed the printer, William Ponsby, to place the poet's true name just below the title on the title page of the 1595 octavo edition. No thinly disguised fiction winked its identity at a knowing coterie audience as in the case of Sidney. Spenser's sequence thus stands alone among others of its kind in expressing the poet's love for his newlywed bride.

From the very beginning the reader is alerted to the happy resolution with which the sequence will end. Along the way the sequence represents the many moods and pangs of this passionate lover as prelude to his consecrated marriage. The first sonnet uses the lyric present and a complex form of indirect address to make the poem a repeatable event, connecting the poet's life and his book while anticipating his eventual happiness when his mistress accepts the gift of his poetry:

> Happy ye leaves when as those lily hands   *i.e., pages; when*
>   Which hold my life in their dead-doing might   *power to cause death*
>   Shall handle you and hold in Love's soft bands, *fetters*
> 4 Like captives trembling at the victor's sight;
> And happy lines, on which with starry light
>   Those lamping eyes will deign sometimes to look *beaming*
>   And read the sorrows of my dying sprite,   *spirit*
> 8 Written with tears in heart's close-bleeding book;   *secretly*
> And happy rhymes, bath'd in the sacred brook
>   Of Helicon whence she derived is,
>   When ye behold that angel's blessed look,

12   My soul's long-lacked food, my heaven's bliss:
   Leaves, lines, and rhymes, seek her to please alone,
      Whom if ye please, I care for other none [*Am* 1].⁴⁹

The opening poem thus intertwines the poet's passionate life and its poetic record using the metaphor of the book of the heart (line 8). Learned but not in an intimidating way, the poem alludes to the mythic river (the "she" of line 10) on Mt. Helicon, sacred to the Muses. The word *derived* is etymologically exact, itself "derived" from *de*, "from" + *rīvus*, "brook." Ever the technical experimenter, Spenser invents his own demanding rhyme scheme (*abab bcbc cdcd ee*) that uses only five rhymes sounds. Thus Spenser blends the Petrarchan and English forms by linking the quatrains with two internal couplets before the final couplet creates strong closure, with the tendency to epigrammatic "point" as we observed in Chapter 2.

Like Sidney, Spenser is a master of using syntax, rhetorical patterning, and rhyme to create balanced structural units. In Sonnet 1, each quatrain functions as a unit. Strong parallelism is created by the successive apostrophes addressed to the poem as material artifact. The play of deictics is especially clever: each reader of the 1591 volume will "handle" its leaves, just as did the book's original recipient.⁵⁰ Instead of triangulated address, we have at least four parties to the communication: poet, leaves, lady, readers. The poems gathered in the pages of the book are available to the eye. The reader's eye inspects the "sorrows" that the poet's eye has written with tears. The "lamping eye" of the first reader (Elizabeth) lights the way for the eyes of later readers, including ours.

The repetition of *happy* at the beginning of each quatrain creates rhetorical balance. Each of the three individual quatrains is an independent unit in sense and syntax. In my punctuation each quatrain ends with a semicolon to suggest they form a series, though in the 1591 print they are closed with full stops. An ascending series—*happy leaves, lines*, and *rhymes*—begins each quatrain and is repeated in the final couplet. These steps make a ladder using the rhetorical scheme of *climax* or *gradatio* (the same device used in *AS* 1). The return of the fourth rhyme sound draws the series of quatrains to a close with the optimistic word *bliss*, which restates the key word *happy*. The final couplet both summarizes the argument of the poem and is capable of standing alone epigrammatically.

Like Sidney, Spenser is a master of using meter for expressive purposes.⁵¹ The poetic line generally is a complete unit of sense, though enjambment does occur (for example, after line 9). Metrical variations, such as offbeats on demoted syllables that would ordinarily take stress, provide additional tension before a hopeful return to greater regularity in the final line:

My soul's long-lacked food, my heaven's bliss[52]
o B   O B o B   o   B o   B

Leaves, lines, and rhymes, seek her to please alone
O   B   o B   O b o B   o B

Whom if ye please, I care for other none
o   b o B   o B   o B o   B

Alternatively, the next to last line could be interpreted as creating an even greater expressive tension before the return to near perfect regularity:

Leaves, lines, and rhymes, seek her to please alone
O   B   o B   [o] B   o-o   B   o B

The verse can even be interpreted as a six-beat line in violation of Spenser's normal rules of scansion to express greater urgency.[53] This possibility is open to more than one realization:

Leaves, lines, and rhymes, seek her to please alone
B [o] B   o   B [o] B   o-o   B   o B
                B   O   B o

The alliteration of the liquid consonant in lines 12–13 (a pattern begun in line 1 and frequently turning up elsewhere) adds further euphony. The final rhyme, it should be noted, would probably have been exact in Spenser's day, creating strong closure in sound and sense.[54]

Amoretti 27 introduces the Renaissance commonplace (topos) of poetry conferring immorality with the claim that "this verse that never shall expire … shall you make immortal" (27.11, 14). Spenser takes up this claim again in one of the most beautiful sonnets in the sequence, the widely anthologized Sonnet 75. The poem contains a brief dialogue between the poet and his future bride:

    One day I wrote her name upon the strand,   *shore*
      But came the waves and washèd it away:
      Again I wrote it with a second hand,
4   But came the tide and made my pains his prey.
    "Vain man," said she, "that dost in vain assay
      A mortal thing so to immortalize,
      For I myself shall like to this decay,
8   And eek my name be wipèd out likewise."   *also*
    "Not so," quod I, "let baser things devise   *said*
      To die in dust, but you shall live by fame:
      My verse your virtues rare shall eternize,
12   And the heavens write your glorious name.
    Where when as death shall all the world subdue,
      Our love shall live, and later life renew" [*Am* 75].

Before the twentieth century it was relatively uncommon for lyric poems to narrate an incident in the past tense. Culler offers this example to illustrate how Spenser employs this unusual strategy. A narrative of a past event frames an account in the present tense of what was said at the time. The dialogue conveys thoughts that continue to have significance in the "lyric present."[55]

Could there be more at stake in the play of past and present tenses? Hans-Georg Gadamer speaks of the uncanny "magic" by which a text handed down by tradition from a distant world in the past seems to speak to us in the present. Such poems give readers the sensation of leaping over space and time. Gadamer writes, "People who can read what has been handed down in writing produce and achieve the sheer presence of the past." Spenser's poem works deictic "magic" by cleverly exploiting the "presence effect."[56]

The conversation took place in the lovers' present time (*now*). But that time is past (*then*) at the present time (*now*) of the narration. The text survives in a succession of written versions, from manuscript to 1595 octavo, to modern editions derived from the early print, to my computer screen, to the book you are reading. This handing down by tradition allows the poem to perform a self-fulfilling prophecy. Over four hundred years later, the sonnet connects us here and now to the then-and-there (*one day*) of the poet's repeated action of writing in the sand (*wrote*, past tense). It connects us here and now to the past conversation conveyed in the present tense (*dost*), reported as already having taken place (*quod*). The present tense shared by the conversation and the writing converge in a shared future tense (*shall*) when Elizabeth foretells her inevitable death.

The poet answers by foretelling a future in which the poem long survives the couple. His prophecy turns out to be true. It prefigures us, among others. William Waters comments on the situation of lyric poems that are passed down through generations of readers who encounter the mark of poets long dead in their second-person addresses. He writes, "Where the continuance of readers and the cessation of the writer occupy the same ground, poetry's touch, and so poetic address, matter the most."[57]

In addition to projecting us as future readers, Spenser's sonnet creates an even greater sense of futurity through the shift to the eternity of heaven. Not only does the individual life take place as a succession of present moments that recede into the past, so also do the collective lives of human history. Even the *world* itself and all the books it contains will end (according to Christian faith) with the Last Judgment.[58]

The complex play of time governs the dramatic arrangement of syntactic and poetic units. The futility of the poet's action of writing her name in the unstable medium of sand is reinforced by the parallelism of *but came*

(2, 4). The first quatrain is devoted to his futile action. The second quatrain is devoted to Elizabeth's moralizing speech. The third quatrain is devoted the poet's response, balanced equally against the previous quatrain. The final couplet provides epigrammatic point that feels like a summary of the argument of the poem. However, by not explicitly mentioning poetry as a vehicle for immortality, the poem concludes as though the Christian idea of heavenly glory has overtaken the classical motif of poetic fame.

The rhyme words, once again, bear much of the weight of the poem's meaning. Spenser is more willing than Sidney to use words with more than one syllable in rhyme position. In the original spelling these run: *strand, way, hand, pray, assay, immortalize, decay, lykewize, devize, fame, eternize, name, subdew, renew*.

Other sound patterns also help bind together the sonnet's parts. Alliteration is insistent without being overbearing (note especially the repeated *w*, *p*, and *d* throughout the poem and the four instances of *l* in the final line). The two most prominent vowel sounds, appearing in three rhyme positions and internally in nearly every verse, are the long *a* sound (as in *name*); and the long *i* sound (as in *lykewize*).[59] Less noticeable than the syntactic patterning, the subtle patterning of consonants and vowels (consonance and assonance) may register below the threshold of conscious attention to help produce, along with the metrical beat, a sense of emotional satisfaction and presence.

The seashore setting of the dialogue, it has recently been suggested, may be identified with Youghal strand in Ireland, near where Elizabeth probably lived.[60] Yet the central image of the futile gesture of writing in the sand also seems to have a literary inspiration. In all likelihood it provides a witty response to Sidney. The so-called *New Arcadia* had posthumously appeared in print in 1590. Spenser could have read the prose romance in either that version or its unrevised first version, which widely circulated in manuscript. In both versions of the *Arcadia*, Pyrocles, disguised as an Amazon, writes a lyric complaint "in a sandy bank."[61] Spenser reverses the apparent gender roles by playfully making himself the author of a sandy text doomed to oblivion. But the poem also aspires to be an event in the lyric present. As it is remembered and repeated it permanently records that gesture and immortalizes her fame.

The name of Elizabeth—shared by the poet's mother, sovereign, and future wife—has just been given immortal fame in the previous sonnet, which concludes: "Ye three Elizabeths for ever live, / That three such graces did unto me give" (*Am* 74.13–14). Despite the modern habit of anthologizing Sonnet 75 without its companion, the two poems clearly benefit from being read in sequence.

5. The Love Sonnet from Wyatt to Shakespeare

As remarkable as the best sonnets of Sidney and Spenser may be, few critics nowadays would dispute that the sonnet sequence by William Shakespeare (1564–1616) is the highpoint of the Renaissance English sonnet tradition. Yet for nearly two centuries after Shakespeare's *Sonnets* first appeared in the quarto edition of Thomas Thorpe in 1609 (Q), they were virtually ignored.[62]

Shakespeare was born to a family of some means in Stratford-on-Avon and attended its grammar school. At the age of eighteen he married Anne Hathaway, who was twenty-six; it was, perhaps, a marriage of convenience. The couple produced three children, two daughters and a son who died in boyhood. He is best known, of course, as a playwright, but he was also a shrewd business man and pursued a highly lucrative theatrical career in London with only occasional visits home, leading some to suppose the marriage was unhappy. He had social ambition, as witnessed by his purchase of a coat of arms for his father in 1596. He retired from the theater and returned to Stratford c. 1611–12. By the time Shakespeare's *Sonnets* were first printed in 1609 he was well known in literary circles as a narrative poet and successful playwright. By this stage of his career he had completed nearly all his plays. Despite popular misconceptions, few professional scholars nowadays question that Shakespeare was in fact the author of the major works attributed to him (conspiracy theories aside) because of the extensive contemporary record of reliable documentary witnesses.[63]

In the nineteenth and early twentieth centuries, many readers gave in to the temptation to read Shakespeare's *Sonnets* for their assumed autobiographical interest. It was only near the end of the nineteenth century—the period coinciding with the organization of the study of English literature as a university discipline—that criticism began to appreciate the sonnets above all for their aesthetic value. Yet even during the first half of the twentieth century few critics held the *Sonnets* in high regard. Shakespeare's lyric poetry came to be widely appreciated for its artistic merit thanks largely to the shifts in critical taste represented by the New Criticism. After the achievements of twentieth-century literary criticism and the effects of generations of pedagogy, it is difficult to imagine that the poetic value of the sonnets will ever again come to be denied by lovers of poetry.

Thorpe's edition contains 154 numbered sonnets—no other English sequence contains so many—followed by *A Lover's Complaint*, a lyrical narrative in rhyme royal.[64] Most scholars today believe that Shakespeare composed most of his sonnets over several years during the 1590s. He may have revised them later, and some may have been composed in the early years of the seventeenth century. Regardless of when Shakespeare composed the sonnets in Q, scholars have wondered whether the 1609 edition was in some sense authorized by the poet. Unfortunately, the question cannot be answered with any confidence. Early editors assumed that Thorpe had pirated the edition after obtaining the manuscript through back channels.⁶⁵ More recently Katherine Duncan-Jones has argued that Shakespeare, in need of extra income during the closure of the theaters during the plague outbreak of August 1608 to May 1609, "authorized" the edition by selling the manuscript to Thorpe.⁶⁶

We do not know whether the order in Q was Shakespeare's, though many critics, myself included, assume that it is. However, the most contentious structural issue by far concerns the apparent addressees of the sonnets themselves. This issue has long been tied to a closely related one—the extent to which these first-person lyrics may be autobiographically related to Shakespeare's life. Edmond Malone was the first scholar to identify the "I" of the *Sonnets* as referring to Shakespeare the man.⁶⁷ This identification is supported by a number of late sonnets that pun on the name *Will* (numbers 135, 136, 143). Malone also was the first to observe in print that a great majority of the sonnets "are addressed to a man."⁶⁸

Malone's observation marks the beginning of the longstanding critical tradition that views Shakespeare's *Sonnets* as containing two subsequences. According to this view, Sonnets 1–126 are addressed to or written about a younger male "friend" or "fair youth" of higher social station than the poet. The first seventeen poems form a subgroup, the so-called procreation sonnets. Sonnets 127–152, on the other hand, seem to be addressed to or written about the woman most often styled by critics as the "dark lady."⁶⁹

Once the *Sonnets* began to be read in this way, they quickly morphed into a dramatic story that included reference to one or more "rival" poets (Sonnets 76–86), a quarrel and reconciliation between the young man and the poet (91–96), and even a sordid affair between the young man and dark lady (133–44).⁷⁰ The nineteenth century was especially interested in the purported autobiographical revelations contained in the *Sonnets*. John Kerrigan strikes the right balance when he suggests: "Shakespeare stands behind the first person of his sequence as Sidney had stood behind Astrophil—sometimes near the poetic 'I,' sometimes farther off, but never without some degree of rhetorical projection. The Sonnets are not autobiographical in a psychological mode."⁷¹

If the poetic "I" of the sonnets is created by a rhetorical performance, so may be the second-person addressees. Even if real persons that Shakespeare knew stand behind the "thou" and the "you" to whom the sonnets are principally addressed, there is no reason to assume that either the friend or the woman must be loosely modeled (like Stella) on one person. Nor is there any internal evidence confirming that all of the first 126 sonnets concern a male friend or that all the poems of the second subsequence are about a woman. A great many of the poems give no clues about the gender of the second-person addressee. Many critics insist, therefore, that we cannot rule out the possibility that the 1609 volume gathers together poems originally written for different occasions, with different real or fictional persons in mind. Yet reading through the entire sequence in the 1609 order may create the impression that there is only one friend and one woman being addressed or spoken about.

On the other hand, readers who only encounter the best-known sonnets out of context almost always, especially if they are heterosexual themselves, assume that a poem like the frequently anthologized Sonnet 18 ("Shall I compare thee to a summer's day?") must be addressed to a woman. Until recently, most readers have assumed that a poem which gives voice to a passionate, even erotic-sounding love must be describing heterosexual desire. Because this was not necessarily the case in Renaissance England, Shakespeare's sonnets may seem to come from a foreign country of the past. They did things differently there.[72]

Shakespeare also did things differently from his contemporaries. Much of the unprecedented achievement of the *Sonnets* rests in how Shakespeare takes up the nearly exhausted literary form of the sonnet sequence and uses it to explore new possibilities for the performance of lyric moods. One of the most obvious ways that he renews the form is by multiplying the complex relationships among his *dramatis personae*.[73]

This sense of something radically new is evident from the opening of the very first poem. Sonnet 1 would probably have been as disorienting to its earliest readers as it is to us, though not necessarily in identical ways. In a tradition that harks back to Petrarch, most Elizabethan sonnet sequences begin with a poem that serves to introduce the volume as a whole. We already have seen this opening strategy in both Sidney and Spenser. Shakespeare's sequence, however, defies this well-worn tradition.

Nor would the experienced reader of sonnets in 1609 have been prepared to encounter the unexpected topic and implied addressee of the opening poem in Q—an ethical argument for the value of sexual reproduction, apparently directed to a man. On the other hand, the educated reader of lyric poetry in the Renaissance certainly expected to encounter epideictic display, the rhetoric of praise or blame (*encomium* or *vituperation*).[74]

Turning to the first sonnet in Q, such readers would not be entirely disappointed:

From fairest creatures we desire increase,
That thereby beauty's rose might never die,
But as the riper should by time decease,   *but while the riper ones*

```
4   His tender heir might bear his memory:            its/his
    But thou, contracted to thine own bright eyes,    betrothed/shrunken
    Feed'st thy light's flame with self-substantial fuel,  fuel of your own substance
    Making a famine where abundance lies,
8   Thy self thy foe, to thy sweet self too cruel.
    Thou that art now the world's fresh ornament,
    And only herald to the gaudy spring,              chief; luxurious
    Within thine own bud buriest thy content,
12  And, tender churl, mak'st waste in niggarding:    boor; hoarding
       Pity the world, or else this glutton be,
       To eat the world's due, by the grave and thee [1].[75]
```

Thus begins the first coherent group of poems in Q, the so-called procreation sonnets. Except for the fifteenth, each of the first seventeen sonnets urges the young man to marry and have a child—preferably a son—to inherit the patrimony.

Yet this argument only reveals itself gradually to the reader. Although the notion of an *heir* is present here, at first it seems only a metaphor. Later sonnets specifically call for a *child* (2.10), the *womb* in which it should grow (3.5), the urgent injunction *to breed* (6.7), the hope for *a son* (7.14), the *concord* of *unions married*, whether musical or human (8.5–6), the blessings of a family comprising *sire, and child, and happy mother* (8.11).

The procreation sonnets cannot be properly understood if we ignore the rhetorical culture of the Renaissance. First and foremost, the sonnets are sophisticated displays of argumentative skills. Scholars have long understood that the procreation sonnets draw on Erasmus's "Epistle to persuade a young gentleman to marriage."[76] At the same time, the argument is complicated by the gradual revelation of an intense emotional bond between the speaker and auditor.

Even if the procreation sonnets were originally intended to be read independently, they seem to be carefully integrated into the artistic design of Q. Shakespeare (or his fictive persona) delays using first-person singular pronouns until Sonnet 10, where for the first time he hints at his love for the young man as a motive: "Make thee another self for love of me, / That beauty still may live in thine or thee" (13–14). Such emotions potentially clash with the poet's seemingly more objective interest in preserving the species and a lineage. Although the proverbial-sounding opening of Sonnet 1 seems objective at first, the poet's biased interest becomes retrospectively clear with his profession of love.

From fairest creatures we desire increase (1.1). This thesis is echoed by Elaine Scarry in the opening words to her wonderful meditation, *On Beauty*: "the felt experience of cognition at the moment one stands in the presence of a beautiful boy or flower or bird" is that the beautiful object "seems to incite, even to require, the act of replication."⁷⁷ The conventional symbol of impermanent beauty, the *rose*, only becomes identified with the beautiful boy in the second quatrain when the poet directly addresses the fair youth for the first time.

Beauty's rose: the unexpected possessive (genitive) construction directs attention to the rhetorical figure. The rose is not described as beautiful but as a quality of a personified beauty. This effect is even more striking in Q, which italicizes and capitalizes the word *Rose*. The figure of the rose harks back to the allegorical love poetry of the Middle Ages, where the beautiful rose is a symbolic object of desire. But in courtly love poetry the rose stands for a woman. In Sonnet 1, affection quietly seeps out from the oxymoron, *tender churl* (1.12). If Shakespeare addresses a real or imagined nobleman, the epithet *churl* (which originally referred to peasants) takes remarkable liberties, though they are softened by the lovely adjective *tender*.

From the very beginning the sonnets constantly remind us of the passage of time and the inevitability of death, even as they stress the youthfulness of the primary addressee in the present. In the procreation sonnets the juxtaposition of images of natural beauty and vitality with thoughts of their inevitable demise creates some emotional tension. In Sonnet 1 many of the words are related to injury, scarcity, death, or decay: *die, decease, famine, cruel, foe, buriest, waste, niggarding, grave*. These pessimistic notes are counterbalanced by a greater number of more pleasant images associated with the young man: *fairest creatures, increase, beauty's rose, riper, tender heir, bright eyes, light's flame, abundance, sweet self, fresh ornament, gaudy spring, bud, tender churl*.

The *world*, on the other hand, provides the neutral background for these opposing forces. It is the ultimate location of all natural cycles, encompassing both the freshness of spring and the coldness of the devouring grave. Given that the poem launches an ethical argument for sexual reproduction as a strategy for overcoming death, it is also striking that while there are *creatures* in this *world*, there is no mention of a creator. In fact, Shakespeare's sonnets have fewer references to religious ideas, especially Christianity or Christian-Neoplatonism, than many other Renaissance sonnet cycles.

As the metaphors and images almost imperceptibly begin to drift from the plant world to the human one in line four, by the second quatrain the use of flower imagery to describe human beings becomes clear. However, the emotions implied by the images now associated with the young man becomes more complex and ambiguous. It is as though the poet says: "You have marvelously concentrated all your bright qualities in your eyes, but in doing so you have also entered into a marriage contract, rather narcissistically, with your own eyes instead of betrothing yourself to a woman so that the rose of your beauty can bud into an heir. This extreme behavior is unwise, because by feeding the flame of your beauty with its own substance, you will consume all the fuel, like a candle or lamp. Your plenitude of beauty, food for the eye, will soon enough turn to dearth. You are therefore your own worst enemy. Unlike the Petrarchan *sweet foe* or *cruel mistress*, you are cruelest of all to yourself."[78]

The rapid shifting of images and metaphors in ways more rhetorically than logically coherent is characteristic of Shakespeare's verbal mastery. The third quatrain returns to the natural imagery of springtime and buds combined with the threatening image of burial. It also continues the implied moral criticism of the youth's ignoble, churlish waste and his insistence on hoarding himself instead of doing the socially responsible thing by sharing and increasing his metaphorical wealth. The couplet is even more direct in its moral criticism. You are no better than a *glutton* if you allow the grave (itself a personification of gluttony) to devour you unless you leave an heir behind. You owe that to the world. Without this act of *pity*, the world will remain *poor*. Thus the first sonnet mixes hyperbolic praise of the young man's beauty with potential moral condemnation.

This drama of ambiguous praise and blame also plays out in the metrical design of the poem. The first quatrain—a generalized account of beauty, its effect on the beholder, and the desirability of preserving it—is highly regular. But as the second quatrain begins its criticism of the youth, the meter grows much more complex and creates significant tension to express the speaker's discomfort:

> But thou, contracted to thine own bright eyes,
> o B   o   B o b o   B   O   B
> Feed'st thy light's flame with self-substantial fuel,
> B   o-O   B   o   B   o   B o B (o)
> Making a famine where abundance lies,
> B o-o B o   b   o B   o B
> Thy self thy foe, to thy sweet self too cruel
> o   B   o B   o-o   B ô B   o   B (o)[79]

The promoted beats, demoted offbeats, the implied offbeat in the fourth line (combined with alliteration), the variable placement of caesuras: all these rhythmic elements subtly contribute to the sense that these things are difficult for the speaker to say.

Similarly, the implied offbeat in line eleven that falls between the alliterating pair of words *bud* and *buriest* slows down the line by introducing a slight pause before the troubling verb *bury*. This verb foreshadows the even more troubling word *grave* in the couplet. Finally, the implied offbeat inserted between *world's due* in the final line of the couplet, followed by the caesura marked by the comma in Q, slow down the line, emphatically stressing the youth's moral obligations to the *world*.

Once the procreation group concludes, Shakespeare turns to another means for the young man to survive death. Like many other Renaissance poets, Shakespeare explores the theme of how poetry confers a kind of immortality. One of the best known of these poems is Sonnet 55:

> Not marble, nor the gilded monuments
> Of princes shall outlive this pow'rful rhyme,
> But you shall shine more bright in these contents   *i.e., these poems*
> 4 Than unswept stone besmeared with sluttish time.   *slovenly/dirty*
> When wasteful war shall statues overturn,   *destructive/vain*
> And broils root out the work of masonry,   *tumults*
> Nor Mars his sword, nor war's quick fire shall burn   *Mars's; rapid/living*
> 8 The living record of your memory.
> 'Gainst death, and all oblivious enmity   *hostility that causes oblivion*
> Shall you pace forth, your praise shall still find room,
> Even in the eyes of all posterity
> 10 That wear this world out to the ending doom.   *Last Judgment*
> So, till the judgement that yourself arise,
> You live in this, and dwell in lovers' eyes [55].

This poem is an example of how Shakespeare enables the older Italian structure to echo within the English sonnet form. The sonnet also contains some ingenious rhymes, giving the lie to critics who think that he lacked skill in rhyming. The sonnet also uses frequent enjambment, on the one hand to emphasize the onward rush of the destructive power of time, and on the other hand to suggest how the friend remains a living presence.

The claim that fine poetry has the power to make its subject immortal is a Renaissance humanist borrowing from classical poetry.[80] Horace describes his own work as immortal in the famous lines beginning *Exegi monumentum aere perennius*: "I have completed a monument to last longer than bronze, one built higher than the kingly pyramids. Neither pelting storms nor the powerful winter wind will be able to tear it down, not the endless tally of years or escaping time. I shall not completely die, and much of me will avoid death and the grave. I will keep growing anew with the praise of posterity."[81] Ovid makes a similar boast at the end of his *Metamorphoses* (15.871–79).

These Augustan poets tied their grandiose claims of their own poetic immortality to the dominion of the Roman Empire. It is understandable that they would connect their power over words to that of the empire itself. They expected Roman rule to last as long as humanity itself. With the benefit of hindsight, we now can see (as Shakespeare and his Renaissance readers also saw clearly) that the Latin poets were wrong about Rome. Since even the most powerful empire is the work of human hands, no state will last forever.

The sixteen centuries separating Shakespeare from the age of Augustus Caesar spanned an interval about four times the length of the one separating us from Shakespeare's *Sonnets*. If we make an effort at fusing horizons with Shakespeare, who gazed across the vast backward and abysm of time to these Augustan poets, an obvious analogy presents itself.[82] We are to Shakespeare as Shakespeare was to Rome. Although the Romans were wrong about the Eternal City, they were more accurate in their assertions about their poetry. Latin poetry continues to be read, though not always in the original language.

If the Roman poets thought of historical time as stretching into a future beyond what the eye could see, this is because pagan antiquity was not prone to theorizing about the end of the world. Apocalyptic thinking, however, developed among their Jewish contemporaries. For example, in late additions to the canon of Scripture in the Book of Daniel, Jews imagined an end to hostile empires. Such messianic longing in turn led to visions of the end of the world itself as the centerpiece of Christian apocalypse, the final triumph of good over evil on Judgment Day. The gradual revelation of the final shape of history led medieval thinkers to invent the idea of the successive transfer of empires Westward throughout history (*translatio imperii*).

Sonnet 55 is one of the world's great lyric meditations on time and historical change. It goes without saying that Shakespeare's effort to glimpse his place in history as a writer of love sonnets was by definition severely limited. On the one hand, his historical situation allowed him to grasp the irony of the Roman poets' failure to imagine their empire ever coming to an end, though the great poetry of the ancients for him and for other educated readers remained worthy of admiration and imitation. On the other hand, he and his compatriots could not have foreseen that within only a few hundred years the English tongue, more than the Latin ever did, would extend its reach over much of the globe until it became a world language of unprecedented scope.

However, like others of his generation who cared about English poetry, Shakespeare could look back at its recent development and recognize that something remarkable was taking place, something that gave him the confidence to prophecy the permanence of his work. That much, at least, he could see clearly. Although what we see when we look back is different, the shared situation of being limited by our own historical horizon offers us an opportunity to fuse horizons in search of understanding—not to overcome temporal or spatial distance entirely (we cannot), but to take it properly into account.

In his commentary to Sonnet 55, Stephen Booth reminds us that the power of the written word to outlast stone monuments is a topic raised in two entries from Geoffrey Whitney's *A Choice of Emblemes*, published in London in 1586.[83] In one emblem, Whitney's motto *Scripta manent* ("Writings remain") is accompanied by an illustration that shows in the foreground a desk upon which some books have been placed, against a background of classical architecture in the process of collapsing. The English poem below the emblem explains that without books our knowledge of ancient civilizations and heroic feats would vanish: "time ... eates the steele, and weares the marble stone / But writinges laste."[84]

The other emblem includes the motto *Pennae gloria perennis* ("The everlasting glory of the pen"). The picture shows winged Fame blowing a trumpet, flying over a building, with three pyramids in the background. Given the commonplace nature of emblem books, it is difficult to prove that Shakespeare had these specific emblems in mind when he wrote the similarly themed Sonnets 55, 65, 81, 107, and 123, though scholars have long believed that Shakespeare knew Whitney's book. If he opened it to the second entry on the same topic, he would find in the accompanying English poem a poignant meditation on recent English literary history, the death of poets, and the immortality of poetry.[85]

The poem, composed in fourteeners, is an elegy that begins by describing how the fate Atropos (to use her Greek name) ended the life of the noble Earl of Surrey, who as the gloss reminds its readers, "wrat [*wrote*] the booke of Songes and Sonettes." The title page of that milestone of Tudor lyric poetry known as *Tottel's Miscellany* advertises Surrey's role as principal author. But "all times do chaunge," we are reminded by Whitney's elegy. After the Muses and gods of poetry and music mourned Surrey's loss, "behold," Sidney was born: "More sweete then honie, was his stile, that from his penne did flowe." After celebrating Sidney's verse and praising Sir Edward Dyer (the dedicatee of the emblem, a minor Elizabethan poet and a friend of Sidney's), Whitney affirms that "writinges last when wee bee gonne, and doe preserve our name," just as Homer's name and poetry are still trumpeted by Fame. "Ægypte spires bee gonne, and Rome doth ruine feede," but the writer's "braine" can "bequeathe the world a monument" that outlasts the work of monarchs, "[o]f marble, or of adamant."

Whitney's effort to promote the transcendence of time through the poetic word is itself (as all our efforts must be) thoroughly time-bound. We should note one additional historical irony: though Sidney is not described as dead, we might notice with the benefit of hindsight that Whitney's emblem book was published in the same year as Astrophil's death.

When we make the effort to understand Shakespeare's poem, we begin to fuse horizons with his meditation on time, love, and poetry. Seeing history in retrospect—Shakespeare looks back at Rome, we look back on Shakespeare looking back at Rome—always involves a limited, perspectival vision. Our historical existence not only demands retrospective vision but also affords partial glimpses of the future in ways that cannot be predicted in advance. In retrospect, we see that Shakespeare was correct when he confidently proclaimed, *You live in this, and dwell in lovers' eyes*. But he could not have known in advance all of the human efforts (copying with a quill pen, printing, editing, anthologizing, annotating, archiving, selling, buying, transmitting electronically, reading, studying, teaching, loving) that would be involved in preserving his *pow'rful rhyme* in human memory.

According to Colin Burrow, when Shakespeare takes up the common Renaissance idea of poetic fame overcoming death in Sonnet 55 and elsewhere, he modestly "immortalizes not himself, as Horace and Ovid do, but the friend."[86] Yet the poet confidently asserts in a later poem that the immortality of the youth depends on the *virtue* (power) that *hath my pen* (81.13). It is only his poetry that will enable the yet-unborn "tongues to be your being to rehearse" so that his beloved will live "even in the mouths of men" (81.11, 14). The claim that his beautiful friend will be immortal because of this poetry suggests that the poet has placed a considerable stake on his poetic fame. As the memory of the young man is passed down through the generations by word of mouth, Shakespeare would have us remember that he is the author of those words.

More significant in Sonnet 55 is how Shakespeare blends the pagan theme of fame with a Christian sense of history. Yet the precise effect of this cultural synthesis is open to question. The poet imagines that his friend will survive death in this *living record*, which will allow him to *pace forth* as his *praise* finds its place *in the eyes of all posterity* until Judgment Day itself, the end-time glimpsed in Christian apocalypse. According to Vendler, there is tension in the three quatrains over the question of how the beloved survives death. "The couplet," she suggests, "solves the tension by assigning 'real' living to the day of the Last Judgment."[87]

Yet the poem may fall short of offering Christian consolation. The poet expresses no faith in the immortality of the soul or hope for eternal salvation. The poem makes no reference to the time when Christ "shall come to judge the quick [cf. line 7] and the dead," as the three major Creeds state.[88] Similarly, the *fire* of the sonnet is not the eternal fire reserved for sinners in the Athanasian Creed but the fire of *wasteful war*. This worldly fire will have no destructive power over the *living record* of the friend, who *dwell[s] in lovers'* eyes until there is, literally, no more time. The poem is conspicuously silent about what happens *after* the Day of Judgment. It thus appears simply as a temporal marker for the endpoint of human history, after which the sonnet will no longer be read by lovers and the beautiful youth will no longer need a *living record*. Unlike Dante imagining his reunion with Beatrice in the communion of saints, Shakespeare does not write of a faith that he will cavort in Heaven with his sweet boy.

Part of the extraordinary power of the sonnet arises from Shakespeare's extraordinary gift for making words and phrases point simultaneously in different directions. Booth's commentary (and ultimately, the entire Empsonian tradition of reading for ambiguity of thought, feeling, and expression) is especially useful for helping us grasp how the *Sonnets* are saturated with meaning. For example, in the line *That wear this world out to the ending doom*, we hear both the verb *wear out*, as in the world growing old until it is consumed with age; and the prepositional phrase *out to*, as in proceeding until reaching the goal. An older sense of *wear out* gives the meaning "holding out against."[89] Or, to take another example: the word *that* in the phrase *till the judgement that yourself arise* by a common Elizabethan construction means "when." The entire phrase, as Booth observes, thus "acts like an appositive to *to the ending doom* and reaffirms the idea of triumph over death." In addition, "the construction *judgement that* shifts the focus from the time of the Last Judgment to the judgment itself."[90] To ignore the pressure placed on the meaning by this other grammatical construction (as some recent editors do) impoverishes our reading.

Even tiny prepositions can do double semantic duty. Recent editors and commentators have generally not noted how the preposition *of* in line eight (*living record of your memory*) exploits a common syntactic ambiguity. Is the construction an objective or subjective genitive? If the former, the emphasis is on the agency of the poem as a *record* that preserves the *memory* of the friend. If the latter, the emphasis falls on the agency of his *memory* that serves as a *living record*. In short, this ambiguity leaves us uncertain who is more powerful: the poet or the friend.

The sonnet closes by affirming that it is *in lovers' eyes*—our eyes—where both the beloved and the poet *dwell*, even still. For this reason, the perfect metrical regularity of the final verse helps emphasize this effect of presence:

    You live in this, and dwell in lovers' eyes
     o B o B   o   B   o B o B

In contrast to this bold affirmation of the uncanny power of the poetic word to confer immortality on his subject, another frequently anthologized sonnet speaks out of a much darker mood. Sonnet 73 is one of the most beautifully haunting love poems in the language:

> That time of year thou mayst in me behold
> When yellow leaves, or none, or few, do hang
> Upon those boughs which shake against the cold,
> 4 Bare ruined choirs, where late the sweet birds sang.   *choir stalls*
> In me thou seest the twilight of such day
> As after sunset fadeth in the west,
> Which by and by black night doth take away,
> 8 Death's second self, that seals up all in rest.
> In me thou seest the glowing of such fire
> That on the ashes of his youth doth lie,
> As the death-bed whereon it must expire,
> 12 Consumed with that which it was nourished by.
> This thou perceiv'st, which makes thy love more strong,
> To love that well, which thou must leave ere long [73]. *Forego/depart from*

This elegant sonnet is masterful in its arrangement of the conventional 4+4+4+2 structure. These divisions support a logical and emotionally compelling progression of images. The poem combines syntactic clarity and surprise while carefully patterning sound. Some of the best literary critics have risen to the challenge of commenting on the poem.[91]

The sonnet focuses on the sense of sight, though hearing and touch have secondary importance. Each quatrain draws an extended comparison between the poet's aging process, already well advanced, and an analogous process from the natural world. An aging man is like the declining seasons, the setting sun, a fire burning itself out. The argument develops concrete variations to an abstract proposition. If you see *x*, then you also see *y*. But sight is not merely a matter of visual perception. Seeing is also an intellectual mode of understanding. The logical implication of the formal argument is that that seeing *y* helps you understand *x*. This is, according to the conventional view, how a good metaphor works. The thing used to make a comparison (the vehicle) conveys a new perspective on the thing being compared (the tenor). Aristotle, in his remarks on metaphor in the *Poetics* (1459a), identified the ability to invent good metaphors as a sign of natural genius.

Yet the deictic play between *here* and *there*, *now* and *then*, creates uncanny slippage between presence and absence. The repeated proposition *thou seest me* uses the second-person, singular subject pronoun (*thou*) and the present tense of the verb in the indicative mood. In a grammatical operation as old as the ancestral Indo-European language and common to all Western languages derived from it, the form of the personal pronoun *me* agrees with its function as a grammatical object. Each word of the basic sentence *thou seest me* (including the second-person singular ending of the verb, *–est*) uses a "shifter." The meaning of every shifter depends on the relative positions of the speaker and addressee during the speech act. The speaker *here, now*, is asking another person to *see, here, now* (that is, *to understand*) the poet's mortality in relation to a series of natural processes.

By bringing this truth to light, *I* ask *you* to *see* my growing old as similar but not identical to the trees' loss of foliage as the seasons advance through autumn and winter; to the fading of light as the day passes through twilight to night; to the gradual loss of heat as a fire goes from blazing coals to glowing embers and eventually to cold ashes. As *you behold me now* in your vision, I want you to imagine that you are also seeing, one at a time, three other temporal processes that serve as illustrations (literally a "bringing-to-light").

These three analogous objects cannot physically be present simultaneously to your sight as you gaze upon the world. But they can easily be held in the mind, almost during a single instant, as you look at me *now* while I am currently speaking, or as you remember what I looked like *then*, as you are reading the poem *now* or remember reading it *then*. This cascading of different sights present to the eye (me *here*, those things *there*) takes place (though in different ways) regardless of whether we imagine the poet is speaking aloud while his friend watches him or the friend is reading the poem in his absence while he holds the living poet present in his mind's eye.

Because the poet *now* (but for us, *then*) projects a future of uncertain date in which he will no longer be present as a living being, an uncanny effect of presence comes to light, but only for us. The poet and his friend lived in their own present time but are both now long dead; we live in our own present world but will die sometime in the future. The shifter *thou* reaches out to us as we inhabit the present tense *now*.

So long as men can breathe or eyes can see, to quote an earlier sonnet, the poem remains a presence, just as the natural processes it describes continue to remain objectively present. Trees lose their leaves, day turns to night, and a fire consumes its fuel. The present tense in the previous sentence is the grammatical mark of a *general truth*. In modern English, we use the simple present tense "where there is no limitation on the extension of the state through the present into the past and future time. This category includes 'eternal truths,' which do not refer specifically to the present but are general timeless statements."[92] One uncanny effect of presence thus occurs when we notice that Shakespeare exploits two different functions for present-tense verbs. *Thou seest me; sunset fadeth in the west*. We live now, Shakespeare lived then, but the same sun still sets below the horizon, just as it did long before he was born and after we die. *Now goth sonne under tree*. The present tense of general or eternal truth undergirds all our specific presents.

Every natural event is, strictly speaking, unique. However, each one in an ongoing series so closely resembles the next that (in most situations) we view them as essentially the same. Although each of the three natural processes described by the sonnet is repeatable, only the first two (seasons and days) are conventionally perceived as cyclical. Whether we regard seasons and days as linear or cyclical processes, when the poem employs them as metaphors for human life, a gap still remains between the vehicle and tenor, and this gap makes a crucial difference. Unlike an individual life, the natural events portrayed in the first two quatrains repeat themselves over and over.

A fire, on the other hand, may occur naturally if lightning strikes a tree, or it may be kindled by human hands (for example, in a hearth). Each fire is a unique event, unlike the setting sun or falling leaves. Even though we habitually speak of life itself as part of a natural cycle, your life and my life, though subject to nature, are not repeatable events and cannot literally begin again. *This thou perceiv'st, which makes thy love more strong, / To love that well, which thou must leave ere long.*

Fusing our horizons with those of the poem, we understand its effect as uncanny in the following way. The poem discloses the eternal truth that what the poet once was, so now are we; as now he is dust, so shall we be. Read like this, the poem serves as a kind of epitaph. In modern spelling and punctuation, Shakespeare's epitaph in Stratford reads: "Good friend, for Jesus' sake forbear / To dig the dust enclosèd here; / Blessed be the man that spares these stones, / And cursed be he that moves these bones." In short, given the sonnet's theme of human mortality, the presence effects of its language allow it to function as a reminder of death (*memento mori*) like no other.

The poem is justly praised for its facility with metaphor and other kinds of description. In the first quatrain, the image of the trees with *yellow leaves, or none, or few* startles us with the unexpected order of the series. Shakespeare's mind is adept at gliding effortlessly from one metaphor to the next to provide fresh perspectives on human experience. The branches of the trees are vividly seen shivering in or in expectation of the winter wind, and we are invited to *behold* something about the poet's advanced age in that scene. But no sooner has the metaphor begun to operate than the vehicle becomes the tenor of a new metaphor, and the interruption of the syntax at the beginning of line four surprises us (*boughs* is syntactically parallel or in apposition to *choirs*). The *sweet birds* thus do double duty as both literal birds in the vehicle of the first metaphor, and singers at the east end of a church in the second.

Ever since Steevens first proposed the idea in the eighteenth century, critics have debated whether Shakespeare intended to remind us of the dissolution of the monasteries by Henry VIII (the sight of monastic ruins was common in Shakespeare's day).[93] In any case, the metaphor-within-a-metaphor calls attention to an absence in the present (the birds of summer are no longer singing) that may provide a way of *beholding* the speaking "I." The helping verb or modal auxiliary *mayst* is not usually glossed by editors, but in Early Modern English it is in fact ambiguous: it can convey either ability or possibility.[94] The speaker declares: *That time of year thou mayst behold in me*, but does his younger friend actually see him that way? We cannot say.

The modal auxiliary *may* drops out in the second and third quatrains, making the friend's sight seem more certain in what it grasps or *beholds*. The opening phrase *in me* in line five creates a clear grammatical parallel with line one (the substitution of *see* for *behold* provides an elegant variation of the verb). The second quatrain also imitates the previous one by offering another nested metaphor within a metaphor at the beginning of line eight. The *black night* syntactically parallels or is in apposition with *death's second self*, a metaphor for sleep.

If the repetition of a grammatical apposition in the same position in the second quatrain leads us to expect it again in the third quatrain, we will be surprised once more. The beautiful description of the slow progression, *day*, *sunset*, *twilight*, and *night*, is made more vivid and surprising by rearranging the natural order. The sound patterns contribute to the mood of the poem, too. In addition to rhyme and meter, the ear hears repeated vowel sounds (*set, west; twilight, by, night*) and alliteration (*by, black; second self, seals*). After finding sleep described as the twin of *death*, we can scarcely avoid thinking of a coffin when we are presented with *black night that seals up all in rest*.

The third quatrain begins with the grammatical parallel: *in me thou seest* and repeats the word *death*; the compound *death-bed* carries over the association with *rest* from the previous quatrain. The kind of death described here seems easeful, a gradual loss of vital heat, with no one raging against the dying of the light. The vehicle of the extended metaphor is a fire (presumably in a hearth) that is already in decline: *ashes* are already accumulating beneath the flame, and soon the fire will extinguish itself. Even the *glowing* embers will darken and eventually grow cold when they are choked of air by their *ashes*.

Again Shakespeare creates layers of metaphor. The metaphor in line twelve is of feeding: *consumed, nourished*. The personification of the fire (*his youth*) and the metaphor of feeding allow the vehicle to represent the tenor (the poet) in a new light. Shakespeare's vital heat will cool in old age until, like the fire, *it must expire*, and the poet breathes his last (though he seems to come to life again each time the poem is repeated in the lyric present).

But for now he is still *glowing*. Duncan-Jones observes that it is difficult to know how we should understand the rhetorical force of the closing couplet. Does the poet describe a present reality or does he express such a hope for the future?[95] Taken in isolation, the sonnet may seem a cautiously optimistic celebration of reciprocated love, all the more precious because it cannot last. Taken in the context of the larger sequence, however, the poem might seem to strike a note of quiet desperation. Fusing our horizons with those of the poem, we may read it as bringing more clearly to light the unique value of our non-repeatable lives and the lives of others.

Many readers find an equally powerful affirmation of love in Sonnet 116, which provides a general definition of love.

	Let me not to the marriage of true minds	*May I never*
	Admit impediments; love is not love	*legal obstacles*
	Which alters when it alteration finds,	
4	Or bends with the remover to remove.	*moves in the direction of the other*
	O no, it is an ever-fixèd mark,	*landmark/seamark/beacon*
	That looks on tempests and is never shaken;	
	It is the star to every wandering barque,	i.e., *North star; lost boat*
8	Whose worth's unknown, although his height be taken.	*its; measured*
	Love's not Time's fool, though rosy lips and cheeks	
	Within his bending sickle's compass come.	*Time's; range*
	Love alters not with his brief hours and weeks,	*Time's*
12	But bears it out even to the edge of doom.	*endures; Doomsday*
	If this be error and upon me proved,	*legally proven against me*
	I never writ, nor no man ever loved [116].	

This poem clearly demonstrates Shakespeare's mastery of the English sonnet. Each quatrain is syntactically independent while the couplet comments on the previous reflections. Both the opening and the reference to the Last Judgment in line twelve allude to the marriage service in the Book of Common Prayer, when the minister warns: "I require and charge you (as you will answer at the dreadful day of judgment, when the secrets of all hearts shall be disclosed) that if either of you know any impediment, why ye may not lawfully be joined in matrimony, that ye confess it."

Although this poem is often recited nowadays during wedding vows, its placement within the first subsequence of Q strongly suggests that it is about something other than heterosexual love leading to marriage and lawful issue. Kerrigan suggests that lines 2–12 resemble "a secular variation on St. Paul's account of love in 1 Corinthians 13," but he offers a substantially darker reading, interpreting the poem as "about what cannot be attained," an absolute goal so lofty as to be out of the reach of ordinary mortals.[96] After the absolutism variously expressed in the previous sonnets, this would be a bracing admission indeed for the poet to make.

In his General Note on the poem, Booth suggests that "its first clause aside, it is one of the few Shakespeare sonnets that can be paraphrased without brutality."[97] We may test this idea by attempting to translate the poem's reasonably plain sense into prose: "I do not wish to allow any obstacles (or even concede that they may exist) that might prevent the permanent union of two minds that share absolute integrity. It is not true love if a lover responds to changes in the beloved (or external circumstances) by changing accordingly. It is not true love if a lover shows a willingness to shift ground by joining the beloved in a new location, emotionally speaking. Absolutely not: real love is established forever in one place, a beacon or lighthouse that faces storms and does not totter. It is the distant, mysterious North Star that every lost vessel can use to navigate by measuring how many degrees it appears above the horizon. True love is not the laughing stock of Father Time, even though the bloom of youth lies within his destructive reach. True love does not change over the course of time but endures as long as the world itself shall last. If anything I have just said can be found to be a mistake (or a heretical belief) in a court of law, I will stop claiming to be a poet and will accept the idea that there's no such thing as a true lover."

That seems to be more or less what the poem "says." Yet any prose paraphrase must fall short of the incomparable grandeur of Shakespeare's poetic language. Its careful organization of a complex but coherent line of thought, its apt metaphors and personifications, its persuasive and insistent tone, and its sonorous cadences: all these combine to make the poetic argument highly compelling and memorable. How does it manage to do so in such a marvelous way?

The poem offers a singular combination of poetic technique and rhetorical force. The visual immediacy of its images (the quality that Renaissance rhetoricians called *enargia*) and its vigorous expression (what they called *energia*) enable the sonnet to speak persuasively to so many readers. To take just one example we could consider lines 9–10. The combination of abstract personification and concretely visualized action, along with the expressive use of versification, emphasize the damaging effect of time on the human body. Metrically subordinated stress is marked [s] while emphatic stress is marked **s**:

```
[s]   s   [s]   +s
```
Love's not Time's fool, though rosy lips and cheeks
```
O   B   O   B    o   B o B o   B
```

Within his bending sickle's compass come
```
o  b  o  B   o   B o   B  o   B
```

The complexity of the rhythm at the beginning of the first line expresses the poet's sense of superiority over time with the emphatically defiant stress on the word *not*. The shift back into regular meter halfway through the first line and the enjambment add to our sense of the impetuous rush of time.

As the regular meter continues in the next line, it conveys the swift and repeated action of the grim reaper harvesting bodies after they have lost the bloom of youthful vitality. Yet the beauty of the startling image of Time reaching out to his victims, who fall *within his bending sickle's compass*, could almost make us half in love with easeful death as we momentarily fall under the trance of the enticing rhythm. It was precisely the bewitching, sonorous power of well-crafted language (so feared by Plato) that Gorgias celebrated in *A Defence of Helen* (see Chapter 1 above).

Sonnet 116 effectively captures the process of looking at what appears visible to human sight. We perceive colors but our eyes cannot see well in the dark or over large distances during the day. In daylight we perceive the color of a beautiful human face (*rosy lips and cheeks*). We hold in special regard the face of another whom we love, whose *worth* (unlike that of a distant star) is *known*. Through a revealing personification, the *mark looks on tempests*, though it is we who sight a *landmark* (for example, a tower erected to guide sailors) by day or a *seamark* or beacon by night.[98] We stand upright on two feet but cannot move through the air. Standing erect, we look up at the *star*. Not being fish, we must use a seaworthy vessel to travel far on a body of water.

But above all, the sonnet speaks out of a shared mood of being in love in ways that continue to resonate powerfully. To claim that the concerns of Shakespeare's sonnet remain alive today is not necessarily to claim that such poems ever transcend the historical conditions of their existence. Such historical variables as sex, class, gender, race, ethnicity, social status, age, physical and mental disability, religion, geographical location, etc., always influence who and what we are. We are social beings by definition. However, my decision not to focus exclusively on the social and historical context of lyric poetry at the expense of universal themes and formal technique is not based on sharing Vendler's impatience with scholars who read lyric poems in terms of their "social matrix" instead of as works of poetic art. She also objects to critics who read "a poem as though it were an essay, governed by an initial topic sentence," and she insists that we should not approach "the *Sonnets* as discursive propositional statements rather than as situationally motivated speech-acts."[99] If Vendler were more sympathetic to a historical understanding of the rhetorical culture of the Renaissance, she might acknowledge that the sonnets were written more for epideictic *display* than for forensic or deliberative *argument* (to recall Aristotle's distinctions).

In other words, the choice between reading for discursive propositional statements and a mimesis of speech acts is a red herring. Classical, medieval, and Renaissance rhetorical theory recognized that the art of rhetoric is a *performance* art, an art that requires a sophisticated understanding of what are now called speech acts.[100] Vendler claims that lyric poetry "deliberately strips away most social specification" so that anyone may voice a lyric. But her appeal to this "normative form" ignores how some poems omit more details of social identity than others.[101] We have only to compare Shakespeare's sonnets with those of Sidney and Spenser to recognize how variable this social specification was, even within in a single subgenre during the same historical period in the same geographically restricted area. In the final analysis (*even to the edge of doom*), I believe masterpieces of early lyric poetry still matter because they articulate, in persuasive and pleasing forms, what it is like to live in the world with others and with ourselves.

The final sonnet that I have selected is one from the second subsequence, evidently addressed to the woman. The astonishing Sonnet 129 creates a major shift of mood, ringing out with a ferocity not previously encountered in the volume:

```
    Th'expense of spirit in a waste of shame    loss; vitality/energy/vital fluid
    Is lust in action, and, till action, lust
    Is perjured, murd'rous, bloody, full of blame,    false to oaths
4   Savage, extreme, rude, cruel, not to trust,
    Enjoyed no sooner but despisèd straight,
    Past reason hunted, and no sooner had,    beyond reason/intemperately
    Past reason hated as a swallowed bait    i.e., one that is poisoned
8   On purpose laid to make the taker mad;    insane
    Mad in pursuit, and in possession so,
    Had, having, and in quest to have, extreme,
    A bliss in proof, and proved, a very woe,    when experienced/tested
12  Before, a joy proposed, behind, a dream.    anticipated
    All this the world well knows, yet none knows well
    To shun the heaven that leads men to this hell [129].
```

This disturbing sonnet is like no other in the tradition. I have adopted Kerrigan's lighter punctuation, which better reflects what he describes as the "rapid, almost frenetic" pace of the "pursuit of lust, satiety, and despair." As he observes, "only 94 compares with this in impersonal profundity, in its illumination of the sequence by means of indirect because general statement."[102] Its impersonal mode of address (no "I" or "thou" is indicated) allows the poem to be read as an exceptionally eloquent moral sermon against one of the chief biblical sins (see Matthew 5:28). The poem also parallels a number of proverbs, including "Short pleasure, long lament."[103]

Despite its impersonality of address, however, when read in the context of the larger sequence it is difficult not to associate this utterance with the same first-person speaker who has told us of his love for a young man and a "black" mistress. For this reason, the poem may be read as a lucid moment of self-criticism that stands at a critical distance from an intimate drama of private feeling. Vendler, in fact, argues that it best understood "as a representation of decisive changes of mind about the experience it treats, changes predicated of a single sensibility ... and its changes of heart."[104] But her mimetic-expressive theory of lyric has its limitations. The world out of which the poem speaks to us is an ethical-rhetorical one. Poetry was often defended, as we saw in Chapter 1, because it presented lively images of the human person, teaching audiences which virtues to imitate, which vices to shun. Sonnet 129 clearly speaks out of this public concern at the same time that it *seems* to speak out of the personal agonies of private experience.

Like Sonnet 116 (its polar opposite in its theologically resonant vocabulary and doctrine) 129 is another definition poem.[105] Vendler suggests that the sonnet employs "an analytic rather than a descriptive model of definition." In addition, she argues that the poem "initially mimics a philosophical or homiletic tone," but "[b]y the third quatrain, any pretense of the homiletic has been discarded."[106] For her, the crucial aesthetic choice Shakespeare makes is to shift from the judgmental self-loathing of the octave to an entirely different perspective on lust in the third quatrain, "representing it *as it was felt at the time*. It can then move, in the couplet, to a totalizing encompassing of its previous differentiations."[107] In other words, the couplet brings together the conflicting perspectives of the poem. However, her interpretation depends on assumptions that not all readers will share, including her understanding of the relation between lyric poetry and the mimesis of a mind at work. Her brilliant display of close reading is unrivaled among contemporary literary critics, but it is sometimes difficult to distinguish where the poet's mind ends and the critic's begins.

Attention to historical genres, on the other hand, provides a more substantial anchor that may prevent a critic from drifting too far on the high seas of ingenuity. The originality of Shakespeare's *Sonnets* as works of art cannot be appreciated apart from measuring it against others of its kind.

Both content and style weigh heavily in this kind of understanding. In traditional rhetorical terms, these roughly correspond to the discovery (*inventio*) and arrangement (*dispositio*) of matter and the selection of words (*elocutio*).

Sonnet 129 seems unique in the way its three quatrains contain a total of only two finite verbs (that is, not participial or infinitive forms). Both of the verbs are the word *is*. Grammarians call this special verb a "copula" because it joins the grammatical subject with something that complements it.[108] As understood by grammarians, copulas in general create a "co-reference relation between the subject and the subject complement." For example, *lust* (S) *is* (V) *perjured* (SC). "The typical, colorless copula" in English "is BE, which expresses essence."[109] From a grammatical point of view, the main syntactic structure employed by the sonnet creates a complex definition of lust. Shakespeare tells us what lust "is" by making an extended declarative statement, piling on a string of adjectival and participial complements of the subject.

Equally striking stylistically is the unusual number of figures of speech. Brian Vickers suggests that the poem is "perhaps the finest example of rhetoric controlling, and being controlled by, emotion."[110] Examples of figures of speech include antithesis (for example, *bliss/woe, heaven/hell*); chiasmus (*lust action : action lust; bliss proof : proved woe; knows well : well knows*); synonymia (the list of adjectives in lines 3–4); anadiplosis, or the use of the same word to end one clause and begin the next (*mad, mad*), and polyptoton, words sharing the same root with different endings (*had, having, to have*).[111] Shakespeare's unusual care in employing rhetorical figures as ornaments for his definition is probably no coincidence. As Douglas Peterson demonstrated over half a century ago, it appears nearly certain that Shakespeare drew on a specific passage in Thomas Wilson's *The Arte of Rhetorique* (1560), since the passage and the sonnet share both the general theme (lust overcoming reason) and a number of specific rhetorical schemes.[112]

Even if these similarities are coincidental, Peterson's general point that Shakespeare was thinking rhetorically in his formal arrangement of words and sentence patterns is beyond doubt. Once again, we see the weakness of Vendler's tendency to divorce aesthetic design from the Renaissance art of rhetoric, as though the two practices were mutually exclusive. The prejudice against rhetorical ornamentation is an old story that may be traced back to the romantic poets, especially in William Wordsworth's famous complaint against poetic diction in the *Preface* to the second edition of *Lyrical Ballads* (1800).

Shakespeare's heavy investment in rhetorical tradition suggests that many of the one-of-a-kind verbal patterns that Vendler finds in the *Sonnets* may be more the product of her imagination than of Shakespeare's conscious design. But when Shakespeare's arrangement of words conforms to the standard definitions in rhetorical handbooks, such patterns clearly suggest the poet's deliberate artistry. Although these rhetorical features are part of the generic repertoire of the Elizabethan love sonnet, yet Shakespeare uses them in such innovative ways that the sonnet is barely recognizable as an example of the subgenre.

Sonnet 129 also devotes much of its stylistic ingenuity to its mixture of imitative and innovative diction. It is especially difficult to provide marginal glosses for this poem because so much of the vocabulary is ambiguous and especially rich in connotations. Here a prose paraphrase of the basic sense of the poem can only provide a few alternative suggestions: "Lust that has been acted upon amounts to the expenditure of vital spirit, or mental energy, or vital fluid (semen), in a shameful waste, or a futile disgrace, or act of shame or modesty, or a desert of shame, or an immodest waist. And until the action of lust takes place, Lust breaks oaths, is murderous, brutally violent, blameworthy, or quick to recriminate others, wild, excessive or violent, uncivilized, vicious, untrustworthy. As soon as lust enjoys its voluptuous pleasure, it is immediately loathed. Its object is irrationally pursued, and as soon as the object is possessed or sexually enjoyed, lust is hated like poisoned bait that has been left to make its prey insane. Lust is insane in following its prey and equally insane when it gains control of its sexual object. It is excessive after, during, and before it possesses its object. It is ecstatically enjoyable during the experience and a true misery after the test. In advance it promises or anticipates happiness. Afterwards, it is unreal, illusory, insubstantial. Everyone knows that everything stated here is true, but no one is wise enough to avoid the bliss that directs people, or men, to this infinite pain, or damnation (or directs men to this vagina)."

If we aim toward fusing horizons with the historical world from which this slippery poem emerges, a few obvious points emerge. Ancient medical doctrine, generally accepted by educated Elizabethans, taught that semen was rarified blood and contained a concentrated dose of an animal's vital spirit. Therefore, it was believed, every seminal emission represented a potentially dangerous drain on a finite amount of life-energy. John Donne, a younger contemporary of Shakespeare's, refers to this belief: "since each such Act, they say, / Diminisheth the length of life a day."[113] Aristotle was less precise, observing in *On Length and Shortness of Life* (466b) that males who copulated frequently do not live as long as females. In *On the Generation of Animals* (725b) he notes the conspicuous exhaustion caused by the loss of semen. Other kinds of harm from loss of vital spirit were also recorded by medical authorities. Francis Bacon noted that the emission of seed weakened the eyesight: "It hath been observed by the ancients, that much use of Venus [i.e., sexual intercourse] doth dim the sight." He explains that "the cause of dimness of sight ... is the expence of spirits."[114] Although the medical understandings of the danger of excessive sexual activity are now outdated, such fears still have the power to speak to our concerns because of our scientific knowledge of sexually transmitted diseases and the risks of unprotected sex. Our understandings of the body's vulnerability to disease provides one way to fuse horizons with the past.

In addition to the medical background of the sonnet, a theological world stands clearly within the poet's moral horizon in ways that continue to show up within the horizon of many twentieth-first-century readers. The key word *lust*, as indicated above, is the English name of a biblical sin that continues to be a concern for many English speakers today. Yet it is an extremely rare word in the major Elizabethan sonnet sequences, falling well outside the normal vocabulary that forms part of the generic repertoire of love poems. Of the eight times that the base word *lust* or one of its variations appears in the six canonical sequences, three are by Shakespeare.[115] In most of its other occurrences outside Sonnet 129, *lust* is used either in contrast to the supposedly purer love of the poet-lover or appears unambiguously in a non-theological older sense that requires a basic knowledge of the history of English to detect since these meanings are now obsolete.

The root word has a long and complex history in English and other Germanic languages. Its oldest senses in English, according to the *OED*, include "pleasure, delight" (1) and "desire, appetite" used in a morally neutral sense (2). Only from late in the Old English period (c. 1000) is the word first documented "in Biblical and Theological use: Sensuous appetite or desire, considered as sinful or leading to sin" (3); also beginning c. 1000 it is used in the closely related sense, "sexual appetite or desire. Chiefly and now exclusively implying intense moral reprobation: Libidinous desire, degrading animal passion" (4). For several centuries both neutral and pejorative senses of the word continued to have currency in English usage, and the intended meanings could only be understood from the context of a specific occurrence of the word in speech or writing. The adjectival form *lusty* occurs only three times in the six major sonnet sequences, two by Shakespeare. In the sixteenth century the adjective retained (perhaps most of the time) its non-pejorative range of meanings: "joyful, merry, jocund; cheerful, lively" (*OED* 1); "pleasing, pleasant" (2); "full of desire" (3); "full of healthy vigor" (5). The pejorative sense is documented from the later fourteenth century: "full of lust or sexual desire" (4); from the mid-sixteenth century an unexpected pejorative sense unrelated to sexual behavior turns up: "insolent, arrogant, self-confident" (6). Finally, a new neutral sense comes in as early as 1576: "Of inanimate agencies (e.g., a fire, wine, poison, a disease): strong, powerful" (7). For an example in Shakespeare's *Sonnets* of a non-pejorative use of the adjective, we find: "Sap checked with frost and lusty leaves quite gone" (3.7).

Editors generally do not bother to gloss the word *lust* in Sonnet 129 because present-day speakers will automatically assume that it is being used in a theological or moral sense, the only sense with which they are familiar unless they have special awareness of the word's complex history. And in fact there can be no doubt that Sonnet 129 uses the word exclusively in this pejorative sense because of the context established by the first line. However, when the speaker implies that he has not only personally experienced this illicit passion but also shamefully acted upon it, the historical genre of Elizabethan love sonnet unexpectedly suffers a sea-change into something rich and strange. Shakespeare's earliest audience could easily have grasped this unprecedented change from their background experience as readers. Recovering some of that sense of shock is one of the most important fruits of our effort to fuse horizons with the poem.

The poem is also innovative in its inclusion of other words that lie outside the normal range of sonnets, and some of these words are surprisingly rare. Although we might have expected the word *savage* to appear elsewhere in the tradition as a description of the cruel Petrarchan mistress, it is a unique occurrence in the six major sequences. However, putting *savage* near *rude* has Shakespeare's fingerprints on it, as we see from *Love's Labor's Lost*: "Like a rude and savage man of Inde" (IV.iii.222). *Extreme* is also unexpectedly rare, only appearing in its base form in this poem (other forms of the word are equally rare in the main sequences). Sonnet 129 includes other words that are more predictable in their infrequent appearance elsewhere in the major sequences: *murderous* only appears a total of three times, all in Shakespeare (129.3, 9.14, 10.5). Sonnets 9 and 10 are part of the prosecution's case against the young man in the procreation sonnets.

The words *shame* and *waste* also appear in the first of that pair of procreation sonnets (9.11, 14), while *shame* appears in the second (10.1). But in 129, the poet strongly implies that shame and waste belong to him, and he hyperbolically projects his guilt as shared by *all the world*. The adjective *bloody* (though not the base word *blood*) is rare in the major sonnet sequences, appearing only nine times, one third of them by Shakespeare. Finally, one other word has Shakespeare's unique signature on it. *Perjured* only appears three times, all in the second subsequence (129.3, 152.6, 152.13). The last instance occurs in the phrase *perjur'd eye*, which plays on the identical sound of *eye* and *I*. (The phrase is taken up in Fineman's title for his influential study of poetic subjectivity.) In short, close study of the poem's vocabulary in relation to a large body of Elizabethan love sonnets by major poets helps refine our understanding of how Shakespeare's diction, along with his syntax and rhetorical figures, presents radical innovations of style for a sonnet sequence.

The sound patterns of the poem add to its forceful impact on our ears and in our musculature, even in a silent reading. Alliteration on the plosives *p* and *b* is especially prominent, contributing to our perception of vehement denunciation. There is repetition of the long vowel *ā*, which appears in the rhyme pairs *shame/blame* and *straight/bait*, and internally in *hated, laid, taker*, and possibly in the second syllable of *savage*.[116] This assonance creates a web of sound that ties together the poem's denunciation of *waste, shame, blame, hated, bait, laid, taker*. The poet did not need the modern science of phonetics to be able to perceive a similar degree of muscular tension in the mouth and use it to bind these vehement words together (nor do we need to posit a fully conscious intention here).

Finally, the versification includes lines of rhythmic complexity that create emotionally expressive tension. The symbol **s** in the scansion given below marks what Attridge calls "emphatic stress," which occurs when a word seems to require especially strong rhetorical emphasis:

             s
Savage, extreme, rude, cruel, not to trust
B   o-o   B   O   Bo   B   o   B

Had, having, and in quest to have, extreme
O   Bo   bo   B   oB   o   B

Attridge scans the bitterly cynical final verse for us (*heaven* is one syllable):

To shun the heaven that leads men to this hell
             B ô B   o-o   B

"Metrical demands," he comments, "also heighten the semantic coloring" because "a misplaced emphatic stress on 'men' would produce a four-beat line, whereas the proper emphasis on 'leads' yields a firmly conclusive pentameter."[117] If we agree with his scansion and avoid emphatic stress on *men*, this lessens the chance that we will hear an Elizabethan slang term for vagina in the word *hell*. Although Shakespeare often uses bawdy wordplay in his writing, I do not believe he does so as frequently as commentators like Booth and Duncan-Jones suggest. In all, the sonnet is one of the most remarkable poems in the language, both in formal technique and profundity of meaning. There are many other remarkable poems in Shakespeare's *Sonnets*, but before his embers fade we must end this chapter on love sonnets with this astonishing example.

6

The Country House Poem: Lanyer and Jonson

In England during the early years of the seventeenth century, a new kind of lyric poem was born.[1] Defined by its subject matter rather than its external form, the country house poem writes about the mansion and surrounding estate of a socially privileged family and their rural way of life. In praising their wealthy patrons, how could poets keep from sounding too groveling on the one hand and too sentimental or nostalgic on the other? What kinds of enjoyment does the country house or estate poem offer to later readers, who may be turned off by the rigid class and gender system of early modern England?

In this chapter we will answer these questions by looking at two of the earliest examples of estate poem: Ben Jonson's "To Penshurst," first published in 1616 but composed a few years earlier, and the more recently canonized work by Aemilia Lanyer, "The Description of Cookham," published in 1611.[2] New literary genres do not emerge out of thin air. They develop instead by selecting from the generic repertoires of existing forms. The country house poem—part descriptive and part meditative—glances back at a number of classical and Renaissance literary antecedents. These include the "topographical encomium, descriptive poem, epigram, epistle, and such classical motifs as praise of hospitality, or the symbolic tree of family greatness."[3]

More broadly, the seventeenth-century country house poem reworks poetic modes that go back to ancient literature. While pastoral poetry imagines the lives and loves of shepherds, georgic poetry describes the seasonal labor of farmers growing crops, cultivating fruit trees, raising cattle, and keeping bees. Both of these older literary modes are readily taken up in estate poems. In addition, satire and writings about the Golden Age help define the moral stance assumed by poets in the country house poem.[4]

At the same time, country house poems cannot be understood in isolation from social relations during a particular phase in the development of early modern British society. For this reason the genre has proven fruitful for politically engaged critics interested in class and gender.[5] Such critics read this kind of poetry with their eyes on how such writing supports the dominant ideologies of its society. They point to how existing relations of power are assumed without question to be natural, God-given, and worthy of praise.

The rediscovery of *Salve Deus Rex Judaeorum* (1611), the only surviving volume of poems by Aemilia Lanyer, is one of the triumphs of feminist literary scholarship of early modern England since the 1970s.[6] Lanyer was proposed as the real-life model for Shakespeare's Dark Lady by the historian A. L. Rowse, though his identification has been almost universally rejected by other scholars.[7] Aemilia Bassano Lanyer (1569–1645) was the daughter of an Elizabethan court musician of Italian origin. Her position brought her to the attention of Henry Cary, Lord Hunsdon. As Lord Chamberlain, he was one of the most powerful men in the realm, and for several years she was his mistress. She was carrying his child at the time of her hastily arranged marriage in late 1592 to another court musician, Alphonso Lanyer.

As a commoner, her life is not well documented, but she claimed to have served during her youth in the household of Susan Bertie Wingfield, Countess of Kent. In her dedicatory poem to the Dowager Countess of Kent in *Salve Deus*, she describes her as "the mistress of my youth, / The noble guide of my ungoverned days" (1–2).[8] Perhaps educated in a noble household, she had at least some Latin and was acquainted with classical literature and rhetoric as well as the Bible.[9]

Lanyer was an accomplished and ambitious poet, a rarity for a woman of any social class in early modern England, but especially so for a commoner. However, she struggled financially for most of her life. Her marriage to Alphonso Lanyer had not provided financial security. A great deal of what we know about Aemilia Lanyer's life and how she viewed her experiences is based on the diary of the unscrupulous astrologer Simon Forman. She consulted him several times between 1597 and 1600, and he tried to seduce her.[10]

Lanyer knew from firsthand experience what is was like to be a "kept" woman, dependent on an older, more powerful man only to be cast aside when the affair no longer proved convenient. She endured a marriage to an unthrifty and possibly abusive husband and suffered multiple miscarriages and the heartbreak of losing an infant child. She knew what it was like to be taken advantage of by a sexual predator with whom she had shared intimate personal information during professional consultations. She found her valiant efforts to support herself thwarted by a powerful lawyer who exploited her financial weakness. Such forms of abuse and oppression by men were hardly unusual for women in early modern England. But in Aemilia Lanyer these experiences found an exceptionally eloquent voice. Her poetic project must be understood as an explicitly feminist one. She uses her poetry not only to protest against the misogynistic prejudices of her culture but also to imagine the possibility of emotionally satisfying relationships among women—even women separated by the social divisions of class.[11]

To understand "The Description of Cookham" some background information about the estate and the people mentioned in the poem will be helpful. The manor house of Cookham was situated on a wooded estate near Maidenhead in Berkshire along the Thames. The estate had been a Crown possession for centuries and was annexed to Windsor Castle in 1540.[12] During the 1590s and early 1600s Cookham was held by William Russell of Thornhaugh, though (to judge from the poem) it was sometimes occupied by his sister Margaret Clifford, Countess of Cumberland.[13] In 1577, Margaret Russell had married George Clifford, the 3rd Earl of Cumberland, a "dashing Elizabethan sea adventurer, flamboyant courtier, and notorious womanizer."[14] The marriage was unhappy, and Margaret was estranged from her husband long before he died in 1605. The surviving record does not indicate exactly when the Countess of Cumberland resided at Cookham. Evidently she lived there after separating from her husband and perhaps during the first part of her widowhood.[15] After the death of the couple's two sons, the only surviving child was Anne Clifford (born 1590). Anne married Richard Sackville, Earl of Dorset in 1609.

Composed shortly after Anne's marriage and appearing as the final poem in *Salve Deus*, "The Description of Cookham" reflects back on a happy period the poet spent in the company of these two noblewomen on the estate. Because George Clifford's only surviving legitimate child was a daughter, the earl provided for his estates and title to pass on to his younger brother in the event of his death. They would revert back to Anne if his brother failed to produce a male heir. This arrangement led to a long and bitter legal dispute in which Margaret Clifford and then Anne spent years litigating the case.

Although family histories and gender politics brought about the departure of the two noblewomen from the estate, the poem aims to keep alive fond memories of female companionship. In recalling the daily rhythms of country life, the poet deliberately engages in an act of poetic mythmaking. Lanyer describes Cookham in terms meant to remind the reader of the passing of a golden age or loss of Eden. She praises the virtues of the countess and her daughter, but at the same time she tactfully yet insistently inserts herself into the idealized portrait of her social superiors. The poem thus does more than simply flatter a patron in hope of material reward.

The early seventeenth-century social conditions celebrated in "The Description of Cookham" may seem like a relic from another time. However, the poem speaks to social concerns that remain alive whenever we interact politely across social distances, regret the passing of happy times, and attempt to compensate for such losses by shaping our lives into the stories we tell. Although the poem may come close at times to sounding sentimental, Lanyer generally avoids this fault through her self-deprecating humor and understated assertions of her poetic gifts. She shows awareness of the social and poetic risks she takes and uses an innovative poetic form to overcome them.

The introduction (lines 1–16) opens with a complex sentence of six lines announcing the principle theme in a way that both respects social distance and makes clear the poet's power:

> Farewell, sweet Cookham, where I first obtained
> Grace from that grace where perfit grace remained,   *perfect*
> And where the Muses gave their full consent
> I should have power the virtuous to content;
> Where princely palace willed me to indite   *write*
> The sacred story of the soul's delight.

With its triangulated address to Margaret and Anne and other potential patrons and readers of her volume of poetry, this apostrophe to the estate presents all the hallmarks of lyric poetry identified by Jonathan Culler. The poem is an epideictic performance. Its voicing makes the lyric an event rather than the representation of one, using language that is both ritualistic and hyperbolic.[16]

The delicate mood of the poem is evident from the opening farewell. The play on several senses of the word *grace*—a figure of speech known as ploce—strikes a careful balance between social deference and rhetorical self-display typical of the poem as a whole. The second *grace* is the honorific form of address for the Dowager Countess of Cumberland, yet the syntax emphasizes the first-person speaker and the gifts she has received from both her patron and the muses. Although few women in Lanyer's day had the self-confidence to claim inspiration from the muses, she tempers this boast with the suggestion that she writes to praise her superior, not to give herself glory. To praise and please the *virtuous* indirect addressee is a special *power* given to the poet.

The final verse of the opening sentence is open to multiple interpretations. Whose soul takes delight and in what "sacred story"? The souls of the patron and poet share in the communion of the faithful. The story of the Passion narrated earlier in the volume informs the spiritual life of meditation and prayer recalled in this final poem. The poet bids farewell to the "sweet place" (7) and records her personal loss: "Never shall my sad eyes again behold / Those pleasures which my thoughts did then unfold" (9–10).

But the poet's sense of loss is coupled with her acknowledgment of the unhappy circumstances of Margaret. In calling her the woman "whose desires" led to "this work of grace" (12), she implies that the countess herself requested the poem. Indeed, this suggestion is restated more directly at the conclusion, when the poet announces that she has "performed her noble hest" (207). If Lanyer in fact composed the poem at the countess's behest, this might explain the poet's boldness in offering consolation in the form of advice. However socially inferior a poet may be to an aristocratic patron, the poet's traditional role was to offer wisdom in elegant form—to please and instruct. Thus Lanyer draws on religious commonplaces to place earthly pleasure and its loss in two conceptual frameworks. Transitory joy may be viewed both as a proof of the vanity of all earthly goods, and as a foreshadowing of heavenly glory (13–16).

After the introduction, the poem devotes the next section to recalling how the arrival of the countess transforms the estate (lines 17–52). There is only one reference to the house in this section of the poem, though it is not directly described. Since neither the countess nor her family owned the royal mansion, this lack of detail seems a decorous acknowledgment of the social circumstances of the primary audience.[17] However, to my knowledge no one has pointed out that the couplet about the house is structurally crucial, since it is closely echoed (including the identical feminine rhymes) in the leave-taking conclusion to the poem:

> The house received all ornaments to grace it,
> And would endure no foulness to deface it [19–20].
>
> The house cast off each garment that might grace it,
> Putting on dust and cobwebs to deface it [201–02].

The *dust and cobwebs* resulting from the house's abandonment are precisely the kind of *foulness* that it refuses during the welcoming phase. If lyric poetry tends to exploit a ritualistic quality to language (as Culler suggests), in this poem the unfolding rhythm of arrival and departure calls to mind a stately procession. The graceful *ornaments*—whether furnishings, decorations, or flowers—will not outlast the presence of the countess and her daughter. The poem itself will prove a more lasting ornament.

Aside from the brief mentions of the house itself, the poem is set entirely outdoors, concentrating our attention on the natural beauty of the "delightful place" (32)—the phrase translates the classical term *locus amoenus*. The main poetic device in the opening and closing sections of the poem is the so-called pathetic fallacy. Borrowed from ancient pastoral elegy, this convention depicts nature responding sympathetically to human emotion. Although the device has often been dismissed as artificial (in the bad sense) since the nineteenth century, the poet's repetition of the phrase "Oh how methought" (17, 33) signals her awareness that the description of natural sympathy is a playful work of imagination not to be taken too seriously. "The trees with leaves, with fruits, with flowers clad, / Embraced each other, seeming to be glad" (23–24). The word *seeming* indicates that this is a subjective perception rather than an objective reality.

The songbirds add to nature's joyful welcome: "The little birds in chirping notes did sing, / To entertain both you and that sweet spring" (29–30). It makes a pleasing picture. Yet the natural bond between the countess and the landscape takes on greater dignity as the hills themselves eagerly desire to receive her. The hills perform a double movement: they *descend* in deference to her social standing, but they simultaneously *rise* in gladness from the earth to meet her steps halfway (35–38). Her walking thus becomes a collaborative effort with the hills, which seem alive. It is a delicately imagined touch.

The next section of the poem (lines 53–90) introduces the central image of a majestic oak, the prospect it afforded, and the meditations it inspired: "Now let me come unto that stately tree, / Wherein such goodly prospects you did see" (53–54). Here the first description of the emotionally charged oak tree is announced by the word *now*. The lyric present tense marks the moment of writing (and reading) to compensate for the loss of Cookham. The deictic *now* structures the temporal design of the entire poem and will become even more prominent during the departure section.

More an event than the representation of one, the oak takes on mythic proportions, towering over its peers as much as "lofty trees" over the humble grass.[18] The countess often visited this welcoming oak, which shielded her from the sun. Seated beneath it, she "might plainly see / Hills, vales, and woods, as if on bended knee / They had appeared, your honour to salute" (67–69). The poet comes close to suggesting that the countess possesses an almost regal majesty. From her seat beneath the oak Margaret surveys: "A prospect fit to please the eyes of kings: / And thirteen shires appeared all in your sight; / Europe could not afford much more delight" (72–74). Yet insofar as "The Description of Cookham" is capable of reactivating this gorgeous panorama in the lyric present, the poet's power over language is what places the countess in the position of sovereign.

The beauty of the scene, the poet recalls, led the countess to spend "time in meditation" on the "Creator's power" (76–77). Divine goodness is visible in the natural order of created things: "in their beauties did you plain descry / His beauty, wisdom, grace, love, majesty" (79–80). The idea that we may know the Creator by studying the creation is an ancient one.[19] These meditations brought the countess into sacred conversation, "With Christ and his apostles there to talk, / Placing his holy writ in some fair tree" (82–83). In a similar vein, she mounted the holy hill with Moses, sang holy hymns with David to delight her soul "in sweet music" (89), and fed her "pined brethren" with Joseph by her side (92). If this last detail is a humorous word-play that refers to feeding the woodland fauna, it suggests more of the playful touch that the poem balances against the heavy theme of paradise lost.

The next section of the poem (lines 93–126) introduces Anne, Countess of Dorset (Margaret's recently married daughter) and begins to shift the mood to sorrow. The emphasis, however, is as much on the poet herself as on Anne. Lanyer describes their friendship as having flourished on the estate despite the vast social distance between them. This section begins with elaborate praise of the lady's family lineage and moral virtue, standard topics of praise poetry (encomium) since antiquity. Above all, the poet "grieves" now that she can no longer "be / Near unto her" (99–100), since marriage has taken Lady Anne to another aristocratic household. The poet blames "Fortune … / Who casts us down into so low a frame, / Where our great friends we cannot daily see, / So great a difference is there in degree" (103–06). That is, the poet claims friendship with the great lady while acknowledging that the difference between their social ranks must limit their intimacy.

Previous critics do not seem to have noticed that the lines lamenting the social context of the poet's inability to maintain daily converse with her "great friends" form the central couplet of the poem. If Renaissance poets often inscribed an emblem of sovereignty at the numerical center, here Lanyer poignantly reserves the center to emphasize the emotional cost of *degree*.[20] The poet tactfully wishes that female friendship might survive against the odds. Her utopian desire remains moving even in a more democratic age.

At the same time, she recognizes the need to avoid suggesting that the lady's sentiments toward her are stronger than they are in fact. There can be no equality of affection, since the poet can never mean to Anne what the noblewoman means to this commoner. The difference in rank inclines the poet's love to exceed that of her social superior, who is far more worthy of receiving it. This too is a potentially risky claim. She nervously calls the idea into question before deciding to stand by it after all. The great are

Nearer in show, yet farther off in love,
In which the lowest always are above.
But whither am I carried in conceit?
My wit too weak to conster of the great.²¹ *interpret/understand*
Why not? Although we are but born of earth,
We may behold the heavens, despising death;
And loving heaven that is so far above,
May in the end vouchsafe us entire love [109–16]. *grant*

This is a remarkable passage of epideictic rhetoric. The poet claims a kind of superiority of the heart to that of her social superior, but she uses the modesty topos to register awareness of her potential breach of etiquette. However, she immediately defends the conceit by offering another that simultaneously displays both humility and self-confidence. She flatters the Countess of Dorset by positioning her grace as far above her as heaven is to earth. Yet the humble poet suggests that (like all human beings) both women are lowly creatures in the sight of God. Both women equally hope that loving him will be repaid by his reciprocal love toward his creatures.

In preparation for the valedictory movement of the final section, the poet now focuses on her own loss, with an apostrophe to her own "sweet memory" (117), bidding it to remember "pleasures past" (117–18). The poet also reminds the Countess of Cumberland and her daughter of her own participation in Anne's innocent recreations and of the love she still bears toward both women. She understands that it would be impertinent to speak of their grief too directly. In locating the grief within herself, she stands as their surrogate: "deprived, I evermore must grieve" (125). The poet's own grief introduces the final movement of the poem—the departure. "And you, sweet Cookham, whom these ladies leave, / I now must tell the grief you did conceive / At their departure" (127–29). For the first time since the introduction, the poet addresses the estate directly by name. The poet marks the transition to the theme of departure and grief with another *now* for the present-time of writing. Again Lanyer introduces the pathetic fallacy with "methought" as she describes how "each thing did unto sorrow frame" (132). The trees lose their flowers and fruit in response to the ladies' preparation for departure. The leaves wither, change color, and fall. Amidst this autumnal scene of nature in mourning, the trees weep but remain "speechless," unable to prevent the women's departure: "But your occasions called you so away, / That nothing there had power to make you stay" (147–48).

The poem reaches its emotional climax in its most famous passage, the description of Countess Margaret bidding farewell to the beloved oak tree:

> You did repeat the pleasures which had passed,
> Seeming to grieve they could no longer last.
> And with a chaste yet loving kiss took leave,
> Of which sweet kiss I did it soon bereave,
> Scorning a senseless creature should possess   *inanimate*
> So rare a favour, so great happiness.
> No other kiss it could receive from me,
> For fear to give back what it took of thee:
> So I, ingrateful creature, did deceive it
> Of that which you vouchsafed in love to leave it [163–72].

The poet audaciously imagines the tree mediating a kiss exchanged between the women. In her precarious social position, Lanyer must balance her desire to maintain a relationship with the countess (who may yet provide further patronage) with her recognition that a more direct expression of affection might seem offensive. Instead of falling into sentimentality, the passage expresses the poet's self-confidence in negotiating the socially sensitive relationship. Taking possession of the kiss is thus an act of self-affirmation: "Yet this great wrong I never could repent" (174). Far from regretting her audacious act, she immortalizes it in the poem.

Now the springtime scene of nature's flowering at the arrival of the countess and her daughter is reversed, as autumn transforms the landscape. In the final section of the poem, the seasons have progressed and nature responds sympathetically to the women's sorrowful departure from the Edenic landscape. Flowers, grass, brooks, and birds all register their extravagant sense of loss. As winter approaches, the reminders of mortality become more insistent, and the poetic rhythms more expressive of the elegiac mood:

> Each arbour, bank, each seat, each stately tree,
>   o B o B   o   B   o   B o B
>
> Looks bare and desolate now for want of thee;
> o   B   o B o-o b o   B   o   B
>
> Turning green tresses into frosty gray,   *i.e., leaves*
> B   o-O   B o b o B o B
>
> While in cold grief they wither all away.
>   o-o   B ô B o   B   o B o B [191–94].

Always careful in her use of poetic rhythm, Lanyer shows particular metrical skill in these beautiful lines. The implied offbeat between *cold* and *grief* emphasizes the feeling of sadness.

It is finally left to the poet to bid a last farewell to the estate. The conclusion of this happy period of her life coincides with the close of the poem.

But thoughts of her mortality are accompanied by a claim to have completed a poem that matters:

> This last farewell to Cookham here I give:
> When I am dead thy name in this may live,
> Wherein I have performed her noble hest,
> Whose virtues lodge in my unworthy breast,
> And ever shall, so long as life remains,
> Tying my heart to her by those rich chains.
>   B o-o   B   o b   o-o   B ô B [205–10].

With her performance complete, she hopes the poem has strengthened the emotional bonds that join the sorrowful women despite their difference of rank. Borrowing from the Renaissance commonplace, the poem claims it has made eternal the place, the patron, and the poet. Over all, this elegant lyric shows admirable skill in its structure, rhetorical design, imagery, and versification. "The Description of Cookham" is not only an important breakthrough in the history of early modern women's writing, it is also a moving testament to poetic artistry.

A very different set of lyric effects is achieved in the Jonson's ode "To Penshurst." Ben Jonson (1572–1637) was born into humble circumstances but managed to use his education, talent, and industry to become the foremost literary figure of his time.[22] A poet, playwright, and maker of court masques, Jonson was the first professional writer in England to make a living from his pen.[23] He studied at Westminster School under William Camden, the humanist educator and antiquarian. The poet later memorialized his former teacher in an epigram that describes him as the man "to whom I owe / All that I am in arts, all that I know."[24] Given the importance of his classical education to his self-definition as an author, this extravagant praise is not much of an exaggeration. Jonson's classicism—his sensitivity to ancient standards of poetic excellence—marks a new turn in the history of English poetry.[25] Although he wrote many fine stanzaic poems, the iambic pentameter couplet was his preferred non-dramatic form.

Jonson's ambitious effort to make himself the unofficial poet laureate was capped by the publication of *The Workes of Benjamin Jonson* in the folio edition of 1616.[26] The Latin motto (adapted from Horace) insists on Jonson's desire to secure a small but discerning readership. We have already noted that the 1616 edition of Jonson's *Workes* helped complete the shift from manuscript to print for lyric poetry in early modern England.[27] But the 1616 folio was unprecedented in the history of English letters. This was the first time a living author had authorized a monumental printed edition of his collected writings. Jonson even dared to include dramatic works at a time when plays were not yet considered to be a form of serious literature. The death of Shakespeare in April 1616, followed by the publication of Jonson's *Works* in November of that year, secured his reputation as the greatest living English author—not bad for a boy raised in poverty who had once worked as a bricklayer. The great could live off the fruit of their lands but not so the professional man of letters, an identity Jonson practically invented through his own toil and sweat. He died in August 1637 and was buried in Westminster Abbey beneath the inscription: "O Rare Ben Jonson." William Drummond, a Scottish poet who made a record of their conversations when Jonson journeyed to Edinburgh in 1618, privately noted: "In his merry humour he was wont to name himself The Poet."[28] Jonson plays this role to perfection in his great country house poem, "To Penshurst."

Unlike the mansion celebrated in Lanyer's "Description of Cookham," the house at Penshurst Place in Kent still survives, largely preserved as it stood during the seventeenth century. The estate is still owned by a descendant of the Sidney family, the Viscount De L'Isle. The oldest portion of the manor house was built by a successful London merchant in the fourteenth century.[29] Penshurst reverted to the Crown in 1521 before it was given by Edward VI to Sir William Sidney in 1552. His son, Sir Henry Sidney (father of the poet Sir Philip Sidney) inherited the estate in 1554 and oversaw a major renovation and expansion of the house and gardens.

The poet's younger brother, Sir Robert Sidney (1563–1626), inherited Penshurst after their father died in 1586, six months before Philip (who would have been heir) succumbed to his wounds in Zutphen. Sir Robert, who continued to oversee improvements to the house and estate, was made Baron Sidney by James I in 1603, Viscount Lisle in 1605 (his title at the time Jonson composed his poem), and Earl of Leicester in 1618. Despite his eventual rise into the upper nobility, Robert was constantly in financial difficulty, having inherited large debts from his father and incurring more of his own. In 1584 he had defied Queen Elizabeth's wishes and married Barbara Gamage, a Welsh heiress, shortly after her previous husband died.[30]

Although Sir Robert and his wife Barbara are not mentioned by their first names in "To Penshurst," the poem's title clearly alerted readers of the 1616 folio to the identity of the lord and lady of the manor. Moreover, their family names occur in descriptions of the "copse … named of Gamage" (19) and "Sidney's copse" (26). This naming strategy suggests that the poem is as much about the lineage as about individuals. Members of the Sidney family were especially prominent among the many aristocratic families whose patronage was sought by Jonson. "By making public his many links with the Sidney dynasty," writes David Norbrook, "Jonson was establishing himself as an heir of the Elizabethan tradition of public poetry."[31] For an ambitious writer in the early seventeenth century, it would be difficult to succeed without noble patrons, and the Sidney family were well known for their support of literary pursuits.

Jonson's "To Penshurst" celebrates Robert Sidney and his family by presenting an idealized image of their way of life, in contrast with more ostentatious displays of wealth by other (unidentified) noble families. The proper stewardship of the estate and the lord and lady's admirable hospitality are the main subjects of this praise poem (encomium). Jonson's gracefully composed poem of 102 lines of iambic pentameter couplets is one of his finest poetic accomplishments. Highly polished in style and carefully structured, his encomium deserves to be read closely for its mastery of poetic form, though in recent decades critics have devoted more attention to its political significance.[32]

Jonson shared with his readers a Renaissance understanding of poetry as a branch of epideictic rhetoric, which gives delight and instruction by praising virtue and condemning vice. In his commonplace book *Discoveries*, Jonson describes the poet (adapting Quintilian's definition of the orator) as "he which can feign [imitate] a commonwealth.... We do not require in him mere elocution, or an excellent faculty in verse, but the exact knowledge of all virtues and their contraries; with ability to render the one loved, the other hated, by his proper embattling them" (setting them in array).[33] The study of poetry, Jonson explains, "offers to mankind a certain rule and pattern of living well and happily, disposing us to all civil offices of society."[34] Jonson assumes that his readers understand the theory and practice of epideictic rhetoric when he contrasts the relatively modest design of the Sidney mansion with houses belonging to other contemporary noblemen who remain discreetly unnamed in such a public poem.

Jonson thus opens the poem with his "proper embattling" of so-called prodigy houses like Theobalds or Knole (which lay only eight miles from the Sidney estate). Such houses were more ostentatious than Penshurst in their conspicuous display of wealth.[35] The first six lines make this contrast between virtue and vice clear while introducing the principle rhetorical device of the poem, the lyric figure of apostrophe:

> Thou art not, Penshurst, built to envious show
>   Of touch or marble, nor canst boast a row   *black marble or touchstone*
> Of polished pillars, or a roof of gold;
>   Thou hast no lantern whereof tales are told,   *turret with windows*
> Or stair, or courts; but stand'st an ancient pile,   *small castle*
>   And these grudged at, art reverenced the while [1–6].

The syntax of the final couplet is difficult because of its compression. As the second-person verb endings make clear, the two parallel main verbs (*stand'st* and *art*) are governed by the implied subject pronoun *thou* carried over from line four. The clause "these grudged at" is an absolute construction (equivalent to the Latin ablative absolute). The sense is "while these [i.e., vainglorious houses] are complained about." The contrast between Penshurst and the garish houses of wealthier neighbors strikes a chord that still resonates today, despite the social changes that have occurred over the centuries. The poem achieves this ongoing resonance not because it transcends all historical circumstances but because it captures a durable public mood.

Although critics disagree about some details, the poem's intricate design is clearly intended to imitate the structure of the cosmos.[36] Paul Cubeta seems to have been the first critic to notice that the poem is divided roughly in two. The first half of the poem describes the fruitful outdoors of the estate. The poem then shifts indoors at line 48 to focus on the theme of hospitality.[37] Don Wayne divides the poem into four sections: lines 1–8 (introduction), 9–44 (description of estate), 45–88 (inside the house), and 89–102 (epilogue).[38] For our purposes, it will be convenient to follow this four-part structure.

We have already examined the first six lines. The next couplet completes the introduction by alluding to the old cosmological theory of four primal elements (earth, water, air, fire). Thus the estate and poem become a microcosm of the universe: "Thou joy'st in better marks, of soil, of air, / Of wood, of water; therein thou art fair" (7–8; here "marks" are distinctive features). The element of fire, which remains potential in the wood, is made actual later in the poem when the hearth is seen as a beacon by the king and prince (77–78). Symbolically, then, the poem imitates the hierarchical order of the macrocosm and of human society or what used to be known as the Great Chain of Being.[39]

This hierarchy is made clear by the description of the estate in the second section, which surveys the trees (12–19); the animals on land (20–30) and in water (31–38); then, moving closer to home, the gardens and orchards with their fruits (39–44). The third section of the poem reveals the hierarchy of the human world, with the farmers and peasants at the bottom, the lord and lady above them, the poet himself in an intermediary role, then finally the king and prince at the top. The poem thus reveals a deep commitment to the principle of hierarchical social order (on this point, traditional critics and Marxists agree).[40]

Yet poetry and the figure of the poet have a special role to play in this display of hierarchy, a role that becomes more visible in the second half of the poem. In this earlier section, the references to classical nature deities, from the dryads (woodland nymphs), Pan, and Bacchus (10–11) to satyrs and fauns (17–18), allude to classical mythology handed down by ancient poets. Jonson blends family history with classical imitation to suggest that this particular landscape literally has been shaped by the figure of the poet, referring to the legend that an oak tree was planted at the birth of Sir Philip Sidney (13–18). The oak that stands as a memorial to the great poet becomes a writing surface that local spirits (Sidney children?) use to carve their names.

The innocent joys of this pleasant place (*locus amoenus*) recall the Golden Age, a topic borrowed from georgic poetry.[41] Thus the description (20–44) catalogues an abundance of foods that require little or no human effort to enjoy. The copse lying to the north of the house "never fails to serve thee seasoned deer / When thou wouldst feast or exercise thy friends" (20–21). Here, in what may be the most delightful section of the poem, everything delicious and wholesome generously offers itself for food. The copse,

> To crown thy open table, doth provide
>   The purple pheasant with the speckled side;
> The painted partridge lies in every field,
>   And for thy mess is willing to be killed [27–30]. *meal*

The classical motif employed here is known as *sponte sua* (of its own free will), imitated from poems by Vergil, Martial, and Juvenal. The reader is meant to be delighted by the extravagant hyperbole as carp "run into thy net" (33) and pike freely offer themselves as food. "Bright eels, that emulate them" also "leap on land / Before the fisher, or into his hand" (37–38). The "painted partridge" is a direct translation of Martial's *picta perdrix* (*Epigrams* 3.58.15). Jonson's description of the gardens and orchard thus offers a catalogue of vividly imagined details.

Jonson delights in how poetic language can be called upon to manifest the things of this world. His sensuous description of fruit anticipates Keats's ode "To Autumn":

> Then hath thy orchard fruit, thy garden flowers,
>   Fresh as the air and new as are the hours:
> The early cherry, with the later plum,
>   Fig, grape, and quince, each in his time doth come;
> The blushing apricot and woolly peach
>   Hang on thy walls, that every child may reach [39–44].

Again the tableau of seasonal fruit is drawn as much from earlier literature as from the poet's empirical observations. Documentary evidence records that each of the fruits mentioned in the poem was in fact cultivated on the estate, and that Robert Sidney planted cherry and quince trees imported from the Continent. But Jonson also expects his readers to recognize his allusion to a description in Vergil's *Georgics*, where the fortunate farmer "plucks the fruits which his boughs, which his ready fields, of their own free will (*sponte sua*), have borne."[42] In Jonson's poem, the *hours* are the Latin *Horae*, the three goddesses in charge of the seasons. The emphasis on the seasonal rhythms of the ripening fruit suggests the care with which the poem imitates the orderly process of time in the natural world. In effect, the fruitfulness of the Penshurst estate, because it is cultivated through the good stewardship of its owner, offers a glimpse of the Golden Age whose passing is lamented in classical literature.[43]

The description of the fruit trees overhanging the stone wall prepares us for the second half of the poem and introduces us to the third section. Here, the poem shifts from describing the surrounding estate to praising what happens inside the house. We should keep in mind that throughout the poem, the feigned second-person addressee is Penshurst, not Lord Lisle. In an influential essay Charles Molesworth suggested over forty years ago that the country house poem in general performs its function as epideictic rhetoric through the panegyric strategy of praising the owner indirectly by praising his estate.[44] The ethical assumption behind the genre is that the material prosperity of a man's estate shows that God rewards moral virtue.

The introduction of the poem, with its satire of the architectural excesses of the other mansions, implies positive moral standards that allow Penshurst to be "reverenced." This moral understanding, proper to georgic poetry in general, remains implicit in the description of the fruitful estate. The poem assumes the "responsible stewardship" of the providentially chosen landowner.[45] Now, in the transitional passage leading the reader indoors, the moral argument comes into more direct view:

> And though thy walls be of the country stone,
>   They're reared with no man's ruin, no man's groan;
> There's none that dwell about them wish them down,
>   But all come in, the farmer and the clown,   *peasant*
> And no one empty-handed, to salute
>   Thy lord and lady, though they have no suit   *formal request* [45–50].

At almost precisely the numerical center of the poem, the lord and lady are directly mentioned for the first time.[46] The benign description of the local population's acceptance of the wall offers an idealized view, to be sure. No one should expect Jonson to present a historically accurate depiction of landlord-tenant relations at Penshurst Place. And though the Lord Lisle may not have caused economic "ruin" (46) to local peasants by enclosing their lands, the real workers on the Sidney estate undoubtedly "groaned" often enough as they performed their year-round agricultural labor. Jonson's word nicely carries a double meaning: *groan* is both the sound made during strenuous exertion and a synonym for protest (*OED*).

As the lord and lady of Penshurst welcome the rural laborers to their home, their guests bring generous gifts in return. The scene of hospitality is designed to give the impression of malice toward none and charity for all. The final three lines of this description obviously reveal the tendencies in Jonson's patriarchal culture to value women chiefly for their role as potential mothers:

> Some bring a capon, some a rural cake,
>   Some nuts, some apples; some that think they make
> The better cheeses, bring 'em; or else send
>   By their ripe daughters, whom they would commend
> This way to husbands; and whose baskets bear
>   An emblem of themselves, in plum or pear [51–56].

To be sure, women were oppressed in a variety of ways in early modern England and were subject to the authority of men. Yet the prospect of a good marriage offers their daughters an opportunity to improve their economic station. The word *emblem* is carefully chosen by Jonson, who draws not on empirical observation but on the conventional meanings of Renaissance emblem books (we considered one such book in Chapter 5).[47]

The poem may still delight and instruct its readers through the poetic imitation of what people are like, as Aristotle and Horace insisted and Jonson agreed a good poem should do.[48] Thus in the passage above we might pause to admire what in his *Timber, or, Discoveries* Jonson calls *poesy*, the poet's "skill or craft of making."[49] We might note his skillful use of enjambment or his repetition of the word *some* (anaphora). The sensuousness of the language is further emphasized by the plosive alliterations of hard *c*, *b*, and *p*. But more than poetic technique is involved here. Even though the details change over time, as long as there are guest-host relations governed by rituals of politeness, "To Penshurst" will continue to reveal something valuable about the human condition.

The poet makes clear that the gifts offered by the farmers and their daughters are not needed by the lord and lady, given the fruits of the estate. Instead, the peasants' gifts "express their love" (57) to the Sidney family, "whose liberal board doth flow / With all that hospitality doth know!" (59–60). Hospitality was a live political issue under James I. The king was troubled by what he called the "decay of hospitality" at a time when many aristocrats preferred to live in London instead of on their country estates. A royal proclamation dated 9 December 1615 attempted to restore the practice of hospitality in the countryside by ordering noblemen and gentleman back to their estates.[50] Jonson thus praises the generous form of hospitality extended at Penhurst. Each guest, regardless of social rank, "is allowed to eat / Without his fear, and of thy lord's own meat" (61–62). The portrayal of mealtime is obviously idealized. In fact, "the actual rule at Penshurst required everyone to attend meals in the hall 'according to their rancke and order.'"[51] Social hierarchy was deeply ingrained in everyday practices.

Although Jonson is silent about such details, in a noble household the steward was responsible for the day-to-day operation of the household, indoors and out. He was charged with making sure proper form was maintained by the domestic staff during the rituals of hospitality. At Penshurst the steward was under the authority of Lady Lisle while her husband was away, as often happened. A letter from Robert to his wife advises her about the steward's essential role: "The steward of a man's house of my quality must both have the spirit and knowledge to command and experience of all things that belongs [sic] to the house, both within doors and without…. Besides, he must know how to give entertainment to strangers according to their qualities [i.e., their rank], which is not easily found in one where such courses are not used."[52] Lord Lisle insists that a well-trained steward's knowledge of hospitality is acquired by experience.

Jonson conspicuously inserts himself into the poem, praising his host for allowing him to eat the same food and drink the same wine as the lord (63–66). Critics often repeat Jonson's story told to Drummond about how on one occasion he had complained about not being served the same food as his host, the Earl of Salisbury.[53] In the poem, the waiter does not look on with envy since "below he shall find plenty of meat, / Thy tables hoard not up for the next day" (70–71). Jonson's tone is playful as he mocks his own "gluttony" (68) while paying a compliment to his host's generosity. Everyone present in this scene behaves with perfect decorum. Moreover, by inserting himself into the poem as a fellow guest, Jonson subtly implies that the poem itself is a return gift, his best way of thanking the host for his hospitality.

Further hospitality is extended when the poet is shown to his room for the night. The thoughtful host prevents his guest from having to ask for anything because he is treated like a king. The poet need not call

> For fire or lights or livery: all is there,   *provisions*
>   As if thou then wert mine, or I reigned here;
> There's nothing I can wish, for which I stay.
>   That found King James, when, hunting late this way
> With his brave son, the Prince, they saw thy fires
>   Shine bright on every hearth … [73–78].

Jonson's seemingly effortless control of his material is remarkable as he unexpectedly brings the real king into the poem. The royal sovereign sits at the head of the descending Great Chain of Being in human society. James

I, a poet and patron of the arts himself, within a few years would award Jonson a pension for his service.

Although the poem may have been composed before the death of Prince Henry in November 1612, by the time it was published in 1616 the acknowledgment of the late heir apparent to the throne would serve as a memorial. In any case, Jonson uses the occasion to compliment Penshurst's "good lady," Barbara Gamage, for her "high housewifery" (84–85). She is such an effective manager of the household that she did not even need to be physically present during the unexpected royal visit. She had already made sure "to have her linen, plate, and all things nigh / When she was far; and not a room but dressed / As if it had expected such a guest!" 86–88). The poet's compliment to the lady's attentiveness closes the third section of the poem, thus preparing the reader for the eloquent conclusion.

In the concluding paragraph, the poem's epideictic function is directly signaled for the first time by the word *praise*: "These, Penshurst, are thy praise, and yet not all" (89). *These* refers to everything that has been described in the poem thus far about the proper stewardship of the idealized estate. Now we are told that Robert Sidney's crowning glory is his excellent wife and the children she gave birth to and takes responsibility for nurturing. Barbara Gamage was certainly "noble, fruitful, chaste" (90); she gave birth to at least eleven children, though many died in infancy (only one son survived his father).[54] The letters she exchanged with her husband suggest that she was an exceptionally devoted mother. In contrasting her sexual fidelity with its lack in other noblewomen, Jonson briefly returns to the satiric bite of the poem's opening, epigrammatically pointing his barb in the bitter (*fel*) mode, according to Renaissance literary theory.[55]

The next three couplets focus on the nurture and education of the children:

> They are and have been taught religion; thence
>   Their gentler spirits have sucked innocence.
> Each morn and even they are taught to pray
>   With the whole household, and may every day
> Read in their virtuous parents' noble parts   *qualities*
>   The mysteries of manners, arms and arts [93–98].   *skills or truths*

The stylistic effect here is in part a function of the careful mixture of native and Latinate diction. One example must suffice: *sucked innocence* weds the Old English verb with the Latinate noun. The delicate poise of these lines is largely achieved by the skillful handling of poetic rhythm. Most of the lines are enjambed, creating a more relaxed, conversational tone. Yet the syntax of the last three lines creates a miniature drama of suspense by postponing the resolution of the sentence. The subject of *may* is carried over from the preceding line, while this auxiliary verb is separated by a line break from the main verb it governs (*read*). In addition, the object of *read* is delayed until the following line.

But the drama is not over yet: the evocative word *mysteries* could mean any number of things (the earlier use of the word *religion* might seem to point in one direction), until the modifying prepositional phrase supplies the missing terms. It is important to hear the older meaning of the word *manners* here. Its reference is not to the current meaning of polite behavior; instead, the word refers to "habitual behavior or conduct, especially in reference to its moral aspect."[56] The boys especially learn about martial prowess (*arms*) from studying their father's virtues, since he (like his older brother) was a brave soldier. Both the sons and daughters benefit from learning the various *arts*. Judging from the example of Mary Sidney, the future author, it was not just the boys who received tutoring in the arts at Penshurst. The description of the entire household joining together in prayer is no fiction: the household rule required the family and staff to attend prayers in the chapel both morning and evening.[57] Moreover, religious piety was a Sidney family tradition: Sir Philip died a martyr to the Protestant cause, and his sister Mary, Countess of Pembroke, completed the translation of the Psalms that he began.

Critics often remark on the brilliant ending, but few have managed to explain it in formal terms. The remaining two couplets offer one last apostrophe, capturing with epigrammatic point what was unfolded in the previous lines. Don Wayne has drawn attention to the instability created by the word *now*, which implies that the preceding narrative took place *then*.[58] But the ending also uses other devices to create—then resolve—this instability. The beautifully resonant ending, masterful in its control of poetic rhythm, returns us to the opening contrast between the prodigy houses and the less grandiose Sidney house. Once again, Jonson is imitating Martial (12.50.8), who satirizes the builder of a pretentious but uncomfortable mansion: "How well you do not dwell" (*Quam bene non habitas*). Jonson shows the contrast in a new light:

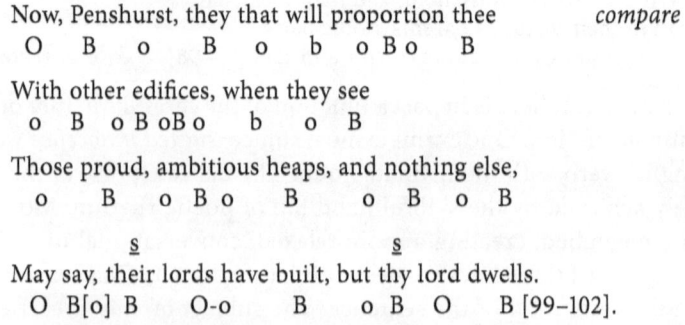

Now, Penshurst, they that will proportion thee   *compare*
  O   B   o   B   o   b   oBo   B

With other edifices, when they see
  o B oBoBo   b   o B

Those proud, ambitious heaps, and nothing else,
  o   B   o Bo   B   o B o B

       s   s
May say, their lords have built, but thy lord dwells.
  O B[o] B   O-o   B   o B O   B [99–102].

The strongest pauses (caesuras) in the first couplet are placed unexpectedly after the third and seventh syllable respectively. By contrast, the caesuras in the final couplet both fall after the sixth syllable, the more normal position.

When the four lines are considered as a group, there is a strong rhythmic contrast between the three regular lines and fourth line, the most irregular of the group. The rhythmic tension thus increases in the final line, which coincides with the emotional pitch of the closing triumphant statement. Normally taking stress, the plural and singular variants of the word *lord* are demoted to an offbeat. The two possessive adjectives (*their*, *thy*) must take emphatic stress to make the contrast clear. This rhetorical pattern is reinforced by placing the first two beats next to each other, creating a virtual offbeat at the syntactic break after "say." Finally, the epigrammatic point of the contrast is sharpened by marking the difference between merely building and truly dwelling. The strong poetic closure of this four-line sentence provides a fitting end to this lyric masterpiece.

The poem thus celebrates the satisfaction of bodily needs, the comforts of domestic routine, and the love of family. If the poet glamorizes aristocratic privilege in a historical world that has almost entirely passed away, his delightful image of human thriving still offers a kind of wisdom. Thanks in no small part to their self-conscious artistry, the country house poems of Lanyer and Jonson touch on what continues to matter in our lives here and now. Despite the cultural distance that separates us from seventeenth-century England, the world in which we dwell is not utterly alien to theirs. Standing at a middle distance from our world, just as their world looks back to Rome, their lyric poems still have the power to please, instruct, and move us through their depiction of everyday life in the company of friends and family.

7

The Pastoral Elegy: Milton's "Lycidas"

Our final chapter turns to John Milton's "Lycidas," first published in 1638 and reprinted by the author in the 1645 edition of his collected *Poems*. Although each of the previous chapters offers at least two different poems to illustrate a distinctive lyric kind, the present chapter concentrates on a single poem to represent the subgenre of pastoral elegy. There are good reasons, both qualitative and quantitative, for reserving a whole chapter to this one lyric. Few critics would dispute that "Lycidas" is the greatest pastoral elegy in English. Yet the poem easily sustains an entire chapter not only because of its poetic excellence but also its unusual length. At 193 lines, the elegy is longer than all but one of the lyrics discussed so far and is nearly twice the length of Jonson's "To Penshurst." Lanyer's poem may be slightly longer, but Milton's dense language and his network of poetic allusions—his way of calling to mind centuries of poetic tradition—cry out for sustained commentary.

Although "Lycidas" may seem difficult and strange for twenty-first-century readers, it is a poetic masterpiece that repays the effort to appreciate and understand it. Its technical virtuosity may be unrivaled, but even more important, it explores a topic of universal human significance. How can a great poem help sharpen our understanding of mortality as a part of the human condition? How can a formal elegy help honor the dead and console the living? What resources of language might lead people turn to poetry in response to grief? How might we come to terms with the fact that our time on earth is limited? Does an apparently meaningless death suggest that life itself may be futile? These are some of the big questions that Milton's poem asks.

Pastoral elegy was only one kind of formal elegy available to English and Continental poets in the early modern period.[1] With Milton's "Lycidas" we encounter a poem steeped in poetic conventions that are unfamiliar to most readers today. His elegy poses serious obstacles to a sympathetic reading in the twenty-first century.² In fact, as early as the mid-eighteenth century its pastoral conventions became the target of Samuel Johnson's scathing response to the poem in *The Lives of the Poets* (1759). "Its form," wrote Dr. Johnson, "is that of a pastoral, easy, vulgar, and therefore disgusting." He alleged that the poem's reliance on pastoral convention demonstrates its lack of "real passion."³ Milton's great elegy clearly cannot be appreciated without an understanding of how he revived the ancient conventions of pastoral elegy and took them to new heights. The result is arguably the greatest lyric poem in the English language. Before we locate the poem in the context of Milton's career, and before we glance at the earlier history of pastoral elegy, it is worth pausing to consider how shifts in taste over the years have influenced the reception of Milton's elegy and judgments of its poetic value.

Until recently, generations of critics praised the unrivaled excellence of the poem. Such statements began in the eighteenth century and reached a peak in the mid-twentieth century. Joseph Warton (1752) suggested that if Milton had written nothing but "Lycidas," "L'Allegro," and "Il Penseroso," these would be sufficient "monuments of his genius" to have ensured that "his name had been immortal." William Hazlitt (1815) defended the poem against the criticism of Dr. Johnson: "Of all Milton's smaller poems, *Lycidas* is the greatest favourite with us." After quoting the apostrophe on fame, he exclaims: "If this is art, it is perfect art." Estimates of the poem continued to grow in the nineteenth century. John Ruskin wrote a well-known appreciation in 1865. Mark Pattison (1887) described it as "the high-water mark of English Poesy." Arthur Machen (1907) suggested that it "is probably the most perfect piece of pure literature in existence because every word and phrase and line is sonorous, ringing and echoing with music."⁴

Despite some exceptions—an often-cited essay by John Crowe Ransom being the most famous—twentieth-century critics generally assumed and often expressly stated the greatness of the poem, at least before the decline of evaluative criticism. M. H. Abrams (1983) sums up the received view of the poem's value by calling it "the lyric of lyrics."⁵ From the eighteenth through the mid-twentieth century, then, most commentators viewed "Lycidas" as unequaled in poetic excellence. However, few critics in recent decades have echoed earlier claims about its supreme value.⁶

Knowing something about the earlier history of pastoral elegy adds to our appreciation of Milton's poem. But it also helps to view "Lycidas" in the context of the poet's life and to understand the circumstances of its composition and publication. John Milton (1608–74) is best known to students of English literature as the author of *Paradise Lost*.⁷ He grew up in London, the son of a prosperous scrivener. His father (also named John) devoted significant financial resources to Milton's education. He hired tutors before his son was old enough to enter school, then paid for him to attend St. Paul's School and Cambridge University. He generously supported the young poet for five years of intensive private study after completing his master's degree in 1632. Upon graduation Milton moved into his father's household in Hammersmith, at that time a village near London, before the family relocated to Horton, Buckinghamshire.

Preparing to become a great poet, Milton made himself into a formidable scholar. He read ancient Greek, Latin, and Hebrew, as well as French and Italian. In all of English literature Milton is without doubt the most learned author. During his postgraduate study he completed his reading of virtually all the ancient Latin and Greek literature that was available in his day. He also read widely in French, Italian, and Renaissance Latin literature. The linguistic density and richness of his style, the complexity of his literary allusions, and the demands made by his encyclopedic knowledge all tend to make his poetry intimidating to many modern readers. To a much greater extent than the other poets discussed in this book, Milton demands to be read in an annotated edition. But his learned and allusive style should not blind us to the personal dimension of his poetry. His mother Sara died less than a year after the family moved to Horton in January 1637. When Milton composed "Lycidas" at the end of that year, his grief for his mother was still fresh and doubtless contributed to the emotional intensity of the elegy.[8]

In 1638, the year the poem was published, Milton traveled to Italy to acquire firsthand knowledge of Italian literature and culture and to meet with some of the leading intellectuals of the day. In 1639 while still in Italy he received news of the death of his closest friend, Charles Diodati, whom he had met at Cambridge University. By the end of the year he composed a Latin elegy, "Epitaphium Damonis" in honor of his friend. But the beginning of the Bishops' War (1639–40) soon led him to interrupt his travels. As he was later to write, "I thought it shameful, while my countrymen were fighting for their liberty at home, that I should be peacefully travelling for culture."[9]

Although it is unclear when Milton became a committed antiroyalist, he soon threw himself wholeheartedly into the revolutionary cause. He wrote polemical tracts during the Civil War and served in the republican government following the execution of Charles I in 1649. Milton's political activism, including service as Latin secretary to the government of Oliver Cromwell, led to a two-decade interruption of his lifelong plan to make himself into a great poet. As he famously wrote in 1642, he desired to "leave something so written to aftertimes, as they should not willingly let it die."[10]

By 1652, however, Milton was completely blind. Shortly after the restoration of the monarchy in 1660 he was imprisoned. His safety, even his life, were briefly in danger. Fortunately for students of English literature, he was pardoned, allowing him to rededicate himself to poetry once more. He lived his final years with his third wife, managing to complete two editions of *Paradise Lost* (1667, 1674). He also published *Paradise Regained* (a brief epic about the temptation of Christ) and the tragedy *Samson Agonistes* in late 1670, though the title page gives the following year. His blindness and his struggle against tyranny encouraged him to identify with the blind Israelite hero. He died in November 1674, only a few months after the second edition of *Paradise Lost* was published. With his passing, the last of the great Renaissance humanists in English literature was laid to rest.

For readers coming to "Lycidas" for the first time, a brief summary of its occasion may prove helpful. The earliest witness to the poem (his poetry notebook known as the Trinity MS) contains an added headnote, which states: "In this Monodie the author bewails a lerned friend unfortunately drownd in his passage from Chester on the Irish seas 1637."[11] The poem was composed in November 1637 (the date is crossed out in the manuscript). The "learned friend" was Edward King, an Anglo-Irishman from a prominent family, who was three years younger than Milton. They had met at Christ's College, Cambridge, when King matriculated at the age of fourteen in 1626 during Milton's second year at university. There is no evidence, however, that the two men were ever personally close. Unlike Milton, King became an ordained minister in the Church of England. He was elected a fellow of Christ's College in 1630 and still held the post at the time of his death during a voyage to Ireland, when his ship struck a rock off the Anglesey coast in Wales. His body was lost at sea, a detail that would add to the pathos of the Milton's elegy. King had published ten poems in Latin, which conveniently allowed Milton to draw on the pastoral tradition of lamenting the death of a shepherd-poet.[12]

A group of King's university associates organized a memorial volume, printed in 1638. The first part, whose title in translation reads *Obsequies by mourning friends, in loving memory and remembrance, for Edward King, drowned*, includes twenty-three Greek and Latin poems. The second part of the volume includes thirteen poems in English, printed after a separate title page: "Obsequies to the memorie of Mr. Edward King, Anno Dom. 1638." "Lycidas," the longest English poem, appears last and is signed "J.M."[13] Nothing is known about how the book came to be assembled or whose idea it was to invite Milton to contribute.

Although Milton had written poetry since his student days, he had only published two poems in English at this stage of his career—a short poem on Shakespeare for the Second Folio edition (1632) and *A Maske Presented at Ludlow Castle* (known as *Comus*), which had been performed three years earlier and was printed in the month of King's death.[14] "Lycidas" was published two more times during Milton's lifetime: as the final poem in *Poems of Mr. John Milton, Both English and Latin* (London, 1645, actually published in January 1646), and in the second edition of his collected poems (1673). When the poem was printed in 1645 during the Civil War, Milton inserted the one-sentence epigraph from his manuscript, adding the following sentence: "And by occasion foretells the ruine of our corrupted Clergie then in their height." The primary reference of the new sentence is to the execution of William Laud, the royalist archbishop of Canterbury, in January 1645. Writing during the Civil War, Milton retrospectively placed himself in the role of a divinely inspired prophet whose powers had been confirmed by later events.

Although pastoral elegy had been much in vogue in sixteenth-century English and Continental poetry, by the time Milton composed "Lycidas" this was no longer the case. To encounter a pastoral elegy at the end of the volume would have come as a bit of a shock to readers in the fourth decade of the seventeenth century. On the other hand, Milton in his twenty-ninth year was drawn to the form because it implicitly announced his intention to follow in the footsteps of Vergil. Like Spenser before him, Milton imitated the greatest Roman poet, who began his poetic career with pastoral as preparation for writing an epic.[15] Pastoral elegy, moreover, was a genre that explored the topic of poetry and its place in the world. For a relatively young writer who was as self-conscious about his poetic career as Milton, the form held an irresistible attraction.[16]

Since Milton's immediate audience consisted primarily of other classically trained readers like himself, he expected them to recognize his many borrowings from the pastoral tradition. Indeed, virtually every line of the poem contains verbal echoes of earlier poetry.[17] Literary historians trace the beginnings of pastoral poetry to the *Idylls* of Theocritus (c. 310–250 BCE), a Sicilian Greek poet based in Alexandria during the Hellenistic age. Theocritus's bucolics (the label refers to fictional speakers who are herdsmen) are composed in dactylic hexameters, the meter used by epic poets, though Theocritus's poetry was "a conscious reduction of Homeric verse to the felt range and possibilities of poetry in a post-heroic, cosmopolitan world."[18] From its origins, then, pastoral poetry was urbane and sophisticated, with a high degree of literary self-consciousness. William Empson famously defined "the pastoral process" as "putting the complex into the simple."[19] If Theocritus inaugurated this mode of writing, Vergil took pastoral to new heights in his first major work, a collection of ten poems known as the *Eclogues*, written in imitation of Theocritus.[20]

Although a detailed account of the history of pastoral elegy would be out of place, a brief sketch of the tradition may explain some puzzling features of the elegy.[21] The first *Idyll* of Theocritus initiates the convention of a shepherd singing a dirge in memory of a fellow shepherd-singer. Thyrsis is asked by a goatherd to sing of Daphnis, the son of the god Hermes and a nymph. Daphnis had won the love of the most beautiful nymph and boasted of his ability to resist any new love. This hubris proved to be his undoing when Love (Eros) overpowered him with a new passion. The shepherd preferred death to being unfaithful. Thyrsis begins his song by asking, "Where, ah! where were ye when Daphnis was languishing; ye Nymphs, where were ye?"[22] This rhetorical gesture begins the pastoral convention of questioning divinities who failed to prevent the shepherd's untimely death.[23]

The first *Idyll* also employs the "pathetic fallacy" (the idea that nature sympathetically responds to human loss) when the animals of the forest lament. As Daphnis languishes, a procession of gods and herdsmen arrives on the scene. The only one to whom Daphnis responds is the goddess of love, Cypris (Aphrodite), who reminds him of his ill-considered boast. He responds in frustration, bidding farewell to the forces of nature, including Arethusa (the same Sicilian river that Milton will address by name in his poem). Daphnis cries out: "'Ye wolves, ye jackals, and ye bears in the mountain caves, farewell! The herdsman Daphnis ye never shall see again, no more in the dells, no more in the groves, no more in the woodlands. Farewell Arethusa, ye rivers, good-night, that pour down Thymbris your beautiful waters'" (19). Daphnis reminds Cypris of her love affairs with mortals and alludes to the death of Adonis, Aphrodite's favorite, whose fatal encounter with a boar has yet to take place. With this figure Theocritus evidently draws on ancient fertility rituals associated with the myth of a dying vegetation god.[24]

Sensing that his death draws near, Daphnis bequeaths his "fair pipe, honey-breathed with wax-stopped joints" to the god Pan before calling for violets and "fair narcissus" to bloom in remembrance (20). Tragically, not even Aphrodite has the power to save the dying shepherd, whose corpse floats downstream until "[t]he whirling wave closed over the man the Muses loved" (21). With his song complete, Thyrsis is awarded a beautifully decorated bowl promised by the goatherd as reward for singing his celebrated "Affliction of Daphnis." Thus the death of the ideal shepherd-singer becomes the occasion of an exchange of aesthetic artifacts, both handiwork and song, that substitute for the lost shepherd. By staging the poem as a dramatic dialogue between Thyrsis and the goatherd, Theocritus invented a new poetic form that builds into its design the expression of communal grief.

The death of Adonis alluded to by Theocritus became the subject of "The Lament for Adonis" (*Idyll* 1), an elegy attributed to Bion, who is thought to have died c. 300 BCE, though he may have lived two centuries later. (Students of English Romanticism will recognize that "Adonais," the title of Shelley's elegy for Keats, derives from this work.) Bion's poem, not strictly speaking a pastoral elegy since it does not concern herdsmen, imagines the dead Adonis lying on his funeral bier. He is visited by a procession of mourners, including Echo, Eros, and Cytherea (Aphrodite). The flower imagery that made a brief appearance in *Idyll* 1 of Theocritus now becomes part of an elaborate funeral ritual. Bion writes: "Ah, even in death he is beautiful, beautiful in death, as one that hath fallen on sleep. Now lay him down to sleep in his own soft coverlets ... though sad he is to look upon. Cast on him garlands and blossoms: all things have perished in his death, yea all the flowers are faded" (24).

The genre of funeral elegy was soon transformed in "The Lament for Bion," traditionally attributed to Moschus.[25] This is the first pastoral elegy written in response to the death of a historical poet. It is also the first time the singer of the lament takes up the poetic mantle of the dead poet. The singer explains that he is "no stranger to the pastoral song, but heir of the Doric Muse which thou didst teach thy pupils. This was thy gift to me; to others didst thou leave thy wealth, to me thy minstrelsy" (29). The poem opens by calling on the woods and waters, the flowers and birds, to mourn Bion. As the elegy proceeds, the gods join in the general lamentation. Even towns associated with individually named Greek poets, including Sappho and Theocritus, join in grieving Bion's passing. The singer holds out the possibility of new life to the dead poet. Persephone, the queen of Hades, will allow him to return to his familiar landscape as she did the legendary poet Orpheus: "as once to Orpheus's sweet minstrelsy she gave Eurydice to return with him, even so will she send thee too, Bion, to the hills" (30). The myth of Orpheus, as we shall see, plays an important role in Milton's poem.

When the Roman poet Vergil (70–19 BCE) breathed new life into the form, he raised pastoral to a dignity and resonance that would prove highly influential throughout the Renaissance and beyond.[26] Vergil composed the *Eclogues*, his first major work, between the years 42 and 37 BCE. In other words, the collection was created during the civil war that eventually ended the Roman Republic. Octavian (the poet's future patron) was to emerge victorious after the battle of Actium in 31, when he took the title of Caesar Augustus. Vergil incorporated allusions to contemporary politics into the pastoral mode, a move destined to prove influential during the Renaissance.

Two of Vergil's eclogues are especially relevant to understanding "Lycidas." *Eclogue* 5 adapts Theocritus's first idyll by returning to the theme of grieving for Daphnis. From the time of the Latin grammarian Servius, the traditional view is that Vergil's Daphnis allegorically represents the recently deified Julius Caesar.[27] Vergil's poem takes the form of a poetic dialogue between two shepherds, Menalcas and his younger companion Mopsus. In Mopsus's song, the death of Daphnis has damaged nature. The singer calls for a tomb to be engraved with an epitaph voiced by the dead shepherd.

The polished style, rhetorical balance, and musicality of the Latin verse are typical of Vergil's art, though these effects cannot be reproduced in translation: "Instead of the soft violet and purple narcissus, only the thistle and thorn bush with sharp needles arise. Scatter the earth with leaves, O shepherds, and shade the springs—Daphnis commands such things to be done for him—and build a tomb and place these verses on it: 'I was Daphnis in the forest, known from here to the very stars; I was the guardian of the beautiful flock and was even more beautiful myself.'"[28] Through the dramatic dialogue between the two grieving shepherds, Vergil takes up a public mood of grief for the dead companion, a poetic mode begun by Theocritus.

Menalcas responds with praise for his companion's consoling song before announcing: "I shall raise Daphnis to the stars, because Daphnis loved me, too" (5.52). The older shepherd imagines Daphnis becoming godlike through the process known as apotheosis. Daphnis stands radiant at the threshold of Olympus, gazing in wonder at the clouds and stars beneath his feet. Menalcas vows to institute an annual ceremony in honor of Daphnis: "These rites will always be performed for you, when we offer our solemn vows to the nymphs and purify our fields. For as long as the wild boar loves the mountain ridges, fish love the rivers, the bees feed on thyme and cicadas on the dew, your honors, name, and praises shall endure forever" (5.74–78). It would be unbearable to imagine the world without a living memorial to his departed friend. The eclogue concludes with the exchange of gifts by the two shepherd-singers. Menalcas receives a decorated sheep-crook from Mopsus in exchange for his reed pipe, emblems of herding and singing, the activities they shared with their former companion. The mourners thus preserve the memory of their dead friend and offer themselves and their ceremony as substitutions.[29]

The other eclogue of Vergil that is closely connected with "Lycidas," especially in narrative structure, is the tenth. The final poem of the series is written in honor of Vergil's friend, the solder, statesman, and poet C. Cornelius Gallus. At the core of *Eclogue* 10 is a love lament in the voice of Gallus. He is an Arcadian shepherd who is also under the sway of "mad love" for Mars (10.44), in a nod to the historical Gallus's military service. Vergil creates an external frame for the eclogue, a device Milton imitates in the final eight lines of "Lycidas." In the first eight lines Vergil fuses his own voice with that of the persona of his shepherd-singer. He calls on Arethusa as his muse to assist him in this "final labor" (1), a song "for my Gallus, but which Lycoris herself may read" (2). "Begin," he prays, "let us tell the anxious loves of Gallus" (6). The opening frame suggests a poet in his full power: "We do not sing to the deaf: all the woods resound" (8). Vergil returns to the external frame in the final eight lines of the poem, which symmetrically mirrors the opening. He announces to the goddesses (Muses) that "these lines will be enough for your poet to have sung" (70). As the shadows lengthen and the evening star appears, the shepherd-poet arises and calls on his goats to return with him to the safety of home.

The main body of the poem begins by questioning the Naiads (water nymphs) where they were when Gallus was "suffering for an unworthy love" (9–10). The other shepherds and the natural beings respond sympathetically to his grief at being abandoned by Lycoris. Even Apollo, patron god of singers, and the woodland deity Pan arrive to express their concern. Eventually, Gallus himself replies in his own voice, imagining his consolation after death if his memory is kept alive by the other shepherds: "But that mournful man said, 'Yet you will sing, Arcadians, these verses to your mountains, Aracadians who alone are expert at singing. O how softly my bones would rest then if your reed pipe might tell of my suffering in love once upon a time'" (31–34).

After expressing his concern for the well-being of his unfaithful mistress, he resigns himself to the inevitability of his fate as an unhappy lover: "Love conquers all: let even us yield to Love" (69). To an even greater extent than the writers whose pastoral elegies he imitated, Vergil demonstrates the value of this lyrical form for expressing grief while celebrating the power of human fellowship.

The moods expressed in pastoral elegy are thus public and shared. Poetry that uses shepherds to speak about the general human condition may seem highly artificial and even distasteful to modern readers. Yet this effect is deliberate. Pastoral poems wear their artifice on their sleeves. In dramatizing the desire to reach out to others during times of loss and grief, pastoral poetry seeks to distil in memorable, persuasive language an understanding of human community.

Although I have focused on the tradition of pastoral elegy in Greek and Latin poetry, readers of "Lycidas" should also be aware of at least one later development.[30] In the Renaissance, starting with Petrarch and Boccaccio and followed by Mantuan, pastoral poets began to imitate Vergil's disguised references to contemporary politics. Milton's denouncing of the corrupt clergy in a notorious passage (lines 108–31) is not a digression (as many earlier critics believed) but instead draws on a recognizable convention.[31] Milton follows other Renaissance poets who used pastoral for satire against clerical corruption and the present state of the church.[32] We may now turn to the complex formal structure of "Lycidas" and some of the problems it has raised for criticism.

The gradual appreciation of the intricate design of "Lycidas" was one of the triumphs of mid- to late-twentieth century criticism of the poem. Dr. Johnson had condemned the poem not only because he thought pastoral conventions were a poor substitute for genuine emotion. He also thought the poem was poorly crafted from a technical point of view. Johnson wrote: "the diction is harsh, the rhymes uncertain, and the numbers," that is, the meter, "unpleasing."[33] It is no accident that one of the first twentieth-century critics to write about the elegy's formal technique was the New Critic John Crowe Ransom.[34] His provocative essay helped stimulate other critics to take issue with his account, and many responded with new evidence for the unrivaled artistry of the poem.

To appreciate the Milton's craftsmanship, it is best to begin with basic matters of external form. Most of the 193 lines are ten syllables long (decasyllabic). There are also thirteen shorter lines of six syllables. Although there are exceptions, most of the decasyllabic lines take five beats (iambic pentameter). The poem divides into eleven verse paragraphs of differing lengths and rhyme patterns. The paragraphs correspond with major divisions in the argument. The short lines always rhyme with one of the preceding verses. In all but four cases they rhyme with the long line immediately before the short one.[35] Ten lines, however, are unrhymed.[36] The final eight-line verse paragraph creates a perfect stanza rhyming *ababbcc*. This stanza goes by the Italian name *ottava rima* (Chaucer was the first to use the form in English). All these formal features show that Milton wanted his readers to pay close attention to how he arranges language and to notice when he violates their expectations.

As for the so-called inner form of the poem, the analysis of Arthur Barker has proven to be highly influential over the years. He identified a pastoral introduction and conclusion that frame the main body of the poem. He then divided the body into "three movements, practically equal in length and precisely parallel in pattern." The first two movements, according to Barker, voice laments for Lycidas, first in his role as poet-shepherd and then as priest-shepherd. In each section a specific problem is identified and temporarily resolved. The third movement resolves the poem as a whole with the apotheosis of Lycidas. The return to the pastoral frame in the conclusion creates a "calm finality" that is "achieved through the resolution of emotional conflicts."[37] Many readers have found that Barker's brief analysis of the poem's complex structure helps them follow the argument. I will follow his lead to organize my own reading of the poem.

By referring to the *argument* of the poem, I mean to highlight its relation to the Renaissance art of rhetoric. Traditional rhetorical doctrine recognized that the art of persuasion could be used to console mourners and to encourage them to accept loss and avoid excessive grief. *The Arte of Rhetorique* (1560) of Thomas Wilson, for example, offered general precepts on how "grief might be assuaged, and the passions of man brought under the obedience of reason. The use hereof is great as well in private troubles, as in common miseries."[38] It is striking how many of the commonplaces that Wilson rehearses—some borrowed from classical culture and others based on Christian faith—remain in use today. It is God's will, which must be patiently endured; the departed have gone to a better place; their short lives were a blessing, etc. But in the hands of a skilled poet, an elegy could provide a powerful vehicle for offering sympathy and assuaging grief, for turning the commonplaces of consolation into the highest form of verbal art.

As Milton signals in his headnote, his poem is a "monody" in which "the author bewails" his friend. George Puttenham provides a convenient definition of this technical term in his discussion of ancient funeral practices, explaining that they included "poetical mournings in verse. Such funeral songs were called *epicedia* if they were sung by many, and *monodia* if they were uttered by one alone."[39] Renaissance theories of poetry that expresses private or public grief viewed it from both a rhetorical and a medicinal standpoint. As Puttenham explains, the poet must "play also the physician, and not only by applying a medicine to the ordinary sickness of mankind, but by making the very grief itself (in part) cure of the disease." Similarly, Scaliger observes: "A discourse of consolation restores the mind of the mourner to tranquility." However, for it to prove therapeutically effective "it can proceed only from a friend," who shares the same sorrow: "we are better able to persuade a listener to quiet his grief if he sees us, too, bear it with equinamity."[40]

Yet unlike a friend's consoling words, elegiac poetry occupies a more public space for an audience that stands at some distance from the original speaker. A successful poetic meditation on death may continue to offer effective consolation long after both the poet and the bereaved have turned to dust. Rosamund Tuve recognizes the continuing persuasive power of "Lycidas" as "the most poignant and controlled statement in English poetry of the acceptance of that in the human condition which seems to man unacceptable."[41] Thomas Wilson attempts to console by evoking a religious commonplace: "GOD hath ordeined all to dye, according to his appointed will."[42] By contrast, Milton persuades his readers by inventing new ways of drawing on rhetorical commonplaces and pastoral form.

If "Lycidas" may be understood as an exceptionally skillful rhetorical performance meant to persuade the reader to accept the troubling fact of a particular death, the poem may also be understood (to evoke once again the traditional categories discussed by M. H. Abrams) in both mimetic and expressive terms. In fact, the poem defies easy categorization, a feature that led to some notable critical debates. On the one hand, the epigraph seems to point to an *expressive* theory—we are invited to read the poem as the expression of John Milton's (or J.M.'s) grief when we read the statement "In this Monody the author bewails a learned friend." Despite Dr. Johnson's belief that the pastoral mode is too artificial to provide a convincing vehicle for real "passion," there is no good reason to doubt that Milton joined the other contributors to the memorial volume in expressing his personal sadness at King's untimely death. Nor is there any reason to doubt that Milton was expressing personal anxieties about the possibility of a premature death before he could answer his true calling as a poet, an interpretation first proposed by E. M. W. Tillyard.[43]

Although both rhetorical and expressive theories shed light on "Lycidas," a mimetic theory of poetry allows another important aspect of the poem to stand out. By drawing on the conventions of pastoral elegy, the poem seems to represent the thoughts and speech of a fictional shepherd speaking to other shepherds, although this identity is only gradually revealed. The poem seems to imitate a mind disturbed by a shocking death and then resolving its mental anguish. During the period when New Criticism enjoyed its greatest influence, the most common way to read "Lycidas" (and indeed all lyrics) was as a dramatic utterance by a fictional persona. The first-person speaker must not to be identified with the poet, New Critics believed. M. H. Abrams clearly articulates this principle when he rejects Tillyard's notion that the poem takes Milton's fear of premature death as its true subject. We simply cannot know "what Milton himself thought and felt," Abrams insists. "But we know precisely what the uncouth swain thought and felt, because the expression of his thoughts and feelings constitutes the poem."[44]

However, even by New Critical assumptions, the situation is more complicated than a straightforward expression of the swain's thoughts and emotions. The pastoral singer is interrupted by other dramatic voices (Phoebus Apollo and St. Peter) during the course of his lament. The intrusion of other voices seems at first blush to contradict the received idea of monody.[45] However, the normal New Critical reading was untroubled by the representation of Apollo and St. Peter as speakers in the fictional world of the poem who interrupt the swain's song.[46] A few critics suggested that these alien voices represent either an inner dialogue within the fictional speaker himself, or what could be viewed as aspects of his own self-doubt, fear, moral outrage, etc.[47] However we interpret these voices, most critics agree that the closing eight lines unexpectedly introduce a new narrative voice. This final voice identifies the "uncouth swain" in the third-person (line 186), announces the end of the shepherd's song, and describes his calm state of mind as he returns home at the end of the day.

In one of the most subtle essays on the poem, Paul Alpers draws on the history of pastoral literature to argue that the poem significantly revises the conventions of representing the speaker as a shepherd. His account of the speaker, in fact, pushes mimetic theory to its limit. Alpers insists on "the unusual openness and flexibility of the speaker of this poem" and the speaker's "identification with things real, remembered, and imagined."[48] According to Alpers, "Lycidas," unlike earlier pastoral elegies, does not represent any "gathering of shepherds to lament their dead fellow." This omission "makes the poem less predictable and rule-governed than earlier pastoral elegies, but the effect is to enhance the depth and energy with which it reveals the significance of their conventions."[49] His point seems to be that the mimesis of the speaker's presence in the poem is inseparable from, or vanishes into, the textuality of the poem.

For convenience I shall follow the critical convention of referring to the "speaker" or "singer" of the poem. Yet we should not understand this figure (the "uncouth swain") as a fictional persona who is fully distinct from the narrative voice that seems to emerge in the final verse paragraph. Nor should we understand the speaker as a coherent fictional character who stands at a specific distance from the historical poet, John Milton, in 1637, 1645, or 1673. Instead, the principle speaker and the other voices we think we "hear" in the poem are best understood as figures of *lyric voicing*. There is no need to assume that such voicing requires a unified self (real or fictional). In other words, the poem weaves together in writing, or encodes, textual signs of subjectivity.[50] Perhaps more than any of the lyrics we have studied so far, "Lycidas" demands to be understood as an act of writing that ultimately challenges both the notion of imitation and the belief in a stable difference between speech and writing. To put the matter another way, "Lycidas" demonstrates the limits of mimetic, rhetorical, expressive, and objective (formalist) theories of poetry. Whether taken in isolation or in combination, the traditional theories fall short of grasping the poem in its entirety.

Whether read as a fictional imitation of the "uncouth swain's" grief or as an expression of the author's inner experience, or something else altogether, "Lycidas" registers in language of unrivaled intensity an imaginative response to an encounter with the sudden death of another. Facing such a death triggers what we would now describe as an existential crisis. The speaker (if there is one) asks searching questions about the meaning of life, friendship, the ideal ordering of society, the suffering of the innocent, and the apparent prosperity of corrupt and powerful men. The poem asks what these worldly concerns indicate about the workings of nature and of nature's God and the ultimate destiny of the soul. In short, the poem takes on grand themes that are of enduring human interest. By the time the poem ends, the crisis has been overcome. Possessed of a new sense of calm, the speaker projects himself into an uncertain future, choosing to lead his life with a newly found meaning and purpose.[51]

The first fourteen lines provide an introductory statement of the occasion of writing and the problem to be addressed. We may begin with the resonant first sentence:

> Yet once more, O ye laurels, and once more
> Ye myrtles brown, with ivy never sere,   *i.e., evergreen*
> I come to pluck your berries harsh and crude,
> And with forced fingers rude,
> Shatter your leaves before the mellowing year [1–5].[52]

The repeated *once more* seems to cast us in the middle of things (*in medias res*). A temporal process has already begun, but what that process may be or when it began remain unspecified. The opening lines create effects of lyric presence in a number of ways. The play of deixis gives us the first-person pronoun and simple present tense verb. The apostrophe to the plants traditionally associated with the poet's garland forms a vivid image before our eyes. The repeated patterns of sound in the rhyme, alliteration, and meter wash over us. All these stylistic devices carve out a strong sense of presence. The poem seeks to be an event more than the representation of one.[53]

Yet the unexpected rhythm of the first line signals to an alert reader the lyric singer's sense of disturbance from the beginning:

> Yet once more, O ye laurels, and once more
> B   o   B [o]B o   B o   b   o   B

Milton, one of the greatest masters of poetic meter, often takes unusual liberties, sometimes pushing the standard iambic pentameter line nearly to the breaking point. I scan the first verse as a six-beat line. A virtual offbeat after the third syllable and a promoted beat on the eighth syllable add further tension to the unrhymed initial line.[54] The next two lines, however, are close to perfectly regular iambic pentameter, and they introduce the first two rhyme sounds (though the reader cannot know this yet). But the rest of the first sentence uses increasingly violent language (*pluck, forced, shatter*) to suggest that there is something disturbing about the act of composing poetry prematurely, "before the mellowing year."

The next lines reveal the reason for the disturbance, naming it as such while intensifying the verbal repetition and alliteration (hard *c* and *d*):

> Bitter constraint, and sad occasion dear   *heartfelt*
> Compels me to disturb your season due:
> For Lycidas is dead, dead ere his prime,
> Young Lycidas, and hath not left his peer.
> 10 Who would not sing for Lycidas? He knew
> Himself to sing, and build the lofty rhyme [6–11].

The announcement of the shepherd's name in connection with his premature death in line eight is attended by metrical and rhetorical exactitude. Rhetorical doctrine taught that repeating the same word or phrase in immediate succession (the figure of speech called *epizeuxis*) heightens the expression of vehemence.[55] The implied offbeat also contributes to the effect of pathos:

> For Lycidas is dead, dead ere his prime
> o B o b o B [o]B   o-o   B

The threefold repetition of the name of the dead poet-shepherd adds further intensity to the emotional effect (the dead man's name alone strongly suggests that he was a shepherd). There may be some further tension implied in the juxtaposition of singing and building. The verb *sing* represents poetry as a fleeting oral performance. However, the architectural metaphor of *build* suggests a monumental construction. Writing creates a solid presence more enduring than an airy song.

The three lines that conclude the first verse paragraph focus our imagination on the horrifying state of the unburied corpse for the first time: "He must not float upon his watery bier / Unwept, and welter [*be tossed*] to the parching wind, / Without the meed [*reward*] of some melodious tear" (12–14). Abandoning the corpse to its dismal fate without a suitable response from the living seems unbearable. Again, the sound quality of the lines contributes to the presence effect. With their almost perfect metrical regularity, the lines convey a sense of resolve. The enjambment after the first line that delays the pause until after the word *unwept* adds to the expression of determination. Consonants formed by the lips (labials) predominate as the plaintive initial *w* appears five times and the *m* alliterates in the last line. The rhyme pair *bier/tear* connects the singer's emotional response with the location he imagines for the corpse.[56]

Although we are now fourteen lines into the poem, the next paragraph marks a new beginning with a formal invocation to the Muses ("sisters") who are placed by tradition beside the well of Aganippe on Mount Helicon. The invocation invites the reader to imagine the poem as a kind of ritual performance on an ancient lyre: "Begin, then, sisters of the sacred well, /

That from beneath the seat of Jove doth spring, / Begin, and somewhat loudly sweep the string" (15–17). The hint of ceremony anticipates the imitation of a funeral procession later in the poem. In calling for poetic inspiration, the singer implores the Muses to play upon the lyre, a request that suggests a metaphor for the poet himself, who would be their instrument.

Soon the speaker projects his imagination into the future, after his own death and funeral (19–22). He hopes that if he successfully completes his solemn poetic task, another poet may remember him at some future date and *turn* (as the short line itself turns) to say a prayer at his grave, just as the present singer now would *bid fair peace* for Lycidas. We cannot miss the parallel between Lycidas and the singer, and thus King and Milton. The final couplet clarifies the nature of the singer's relationship with the dead shepherd: "For we were nursed upon the self-same hill, / Fed the same flock, by fountain, shade, and rill" (23–24). In recalling the bonds of affection that grew from their shared childhood experience, the couplet softens the previously *harsh and crude* music of the verse, especially with the liquid consonant of the rhyme (*hill/rill*), the alliteration on the spirant *f* and the assonance of the repeated vowel in *same/shade*. The vowel repeats the sound in *sable* but now places it in a more idealized pastoral setting, anticipating the nostalgic mood of recalling bygone days in the next paragraph.

The following passage was greatly deplored by Dr. Johnson, who insisted: "Passion plucks no berries from the myrtle and ivy, nor calls upon Arethuse and Mincius, nor tells of rough *satyrs* and *fauns with cloven heel*. Where there is leisure for fiction there is little grief."[57] But the passage serves a necessary function in the poetic economy of pastoral elegy. Instead of the unnatural disturbance of seasons constrained by *sad occasion* in the first paragraph, we now find the typical course of a natural day representing the pastoral way of life.

The idealized picture of peaceful leisure (rural *otium*) pursued from dawn to midday to evening provides a coherent image that may be taken in at once:

25	Together both, ere the high lawns appeared	*open spaces*
	Under the opening eye-lids of the morn,	
	We drove a-field, and both together heard	
	What time the grey-fly winds her sultry horn,	*The time when*
	Battening our flocks with the fresh dews of night,	*fattening*
30	Oft till the star that rose, at evening, bright,	*evening star*
	Toward heaven's descent had sloped his westering wheel.	*its*
	Meanwhile the rural ditties were not mute,	
	Tempered to the oaten flute,	
	Rough satyrs danced, and fauns with cloven heel,	
35	From the glad sound would not be absent long,	
	And old Damaetas loved to hear our song [25–36].[58]	

The speaker and Lycidas are clearly identified as shepherds "battening our flocks." By the time old Damaetus appears, the boys' pastoral identity as shepherd-singers is confirmed: "he loved to hear our song."[59] The description of the idyllic life enjoyed by the speaker and Lycidas is meant to charm us. Their social interactions are framed by time passing from morning to evening, placing human activity within a daily natural cycle that reemerges to such powerful effect at the end of the poem.

The next paragraph marks a major transition in mood, abruptly returning us to the anguish of the present after the gentle recollection of youthful memories. The first thing to notice is the shift in pronouns. For the first time the singer directly addresses the dead Lycidas in the second person. Once more we encounter a powerful instance of Jonathan Culler's master-trope of lyric, apostrophe:

> But O the heavy change, now thou art gone,
> Now thou art gone, and never must return!
> Thee shepherd, thee the woods, and desert caves,
> 40 With wild thyme and the gadding vine o'ergrown,   *wandering*
> And all their echoes mourn [37–41].

The paragraph goes on to describe how the woods and flowers mourn, an instance of the pathetic fallacy loosely modeled after the "Lament for Bion," where the groves lament the poet-shepherd's death.[60] The verbal repetitions in the first three lines quoted above again heighten the pathos, and the images of natural devastation produce a feeling of lush presence and painful loss. The violation of natural word order (hyperbaton) carefully interweaves Lycidas into the sentence and the landscape. He is kept present by the syntactic device of rearranging words and delaying for as long as possible the verb *mourn* as if to ward off the pain by magic. Natural word order would place the subject of the sentence first, followed by the verb and the object (*all their echoes mourn thee, shepherd*).

We know that the effect of this word order is deliberate because in the 1638 print the word *shepherd* was plural. Milton corrected it in later editions to correspond with the reading of the Trinity MS, which gives the word in the singular. The 1638 reading, *thee shepherds*, makes them the first mourners.[61] The corrected reading thus delays the first direct address to the shepherds as a group until line 165, at a crucial moment in the poem. The passage about nature mourning quoted above, moreover, illustrates Milton's tendency to load his style with adjectives.[62] Here the adjectives strengthen the contrast between abundance and lack. The paragraph closes by defining the greatest loss as the breaking of human community. Death has silenced Lycidas's song, which shall never be heard again by *shepherd's ear*.

Now that the consequences of a particular death have been brought to light, the next verse paragraph imitates the pastoral convention (initiated by Theocritus) of questioning the divinities who failed to prevent the shepherd's untimely death:

50	Where were ye nymphs when the remorseless deep	
	Closed o'er the head of your loved Lycidas?	
	For neither were ye playing on the steep,	*i.e., slope*
	Where your old bards, the famous Druids, lie,	
	Nor on the shaggy top of Mona high,	*Anglesey*
55	Nor yet where Deva spreads her wizard stream:	*River Dee*
	Ay me, I fondly dream!	*foolishly*
	Had ye been there—for what could that have done?	
	What could the muse herself that Orpheus bore,	*Calliope*
	The muse herself for her enchanting son	
60	Whom universal nature did lament,	
	When by the rout that made the hideous roar,	*i.e., Bacchantes*
	His gory visage down the stream was sent,	
	Down the swift Hebrus to the Lesbian shore [50–63].	*Greek river; of Lesbos*

The singer's emotional distress is effectively conveyed by the agitated meter of the first two lines:

> Where were ye nymphs when the remorseless deep
> o b o B   o   b o B   o B
> b   o-o   B   ô b o-o   B   o B
>
> Closed o'er the head of your loved Lycidas?
> B   o-o   B   o-o   B ô B o b

After pushing iambic pentameter nearly to the breaking point, the poet follows with four lines of almost perfectly regular meter, coinciding with the lyric speaker's lulling himself into the dreamlike state of imaging that rescue was possible. The effect of emotional agitation is enhanced by the breakdown in syntax in line 57, where the grammatical structure is interrupted and the thought left incomplete (a device known as anacoluthon).

Milton draws on native and classical mythology in this remarkable passage, which he devoted considerable effort to revising in manuscript.[63] Since King died off the coast of Anglesey in Wales, Milton alludes to the Welsh landscape and its association with poet-priests (bards and druids). At the same time, he draws on the myth of Orpheus, son of Calliope, the muse of epic poetry. Orpheus was the greatest of legendary poet-musicians, who famously charmed the wild beasts, trees, and even the rocks with his lyre. He almost managed to rescue his wife Eurydice from Hades until he lost her again by looking back. The myth was most fully recorded by Ovid (*Metamorphoses* 11.1–66), who narrates how the lyric poet in his grief abandoned the company of women and was dismembered for this slight by the frenzied female followers of Bacchus. His head floated down the Hebrus until it reached the island of Lesbos, home of early Greek lyric poets including Alcaeus and Sappho. The connection of Orpheus and King in their shared watery deaths is thus no accident. We have already seen that Orpheus was incorporated into the tradition of pastoral elegy and associated with death and rebirth in the "Lament for Bion." Milton will draw on these associations of death and rebirth in the powerful closing movement of the poem.[64]

Recognizing that his wish for a miraculous rescue is a vain fantasy leads the dismayed singer to question what his friend's death suggests about his own future. Milton finds that his doubts about the value of pursuing the poetic vocation may be expressed most effectively in language drawn directly from Vergil:

	Alas! What boots it with uncessant care	*profits/avails*
65	To tend the homely slighted shepherd's trade,	*simple; disdained*
	And strictly meditate the thankless muse?	*i.e., to be devoted to poetry*
	Were it not better done as others use,	*are wont*
	To sport with Amaryllis in the shade,	
	Or with the tangles of Neaera's hair? [64–69].	

These lines frankly ask whether the sacrifices required of the poet are truly worth the effort. The shepherd-singer's way of life is *slighted* by the world—either looked on with indifference or actively despised. Milton's striking Latinate description of the act of writing poetry as "meditating the muse" echoes Vergil's *musam meditaris* in *Eclogue* 1.2.[65] The close imitation of Vergil's phrase, in fact, enacts what it describes. The line is the product of long meditation on poetry. The speaker ponders the alternative, wondering aloud whether it might not be preferable to abandon the hard road of poetry to settle for an easier life of sensual pleasure.

His initial answer to the question offers a conventional justification for the painstaking effort required to make poetry:

70	Fame is the spur that the clear spirit doth raise	*noble/pure*
	(That last infirmity of noble mind)	
	To scorn delights, and live laborious days;	
	But the fair guerdon when we hope to find,	*reward*
	And think to burst out into sudden blaze,	
75	Comes the blind Fury with th'abhorred shears,	
	And slits the thin-spun life[66] [70–76].	

Although fame is identified as the motivation of a *clear spirit* or *noble mind*, the pursuit of fame is also described in pejorative terms (*infirmity*). More distressing still, Lycidas's untimely death suggests that a similar fate may await the speaker. Indeed, by implication a comparable misfortune could happen to any reader who might suffer a premature death before completing the projects that give meaning to an individual life. The unsettling image used here alludes to the classical myth of the three Fates who spin, measure out, and cut the thread of each individual human life. Milton deliberately conflates Atropos, the third Fate, with a Fury, a figure of vengeance, whom he makes blind, all to intensify the expression of dismay.

Additional distress is conveyed by syntactic inversions (hyperbaton). The object (*guerdon*) of the verb *find* is moved ahead of the conjunction *when*: "But the fair guerdon when we hope to find." The verb is placed before the subject in "Comes the blind Fury." The initial beat on *Comes* works in concert with the word order to add shock to the line, which probably should be read as including an emphatic six beats:

    Comes the blind Fury with th'abhorred shears
     B   o B ô B o b   o   B o B

Although other scansions are possible, the expressive tension of the meter conveys an emotional disturbance. By this point it seems clear that the fear of death triggered by the sudden loss of his younger friend leads Milton to voice anxiety and dread in what sounds remarkably like an existential crisis (though the seventeenth century obviously could not describe it in those terms). In short, the fact of mortality calls into question the meaning of life.

The expression of the singer's despair is not allowed to resonate even for the length of a verse. Midway through the line another voice unexpectedly breaks in to offer a potential solution to the poet's dilemma. The young poet's life may indeed be cut off, the voice concedes,

But not the praise,	
Phoebus replied, and touched my trembling ears;	*Apollo*
Fame is no plant that grows on mortal soil,	
Nor in the glistering foil	*glittering jewelers' foil*
80 Set off to the world, nor in broad rumour lies,	
But lives and spreads aloft by those pure eyes,	*near/in presence of*
And perfect witness of all-judging Jove;	
As he pronounces lastly on each deed,	
Of so much fame in heaven expect thy meed[67] [76–84].	*reward*

Phoebus Apollo in his role as the god of music and poetry defines true fame as a heavenly (not earthly) reward, the result not of human but of divine judgment.

Yet the past tense of *replied* is unexpected and may cause the attentive reader some confusion. At least for the moment, the speaker is represented not as questioning the value of a poetic vocation in the present tense of the discourse that has predominated until now, but as reporting some earlier, unspecified occasion of anxious lamentation when another voice suddenly chimed in.[68] This shift of verb tense, in fact, creates narrative distance in a way that anticipates the ending of the poem. Disorientation of a different kind may result from the description of Jove's act of divine judgment, which is stated in terms that are not necessarily in conflict with Christianity.[69] However we interpret the overlapping voices and the consolation expressed in this passage, the closure of the debate on poetry still leaves many existential issues unresolved. The first major movement of the poem (if we accept Barker's analysis) is complete, but the elegy cannot end until these issues are addressed and other ceremonies are performed.

The first-person voice returns, beginning the second movement of the poem with another apostrophe to divine beings long evoked in pastoral poetry. Arethusa, the Sicilian spring associated with Theocritus's supposed birthplace, is paired with Mincius, the river flowing near Vergil's Mantuan birthplace.[70] This verse paragraph seeks to find out who was responsible for Lycidas's unhappy death. The inquiry into the cause of death is set to the tune of pastoral music:

85	O fountain Arethuse, and thou honoured flood,	
	Smooth-sliding Mincius, crowned with vocal reeds,	
	That strain I heard was of a higher mood:	*melody; musical mode*
	But now my oat proceeds,	
	And listens to the herald of the sea	*i.e., Triton*
90	That came in Neptune's plea;	*i.e., legal defense*
	He asked the waves, and asked the felon winds,	*savage/wild*
	What hard mishap hath doomed this gentle swain? [85–92].	

The passage implies that the speaker heard Phoebus's speech performed as music, but now he listens to a different performance. More precisely, his pastoral flute (silent without the singer's animating breath) comes alive and listens to Triton, the first of a number of internal speakers in this and the following paragraph. Yet the question the herald asks on behalf of Neptune is identical to the question the shepherd wants to ask: why did his friend have to die?

Only the forces of nature seem to be in a position to know what caused his death. Indeed, they may even be implicated in the event. Triton asks the winds, but they proclaim their innocence:

	And questioned every gust of rugged wings	
	That blows from off each beaked promontory;	
95	They knew not of his story,	
	And sage Hippotades their answer brings,	*Aeolus, god of the wind*
	That not a blast was from his dungeon strayed,	
	The air was calm, and on the level brine,	
	Sleek Panope with all her sisters played [93–99].	*a sea nymph*

The gods of wind and sea, the messenger reports, were not personally involved in this death. The winds remained confined to their home, and the sea was smooth enough for the Nereids to sail calmly on, turning away quite leisurely from the disaster.

The graceful beauty of these lines is partly the effect of a more relaxed rhythm created by the only feminine rhymes in the poem: *promontory/ story*.[71] The mystery of the *hard mishap* remains unsolved until the final lines of the paragraph. Yet the solution raises more questions than it answers: "It was that fatal [*mortal/fated*] and perfidious bark [*treacherous ship*] / Built in the eclipse, and rigged with curses dark, / That sunk so low that sacred head of thine" (100–02). The victim's head is described as "sacred" for a number of reasons, including the fact that King was a consecrated minister of the Anglican Church. But who, we might wonder, is speaking here?[72] Who, that is, is in a position to know that the ship was built during an inauspicious eclipse, that it was fated for disaster and rigged out with curses? Who cursed the rigging?[73]

We may find ourselves disoriented by the echoing voices. Aeolus brought the answer from the winds, and perhaps from the sea-nymphs. But why should these minor divinities know about the circumstances of the ship's construction? More disorienting still, this voice—or rather this written imitation of one—seems to address its authoritative pronouncement to Lycidas himself: *that sacred head of thine*. Could it be the voice of Milton himself that resonates here? Who uses this heavily Latinate diction, including the word *perfidious*, first recorded in 1572?[74] Perhaps these are not even the right questions to be asking of a poem whose encoding of textual subjectivity is no respecter of discrete persons.

In the next paragraph the river Cam, the personification of Cambridge University, joins what now resembles a funeral procession. Although the classical deities did not directly express grief over the shepherd's death, the paternal Camus feels a personal loss. At the same time, the suggestive portrait of this stately figure is designed to produce delight, especially for the members of the original audience who were Cambridge graduates:

> Next Camus, reverend sire, went footing slow,
> His mantle hairy, and his bonnet sedge,   *riverside vegetation*
> 105 Inwrought with figures dim, and on the edge
> Like to that sanguine flower inscribed with woe.   *bloody*
> Ah, who hath reft (quoth he) my dearest pledge? [103–7].   *forcefully taken; child*

The *sanguine flower* is the hyacinth, whose red streaks were explained by classical mythology as spelling the Greek letters of Apollo's anguished cry of *AI, AI* (alas! alas!). After accidently killing his beloved Hyacinth, the god transformed the youth into the white flower that bears his name, using the boy's blood to inscribe all his woe.[75] Like each individual life, every death is unique. Yet at the same time, each new expression of grief is *like to* other expressions of grief, bringing to light a shared, public mode of being with others.

More obviously public, however, is the final voice that sounds out in this long paragraph. Signs of its distinctively public nature may be read in the biblical echoes and the increasingly satirical mode. Before St. Peter booms forth his scathing speech, he is introduced as a figure of great power and energy:

	Last came, and last did go,	
	The pilot of the Galilean lake,	
110	Two massy keys he bore of metals twain,	*massive; twin*
	(The golden opes, the iron shuts amain)	*opens; with force*
	He shook his mitred locks, and stern bespake,	*wearing a miter; spoke out*
	How well could I have spared for thee, young swain,	*given in exchange*
	Enow of such as for their bellies' sake,	*Enough of such a kind as*
115	Creep and intrude, and climb into the fold? [108–15].	*sheep pen*

The two keys refer to those given by Christ to Peter in Matthew 16:19. Peter was fishing on the Sea of Galilee when Christ first called him (Luke 5:30–11). He wears a miter as the first bishop.[76] The reference to intruders into the fold echoes John 10:1 ("He that entereth not by the door into the sheepfold, but climbeth up some other way").[77] The image of vulnerable sheep whose interests should be defended by an ecclesiastical figure explicitly transforms classical pastoral into specifically Christian terms for the first time in the poem.

As Rosamund Tuve observes, the purpose of the imagery in St. Peter's speech is "denigration, an almost magniloquent diminishing ... of its subjects—the exact formal parallel and the exact evaluative opposite of the 'praise' or magnification which is the natural function of ... any funeral elegy."[78] In other words, we are fully within the mode of epideictic or display rhetoric that has been discussed in previous chapters. Nowhere does the New Critical interpretative strategy of reading lyric as the dramatic utterance of a fictive speaker seem as impoverished as when we encounter the hallmarks of "display" rhetoric. Such public poetry is designed to persuade its readers, moving them to action in the world.

St. Peter's vehement denunciation of the corrupt clergy rises to a crescendo that ends the second movement of the poem with the threat of divine vengeance:

Of other care they little reckoning make,
Than how to scramble at the shearers' feast,
And shove away the worthy bidden guest;
Blind mouths! that scarce themselves know how to hold
120 A sheep-hook, or have learned aught else the least
That to the faithful herdman's art belongs!
What recks it them? What need they? They are sped;
And when they list, their lean and flashy songs   *wish/choose; trifling,*
Grate on their scrannel pipes of wretched straw,   *thin/harsh (?)*
125 The hungry sheep look up, and are not fed,
But swoll'n with wind, and the rank mist they draw,   *foul*
Rot inwardly, and foul contagion spread:
Besides what the grim wolf with privy paw
Daily devours apace, and nothing said,
130 But that two-handed engine at the door,
Stands ready to smite once, and smite no more[79] [116–31].

Although the precise meaning of the *two-handed engine* is the most highly debated question in Milton scholarship, it need not occupy us here.[80] It is enough to recognize that the apocalyptic image is intended to terrify Milton's readers. The powerful denunciation thus demands to be understood according to something like the theory of the sublime first proposed by "Longinus."[81]

There is no doubt that this voice is indistinguishable from the author's, as the 1645 headnote indicates. The vehemence of Milton's denunciation is strengthened by his use of sound patterns, though space allows for only a few examples. The line "Grate on their scrannel pipes of wretched straw" audibly growls its insult with the repeated *rs*.[82] Alliteration on plosive consonants spits out in contempt (*privy paw, daily devours*; the *d* is picked up with *door* in the next line). The prosody has its own contribution to make. Although the poem is predominantly composed in end-stopped lines, this passage includes several enjambments (after lines 119 and 120, 123, and 128), which drive the attack forward. By contrast, there are moments where the rhythm briefly halts. Two phrases place metrical beats together for greater emphasis: *grim wolf, smite once*. Other sound patterns organize the saint's angry complaint. The rhyme scheme of the last eight lines corresponds to the *ottava rima* of the final paragraph.[83]

In all, the speech warns the clergy under Archbishop Laud that the corrupt Christian pastors will one day face divine judgment—a different kind of doom from that mentioned by Neptune's herald.[84] Thus the second movement comes to a resounding close. In some ways, the historical nature of Milton's political concerns is most evident in St. Peter's denunciation of the Laudian clergy. Although those specific battles are long over, we may fuse horizons with Milton's political passions if we substitute our own examples of intolerable public policy.[85]

The final movement of the poem reverts to the classical mode of pastoral, with an apostrophe to Alpheus, the river deity. According to the myth recorded by Ovid (*Metamorphoses* 5.572–641), Alpheus sought the love of the nymph Arethusa as she bathed in his river on the Greek mainland. Diana changed the nymph into a stream so that she could escape his clutches. Fled into the sea, she reemerged on the island of Ogygia off the Sicilian coast. But Alpheus pursued, and the two bodies of water mingled to form a single fountain. The nymph's name appeared at the beginning of the poem's second movement (85). Now the Sicilian fountain is called again by its masculine name and urged to return after recoiling at the sound of St. Peter's fearsome voice. The first paragraph of the final movement, with its famous catalogue of flowers, is one of the most beautiful descriptive passages in English poetry, with its rich colors, textures, and sounds:

> Return Alpheus, the dread voice is past,
> That shrunk thy streams; return Sicilian muse,
> And call the vales, and bid them hither cast
> 135 Their bells, and flowrets of a thousand hues.
> Ye valleys low where the mild whispers use,   *habitually resort*
> Of shades and wanton winds, and gushing brooks,   *unrestrained*
> On whose fresh lap the swart star sparely looks,   *dark from heat*
> Throw hither all your quaint enamelled eyes,
> 140 That on the green turf suck the honied showers,
> And purple all the ground with vernal flowers.
> Bring the rathe primrose that forsaken dies,   *early*
> The tufted crow-toe, and pale jessamine,   *wild hyacinth (?); jasmine*
> The white pink, and the pansy freaked with jet,   *streaked capriciously*
> 145 The glowing violet,
> The musk-rose, and the well-attired woodbine,
> With cowslips wan that hang the pensive head,   *pale*
> And every flower that sad embroidery wears:
> Bid amaranthus all his beauty shed,
> 150 And daffodillies fill their cups with tears,
> To strew the laureate hearse where Lycid lies[86] [132–51].

As it happens, we know from the manuscript evidence that Milton took great pains with this gorgeous catalogue of (mostly) springtime flowers. The first draft in the manuscript was cancelled. It was then revised (and reduced by two lines) on an additional sheet.[87] Clearly, something is happening here that matters deeply to the poet. We may ask how the presence effects of the catalogue go hand in hand with its meaning effects.[88] The deictic *hither* appears twice to indicate the place toward which the singer calls for the in-gathering of flowers. The sensuous effect of this presence, made lusher by the resonant sound patterns, is to create a bountiful sense of fullness. Not only the growing list of flowers but also the series of modifiers (*all, all, every, all*) and the verb *fill* convey an experience of satisfaction.

Yet the purpose for calling on the animated forces of nature to bring this colorful gathering of flowers only comes to light at the end of the list. The movement toward sadness—the shedding of floral beauty and the filling of empty cups with tears—crests with the order *To strew the laureate hearse where Lycid lies.* The poem, in every sense of the word, *imitates* his funeral. The last time the body of Lycidas was present in the poem, his *sacred head* had *sunk so low* in the water (102). Now we are invited to imagine his body lying before us in its casket, receiving the funeral rituals that are its due. As we have already been told, "He must not float upon his watery bier / Unwept, and welter to the parching wind, / Without the meed of some melodious tear" (12–14). The singer now makes good on this promise, at least in his imagination.

At the same time, readers familiar with the pastoral tradition will recognize that the strewing of the body with flowers is an ancient poetic device going back to Bion's *Lament for Adonis* ("Cast on him garlands and blossoms: all things have perished in his death, yea all the flowers are faded").[89] Yet the link between flowers and funerals is not merely a literary one. Flowers appear in many different parts of the world at times of mourning, though the specific cultural meanings are variable.[90] By alluding to this poetic and cultural practice, the beautiful catalogue of flowers promises to offer the kind of consolation that comes from the observance of a familiar ceremony of mourning. If (as Jonathan Culler suggests) lyric poetry has always shown a tendency toward ritualized effects of language, a strong poet may gain additional lyric power by alluding to real or imagined rituals.

However, any comfort derived from imagining the shepherd's funeral service must be short-lived, since the singer recalls that his friend's body remains absent and its ultimate fate unknown (the geographical references in the passage will be explained below):

> For so to interpose a little ease,
> Let our frail thoughts dally with false surmise.
> Ay me! Whilst thee the shores, and sounding seas
> 155 Wash far away, where'er thy bones are hurled,
> Whether beyond the stormy Hebrides
> Where thou perhaps under the whelming tide
> Visit'st the bottom of the monstrous world;
> Or whether thou to our moist vows denied,   *tearful prayers*
> 160 Sleep'st by the fable of Bellerus old,
> Where the great vision of the guarded mount
> Looks toward Namancos and Bayona's hold;
> Look homeward angel now, and melt with ruth.   *St. Michael; pity*
> And, O ye dolphins, waft the hapless youth [152–64].   *convey safely*

The speaker's *frail thoughts*—the human tendency to experience grief and seek some form of relief—lead him to indulge (*dally*) for a few moments in the fantasy that the body is present. But he suddenly identifies such thoughts as *false surmise*. As Peter Sacks suggests, the same recognition applies to "any elegy, any ... farewell addressed to one who has already gone."[91]

The horror of the dear companion's death in a cold sea returns with a new urgency. Indeed, the rhyme pairing of *ease* and *seas* neatly captures the contrasting moods of this movement in the poem. *Ease* represents all that is human, temporary, artificial, unsustainable, and false; *seas* points to everything that is inhumane, permanent, natural, real, yet intolerable. The bones were imagined at the beginning of the elegy as dried by "the parching wind" (13), in contrast to the singer's wet "melodious tear" (14). The bones are now imagined churning beneath the ocean's surface to join the monsters of the deep. Or else the body has been cast onto land, the bones left to dry on some desolate shore, in contrast to *our moist vows*. Yet even the horror of Lycidas's unknown fate is eased by the gentler verbs *visit* and *sleep*, as if to soften the blow or even deny his loss.

Above all, it is the uncertainty of his fellow shepherd's final resting place that most agitates the singer. Milton transforms this unsolvable mystery into a source of sublime poetic power. As T. S. Eliot (generally no admirer of Milton) commented, "the effect of magnificence" created by the use of proper names in this passage creates a "grandeur of sound" than which "there is nothing finer in poetry."[92] But Milton's achievement is not based merely on a mastery of sonorous diction. The *Hebrides*, the western islands of Scotland, lie far to the north of where the ship went down. *Bellerus* is Milton's invention for the eponymous origin of the Latin name for Land's End in Cornwall, the extreme southwestern point of Britain. This rapid sweep of geography, made possible only by the power of our minds, creates what Kant calls the "mathematically sublime." It occurs when the mind grasps how nature's expanse lies beyond comprehension by means of the senses.[93]

Completing the vast geographical picture is *the guarded mount*, St. Michael's Mount in Cornwall. The peak is guarded by the archangel who casts his *great vision* toward Spain, as the geographical distance multiplies toward infinity. (*Namancos* is an old name for a district in northwestern Spain; *Bayona* is a fortress town near Cape Finestre in Galicia.) The *angel* who is implored to *look homeward*, as Warton recognized in the eighteenth century, is St. Michael (not Lycidas).[94] The guardian angel is thus urged to turn his protective gaze away from Spain (England's Catholic enemy) towards Britain and to look with compassion on the unfortunate victim.

Finally, the verse paragraph concludes with the singer calling on the dolphins of myth to rescue the youth and bring him safely to shore. Readers familiar with the ancient myth will recall the dolphins that rescued Arion, the legendary musician.[95] Both the angel's gaze and the dolphins' action, if the singer's hopes come true, will move in the direction of Lycidas's earthly home, anticipating the final resolution of the poem.

The remainder of the third and final movement of the elegy proper (to draw on Barker's scheme one last time) abruptly shifts the poem to an explicitly Christian consolation. This triumphant conclusion, which affirms the hope in eternal life, has been carefully prepared for in advance. It may well have been expected, at least by readers who bring some background knowledge of pastoral convention. Yet the apparent lack of transition to this verse paragraph has troubled some critics.[96] In any case, for the first time the singer directly addresses other shepherds, the pastoral community that has remained at best an implied presence until now:

165	Weep no more, woeful shepherds weep no more,	
	For Lycidas your sorrow is not dead,	*i.e., cause of sorrow*
	Sunk though he be beneath the watery floor,	
	So sinks the day-star in the ocean bed,	*the sun*
	And yet anon repairs his drooping head,	*in a moment; renews*
170	And tricks his beams, and with new spangled ore,	*trims; i.e., gold*
	Flames in the forehead of the morning sky:	
	So Lycidas sunk low, but mounted high,	
	Through the dear might of him that walked the waves;	*Christ*
	Where other groves, and other streams along,	
175	With nectar pure his oozy locks he laves,	*washes*
	And hears the unexpressive nuptial song,	*inexpressible*
	In the blest kingdoms meek of joy and love [165–77].	

One of the signs that this shift marks a fresh beginning for the poem is metrical. The six-beat rhythm of line 165 is virtually identical to that of the opening line of the poem. The similarity becomes clear when the two lines are put next to each other:

> Yet once more, O ye laurels, and once more
> B   o   B[o]B o B o   b   o   B

> Weep no more, woeful shepherds, weep no more
> B   o   B [o]B o B   o   B   o   B

Although other scansions are possible, the only rhythmic difference between the two lines is slight.[97] The fifth beat is promoted in the first case. Otherwise the scansion is identical, including the placement of a virtual offbeat between the second and third beats of both lines. The rhythmic echo is also clear from the identical placement of the word *more* in the two most metrically emphatic positions in both lines. Other sound patterns contribute to the lyric effect of the sentence as a whole, including alliteration (*flames/forehead, walked/waves, locks/laves*).

Rarely (if ever) in the history of poetry has the traditional symbolism of the setting and rising of the sun as analogous to death and rebirth been used to such great effect.[98] To help mark this movement, the poem repeats the word *sunk*, used earlier to describe the fatal outcome of the ship's foundering ("sunk so low that sacred head of thine" [102]). Now the same verb leads directly to the shepherd's rising: "So Lycidas sunk low, but mounted high." The *might* that enables his soul to ascend to heaven is not his own but Christ's. The indirect way of naming Jesus is carefully chosen: "him that walked the waves."[99] The *groves* and *streams* where Lycidas now finds peace are not the sylvan woods of pastoral poetry but the Christian heaven foreshadowed by the pagan myth of the Elysian Fields.

Equally impressive is Milton's fusion of classical and Christian images when Lycidas washes *his oozy locks* with *nectar*, the drink reserved to the Olympian gods.[100] The troubling idea of Lycidas's corpse *under the whelming tide* is now rendered harmless with the playful image of washing the brine from his hair. Even the alliterative pattern has been redeemed: the repeated liquid consonant of *laureate hearse where Lycid lies* returns with the more comforting phrase *locks he laves*.

As the third and final movement of the elegy draws nearer to its triumphant close, Milton's vision of heaven offers a Christian transfiguration of the pastoral gathering of shepherds:

> There entertain him all the saints above,
> In solemn troops, and sweet societies
> 180 That sing, and singing in their glory move,
> And wipe the tears for ever from his eyes [178–81].

Here Milton fuses two passages from the Book of Revelation, the description of the marriage supper of the Lamb (19:6–7) and the song of the 144,000 (14:1–4). He exercises some poetic license, however, in having the saints in heaven "wipe the tears for ever from his eyes." In the Bible, God performs this consoling act by himself: "And God shall wipe away all tears from their eyes" (Rev. 7:17). In affirming an article of Christian faith, Milton emphasizes the durable bonds of human community, bonds capable of outlasting even death.[101]

After these resonant and authoritative words of Christian consolation, the poet addresses Lycidas directly for the first time in this climactic paragraph, prophesying that in the future the shepherd will protect friends and strangers. Or rather, the poet *makes* it happen through the power of his word: "Henceforth thou art the genius [*protective deity*] of the shore, / In thy large recompense, and shalt be good / To all that wander in that perilous flood" (183–85).[102] The phrase *in thy large recompense* carries two meanings. Lycidas is transformed into the genius of the shore to reward him for his virtuous life, and this change compensates his survivors for his loss. The idea of the dead shepherd "imagined as a god, being good to his worshippers" echoes Vergil's fifth eclogue: *sis bonus o felixque tuis* ("O be good and favorable to your own people" [*Ec.* 5.65]).[103] Once again, the network of poetic allusions defies any attempt to read the lyric as the dramatic utterance of a single fictive speaker. Yet it is precisely at this point that the most surprising shift in the elegy occurs. The unexpected narrative coda seems to insist on the presence of just such a speaker, who is now described as the singer of the song we have just heard.

We have already noted that the final paragraph, equivalent to a perfect stanza of *ottava rima*, provides an external frame that was not anticipated in the poem's opening lines. In the beginning the author himself (as the epigraph insists) seems to speak in the first person. The effect of closure created by the final paragraph has been compared to the coda of a Beethoven symphony.[104] Here are the final eight lines:

Thus sang the uncouth swain to the oaks and rills,	*unknown/rustic*
While the still morn went out with sandals grey,	
He touched the tender stops of various quills,	*finger holes; reeds*
With eager thought warbling his Doric lay:	*dialect of Greek pastoral*
190 And now the sun had stretched out all the hills,	
And now was dropped into the western bay;	
At last he rose, and twitched his mantle blue:	
Tomorrow to fresh woods, and pastures new [186–93].	

Milton provides narrative distance on the struggles of the grieving shepherd to find consolation. Thus we return to the pastoral landscape on earth after a brief journey to heaven in our imaginations, and thus the poem returns to the image of the setting sun as both religious symbol and natural wonder.

However, the passage of time in the stanza does not align perfectly with how it appears in the rest of the poem (and we have already noticed the inconsistent use of verb tenses above). In a few swift lines we seem to be propelled from morning to sunset. It is as though the swain has been singing and piping for an entire natural day (though a recitation of the poem would take only a few minutes) until the shadows of the hills lengthen and the sun finally sinks below the horizon. As the fictional swain played musical notes on his pipe of *various quills*, Milton composed the poem with his own kind of quill, whose marks have survived in the Trinity MS.

Once again Milton calls on his learned readers to hear a Vergilian echo from the close of the first eclogue: *maioresque cadunt altis de montibus umbrae* ("and greater shadows fall from the high mountains" [*Ec.* 1.83]). The sunset over the sea repeats the water imagery that so many of the poem's critics have discussed, but it also reminds us that Edward King died off the western coast of Britain. It is as though the swain's gaze now joins with that of Milton; both contemplate one last time a fellow poet's final moments of mortal life.

But the sunset is a symbol not merely of death but also of new hope. It will rise again in the morning, just as the shepherd will rise with each new day. With calm of mind (all passion spent) the shepherd adjusts his *mantle blue* (most often read as a symbol of hope, though the color also reminds us of water as a symbol of renewed life). Ready to return home, he stands newly open to the world, better prepared to encounter *fresh woods, and pastures new*. As the swain projects himself into future possibilities, his authorial double offers him as a model for a virtuous form of life in which one might be at home in the world of purposeful activity. Indeed, such a life seems to have been chosen by Milton. Within a few short months of completing the elegy for Edward King, Milton was on his way to Italy to advance his humanist education, where he was to remain until called back home by his sense of duty to the English Revolution.

Coda: The Irish Dancer

With the somber tones of Milton's oaten flute fading as the sun goes down, we end on a gayer note by returning yet once more to the early years of the lyric in English. An anonymous fourteenth-century voice urges us to recall the ancient bond of lyric poetry, song, and dance. We do not know whether these lovely verses constitute a complete lyric or merely a fragment:

Ich am of Irlaunde,   I
And of the holy londe
Of Irlande.
Gode sire, pray ich thee,   Good sir, I pray thee,
For of sainte charitee,   For the sake of holy charity,
Come and daunce wit me   with
In Irlaunde.[1]

Despite its being copied out as prose on a four-inch-wide strip of vellum in an early fourteenth-century hand (MS Rawlinson D.913), its rhyme and meter indelibly mark this mysterious text as verse. Its reference to dancing suggests that it forms all or part of a carol in that word's original sense, a song to accompany a ring-dance. The editors italicize the first stanza to indicate that it forms the repeated burden, perhaps sung by the group of dancers before a soloist sings each stanza.[2]

The same vellum strip includes five other short Middle English lyric fragments that read like love poetry, described by R. H. Robbins as "among the freshest and most charming of all early English compositions."[3] William Butler Yeats was charmed by the Irish dancer, adopting the lyric for his volume *Words for Music Perhaps* (1933), though he inserts a line in the burden to incorporate a *carpe diem* theme: "'And time runs on,' cried she."[4] His creative act reminds us that the most typical response to beauty, as Elaine Scarry maintains, is the urge to copy or reproduce it.[5]

Like many popular songs from the Middle Ages and Renaissance, the Irish dancer poem is unmoored from any firm historical or social context beyond the manuscript and linguistic ones. The French catchphrase *sainte charitee* and the loanword *dance* (first recorded in English c. 1300) bear witness to the linguistic consequences of the Norman Conquest, just as the reference to Ireland serves as a reminder that the earliest English colonial enterprise began there in the twelfth century. From such a shadowy context, the female voice of the song rises to greet us, a first-person utterance directed to a Thou.

The kindly greeting has been used since the time of Plato or even Homer as a metaphor for the appearance of beauty before our eyes. "At the moment one comes into the presence of something beautiful," Scarry writes, "it greets you. It lifts away from the neutral background as though coming forward to welcome you—as though the object were designed to 'fit' your perception."[6] The texture of the language, the duplication of the final syllable in the three lines of the chorus, and the repetition of *Ireland* strike the ear with an almost hypnotic effect. Major theorists of lyric poetry from Aristotle and Sir Philip Sidney to Northrop Frye and Jonathan Culler have thought they could hear in the lyrics of their own time distant echoes of a ritual past, rooted in the oral cultures of archaic Greek and Hebrew poetry and beyond.

This rhythmic fragment of Middle English song, though we cannot know what music may have accompanied it, reaches out as if to cast a spell and charm us into accepting the invitation to dance. Although it is difficult to be sure how to scan the meter, its rhythmic pulse brings to mind a rope-skipping chant on a playground. A voice sings, bodies move to the music. Though we do not know where the song was composed, Ireland must have seemed an exotic place not only to inhabitants of England but even to its English or French-speaking colonists surrounded by a sea of Gaelic voices. The addition of the adjective *holy* in the second line reminds us that Christianity came early to this land of saints and scholars.

The religious coloration to the language continues in the second stanza, with its courteous address to the male listener and the French petitionary formula. Yet none of this prepares us for the unexpected request for a dance, reinforced by the falling rhythm of the crucial line. By the time the final verse rings out *Ireland* one last time, its meaning has undergone a sea-change. Ireland has become a land of secular joy, a place of shared sociality, of being-with-others in the world. By hearing or reading the song, perhaps even by dancing to its music, its audience steps into that festive world. Scarry suggests that the "willingness continually to revise one's own location in order to place oneself in the path of beauty is the basic impulse underlying education. One submits oneself to other minds (teachers) in order to increase the chance that one will be looking in the right direction when a comet makes its sweep through a certain patch of sky."[7]

All together now...

Appendix: A Modified Version of Attridge's Scansion Symbols

Derek Attridge's system, at its most basic, distinguishes beats (**B**) from offbeats (**o**). You already do this when you tap your foot to music. When your foot goes down, it marks a beat. When your foot goes up, it marks an offbeat. A beat may also be realized by *promoting* an unstressed syllable (marked by lower-case **b**). Similarly, an offbeat may be realized by demoting a stressed syllable (marked by an upper case **O**).[1]

Attridge also accounts for an *implied* offbeat.[2] The idea of an implied offbeat departs from traditional systems of scanning meter because an implied offbeat falls on the silent interval between two beats. It is *perceived*, even though it remains unrealized (is silent). (In *Moving Words* he modifies his theory of implied offbeats, distinguishing them from *virtual* offbeats, which occur at a syntactic break often marked by punctuation.)

Here is a chart of my modified version of Attridge's symbols to mark beats and offbeats[3]:

B	beat
o	offbeat
(o)	optional offbeat
o-o	double offbeat
o-O	double offbeat with demotion of stressed second syllable
O-o	double offbeat with demotion of stressed first syllable
o-o-o	triple offbeat
[B]	virtual beat
[o]	virtual offbeat
ô	implied offbeat
b	beat by promotion of unstressed syllable
O	offbeat by demotion of stressed syllable

Finally, here are Attridge's symbols for stress patterns.[4] These symbols may be used above a line of verse whenever we wish to mark the relation of **linguistic stress** to **beats**:

+s	stressed syllable
−s	unstressed syllable
s	indefinite stress, may replace either +s or −s
<u>s</u>	emphatic stress, may replace +s
[s]	metrically subordinated stress; may replace −s
(s)	elision by contraction to omit syllable

Chapter Notes

Introduction

1. See Kathryn Zickuhr, "New Reading Data from the NEA's Survey of Public Participation in the Arts," *Pew Internet & American Life Project*, October 3, 2013, available at http://libraries.pewinternet.org/2013/10/02/new-reading-data-from-the-neas-survey-of-public-participation-in-the-arts/ (accessed 9 April 2016). The current state of reading poetry was the topic of *Poetry in America: Review of the Findings* (2006), a study of attitudes and experiences of poetry conducted by scholars at the University of Chicago and sponsored by the Poetry Foundation, available at http://www.poetryfoundation.org/foundation/PoetryinAmerican_FullReport.pdf (accessed 9 April 2016).

2. *Poetry in America*, 37–38.

3. For a useful anthology on the contemporary debate on literary canons, see Lee Morrissey, ed., *Debating the Canon: A Reader from Addison to Nafisi* (New York: Palgrave, 2005).

4. On the history of literary canons, see Jan Gorak, *The Making of the Modern Canon: Genesis and Crisis of a Literary Idea* (London: Athlone, 1991); Gorak, ed., *Canon vs. Culture: Reflections on the Current Debate* (New York: Garland, 2001); E. Dean Kolbas, *Critical Theory and the Literary Canon* (Boulder, CO: Westview, 2001).

5. See *Poetry in America*, 50–51.

6. Derek Attridge, *The Rhythms of English Poetry* (New York: Longman, 1982). He has made minor adjustments to his approach in recent years; see *Moving Words: Forms of English Poetry* (Oxford: Oxford University Press, 2013).

7. Attridge, *Rhythms of English Poetry*, 3–18; however, there is no doubt that classically educated poets believed that they were composing in metrical feet.

8. For a highly regarded critic who also defends using Attridge's system, see Jonathan Culler, *Theory of the Lyric* (Cambridge: Harvard University Press, 2015).

9. See the video archive available at http://www.favoritepoem.org (accessed 9 April 2016). Fifty selections were chosen from those offered by 18,000 volunteers.

10. "Historicist" is a label used to describe a variety of critical approaches to interpreting literature and culture that emphasize the historical conditions of producing meaning; the term was first widely applied with the advent of the so-called New Historicism in the 1980s. Conventionally, historicism is contrasted with formalism, which stresses the formal features intrinsic to a work of art.

Chapter 1

1. M. H. Abrams, *The Mirror and the Lamp* (New York: Norton, 1958).

2. On the origins and later development of rhetoric in the ancient world, see George A. Kennedy, *A New History of Classical Rhetoric* (Princeton: Princeton University Press, 1994).

3. *Republic* 394b-c; cf. *Poetics* 1448a. I cite Plato's *Republic* and Aristotle's *Poetics* from the excerpts printed in *Ancient Literary Criticism: The Principal Texts in New Translations*, ed. D. A. Russell and M. Winterbottom (Oxford: Clarendon Press, 1972), henceforth abbreviated *ALC*; citations by page number will appear parenthetically. The passage from Plato appears at *ALC* 62; the passage from Aristotle is at *ALC* 92–93. See D. A. Russell, *Criticism in Antiquity* (Berkeley: University of California Press, 1981), 99–113.

4. See G. R. F. Ferrari, "Plato and Poetry," in *The Cambridge History of Literary Criticism*, vol. 1: *Classical Criticism*, ed. George A. Kennedy (Cambridge: Cambridge University Press, 1989), 92–148, esp. 136. Further citations from this multi-volume work are abbreviated as *CHLC*, followed by volume and page number.

5. *ALC* 7. See Jeffrey Walker, *Rhetoric and Poetics in Antiquity* (Oxford: Oxford University Press, 2000), 5.

6. See Walker, *Rhetoric and Poetics*, 12.
7. See Stephen Halliwell, "Aristotle's *Poetics*," in *CHLC* 1:149-83.
8. Daniel Javitch, "The Assimilation of Aristotle's *Poetics* in Sixteenth-century Italy," in *The Cambridge History of Literary Criticism*, vol. 3: *The Renaissance*, ed. Glyn P. Norton (Cambridge: Cambridge University Press, 1999), 53-65 (53).
9. T. S. Eliot, *The Sacred Wood: Essays on Poetry and Criticism*, 2nd ed. (London: Methuen, 1928), viii.
10. W. R. Johnson, *The Idea of Lyric: Lyric Modes in Ancient and Modern Poetry* (Berkeley: University of California Press, 1982), 82; for a different explanation, see Walker, *Rhetoric and Poetics*, 287. The absence of a theory of lyric poetry in Aristotle began to be addressed by Alexandrian scholars during the Hellenistic age, and later by Renaissance scholars.
11. Aristotle, *On Rhetoric: A Theory of Civic Discourse*, trans. George A. Kennedy (New York: Oxford University Press, 1991), 96; subsequent references appear parenthetically.
12. *Rhetoric*, trans. Kennedy, 48 n. 77. For the classical background and Renaissance adaptations of epideictic rhetoric, see O. B. Hardison, Jr., *The Enduring Monument: The Idea of Praise in Renaissance Literary Theory and Practice* (Chapel Hill: University of North Carolina Press, 1962).
13. Jonathan Culler, *Theory of the Lyric* (Cambridge, MA: Harvard University Press, 2015), 115.
14. Kennedy, *New History of Classical Rhetoric*, 89.
15. Kennedy, *New History of Classical Rhetoric*, 89.
16. Russell, *Criticism in Antiquity*, 6
17. English translations from Horace are mine; I quote the Latin and cite parenthetically by line number from the Loeb edition, *Satires, Epistles and Ars poetica*, ed. and trans. by H. Rushton Fairclough (London: Heinemann, 1926); see also *ALC* 279-91.
18. See *English Renaissance Literary Criticism* (Oxford: Clarendon Press, 1999), ed. Brian Vickers, 15, citing Cicero, *De or.* 2.27.115, *Orat.* 21.69. Additional citations to this volume are abbreviated *ERLC*. Limits of space necessitate leaving out Cicero, most of whose mature treatises on rhetoric focus on prose oratory.
19. Vincent Gillespie, "From the Twelfth Century to c. 1450," in *The Cambridge History of Literary Criticism*, vol. 2: *The Middle Ages*, ed. A. J. Minnis and Ian Johnson (Cambridge: Cambridge University Press, 2005), 145-235 (163).
20. The most comprehensive account of the transmission of classical literary culture in the Middle Ages and Renaissance is R. R. Bolgar, *The Classical Heritage and Its Beneficiaries* (Cambridge: Cambridge University Press, 1954).
21. Ann Moss, "Horace in the Sixteenth Century: Commentators into Critics," *CHLC* 3:66-76, esp. 76; Javitch, "Assimilation of Aristotle's *Poetics*," *CHLC* 3:56-57.
22. Quintilian, *The Institutio Oratoria of Quintilian*, trans. H. E. Butler, 4 vols. (Cambridge, MA: Harvard University Press, 1920-22), Bk.1.8.5. Henceforth, references to Quintilian are from this edition; English quotations not translated in *ALC* are from Butler, sometimes silently modified. For the influence of Quintilian's discussions of literature, see Ernst Robert Curtius, *European Literature and the Latin Middle Ages*, trans. Willard R. Trask (Princeton: Princeton University Press, 1953), 436-38.
23. For an overview, see Ann Moss, "Theories of Poetry: Latin Writers," *CHLC* 3:98-105.
24. For the medieval reception of ancient literary criticism and other developments, see Vincent Gillespie, "From the Twelfth Century to c. 1450," *CHLS* 2:145-235.
25. For medieval literary criticism and theory, see *CHLC* 2.
26. St. Augustine of Hippo, *Confessions* I.13.
27. James J. Murphy, "The Arts of Poetry and Prose," *CHLC* 2:42-67.
28. See *CHLC* 2:2.
29. "Introduction to Ovid's *Epistles*," in *Medieval Literary Theory and Criticism, c. 1100-c.1375: The Commentary Tradition*, ed. A. J. Minnis and A. B. Scott, with David Wallace, rev. ed. (Oxford: Clarendon Press, 1991), 20.
30. For sixteenth-century efforts to recover a classical pronunciation of Latin, see Derek Attridge, *Well-Weighed Syllables: Elizabethan Verse in Classical Meters* (Cambridge: Cambridge University Press, 1974), 78-85.
31. For the widely used textbooks by Priscian (c. 510), see James J. Murphy, *Rhetoric in the Middle Ages: A History of Rhetorical Theory from St. Augustine to the Renaissance* (Berkeley: University of California Press, 1974), 71-72.
32. Curtius, *European Literature and the Latin Middle Ages*, 442.
33. For information about the medieval *ars poetriae*, see Murphy, *Rhetoric in the Middle Ages*, 135-93. Not all medieval handbooks discuss prosody, but all cover traditional rhetorical doctrine.
34. Matthew of Vendôme, *The Art of Versification*, trans. Aubrey E. Galyon (Ames: Iowa State University Press, 1980).
35. See Peter Dronke, *The Medieval Lyric* (New York: Harper & Row, 1969). For a brief historical sketch, see *The New Princeton Encyclopedia of Poetry and Poetics*, ed. Alex Pre-

minger and T. V. F. Brogan (Princeton: Princeton University Press, 1993), s.v. *prosody*, 991–92 (henceforth abbreviated *NPEPP*). *The Princeton Encyclopedia of Poetry and Poetics*, 4th ed., gen. ed., Roland Greene (Princeton: Princeton University Press, 2012), henceforth abbreviated *PEPP*, omits the historical survey of prosody.

36. *NPEPP* 992.

37. For a brief sampling with historical background of the *kharzas*, first discovered in 1948, see Dronke, *Medieval Lyric*, 86–90.

38. See Margaret Switten, "Versification and Music," in *The Troubadours: An Introduction*, ed. Simon Gaunt and Sarah Kay (Cambridge: Cambridge University Press, 1999), 141–63.

39. Elizabeth W. Poe, "The *Vidas* and *Razos*," in *A Handbook of the Troubadours*, ed. F. R. P. Akehurst and Judith M. Davis (Berkeley: University of California Press, 1995), 185–97; Simon Gaunt and John Marshall, "Occitan Grammars and the Art of Troubadour Poetry," *CHLC* 2: 472–95 (492–95).

40. See the separate chapters on each line of transmission in Akehurst and Davis, *Handbook of the Troubadours*, 255–305.

41. For a recent overview of the early history of the sonnet, see William J. Kennedy, "European Beginnings and Transmissions: Dante, Petrarch and the Sonnet Sequence," in *The Cambridge Companion to the Sonnet*, ed. A. D. Cousins and Peter Howarth (Cambridge: Cambridge University Press, 2011), 84–104.

42. Michael R. G. Spiller, *The Development of the Sonnet: An Introduction* (London: Routledge, 1992) devotes separate chapters to the Sicilians and the *stilnovisti*.

43. Dante Alighieri, *De vulgari eloquentia*, ed. and trans. Steven Botterill (Cambridge: Cambridge University Press, 1996), henceforth abbreviated *DVE* and cited parenthetically by book, chapter, and line.

44. John A. Scott, *Understanding Dante* (Notre Dame: University of Notre Dame Press, 2004), 45.

45. *NPEPP*, s.v. *lyric*, esp. 713–14.

46. *Boccaccio On Poetry, Being the Preface and the Fourteenth and Fifteenth Books of Boccaccio's Genealogia Deorum Gentilium*, trans. Charles G. Osgood (Indianapolis: Bobbs-Merrill, 1956).

47. See David Robey, "Humanist Views on the Study of Italian Poetry in the Early Italian Renaissance," *CHLC* 2: 626–28.

48. Martin McLaughlin, "Latin and Vernacular from Dante to the Age of Lorenzo (1321-c.1500)," *CHLC* 2:612–25 (614).

49. McLaughlin, "Latin and Vernacular," 618.

50. McLaughlin, "Latin and Vernacular," 619.

51. McLaughlin, "Latin and Vernacular, 622, quoting Landino, *Disputationes camaldulenses*.

52. Robey, "Humanist Views," 630–32.

53. Quoted by Robey, "Humanist Views," 635.

54. Robey, "Humanist Views," 638.

55. Ann Moss, "Humanist Education," *CHLC* 3: 145–54.

56. Richard Waswo, "The Rise of the Vernaculars," *CHLC* 3:409–16 (412).

57. Waswo "Rise of the Vernaculars," 413.

58. Waswo, "Rise of the Vernaculars," 413, quoting Speroni's *Courtier*.

59. See Margaret W. Ferguson, *Trials of Desire: Renaissance Defenses of Poetry* (New Haven: Yale University Press, 1983), 18–53 on du Bellay's defense of the French language.

60. Vickers, *ERLC* 62, n. 21. Excerpts from English literary critics printed by Vickers will be cited parenthetically by page. For a useful anthology, see *Sidney's "The Defence of Poesy" and Selected Renaissance Literary Criticism*, ed. Gavin Alexander (London: Penguin, 2004), henceforth abbreviated *SRLC*.

61. *ERLC* 123. Wilson issued the first edition of the *Rhetorique* in 1553.

62. Attridge, *Well-Weighed Syllables* demonstrates that these prejudices were based on the way Latin prosody was taught in the Elizabethan classroom, where classical Latin was systematically mispronounced.

63. See Martin J. Duffell, *A New History of English Metre* (London: Modern Humanities Research Associates, 2008), 116–36.

64. Parenthetical citations from Gascoigne's *Certayne notes* are from *ERLC*. Alexander, *SRLC* 406 suggests that Donati is probably fictitious.

65. See Wilson, *Arte of Rhetorique*, in *ERLC* 82–84, for epideictic oration; for poetry, see George Puttenham, *The Art of English Poesy: A Critical Edition*, ed. Frank Whigham and Wayne A. Rebhorn (Ithaca: Cornell University Press, 2007), I.10.

66. Hardison, *Enduring Monument*, 30; he observes that "Renaissance lyric is more obviously influenced by epideictic rhetoric than any other genre" (95).

67. Twentieth-century advances in linguistics have greatly complicated traditional approaches to meter; see Attridge, *Rhythms of English Poetry*, 28–55 for an overview.

68. Attridge, *Rhythms of English Poetry*, 77.

69. *SRLC* 407 n. 8. See also William Scott, *The Model of Poesy*, ed. Gavin Alexander (Cambridge: Cambridge University Press, 2013), 203–4, n. 60.25–31.

70. In Puttenham, *Art of English Poesy*, ed. Whigham and Rebhorn, the editors compare

Puttenham's discussion of the three ancient grades of accent with Gascoigne's treatment, noting that Puttenham's is based on sixteenth-century Latin grammars (168 n. 6).

71. *ELCR* 164; I have corrected the two characters for marking accent that are erroneously printed by Vickers in the sentence quoted; Vickers reproduces this error from *Elizabethan Critical Essays*, ed. G. Gregory Smith, 2 vols. (Oxford: Oxford University Press, 1904), 1:49. The 1575 text available in the database *Early English Books Online* (EEBO) shows the correct accent marks.

72. This and the following graphic representation of Gascoigne's scansion is drawn from the digitized version of his 1575 volume *The Posies*, available in *Early English Books Online* (EEBO).

73. For my modified version of Attridge's scansion symbols, see Appendix. Attridge, *Rhythms of English Poetry*, 357–62 provides a synopsis of his metrical rules and original scansion symbols.

74. On the transmission of stable patterns of meter through the generations, see Attridge, *Rhythms of English Poetry*, 149.

75. Attridge, *Rhythms of English Poetry*, 78–79.

76. Attridge, *Rhythms of English Poetry*, 295–300.

77. Attridge, *Rhythms of English Poetry*, 78. Cf. Paul Fussell, Jr., *Poetic Form and Poetic Meter* (New York: Random House, 1965), 6.

78. Attridge, *Rhythms of English Poetry*, 295.

79. The alternate titles derive from the two different prints published in 1595. Parenthetical page citations to this work are from Sir Philip Sidney, *An Apology for Poetry (Or The Defense of Poesy)*, ed. Geoffrey Shepherd; rev. 3rd ed., R. W. Maslen, ed. (Manchester: Manchester University Press, 2002).

80. Scaliger, I, i, 2–6, quoted by Maslen, *Apology*, 143.

81. Following Attridge, *Rhythms of English Poetry*, 19, I have adopted the reading of the other 1595 edition here as being clearer than the alternative *time* retained by Maslen.

82. Puttenham, *The Art of English Poesy*, ed. Whigham and Rebhorn. Another modernized edition is available in Alexander, *SRLC*.

83. Scott, *Model of Poesy*, ed. Alexander; Scott draws extensively on Sidney.

84. *The Works of Thomas Campion*, ed. Walter R. Davis (New York: Norton, 1970), 287–317. For detailed analysis, see Attridge, *Well-Weighed Syllables*, 219–27.

85. An excerpted text is available in *ERLC* 441–53. A modernized edition of the full text is available in *SRLC*.

Chapter 2

1. For more details, see the selection from Gérard Genette, *The Architexte* (1979) in *The Lyric Theory Reader: A Critical Anthology*, ed. Virginia Jackson and Yopie Prins (Baltimore: Johns Hopkins University Press, 2014), 17–30.

2. For a wide-ranging perspective on the Western history and theory of lyric, see Jonathan Culler, *Theory of the Lyric* (Cambridge, MA: Harvard University Press, 2015). For the changing uses of the term *lyric*, see Virginia Jackson, "Lyric," in *The Princeton Encyclopedia of Poetry and Poetics*, 4th ed., Roland Greene, gen. ed. (Princeton: Princeton University Press, 2012), 826–34 (henceforth abbreviated *PEPP*). For more details, see Jackson and Prins, *Lyric Theory Reader*.

3. *The Oxford English Dictionary*, 2nd ed. (Oxford: Clarendon Press, 1989), s.v. *lyric*.

4. M. H. Abrams and Geoffrey Galt Harpham, *A Glossary of Literary Terms*, 9th ed. (Boston: Wadsworth, 2009), s.v. *lyric*.

5. Culler, *Theory of Lyric*, 37, 109–25.

6. David Lindley, *Lyric* (London: Methuen, 1985), 4.

7. Scott Brewster, *Lyric* (London: Routledge, 2009), 2. Brewster offers a useful survey of definitions and origins of lyric poetry (1–42).

8. Roland Greene, "The Lyric," in *The Cambridge History of Literary Criticism*, Vol. 3: *The Renaissance*, Glyn P. Norton, ed. (Cambridge: Cambridge University Press, 1999), 216–28 (216).

9. Heather Dubrow, *The Challenges of Orpheus: Lyric Poetry and Early Modern England* (Baltimore: Johns Hopkins University Press, 2008), 3–4.

10. G. W. F. Hegel, *The Philosophy of Hegel*, ed. Carl J. Friedrich (New York: Random House, 1954), 365; 381–82. For a brief account of Hegel's views on lyric as both "aesthetic form" and "culturally expressive potential," see *PEPP* 831. For more on Hegel's theory of lyric, see Culler, *Theory of the Lyric*, 92–109; he cautions that Hegel's is not "an expressive theory in the modern sense" (100).

11. Culler, *Theory of the Lyric*, 2.

12. M. H. Abrams, *The Mirror and the Lamp* (New York: Norton, 1958); see also *The New Princeton Encyclopedia of Poetry and Poetics*, 3rd ed., ed. Alex Preminger and T. V. F. Brogan (Princeton: Princeton University Press, 1993), s.v. *Poetry, Theories of (Western)*, 942–54 (henceforth abbreviated as *NPEPP*).

13. Culler, *Theory of the Lyric*, 73, quoting Charles Batteux, *Principes de la littérature*. For another discussion of Batteux, see Genette, *Architext*, in Jackson and Prins, *Lyric Theory Reader*, 23–24.

14. William Wordsworth, Preface to *Lyrical*

Notes—Chapter 2

Ballads (1800), in *Criticism: The Major Statements*, ed. Charles Kaplan (New York: St. Martin's Press, 1975), 316.

15. T. S. Eliot, "Tradition and the Individual Talent," *Selected Essays* (New York: Harcourt, 1964), 3–11 (10–11).

16. Jacques Derrida's deconstruction of the primacy of speech over writing ("logocentrism") was influential among avant-garde literary critics in the 1970s and '80s; for his classic statement, see *Of Grammatology*, trans. Gayatri Chakravorty Spivak (Baltimore: Johns Hopkins University Press, 1976).

17. See Émile Benveniste, *Problems in General Linguistics*, trans. Mary Elizabeth Meek (Coral Gables: University of Miami Press, 1971); Roman Jakobson, "Shifters, Verbal Categories, and the Russian Verb," *Selected Writings* (The Hague: Mouton, 1971), 2:130–47.

18. Hans Ulrich Gumbrecht, *The Production of Presence: What Meaning Cannot Convey* (Stanford: Stanford University Press, 2003), 94. On the "lyric present," see Culler, *Theory of the Lyric*, 283–95.

19. Susan Stewart, *Poetry and the Fate of the Senses* (Chicago: University of Chicago Press, 2003), 150.

20. Barbara Herrnstein Smith, *On the Margins of Discourse* (Chicago: University of Chicago Press, 1978), argues that literary works may be understood as "fictive utterances," and that "lyric poems typically represent personal utterance" (8); for Culler's cogent critique, see *Theory of the Lyric*, 110–15.

21. Virginia Jackson and Yopie Prins, "Lyrical Studies," *Victorian Literature and Culture* 27 (1999): 521–30 (523); see Jackson and Prins, eds., *Lyric Theory Reader*, for further details.

22. René Wellek, "Genre Theory, the Lyric, and *Erlebnis*," in *Lyric Theory Reader* 40–52 (48).

23. Abrams, *Mirror and the Lamp*, 97–98.

24. See Sir Philip Sidney, *An Apology for Poetry (Or The Defense of Poesy)*, ed. Geoffrey Shepherd; rev. 3rd ed., R. W. Maslen, ed. (Manchester: Manchester University Press, 2002), 115.33; George Puttenham, *The Art of English Poesy: A Critical Edition*, ed. Frank Whigham and Wayne A. Rebhorn (Ithaca: Cornell University Press, 2007), 134; William Scott, *The Model of Poesy*, ed. Gavin Alexander (Cambridge: Cambridge University Press, 2013), 28.

25. Jackson and Prins, *Lyric Theory Reader* refer to this shift as "lyric reading" or the "lyricization of poetry" (6, 7), which they believe is mostly the invention of twentieth-century literary criticism, especially the mid-century movement known as New Criticism; for Culler's response to this "modern historicist critique of the category of lyric," see *Theory of the Lyric* 83–85 (83).

26. Edgar Allan Poe, "The Poetic Principle," in Kaplan, *Criticism*, 381–401 (382–83).

27. John Stuart Mill, "Thoughts on Poetry and Its Varieties," *Autobiographical and Literary Essays* (Toronto: University of Toronto Press, 1981), 341–70 (348).

28. Culler, *Theory of the Lyric*, 321.

29. See Herbert Tucker, "Dramatic Monologue and the Overhearing of Lyric," in Jackson and Prins, *Lyric Theory Reader*, 144–56. For a critique of the New Critical reduction of all lyric poetry to dramatic monologues, see Culler, *Theory of the Lyric*, 109–10.

30. Northrop Frye, *Anatomy of Criticism: Four Essays* (Princeton: Princeton University Press, 1957), 247 (subsequent page references appear parenthetically). Alastair Fowler, *Kinds of Literature: An Introduction to the Theory of Genres and Modes* (Cambridge, MA: Harvard University Press, 1982), 234–35 points out some of the problems with Frye's theory of radicals.

31. Aristotle, *Poetics* 1450a, *Ancient Literary Criticism: The Principal Texts in New Translations*, ed. D. A. Russell and M. Winterbottom (Oxford: Clarendon Press, 1972), 98.

32. On the musicality of lyric see Robert von Hallberg, *Lyric Powers* (Chicago: University of Chicago Press, 2008), 144.

33. For discussion of Frye's *melos/opsis* distinction, see Culler, *Theory of the Lyric*, 246–58.

34. Culler, *Theory of the Lyric*, 252. See Roland Greene, *Post-Petrarchism: Origins and Innovations of the Western Lyric Sequence* (Princeton: Princeton University Press, 1991), 4–5. Greene notes a variable tension between the ritualistic and fictive poles of the lyric sequence beginning with Petrarch; Culler applies this dialectic to the lyric in general.

35. Frye, *Anatomy*, 17; Frank Lentricchia, *After the New Criticism* (Chicago: University of Chicago Press, 1980), 16–24.

36. Gerald Graff, *Professing Literature: An Institutional History* (Chicago: University of Chicago Press, 1987, 256.

37. *Lyric Poetry: Beyond New Criticism*, ed. Chaviva Hošek and Patricia Parker (Ithaca: Cornell University Press, 1985).

38. Paul de Man, "Lyrical Voice in Contemporary Theory: Riffaterre and Jauss," in Hošek and Parker, *Lyric Poetry*, 55–72 (55).

39. De Man, "Lyrical Voice," 64.

40. De Man, "Lyrical Voice," 69. Cf. de Man's essay from 1969, "Lyric and Modernity," in *Blindness and Insight: Essays in the Rhetoric of Contemporary Criticism*, 2nd ed. (Minneapolis: University of Minnesota Press, 1983), 166–86.

41. Culler, "Changes in the Study of the Lyric," in Hošek and Parker, *Lyric Poetry*, 38–

54 (40). See also Culler's "Apostrophe" in *The Pursuit of Signs: Semiotics, Literature, Deconstruction* (Ithaca: Cornell University Press, 1981), 135–54. Cf. William Waters, *Poetry's Touch: On Lyric Address* (Ithaca: Cornell University Press, 2003), 3.

42. Culler, *Theory of the Lyric*, 187.

43. On "lyric hyperbole" as "a fundamental underlying structure of lyric," see Culler, *Theory of the Lyric*, 258–63 (259).

44. Culler, *Theory of the Lyric*, 31, 82, 176.

45. See H. Aram Veeser, ed., *The New Historicism* (New York: Routledge, 1989).

46. See Marjorie Levinson, "What Is New Formalism?" *PMLA* 122.2 (2007): 558–69. See also the special issue of *Modern Language Quarterly* 61 (2000) devoted to "new formalism."

47. See Joel Fineman, *Shakespeare's Perjured Eye: The Invention of Poetic Subjectivity in the Sonnets* (Berkeley: University of California Press, 1986).

48. Culler, *Theory of the Lyric*, 49; 34, 35, 37, 37.

49. For Culler, *Theory of the Lyric*, 31, even William Carlos Williams' famous "Red Wheelbarrow" is epideixis, "an unorthodox, unfinished version of the poem of praise."

50. Alastair Fowler, *Kinds of Literature* (Cambridge, MA: Harvard University Press, 1982); subsequent page references appear parenthetically.

51. Fowler, *Kinds of Literature*, 58; for fifteen common "features that have been generically organized," see 60–73.

52. Fowler, *Kinds of Literature*, 195–96. On epigrammatic "point," see 198, 199, 200, 201.

53. Fowler, *Kinds of Literature*, 112–13. Here, "liminal" refers to poems spoken at the doorway; "psychomachies" are poems that represent inner struggles as allegorical warfare; *blasons* are descriptions of the beloved's physical beauty; *baisers* are poems about kisses. Many of these Elizabethan subgenres have classical antecedents.

54. The most important ancient authorities for establishing generic hierarchies were Cicero, Horace, Quintilian, and Diomedes (a fourth-century CE grammarian); see Fowler, *Kinds of Literature*, 219 and 317 n. 22. Cf. his table of historic genres as schematized by these four ancient and five early modern English critics (220).

55. See the classic essay by M. H. Abrams, "Structure and Style in the Greater Romantic Lyric," in *From Sensibility to Romanticism*, ed. Frederick W. Hilles and Harold Bloom (New York: Oxford University Press, 1965), 527–60.

56. Fowler, *Kinds of Literature*, 220.

57. Helen Vendler, *The Music of What Happens: Poems, Poets, Critics* (Cambridge, MA: Harvard University Press, 1988), 2 (her italics).

58. Helen Vendler, *Poems, Poets, Poetry: An Introduction and Anthology*, 2nd ed. (Boston: Bedford/St. Martin's, 2002); subsequent page references appear parenthetically.

59. Vendler, *Poems, Poets, Poetry*, 14 (her italics); for Culler's critique of her view, see *Theory of the Lyric*, 110.

60. Vendler, *Poems, Poets, Poetry*, 27; her italics. Cf. Vendler, *Music of What Happens*, 77.

61. Culler, *Theory of the Lyric*, 40; cf. 322.

62. *The New Oxford Book of Seventeenth-Century Verse*, ed. Alastair Fowler (Oxford: Oxford University Press, 1991), 255.

63. Fowler, *Kinds of Literature*, 197, points out that Herrick's *Hesperides* modulates epigram with "an astonishing variety of genres."

64. See Fowler, *Kinds of Literature*, 198.

65. Cf. Fowler, *Kinds of Literature*, 197.

66. See *NPEPP*, s.v. *Poetry*, 940.

67. William Empson, quoted by Frank Kermode, *The Appetite for Poetry* (Cambridge, MA: Harvard University Press, 1989), 45.

Chapter 3

1. The word *masterpiece* was borrowed from Dutch or perhaps German. *The Oxford English Dictionary*, 2nd ed. (Oxford: Clarendon Press, 1989), s. v., records the earliest uses of the word in English from the first decade of the seventeenth century.

2. The poetry of the so-called Alliterative Revival remained alive in the north and west of England throughout the Middle Ages, but it is more associated with epic and romance than with lyric.

3. Ardis Butterfield, "Lyric," in *The Cambridge Companion to Medieval English Literature*, ed. Larry Scanlon (Cambridge: Cambridge University Press, 2009), 95–109 (96).

4. Ralph Hanna, "Miscellaneity and Vernacularity: Conditions of Literary Production in Late Medieval England," in *The Whole Book: Cultural Perspectives on the Medieval Miscellany*, ed. Stephen G. Nichols and Siegfried Wenzel (Ann Arbor: University of Michigan Press, 1996), 37–51 (47). For similar cautions, see Seth Lerer, "Medieval English Literature and the Idea of the Anthology," *PMLA* 118.5 (2003): 1251–67.

5. On the common confusion between a literary canon and a classroom syllabus, see John Guillory, *Cultural Capital: The Problem of Literary Canon Formation* (Chicago: University of Chicago Press, 1993), 33.

6. Text from Maxwell S. Luria and Richard

L. Hoffman, eds., *Middle English Lyrics* (New York: Norton, 1974) no. 190; the standard scholarly edition is Carleton Brown, ed., *English Lyrics of the XIIIth Century* (Oxford: Clarendon Press, 1932), no. 1. I have added the final etymological *e* to *wod*, which is necessary for the rhyme. The final *e* appears in Oxford, St. Johns College MS 190 and British Library MS Arundel 288, two thirteenth-century manuscripts of the Anglo-Norman French work that preserves the lyric; see A. D. Wilshere, ed., *Edmundi Abingdonensis Mirour de Seinte Eglyse* (London: Anglo-Norman Text Society, 1982), 66, 69. The *e* also appears in the thirteenth-century Bodleian MS Digby 20, quoted Brown 166.

7. See Derek Attridge, *Moving Words: Forms of English Poetry* (Oxford: Oxford University Press, 2013), 147–87; for his analysis of this poem, see 147–50. The dolnik provides important evidence for the failure of traditional foot-based prosody to account for some varieties of poetic rhythm.

8. Rosemary Woolf, *The English Religious Lyric in the Middle Ages* (Oxford: Clarendon Press, 1968), 242.

9. Two closely related Latin texts are edited in Helen P. Forshaw, S.H.C. J., ed. *Edmund of Abingdon, Speculum religiosorum and Speculum Ecclesie* (London: British Academy by Oxford University Press, 1973); on French translations, see 1, 15–16; Wilshere, ed., *Mirour de Seinte Eglyse*, x–xi. Translations from French and Latin are mine unless otherwise noted; citations of the Latin and French texts are by page number from the respective editions.

10. See Woolf, *English Religious Lyric*, 242.

11. Cf. Butterfield, "Lyric," 100–1.

12. See Wilshere, *Mirour de Seinte Eglyse*, x–xii.

13. From Latin text of *Speculum Ecclesie* in Forshaw, *Edmund of Abingdon*, 91; cf. *Speculum religiosorum* 90.

14. Hans-Georg Gadamer, *Truth and Method*, 2nd rev. ed., trans. Joel Weinsheimer and Donald G. Marshall (New York: Continuum, 1999), 306.

15. The classic discussion of affective piety in relation to devotional lyrics is Douglas Gray, *Themes and Images in Medieval English Religious Lyric* (London: Routledge, 1972), 18–31.

16. See *Meditations on the Life of Christ: An Illustrated Manuscript of the Fourteenth Century: Paris, Bibliothèque Nationale, MS. Ital. 115*, ed. Isa Ragusa and Rosalie B. Green (Princeton: Princeton University Press, 1961). Recent scholarship suggests that the *Meditationes* was composed c. 1336–64; see Sarah McNamer, "The Origins of the *Meditationes vitae Christi*," *Speculum* 84.4 (2009): 905–55; see also McNamer,

Affective Meditation and the Invention of Medieval Compassion (Philadelphia: University of Pennsylvania Press, 2010).

17. Mary J. Carruthers, *The Book of Memory: A Study of Memory in Medieval Culture* (Cambridge: Cambridge University Press, 1990) and *The Craft of Thought: Meditation, Rhetoric, and the Making of Images, 400–1200* (Cambridge: Cambridge University Press, 1998).

18. *Speculum Ecclesie*, ed. Forshaw, 91, 93; the corresponding passage in *Speculum religiosorum* 90, 92, sticks closer to the Vulgate: 'Call me not Noemi (that is, beautiful) but call me Mara (that is, bitter) for the Almighty hath quite filled me with bitterness'" (I give the Douay-Rheims translation of the Vulgate in this and the following quotation).

19. *Mirour*, 66, from Oxford, St. Johns College MS 190; the Digby MS printed by Brown, *English Lyrics of the XIIIth Century*, 166, uses the present tense, *dit* "says."

20. From Latin text, ed. Forshaw, 93 (my emphasis).

21. Cf. Alan J. Fletcher, "The Lyric in the Sermon," in *A Companion to the Middle English Lyric* (Cambridge: Brewer, 2005), ed. Thomas G. Duncan, 188–209, esp. 201.

22. Jonathan Culler, *Theory of the Lyric* (Cambridge, MA: Harvard University Press, 2015), 16, 283–95.

23. The main differences between Middle English and Modern English pronunciation are the result of the so-called Great Vowel Shift that occurred in approximately the later fifteenth century. In phonetic transcription the short, lax *u*-sound in *sone*, *under*, and perhaps *wode*, is written [ʊ]. By the later fourteenth century, [wʊdə] had changed to [woːd].

24. J. A. W. Bennett, *Poetry of the Passion: Studies in Twelve Centuries of English Verse* (Oxford: Clarendon Press, 1982), points out that the poem contains a "submerged allusion" (37) to the verse in the Song of Songs about the sun-browned beloved cited by Edmund of Abingdon.

25. The first couplet probably rhymes on [-ʊdə]; *rood* is [roːd], from OE *rōd*.

26. The earliest manuscript (Lambeth Palace Library MS 853) is from the first quarter of the fifteenth century. That the original poet's dialect is northern is demonstrated by Felicity Riddy, "The Provenance of *Quia Amore Langueo*," *Review of English Studies* 18 (1967): 429–33. Most modern editions are based on Oxford, Bodleian Douce MS 322. Unless otherwise indicated, I quote from Luria and Hoffman, *Middle English Lyrics*, no. 196; cf. *Religious Lyrics of the XIVth Century*, ed. Carleton Brown, 2nd rev. ed. G. V. Smithers (Oxford: Clarendon Press, 1965), no. 132.

27. It is included in a later fifteenth-century Carthusian miscellany of poetry and prose, British Library Additional MS 37049, fol. 25v-26r, available online at www.bl.uk/manuscripts/FullDisplay.aspx?ref=Add_MS_37049); this copy includes color illustrations discussed below. The Carthusians were the most austere monastic order.

28. On the shared "public language" of Middle English lyrics, see Butterfield, "Lyric," 107.

29. Another Middle English lyric ("In the vaile of restles mynd") uses the same refrain, though the primary speaker is Jesus; see *English Medieval Religious Lyrics*, ed. Douglas Gray (Exeter: University of Exeter Press, 1992), no. 43.

30. Gray, *English Medieval Religious Lyrics*, 137.

31. See Karen Saupe, ed., *Middle English Marian Lyrics* (Kalamazoo, MI: Medieval Institute Publications, 1997), Introduction, available at http://d.lib.rochester.edu/teams/publication/saupe-middle-english-marian-lyrics. On Marian honorific titles as conventional riddles, see Helen Phillips, "'Almighty and al merciable quene': Marian Titles and Marian Lyrics," in *Medieval Women: Texts and Contexts in Late Medieval Britain: Essays for Felicity Riddy*, ed. Jocelyn Wogan-Browne et al. (Turnhout: Brepols, 2000), 83-99; the poem is discussed at 98-99.

32. Brown, *Religious Lyrics of the XIVth Century*, 286.

33. Lines 49-50; following Gray, I have given the more alliterative reading of line 50 from MS Add.; Douce reads "My childe." See Riddy, "Provenance," 430 on the word *barne* 'child' corresponding with the northern dialect of the poet.

34. Lines 52-56; I have omitted the italics that Luria and Hoffman use to mark the shift of address. Saupe, *Middle English Marian Lyrics* (note to lines 53-55), finds the shift "awkward, but it dramatizes Mary's role as intercessor as she first addresses humankind and then Jesus."

35. Saupe, *Middle English Marian Lyrics*, note to line 92.

36. Cf. Woolf, *English Religious Lyric*, 302, who finds the blurring of relationships unartful.

37. Text from Luria and Hoffman, *Middle English Lyrics*, no. 181; cf. *Religious Lyrics of the XVth Century*, ed. Carleton Brown (Oxford: Clarendon Press, 1939), no. 81. Brown and some later editors print the poem in couplets, which helps clarify the four-beat lines.

38. For a sample of critical discussion, see the excerpts by Jemielty, Manning, Halliburton, and Spitzer in Luria and Hoffman, *Middle English Lyrics*, 325-49. Fletcher, "Lyric in Sermon," 208-9 reports that a late fourteenth- or early fifteenth-century preacher quoted the lyric in a Latin sermon and indicated that it "is commonly sung."

39. Brown, *English Lyrics of the XIIIth Century*, no. 31. Lines 3-4 of the earlier lyric read (I modernize letter forms and capitalization): "Of on ic wille singen that is makeles, / The king of halle kinges to moder he hire ches." (Of one I will sing that is matchless; the king of all kings as mother he chose her.) Lines 19-20 read: "Maiden and moder nas never non wimon boten he—/ Wel mitte he berigge of godes sune be." (Virgin and mother no woman was but she; well might she be the bearer of God's son.)

40. Woolf, *English Religious Lyric in the Middle Ages*, 242.

41. Woolf, *English Religious Lyric*, 9.

42. Michael Steffes, "'As Dewe in Aprylle': 'I Syng of a Mayden' and the Liturgy," *Medium Ævum* 71 (2002): 66-73.

43. On the liturgical references, see Woolf, *English Religious Lyric*, 287 n. 1; *Medieval English Lyrics: A Critical Anthology*, ed. R. T. Davies (Evanston: Northwestern University Press, 1964), 17-18 and appendix.

44. Manning, in Luria and Hoffman, *Middle English Lyrics*, 332, 336.

45. Cf. Spitzer, in Luria and Hoffman, *Middle English Lyrics*, 343.

Chapter 4

1. James I. Wimsatt, *Chaucer and His French Contemporaries: Natural Music in the Fourteenth Century* (Toronto: University of Toronto Press, 1991); Ardis Butterfield, *The Familiar Enemy: Chaucer, Language and Nation in the Hundred Years' War* (Oxford: Oxford University Press, 2009). I remain unconvinced by claims that the Italian eight-line stanza known as *ottava rima* was a more important influence on Chaucer's rhyme royal than the more closely equivalent seven-line French stanza.

2. Text from *The Riverside Chaucer*, 3rd ed., Larry D. Benson, gen. ed. (Boston: Houghton Mifflin, 1987).

3. Not all modern scholars accept Stowe's attribution to Chaucer. See *Riverside Chaucer* 1089-90; Geoffrey Chaucer, *The Minor Poems, Part One, The Variorum Edition of the Works of Geoffrey Chaucer*, Vol. 5, ed. George B. Pace and Alfred David (Norman: University of Oklahoma Press, 1982), 187-90.

4. For the full text of Machaut's "Se pour ce muir, qu'Amours ay bien servi" ("If I die because I have served Love well"), see Wimsatt, *Chaucer and His French Contemporaries*, 144-45.

5. See *Squires Tale*, V.644–47; *Riverside Chaucer* 1090 n. gives other Chaucerian uses of this symbolism.

6. See Wimsatt, *Chaucer and His French Contemporaries*, 93–95.

7. Wimsatt, *Chaucer and His French Contemporaries*, 144.

8. See *OED*, s.v. *newfangleness* and *newfangle*. Chaucer perhaps heard the cognate word used in London by Flemish traders, since the Middle Dutch word *nievingel(heit)* is recorded.

9. See *Squire's Tale* V.610, 618; *Anelida and Arcite* 141; *Manciple's Tale* IX.193 ironically attributes the desire for sexual novelty to men in the context of a story about an unfaithful wife.

10. Wimsatt, *Chaucer and His French Contemporaries*, 94.

11. Jonathan Culler, *Theory of the Lyric* (Cambridge, MA: Harvard University Press, 2015), 187, 186; on love poems addressed to a beloved, see 206–11.

12. The grammatical ambiguity of *mirror*, as well as the metrical regularity of the line, is lost in the MS Fairfax 16, which reads *in a merour*.

13. Culler, *Theory of the Lyric*, 258–63.

14. My summary of the evidence for dating the poem is based on *Riverside Chaucer* 1088.

15. The most authoritative biographical study is Derek Pearsall, *The Life of Geoffrey Chaucer: A Critical Biography* (Oxford: Blackwell, 1992). For a highly readable account focusing on one crucial year, see Paul Strohm, *Chaucer's Tale: 1386 and the Road to Canterbury* (New York: Penguin, 2014).

16. Eleven manuscripts are from the fifteenth century; one is an eighteenth-century transcript from a fifteenth-century manuscript before it was damaged by fire. For further information about the text, see *Riverside Chaucer* 1191; Pace and David, *Minor Poems*, 124–27.

17. "An ABC," line 121, in *Riverside Chaucer*. The borrowing was noted by Rossell Hope Robbins, "The Lyrics," in *Companion to Chaucer Studies*, rev. ed., ed. Beryl Rowland (New York: Oxford University Press, 1979), 380–402 (394).

18. For the latter range of meanings, see *Middle English Dictionary*, s. v. *light*, adj. (2), definition 8 a-c (available online at http://quod.lib.umich.edu/m/med/).

19. See *OED*, s.v. *heavy*, adj.[1] definition 3.

20. The same official propaganda is echoed by Chaucer's friend John Gower, who offers the same three claims to the throne in his *Cronica tripertita* (quoted in *Riverside Chaucer*, 1089 n. to line 22–23).

21. The best known example is now available in *The Devonshire Manuscript: A Women's Book of Courtly Poetry*, Lady Margaret Douglas and Others, ed. Elizabeth Heale (Toronto: Centre for Reformation and Renaissance Studies, 2012).

22. For his life, see Susan Brigden, *Thomas Wyatt: The Heart's Forest* (London: Faber, 2012).

23. Arthur F. Marotti, *Manuscript, Print, and the English Renaissance Lyric* (Ithaca: Cornell University Press, 1995), identifies four crucial events that help elevate the prestige of lyric poetry in English in print: *Tottel's Miscellany* (1557); the posthumous printing of Sidney's *Astrophil and Stella* in 1591 and 1592 and his collected works in the 1598 folio; Ben Jonson's 1616 folio of his *Workes*; and the first editions of Donne's and Herbert's works in 1633 (211).

24. Julia Boffey, *Manuscripts of English Courtly Love Lyrics in the Later Middle Ages* (Woodbridge, Suffolk: D. S. Brewer, 1985), 8–9; Marotti, *Manuscript, Print, and the English Renaissance Lyric*, 38–40; Elizabeth Heale, "Women and Courtly Love Lyric: The Devonshire MS (BL Additional 17492)," *Modern Language Review* 90 (1995): 296–313.

25. Marotti, *Manuscript, Print*, 73; cf. Chris Stamatakis, *Sir Thomas Wyatt and the Rhetoric of Rewriting: "Turning the Word"* (Oxford: Oxford University Press, 2012), esp. 15–34.

26. See Jason Powell, "Marginalia, Authorship, and Editing in the Manuscripts of Thomas Wyatt's Verse," *English Manuscript Studies* 15 (2009): 1–40, esp. 28–31.

27. Marotti, *Manuscript, Print*, 218. See also Michael R. G. Spiller, *The Development of the Sonnet: An Introduction* (New York: Routledge, 1992), 98; Matthew Zarnowiecki, *Fair Copies: Reproducing the English Lyric from Tottel to Shakespeare* (Toronto: University of Toronto Press, 2014), 40.

28. Francis Turner Palgrave, *The Golden Treasury of the Best Songs and Lyrical Poems in the English Language*, ed. Christopher Ricks (London: Penguin, 1991). On poetry anthologies, see Anne Ferry, *Tradition and the Individual Poem: An Inquiry into Anthologies* (Stanford: Stanford University Press, 2001).

29. Stamatakis, *Thomas Wyatt*, 3; cf. Cathy Shrank, "'But I, that knew what harbred in that hed': Sir Thomas Wyatt and his Posthumous 'Interpreters,'" *Proceedings of the British Academy* 154 (2008): 375–401.

30. A. C. Spearing, *Medieval to Renaissance in English Poetry* (Cambridge: Cambridge University Press, 1985), 279.

31. Marotti, *Manuscript, Print*, 214.

32. See Richard C. Harrier, *The Canon of Sir Thomas Wyatt's Poetry* (Cambridge: Harvard University Press, 1975).

33. Text from *Sir Thomas Wyatt: The Complete Poems*, ed. R. A. Rebholz (New Haven: Yale University Press, 1979), no. LXXX; I occasionally alter punctuation silently.

34. Alastair Fowler, "Obscurity of Sentiment in the Poetry of Wyatt," in Fowler, *Conceitful Thought: The Interpretation of English Renaissance Poems* (Edinburgh: Edinburgh University Press, 1975), 1–20 (13). Cf. Catherine Bates, "Wyatt, Surrey, and the Henrician Court," *Early Modern English Poetry: A Critical Companion*, ed. Patrick Cheney et al. (New York: Oxford University Press, 2007), 38–47 on how this poem resists any univocal interpretation (42).

35. C. E. Nelson, "A Note on Wyatt and Ovid," *Modern Language Review* 58 (1963): 60–63.

36. Most commentators agree that Tottel's revisions spoil the effect by making it too regular. In the following discussion, Tottel's variant readings are drawn from the critical apparatus in *Collected Poems of Sir Thomas Wyatt*, ed. Kenneth Muir and Patricia Thomson (Liverpool: Liverpool University Press, 1969), 27.

37. Derek Attridge, *The Rhythms of English Poetry* (New York: Longman, 1982), 345; I am indebted to Attridge's analysis of the poem (344–47). See Appendix for my modification of Attridge's scansion symbols.

38. Attridge, *Rhythms*, 346.

39. Attridge, *Rhythms*, 346; I have substituted *themselves* from Rebholz's edition for Attridge's *themself*, which is based on Muir-Thomson's reading *theimself* as witnessed by the Egerton MS. The scansion remains unaffected.

40. The scansion of line eight is mine; Attridge provides the scansion of line nine (346).

41. Attridge, *Rhythms*, 347. The "demotion rule" (#4) here is that a stressed syllable (in this case, *dear*) between two other stressed syllables may be realized as an offbeat.

42. Attridge, *Rhythms*, 347.

43. Attridge, *Rhythms*, 347.

44. For a line-terminal unstressed syllable to be promoted to a beat, according to Attridge's "promotion rule" (#3), it should be preceded by an unstressed syllable, not an implied offbeat (see 359). But as a rhyme sound, *-ness* clearly realizes a beat.

45. I borrow Attridge's scansion of the second line, which he prefaces with the observation that "the syntactic and lexical structures do not always co-operate with the metrical scheme" (345). The first element of the compound noun (written as two words in the Egerton MS) might be better interpreted as a metrically subordinated stress.

46. The meter clearly troubled Tottel, who prints the couplet: "But, syns that I vnkyndly so ame serued / How like you this, what hath she now deserued?"

47. Catherine Bates, *Masculinity and the Hunt: Wyatt to Spenser* (Oxford: Oxford University Press, 2013), 107.

Chapter 5

1. See Thomas Roche, Jr., *Petrarch and the English Sonnet Sequences* (New York: AMS, 1989); Roland Greene, *Post-Petrarchism: Origins and Innovations of the Western Lyric Sequence* (Princeton: Princeton University Press, 1991); Heather Dubrow, *Echoes of Desire: English Petrarchism and Its Counterdiscourses* (Ithaca: Cornell University Press, 1995); William J. Kennedy, *The Site of Petrarchism: Early Modern National Sentiment in Italy, France, and England* (Baltimore: Johns Hopkins University Press, 2003).

2. Jonathan Culler, *Theory of the Lyric* (Cambridge, MA: Harvard University Press, 2015), 315. See E. R. Curtius, *European Literature and the Latin Middle Ages*, trans. W. R. Trask (Princeton: Princeton University Press, 1953), 158 on how medieval lyric themes "were included in the list of epideictic topoi by late antique theory."

3. George Puttenham, *The Art of English Poesy: A Critical Edition*, ed. Frank Whigham and Wayne A. Rebhorn (Ithaca: Cornell University Press, 2007), 134.

4. Anne Ferry, *The "Inward" Language: Sonnets of Wyatt, Sidney, Spenser, Shakespeare, Donne* (Chicago: University of Chicago Press, 1983).

5. See Arthur F. Marotti, "'Love is Not Love': Elizabethan Sonnet Sequences and the Social Order," *English Literary History* 49 (1982): 396–428; Ann Rosalind Jones and Peter Stallybrass, "The Politics of *Astrophil and Stella*," *Studies in English Literature* 24 (1984): 53–68; cf. the response by Katherine Duncan-Jones, *Sir Philip Sidney: Courtier Poet* (New Haven: Yale University Press, 1991), 239.

6. Puttenham, *The Art of English Poesy*, 134; cf. Dubrow, *Echoes of Desire*, 10, who insists that Petrarchan sonnets "are always—and often primarily—about love, desire, and gender," whatever else they may also be about.

7. Susan Brigden, *Thomas Wyatt: The Heart's Forest* (London: Faber, 2012), 312–450 provides a detailed account of his diplomatic missions, especially as resident ambassador to Charles V, Holy Roman Emperor, from 1537–38; she discusses his encounters with French, Italian, and Spanish dignitaries who were also poets.

8. For details of the two imprisonments, see Brigden, *Thomas Wyatt*, 274–90, 542–47; one early source also claims that Wyatt was imprisoned in Fleet Prison in 1534 for homicide (Brigden 205–10).

9. For an account of their relationship, see Brigden, *Thomas Wyatt*, 145–51, 162–64. See also Patricia Thomson, *Sir Thomas Wyatt and His Background* (Stanford: Stanford University Press, 1964), 21–29.

10. Unless otherwise noted, all references to Wyatt's poetry will be to *Sir Thomas Wyatt: The Complete Poems*, ed. R. A. Rebholz (New Haven: Yale University Press, 1979). Examples of identifiable references to court figures include a sonnet (Rebholz XXIX), an adaptation of Petrarch's lament for the death of his patron (*Rime* 269), which many scholars assume alludes to Cromwell's execution (see Brigden, *Thomas Wyatt*, 683 n. 2); and the lament for the execution of Anne Boleyn's alleged lovers (CXCVII). His best-known satire (CXLIX) is addressed to his friend John Poyntz (Poins). See Cathy Shrank, "'But I, that knew what harbred in that hed': Sir Thomas Wyatt and his Posthumous 'Interpreters,'" *Proceedings of the British Academy* 154 (2008): 375–401 for Wyatt's deliberate evasiveness in his works.

11. See Rebholz, *Thomas Wyatt*, 343; Brigden, *Thomas Wyatt*, 162 for references. On imitation and differentiation in this lyric, see Dubrow, *Echoes of Desire*, 95.

12. See Stephen Greenblatt, *Renaissance Self-Fashioning* (Chicago: University of Chicago Press, 1980), 149; cf. Brigden, *Thomas Wyatt*, 162. It is worth noting that "Anna," the solution to the riddle poem "What word is that that changeth not" (LIV), was written in the Egerton MS by a later reader. Catherine Bates, *Masculinity and the Hunt* (Oxford: Oxford University Press, 2013), 86 thinks "the precise nature of Wyatt's relation with Anne" is "probably best left to speculation," though she reminds us that the poet "worked in a court whose king enthusiastically espoused the persona of the noble huntsman."

13. Bates, *Masculinity and the Hunt*, 79–84.

14. See Heather Dubrow, *The Challenges of Orpheus: Lyric Poetry and Early Modern England* (Baltimore: Johns Hopkins University Press, 2008), 96–97 on the interpretive complexities of the final couplet.

15. See Michael R. G. Spiller, *The Development of the Sonnet: An Introduction* (New York: Routledge, 1992), 85; Susanne Woods, *Natural Emphasis: English Versification from Chaucer to Dryden* (San Marino, CA: Huntington Library, 1984), 88.

16. Except for the final line, the Egerton MS supplies no punctuation for line endings of the sonnet; however, syntactically line 10 marks the close of an independent clause.

17. Greenblatt, *Renaissance Self-Fashioning*, 282 n. 63.

18. Douglas L. Peterson, *The English Lyric from Wyatt to Donne: A History of the Plain and Eloquent Styles* (Princeton: Princeton University Press, 1967), 101.

19. *AS* was composed c. 1582. It was first printed in two pirated quartos in 1591. The vastly superior version in the 1598 folio provides the copy text for modern editions. The folio, which was authorized by the poet's sister Mary, Countess of Pembroke, was the first collected works of Sidney. Although manuscripts of the sequence circulated among members of the Sidney-Pembroke circle, not until the first print versions appeared did the vogue for sonneteering really take off. In all, about twenty English sonnet sequences were written or published in the 1590s. Roche, *Petrarch and English Sonnet Sequences*, 518–22 provides a list of the sequences and all the known editions through 1647; see also Spiller, *Development of the Sonnet*, 198–99.

20. For the life, see Duncan-Jones, *Courtier Poet*.

21. On Sidney's coterie, see H. R. Woudhuysen, *Sir Philip Sidney and the Circulation of Manuscripts* (Oxford: Oxford University Press, 1996), 357–83.

22. For Sidney's rhyming practices in comparison with Shakespeare's, see Anne Ferry, *By Design: Intention in Poetry* (Stanford: Stanford University Press, 2008), 33–56.

23. For a sense of his astonishing variety, see the Table of Verse Forms in *The Poems of Sir Philip Sidney*, ed. William Ringler (Oxford: Clarendon Press, 1962), 569–72.

24. I quote Sidney's poetry from *Sir Philip Sidney*, ed. Katherine Duncan-Jones (Oxford: Oxford University Press, 1994), a modern-spelling edition, though I use American punctuation.

25. Ferry, *"Inward" Language*, 125–26.

26. Fraunce defines *climax* as "a reduplication continued by divers degrees and steps, as it were, of the same word or sound" (quoted by Duncan-Jones, ed., *Philip Sidney*, 155).

27. Colin Williamson, "Structure and Syntax in *Astrophil and Stella*," in *Sir Philip Sidney: An Anthology of Modern Criticism*, ed. Dennis Kay (Oxford: Clarendon Press, 1987), 227–42 (233).

28. Eric Jager, *The Book of the Heart* (Chicago: University of Chicago Press, 2000), 147 points out Sidney's implicit use of the metaphor of the heart as book.

29. Ferry, *"Inward" Language*, 128; Rebecca Wiseman, "Introspection and Self-Evaluation in *Astrophil and Stella*," *Sidney Journal* 30.1 (2012): 51–77.

30. Culler, *Theory of the Lyric*, 21.

31. See Katherine Duncan-Jones, "Sidney, Stella, and Lady Rich," in *Sir Philip Sidney: 1586*

and the Creation of a Legend, ed. Jan van Dorsten et al. (Leiden: Brill/Leiden University Press, 1986), 170–92; Duncan-Jones, *Courtier Poet*, 239–47.

32. Quoted Ringler, *Poems of Philip Sidney*, xlix.

33. Ringler, *Poems of Philip Sidney*, 436–37. Sidney puns on her married name in sonnets 24, 35 and 37, the last of which appears in only one manuscript and was first printed in the 1598 folio.

34. Ringler, *Poems of Philip Sidney*, 553. The identification with Lady Rich is also made in Bodleian MS Rawl. poet. 172 (Ringler 473).

35. "Some Sonnets of Sir Philip Sidney," *Last Essays* (1833), quoted by Ringler 440.

36. Bradbook, quoted by Duncan-Jones, "Sidney, Stella, and Lady Rich," 170.

37. Duncan-Jones, "Sidney, Stella, and Lady Rich," 174. On overlap between *energia* (vigor of style) and *enargia* (vividness), see Richard A. Lanham, *A Handlist of Rhetorical Terms*, 2nd ed. (Berkeley: University of California Press, 1991), 64–65.

38. Duncan-Jones, *Courtier Poet*, 246.

39. Other sonnets that address friends include *AS* 20, 21, 23, 27, 51, 69, 88, 92, 104.

40. Derived from medieval Latin for "griffin" (a mythical bird often confused with the vulture), the word *gripe* was certainly a learned word when first introduced to English in the thirteenth century, though it was common in poetic usage in the sixteenth century; see *OED*, s.v. *gripe*, sb².

41. *OED*, s.v. *rhubarb*. Sidney uses the word in *An Apology for Poetry (Or The Defense of Poesy)*, ed. Geoffrey Shepherd; rev. 3rd ed., R. W. Maslen, ed. (Manchester: Manchester University Press, 2002), 95.23.

42. Cf. Anne Ferry's device of printing the rhyme words in a single column to highlight the semantic weight they carry (*By Design* 42).

43. Jonathan Culler, "Changes in the Study of the Lyric," in *Lyric Poetry: Beyond New Criticism*, ed. Chaviva Hošek and Patricia Parker (Ithaca: Cornell University Press, 1985), 38–54 (40). Spiller, *Development of the Sonnet*, 109 calls attention to Sidney's fondness for apostrophe; by his count, sixty-two of 108 sonnets employ the trope, compared with about forty in Petrarch's *Rime*.

44. Culler, *Theory of the Lyric*, 213.

45. David Kalstone, *Sidney's Poetry: Contexts and Interpretations* (New York: Norton, 1965), 164, 192, n. 16, prefers reading it in normal word order.

46. Duncan-Jones, *Philip Sidney*, 160.

47. Williamson, "Structure and Syntax," 239.

48. For biography, see Andrew Hadfield, *Edmund Spenser: A Life* (Oxford: Oxford University Press, 2012).

49. Text based on *The Yale Edition of the Shorter Poems of Edmund Spenser* [henceforth *Yale Spenser*], ed. William A. Oram et al. (New Haven: Yale University Press, 1989), though I modernize the spelling, capitalization, and punctuation.

50. See Dubrow, *Challenges of Orpheus*, 99. For how Renaissance printers used gendered "corporality" in marketing published books of sonnets, see Wendy Wall, *The Imprint of Gender: Authorship and Publication in the English Renaissance* (Ithaca, NY: Cornell UP, 1993), 60–70.

51. Woods, *Natural Emphasis*, 138; cf. Derek Attridge, *Moving Words: Forms of English Poetry* (Oxford: Oxford University Press, 2013), 127–46.

52. My scansion of this line is conjectural, assuming a ten-syllable, five-beat line, though other possibilities cannot be ruled out.

53. Cf. Derek Attridge, *Rhythms of English Poetry* (New York: Longman, 1982), 237 for a Spenserian decasyllabic line that adds a sixth beat. My scansion of *Am* 1.13 uses Attridge's symbol [o] for a **virtual offbeat**. Unlike an implied offbeat, a virtual one occurs at a syntactic break usually marked by punctuation.

54. It is difficult to ascertain Spenser's pronunciation of this vowel (developed from ME ǭ) since more than one possibility seems to have been current in the sixteenth century; see E. J. Dobson, *English Pronunciation 1500–1700*, 2nd ed., 2 vols. (Oxford: Clarendon Press, 1968), 2:671–73, 2:676.

55. Culler, *Theory of the Lyric*, 278–79. This strategy may not be as rare in early lyric as Culler suggests; cf. the Marian lyric "In a tabernacle of a toure" discussed in Chapter 3.

56. Hans-Georg Gadamer, *Truth and Method*, 2nd rev. ed., trans. Joel Weinsheimer and Donald G. Marshall (New York: Continuum, 1999), 163–64; for "presence effects," see Hans Ulrich Gumbrecht, *The Production of Presence: What Meaning Cannot Convey* (Stanford: Stanford University Press, 2003).

57. William Waters, *Poetry's Touch: On Lyric Address* (Ithaca: Cornell University Press, 2003), 106.

58. St. Augustine first explored the analogy between text, individual life, and human history in *Confessions* XI, c. 28.

59. The first vowel was probably pronounced [ɛː] in Spenser's London dialect of Early Modern English; the second vowel was probably realized as the diphthong [əɪ]. See the simplified account in Jeremy J. Smith, *Essentials of Early English: An Introduction to Old, Middle and Early Modern English*, 2nd edition

(New York: Routledge, 2005), 128–30, which aims to describe the pronunciation "of middle-aged, middle-class Londoners living around 1600" (128). For more technical information on the two vowels, see Dobson, *English Pronunciation 1500–1700*, 2:594–603 and 2:659–64.

60. Hadfield, *Edmund Spenser*, 308.

61. Sir Philip Sidney, *The Old Arcadia*, ed. Katherine Duncan-Jones (Oxford: Oxford University Press, 1999), 104; the editor notes that "sand was a stock image of changeability, and especially of women's fickleness" (374). In the *Old Arcadia*, the Amazon's name is Cleophila. Sidney took the image of a woman writing in the sand from a lyric in *Diana* by the Spanish author Montemayor; for Sidney's version, see *Certain Sonnets* no. 28, in Ringler, *Poems of Philip Sidney*.

62. For the early reception of the *Sonnets*, see *Shakespeare's Sonnets*, ed. Katherine Duncan-Jones (London: Nelson, 1997), 69–81. The fullest account is available in *A New Variorum Edition of William Shakespeare: The Sonnets*, ed. Hyder Edward Rollins, 2 vols. (Philadelphia: Lippincott, 1944).

63. See Samuel Schoenbaum, *William Shakespeare: A Compact Documentary Life* (Oxford: Oxford University Press, 1977). Stephen Greenblatt, *Will in the World: How Shakespeare Became Shakespeare* (New York: Norton, 2004) offers a highly readable, though often speculative, account of his life and career.

64. Renaissance sonnet sequences often followed Petrarch's lead in including other kinds of lyric; see Heather Dubrow, "'Dressing Old Words New'? Re-evaluating the 'Delian Structure,'" in *A Companion to Shakespeare's Sonnets*, ed. Michael Schoenfeldt (Malden, MA: Blackwell, 2008), 90–103.

65. See William Shakespeare, *The Complete Sonnets and Poems*, ed. Colin Burrow (Oxford: Oxford University Press, 2003), 94–95.

66. Duncan-Jones, *Shakespeare's Sonnets*, 10–13, 32–41.

67. See Margreta de Grazia, "The Scandal of Shakespeare's Sonnets," in *Shakespeare's Sonnets: Critical Essays*, ed. James Schiffer (New York: Garland, 1999), 89–112, esp. 92.

68. Malone, *Supplement* (1780), quoted by Duncan-Jones, *Shakespeare's Sonnets*, 44.

69. For a brief account of this "story," and its potentially biographical relation to Shakespeare, see Robert Matz, *The World of Shakespeare's Sonnets: An Introduction* (Jefferson, NC: McFarland, 2008), 6–13.

70. For a cautionary note, see Heather Dubrow, "'Incertainties Now Crown Themselves Assur'd': The Politics of Plotting Shakespeare's Sonnets," in Schiffer, *Shakespeare's Sonnets*, 113–33.

71. William Shakespeare, *The Sonnets and A Lover's Complaint*, ed. John Kerrigan (Harmondsworth: Penguin, 1986), 11.

72. See Peter Stallybrass, "Editing as Cultural Formation: The Sexing of Shakespeare's Sonnets," in Schiffer, *Shakespeare's Sonnets*, 75–88. Matz, *Shakespeare's Sonnets*, 65–70, discusses same-sex desire at a time before sexuality was understood in terms of exclusively heterosexual and homosexual identities (according to Foucault and his followers).

73. Cf. Helen Vendler, *The Art of Shakespeare's Sonnets* (Cambridge, MA: Harvard University Press, 1997), 18; Ferry, *"Inward" Language*, 178.

74. See Brian Vickers, *Classical Rhetoric and English Poetry* (Carbondale: Southern Illinois University Press, 1989), 69–73. Joel Fineman, *Shakespeare's Perjured Eye: The Invention of Poetic Subjectivity in the Sonnets* (Berkeley: University of California Press, 1986) shows how Shakespeare responds to the conventions of Renaissance epideictic.

75. Unless stated otherwise, quotations of Shakespeare's sonnets are from Burrow, *Complete Sonnets*.

76. See Katharine M. Wilson, *Shakespeare's Sugared Sonnets* (London and N.Y., 1974), 146–67, cited by Stephen Booth, *Shakespeare's Sonnets: Edited with Analytic Commentary* (New Haven: Yale University Press, 1978), 135. The letter was translated into English by Thomas Wilson in *The Arte of Rhetorique* in 1553. Booth's edition includes a facsimile of Q.

77. Elaine Scarry, *On Beauty and Being Just* (Princeton: Princeton University Press, 1999), 3; she does not mention the procreation sonnets.

78. For a defense of the technique of impersonating the poet, see Lars Engle, "William Empson and the Sonnets," in Schoenfeldt, *Companion to Shakespeare's Sonnets*, 163–82 (172).

79. I have only marked the most likely scansion, though others are possible. See Appendix for scansion symbols.

80. Anne Ferry, *All in War with Time: Love Poetry of Shakespeare, Donne, Jonson, Marvell* (Cambridge, MA: Harvard University Press, 1975), 3–63. Ferry, *"Inward" Language*, 189, points out that none of Shakespeare's references to immortalizing the beloved occurs in the poems thought to be addressed to the woman.

81. Horace, *Odes* 30.1–8 (my translation); for the original Latin and another translation, see Horace, *Odes and Epodes*, ed. and trans. Niall Rudd (Cambridge, MA: Harvard University Press, 2004), 216–17.

82. See the discussion of "fusing horizons" in Gadamer in Chapter 3 above; cf. Hans Robert

Jauss, *Toward an Aesthetic of Reception*, trans. Timothy Bahti (Minneapolis: University of Minnesota Press, 1982), 29–30.

83. I cite Geoffrey Whitney, *A Choice of Emblemes* from the facsimile edition in *The English Emblem Tradition* (*Index emblematicus*), ed. Peter M. Daly et al., Vol. 1 (Toronto: University of Toronto Press, 1988), 79–337.

84. Whitney, *Choice of Emblemes* (facsimile), 223.

85. Whitney, *Choice of Emblemes* (facsimile), 297–98.

86. Burrow, *Sonnets*, 490; cf. Kerrigan, *Sonnets*, 21 and Duncan-Jones, *Sonnets*, 272.

87. Vendler, *Art of Shakespeare's Sonnets*, 269.

88. The 1547 Book of Common Prayer includes this formula from the Apostles' Creed.

89. Booth, *Sonnets*, 229.

90. Booth, *Sonnets*, 229–30.

91. See William Empson, *Seven Types of Ambiguity*, 3rd ed. (New York: New Directions, 1947), 2–3; cf. Engle, "William Empson," 169–70.

92. Randolph Quirk et al., *A Grammar of Contemporary English* (Harlow, Essex: Longman, 1972), 85.

93. See Rollins, *Variorum* II, 190.

94. *May* as expressing ability or power is an archaic sense that was still active in Shakespeare's day; for the two relevant meanings of the word, see *OED* s.v. *may*, 2, 3.

95. Duncan-Jones, *Sonnets*, 256.

96. Kerrigan, *Sonnets*, 333, 53.

97. Booth, *Sonnets*, 387.

98. See *OED*, s.v. *mark*, def. 9. Cf. Booth's analysis of the aptness of the metaphor of a seamark that *looks on tempests and is never shaken* (*Sonnets*, 388); contrast Vendler, *Art of Shakespeare's Sonnets*, who reads the *ever-fixèd mark* as the North Star (489).

99. Vendler, *Art of Shakespeare's Sonnets*, 1, 492. For Culler's response to Vendler, see *Theory of the Lyric*, 110.

100. Culler, *Theory of the Lyric*, 130 suggests that "'performance' is doubtless the best translation of *epideixis*: discourse conceived as an act, aiming to persuade, to move, to innovate." However, by expanding the definition of epideictic to include "general claims about the world" (286), Culler's theory gives short shrift to historically specific practices of teaching and producing rhetorical performances.

101. Vendler, *Art of Shakespeare's Sonnets*, 1–2.

102. Kerrigan, *Sonnets*, 356.

103. Booth, *Sonnets*, 441, citing Tilley P419.

104. Vender, *Art of Shakespeare's Sonnets*, 550.

105. Rollins, *Variorum* I, 330 documents the popularity of definitions of love in Elizabethan poetry.

106. Vender, *Art of Shakespeare's Sonnets*, 551, 550.

107. Vendler, *Art of Shakespeare's Sonnets*, 552 (her italics).

108. On "copulatives" in Shakespeare's *Sonnets*, see Matthew Zarnowiecki, *Fair Copies: Reproducing the English Lyric from Tottel to Shakespeare* (Toronto: University of Toronto Press, 2014), 156–68; for Sonnet 129, see 161–64.

109. Quirk et al., *Grammar of Contemporary English*, 820; the verb *be* (from Old English *beon*) has served this grammatical function since long before the earliest documented stages of English.

110. Brian Vickers, *Classical Rhetoric*, 161. His analysis (160–63) reveals the use of syllepsis, antimetabole (chiasmus), anaphora, asyndeton, epanalepsis, parison, antithesis, isocolon, paromasia, anadiplosis, and polyptoton.

111. On rhetorical figures in the poem, in addition to Vickers, see Booth, *Sonnets*, 443; Peterson 382 in the work cited in the next note; Burrow, *Sonnets*, 638; and Duncan-Jones, *Sonnets*, 372.

112. Douglas L. Peterson, "A Probable Source for Shakespeare's Sonnet CXXIX," *Shakespeare Quarterly* 5.4 (1954): 381–84; also see Peterson, *English Lyric*, 227–31.

113. "Farewell to Love," lines 24–25 in *The Complete Poetry of John Donne*, ed. John T. Shawcross (Garden City, NJ: Anchor, 1967).

114. Bacon, *Sylva Sylvarum* (1627), sec. 693, quoted by Booth, *Sonnets*, 442.

115. Information on word frequencies in the following discussion is based on Herbert S. Donow, *A Concordance to the Sonnet Sequences of Daniel, Drayton, Shakespeare, Sidney, and Spenser* (Carbondale: Southern Illinois University Press, 1969).

116. Cf. Vickers, *Classical Rhetoric*, 162, who notes some of the instances of this vowel, and alliteration on [m]. Middle English *ā* [aː] becomes [ɛː] in Early Modern English. See Dobson, *English Pronunciation*, 2:594–603; Helge Kökeritz, *Shakespeare's Pronunciation* (New Haven: Yale University Press, 1953), 173–80; for a simplified account, see Smith, *Essentials of Early English*, 128–29.

117. Attridge, *Rhythms of English Poetry*, 258.

Chapter 6

1. The label "country house poem" was first applied by G. R. Hibbard in "The Country House Poem of the Seventeenth Century," *Jour-*

nal of the Warburg and Courtauld Institutes 19 (1956): 159–74; for an anthology, see Alastair Fowler, *The Country House Poem: A Cabinet of Seventeenth-Century Estate Poems and Related Items* (Edinburgh: Edinburgh University Press, 1994).

2. For Lanyer's life and work, see Susanne Woods, *Lanyer: A Renaissance Woman Poet* (New York: Oxford University Press, 1999); on uncertainty over which poem was written first, see 184 n. 30.

3. Alastair Fowler, *Kinds of Literature* (Cambridge, MA: Harvard University Press, 1982), 156.

4. See Alastair Fowler, "Country-House Poems: The Politics of a Genre," *The Seventeenth Century* 1 (1986): 1–14; Fowler, *Country House Poem*, 16–17; Barbara K. Lewalski, "The Lady of the Country-House Poem," in *The Fashioning and Functioning of the British Country House*, ed. Gervase Jackson-Stops et al. (Washington, D.C.: National Gallery of Art, 1989), 261–75 (261). Two Roman poems whose influence on the early modern genre is substantial are Horace, Epode 2 (*Beatus vir*) and Martial, Epigram 3.58 (*Baiana nostri villa*).

5. Raymond Williams, *The Country and the City* (New York: Oxford University Press, 1973); Don E. Wayne, *Penshurst: The Semiotics of Place and the Poetics of History* (Madison: University of Wisconsin Press, 1984); Kari Boyd McBride, *Country House Discourse in Early Modern England* (Aldershot: Ashgate, 2001). Less politically engaged studies include William Alexander McClung, *The Country House in English Renaissance Poetry* (Berkeley: University of California Press, 1977); Heather Dubrow, "The Country-House Poem: A Study of Generic Development," *Genre* 12 (1979): 153–79; Hugh Jenkins, *Feigned Commonwealths: The Country-House Poem and the Fashioning of Ideal Community* (Pittsburgh: Duquesne University Press, 1998).

6. See Karen Nelson, "Annotated Bibliography: Texts and Criticism of Aemilia Bassano Lanyer," in *Aemilia Lanyer: Gender, Genre, and the Canon*, Marshall Grossman, ed. (Lexington: University Press of Kentucky, 1998), 234–54. The Latin title means *Hail God, King of the Jews*.

7. See Woods, *Lanyer*, 90–98, for a refutation of Rowse's claim.

8. All quotations of Lanyer's poetry are based on *The Poems of Aemilia Lanyer: Salve Deus Rex Judaeorum*, ed. Susanne Woods (New York: Oxford University Press, 1993); I have modernized spelling, capitalization, and punctuation.

9. Woods, *Lanyer*, 9–14.

10. Woods, *Lanyer*, 20–28.

11. See the essays collected in Grossman, *Aemelia Lanyer*, esp. Barbara K. Lewalski, "Seizing Discourses and Reinventing Genres," 49–59; Janel Mueller, "The Feminist Poetics of 'Salve Deus Rex Judaeorum,'" 99–127. Other important feminist studies include Lewalski, "Of God and Good Women: The Poems of Aemilia Lanyer," in *Silent But for the Word: Tudor Women as Patrons, Translators, and Writers of Religious Works*, ed. Margaret Patterson Hannay (Kent: Kent State University Press, 1985), 203–24, 283–87; Lewalski, "Rewriting Patriarchy and Patronage: Margaret Clifford, Anne Clifford, and Aemilia Lanyer, *Yearbook of English Studies* 21 (1991): 87–106; Lewalski, "Imagining Female Community: Aemilia Lanyer's Poems," in Lewalski, *Writing Women in Jacobean England* (Cambridge, MA: Harvard University Press, 1993), 213–41, 394–99; Lisa Schnell, "'So Great a Difference Is There in Degree': Aemilia Lanyer and the Aims of Feminist Criticism," *Modern Language Quarterly* 57 (1996): 23–35; Kari Boyd McBride, "Remembering Orpheus in the Poems of Aemelia Lanyer, *Studies in English Literature 1500–1900* 38 (1998): 87–108.

12. Lewalski, "Lady of the Country-House Poem," 265.

13. Lewalski, "Imagining Female Community," 216.

14. Lewalski, "Lady of the Country-House Poem," 265.

15. Lewalski, "Imagining Female Community," 216.

16. Jonathan Culler, *Theory of the Lyric* (Cambridge, MA: Harvard University Press, 2015), 34–38.

17. Lewalski, "Imagining Female Community," 237.

18. On the mythic cast of the poem as a description of a lost Eden, see Lewalski, "Imagining Female Community," 237; "Of God and Good Women," 220; "Seizing Discourses," 55.

19. E. R. Curtius, *European Literature and the Latin Middle Ages*, trans. Willard R. Trask (Princeton: Princeton University Press, 1953), 319–26.

20. On sovereign centers, see Alastair Fowler, *Triumphal Forms: Structural Patterns in Elizabethan Poetry* (Cambridge: Cambridge University Press, 1970).

21. *Conster* (accented on the first syllable) is an archaic form of the word *construe*; here, its primary sense is to interpret actions or persons or to understand a person's meaning (*OED*, s.v. *construe*, 6, 8).

22. For the life, see Ian Donaldson, *Ben Jonson: A Life* (Oxford: Oxford University Press, 2011).

23. On Jonson's effort to make himself into

a writer of national importance, see Richard Helgerson, *Self-Crowned Laureates: Spenser, Jonson, Milton, and the Literary System* (Berkeley: University of California Press, 1983).

24. *Ben Jonson*, ed. Ian Donaldson (Oxford: Oxford University Press, 1985), *Epigrams* 14, lines 1–2; unless otherwise noted, all further citations to Jonson's work are to this edition.

25. Richard S. Peterson, *Imitation and Praise in the Poems of Ben Jonson* (New Haven: Yale University Press, 1981).

26. See Donaldson, *Ben Jonson: A Life*, 324–31.

27. See Arthur F. Marotti, *Manuscript, Print, and the English Renaissance Lyric* (Ithaca: Cornell University Press, 1995), 211.

28. William Drummond of Hawthornden, *Conversations*, in Donaldson, *Ben Jonson*, 609.

29. For more detailed information see Wayne, *Penshurst*; McClung, *Country House*.

30. The surviving correspondence between Lord Lisle and his wife reveals the emotional stress caused by his financial difficulties; see J. C. A. Rathmell, "Jonson, Lord Lisle, and Penshurst," *English Literary Renaissance* 1 (1971): 250–60.

31. David Norbrook, *Poetry and Politics in the English Renaissance*, rev. ed. (Oxford: Oxford University Press, 2002), 163.

32. Marxist critique began with Raymond Williams in *The Country and the City* (New York: Oxford University Press, 1973), esp. 32. For a response, see Alastair Fowler, "Country House Poems: The Politics of a Genre," *Seventeenth Century* 1 (1986): 1–14, esp. 6–9.

33. *Discoveries*, in Donaldson, *Ben Jonson*, 549. *Feign* here has the sense of representing something in fiction (*OED* 3), an imitation (mimesis). *Embattle* is used figuratively, meaning "to set (an army) in battle array" *OED* (v.,[1] def. 1); it also carries a secondary sense as an architectural term, "to furnish (a building, wall, etc.) with battlements" (*OED* v.[2]).

34. Jonson, *Discoveries*, in Donaldson, *Ben Jonson*, 583.

35. See Rathmell, "Jonson, Lord Lisle, and Penshurst," 256.

36. See Alastair Fowler, "The Locality of Jonson's 'To Penshurst,'" in Fowler, *Conceitful Thought: The Interpretation of English Renaissance Poems* (Edinburgh: Edinburgh University Press, 1975), 114–34, esp. 125–28 on number symbolism.

37. Paul M. Cubeta, "A Jonsonian Ideal: 'To Penshurst,'" *Philological Quarterly* 42 (1963): 14–24 (17).

38. Wayne, *Penshurst*, 45.

39. Cubeta, "Jonsonian Ideal," 22; Gayle Edward Wilson, "Jonson's Use of the Bible and the Great Chain of Being in 'To Penshurst,'" *Studies in English Literature* (Houston) 8 (1968): 77–89. The classic study in the history of ideas is Arthur O. Lovejoy, *The Great Chain of Being* (Cambridge, MA: Harvard University Press, 1964), first published in 1936.

40. Cf. Fowler, "Locality,"131; Norbrook, *Poetry and Politics*, 168.

41. Fowler, "Politics," 3.

42. *Georgics* 2.501–2, in *Virgil, Eclogues, Georgics, Aeneid I–VI*, ed. and trans. H. Rushton Fairclough (London: W. Heinemann, 1929). Cf. Rathmell, "Jonson, Lord Lisle, and Penshurst," 253 on fruits cultivated on the estate.

43. Jonson makes a more direct allusion to the Golden Age in another poem in praise of country life, "To Sir Robert Wroth" (*Forest* 3.50).

44. Charles Molesworth's "Property and Virtue: The Genre of the Country-House Poem in the Seventeenth Century," *Genre* 1 (1968): 141–57, esp. 145.

45. Fowler, "Politics," 9.

46. Fowler, "Locality," 126.

47. Fowler, "Politics," 9 compares the "ripe daughters" with the emblem of *Fecondità* (fruitfulness) in Cesare Ripa, *Iconologia* (1611).

48. Cf. *Discoveries*, in Donaldson, *Ben Jonson*, 582, 588.

49. *Discoveries*, Donaldson, *Ben Jonson*, 583.

50. The 1615 proclamation is quoted in Jenkins, *Feigned Commonwealths*, 37; cf. McBride, *Country House Discourse*, 95–98.

51. Fowler, "Politics," 11.

52. *Historical Manuscripts Commission*, 77, *De L'Isle and Dudley MSS*, IV, 162, quoted by Rathmell, "Jonson, Lord Lisle, and Penshurst," 250 (ellipsis his); I have modernized spelling and punctuation.

53. *Conversations*, in Donaldson, *Ben Jonson*, 602.

54. Millicent V. Hay, *The Life of Robert Sidney, Earl of Leicester, 1563–1626* (Cranbury: Associated University Press, 1984), 182–86.

55. See Fowler, *Kinds of Literature*, 184 on the subgenres of epigram.

56. *OED*, s.v. manner, 4a.

57. Rathmell, "Jonson, Lord Lisle, and Penshurst," 254.

58. Wayne, *Penshurst*, 178; see 177–79 for other examples of deixis (shifters) in the poem.

Chapter 7

1. See Joshua Scodel, *The English Poetic Epitaph: Commemoration and Conflict from Jonson to Wordsworth* (Ithaca: Cornell University Press, 1991); G. W. Pigman III, *Grief and English Renaissance Elegy* (Cambridge: Cambridge University Press, 1985).

2. Cf. Rosamund Tuve, "Theme, Pattern, and Imagery in *Lycidas,*" in *Milton's* Lycidas: *The Tradition and the Poem, New and Revised Edition,* ed. C. A. Patrides (Columbia: University of Missouri Press, 1983), 171–204, esp. 182–83.

3. See *Milton's "Lycidas," Edited to Serve as an Introduction to Criticism,* ed. Scott Elledge (New York: Harper & Row, 1966), 228–30 (quotations 229). This indispensable collection includes texts of earlier pastoral elegies (in translation for non-English works), historical materials, and critical appraisals from the eighteenth to twentieth centuries.

4. Quotations from Elledge, *Milton's "Lycidas,"* at 227 (Warton), 232 (Hazlitt), 244 (Pattison, Machen).

5. Abrams, in Elledge, *Milton's "Lycidas,"* 345. For further examples, see *A Variorum Commentary on The Poems of John Milton, Volume Two, The Minor English Poems, Part Two,* ed. A. S. P. Woodhouse and Douglas Bush (New York: Columbia University Press, 1972), henceforth cited as *Variorum.*

6. Exceptions include Mark Womack, "On the Value of *Lycidas,*" *Studies in English Literature* 37 (1997): 119–36; Barbara Kiefer Lewalski, *The Life of John Milton: A Critical Biography,* rev. ed. (Malden, MA: Blackwell, 2003), 81; Gordon Teskey, *The Poetry of John Milton* (Cambridge, MA: Harvard University Press, 2015), 166–99.

7. For biography see Lewalski, *Life of John Milton.*

8. Elledge, *Milton's "Lycidas,"* 165–66.

9. *The Works of John Milton,* ed. F. A. Patterson et al. (New York: Columbia University Press, 1931–38), 8:124, quoted by Carey and Fowler, *Poems,* xviii.

10. *The Reason of Church Government Urged against Prelaty,* in Elledge, *Milton's "Lycidas,"* 174–75 (175).

11. The autograph manuscript is owned by Trinity College, Cambridge; a digital version is available online. The one-sentence epigraph in the Trinity MS was not included in the 1638 print, though the memorial volume made the honoree and occasion of his death clear to the original audience.

12. Gordon Campbell, "King, Edward (1611/12–1637)," *Oxford Dictionary of National Biography,* Oxford University Press, 2004; online edn, October 2007, accessed 9 June 2013.

13. Elledge, *Milton's "Lycidas,"* 150.

14. Elledge, *Milton's "Lycidas,"* 165.

15. Spenser published *The Shepheardes Calender* in 1579, a highly innovative series of twelve pastoral eclogues organized by month.

16. For Pindar's odes as another generic model, see Stella P. Revard, *Milton and the Tangles of Neaera's Hair: The Making of the 1645 Poems* (Columbia: University Missouri Press, 1997), 162–204, esp. 165–79.

17. James H. Hanford, "The Pastoral Elegy and Milton's *Lycidas,*" in Patrides, *Milton's Lycidas,* 31–59; cf. Teskey, *Poetry of John Milton,* 189–90. Teskey 178–89 stresses the importance of Theocritus to Milton's conception of the poem.

18. Paul Alpers, *What Is Pastoral?* (Chicago: University of Chicago Press, 1996), 51.

19. William Empson, *Some Versions of Pastoral* (New York: New Directions, 1974), 22; his book was first published in 1935.

20. Vergil borrowed the name *Lycidas* for one of his shepherd-singers in *Eclogues* 7 and 9 from Theocritus 7 and 27; Bion uses it in 2 and 6. For pastoral names as generic markers, see Alastair Fowler, *Kinds of Literature* (Cambridge, MA: Harvard University Press, 1982), 77–82.

21. For further details, see *Variorum* 549–65; for texts, see *The Pastoral Elegy: An Anthology,* ed. Thomas Perrin Harrison; translations by Harry Joshua Leon (New York: Octagon, 1968); and Elledge, *Milton's "Lycidas,"* 15–103.

22. From Andrew Lang's translation in Elledge, *Milton's "Lycidas,"* 17; further page references to Theocritus, Bion, and Moschus are from this edition and appear parenthetically in the text.

23. See Peter Sacks, *The English Elegy: Studies in the Genre from Spenser to Yeats* (Baltimore: Johns Hopkins University Press, 1985), 21–23.

24. On mythic archetypes, see the following in Patrides, *Milton's* Lycidas: Richard P. Adams, "The Archetypal Pattern of Death and Rebirth in *Lycidas,*" 111–16; Northrop Frye, "Literature as Context: Milton's *Lycidas,*" 204–15; and Caroline W. Mayerson, "The Orpheus Image in *Lycidas,*" 116–28.

25. On the identities of Bion and Moschus, see Harrison, *Pastoral Elegy,* 260–61.

26. Alpers, *What Is Pastoral,* 154–74.

27. *Variorum* 553; Alpers, *What Is Pastoral,* 155.

28. For the Latin, see *Eclogues* 5.38–44, in *Virgil, Eclogues, Georgics, Aeneid I–VI,* ed. and trans. H. Rushton Fairclough (London: W. Heinemann, 1929); my translations of Vergil throughout; Latin line numbers appear parenthetically in the text.

29. Alpers, *What Is Pastoral,* 158.

30. See Elledge, *Milton's "Lycidas,"* and Harrison, *Pastoral Elegy* for other Renaissance pastorals that contribute language and imagery to "Lycidas," including eclogues by Sannazaro (1458–1530), an elegy by Clément Marot (1531) that laments the death of Louise of Savoy,

mother of King Francis I of France; and Spenser's pastoral elegy for Sir Philip Sidney, "Astrophel."

31. J. M. French, "The Digressions in Milton's 'Lycidas,'" *Studies in Philology* 50 (1953): 485–90.

32. In England, Spenser followed the example of Mantuan in the May, July, and September eclogues in *The Shepheardes Calendar*, an important influence on Milton; see *Variorum* 555–57, 60. Carey and Fowler, *Poems*, 234 note echoes of Spenserian diction in the poem.

33. Elledge, *Milton's "Lycidas,"* 229.

34. John Crowe Ransom, "A Poem Nearly Anonymous," in Patrides, *Milton's Lycidas*, 68–85.

35. See Alastair Fowler, "'To Shepherd's Ear': The Form of Milton's *Lycidas*," in *Silent Poetry: Essays in Numerological Analysis*, ed. Fowler (London: Routledge, 1970), 170–84, esp. 173–74.

36. The unrhymed lines are 1, 13, 15, 22, 39, 51, 82, 91, 118, 161.

37. Arthur Barker, "The Pattern of Milton's Nativity Ode," *University of Toronto Quarterly* 10 (1941): 167–81 (esp. 171–72), quoted in *Variorum* 576–77. Each "movement" in Barker's scheme begins with an invocation (lines 15, 85, 132).

38. Thomas Wilson, *The Arte of Rhetorique*, ed. G. H. Mair (Oxford: Clarendon Press, 1908), 65 (spelling modernized).

39. George Puttenham, *The Art of English Poesie: A Critical Edition*, ed. Frank Whigham and Wayne A. Rebhorn (Ithaca: Cornell University Press, 2007), 137.

40. Puttenham, *Art of English Poesie*, 135; Scaliger in Elledge, *Milton's "Lycidas,"* 110. Wilson, *Arte of Rhetorique*, 67 speaks of the passions as a disease.

41. Rosemund Tuve, "Theme, Pattern, and Imagery in *Lycidas*," in Patrides, *Milton's Lycidas*, 171–204 (171).

42. Wilson, *Arte of Rhetorique*, 72.

43. E. M. W. Tillyard, from *Milton* (1930), in Patrides, *Milton's Lycidas*, 62–67.

44. M. H. Abrams, "Five Types of *Lycidas*," in Patrides, *Milton's Lycidas*, 216–35 (226).

45. See Ransom in Patrides, *Milton's Lycidas*, 83.

46. See, for example, Cleanth Brooks and John Edward Hardy, "Essays in Analysis: *Lycidas*," in Patrides, *Milton's Lycidas*, 140–56 at 147–48, 151–52. Stanley E. Fish, "*Lycidas*: A Poem Finally Anonymous," in Patrides, *Milton's Lycidas*, 319–40 offers the most vigorous challenge to the New Critical "assumption that the poem is a dramatic lyric and hence the expression of a united conscious" (321).

47. Frye, in Patrides, *Milton's Lycidas*, 207; Jon Lawry, "'Eager Thought': Dialectic in *Lycidas*," in Patrides, *Milton's Lycidas*, 236–45; Alpers, *What Is Pastoral*, 99.

48. Paul Alpers, "*Lycidas* and Modern Criticism," *English Literary History* 49 (1982): 468–96 (481); cf. the revised version in *What Is Pastoral*, 93–112.

49. Alpers, *What Is Pastoral*, 93.

50. See A. C. Spearing, *Textual Subjectivity: The Encoding of Subjectivity in Medieval Narrative and Lyric* (Oxford: Oxford University Press, 2005). The "encoding" is largely a function of linguistic effects like deixis.

51. Cf. Abrams in Patrides, *Milton's Lycidas*, 227–28.

52. All quotations of "Lycidas" are from *The Poems of John Milton*, ed. John Carey and Alastair Fowler (London: Longman, 1968); I silently adjust punctuation and capitalization. The opening alludes to Vergil, *Eclogue* 2.54.

53. Jonathan Culler, *Theory of the Lyric* (Cambridge, MA: Harvard University Press, 2015); on this opening apostrophe see 217.

54. Other scansions of line 1 are certainly possible, including:

Yet once more, O ye laurels, and once more
o B ó B   O-o B   o-o   B ó B

The line's openness to multiple interpretations of its rhythm suggests an unusually high degree of expressive tension.

55. See Puttenham, *Art of English Poesie*, 285; on the effect of pathos created by this repetition, cf. Quintilian, *Institutio oratoria* 9.23.28, who cites Vergil, *Eclogue* 2.69, a text clearly on Milton's mind.

56. On the assumed link between sound and meaning in rhyme pairs, see the famous dictum by Roman Jakobson, "Linguistics and Poetics," in *Language in Literature*, ed. Krystyna Pomorska and Stephen Rudy (Cambridge, MA: Harvard University Press, 1987), 62–94: "In poetry, any conspicuous similarity in sound is evaluated in respect to similarity and/or dissimilarity in meaning" (87).

57. Johnson, in Elledge, *Milton's "Lycidas,"* 229. Satyrs, goat-like creatures from Greek mythology, are associated with Dionysus; the Romans identified them with native fauns, half-man, half-goat sylvan deities associated with Pan (Faunus).

58. The "oaten flute" is a traditional pastoral instrument made of oat straw; cf. Vergil, *Ec.* 1.2.

59. See also line 24; contrast Alpers, *What Is Pastoral*, 96, who argues that the description is missing "the single thing we most expect to find in an eclogue, a shepherd-singer"; cf. his claim that the poem "does not explicitly represent its speaker as a shepherd until the end" (239).

60. "Lament for Bion," in Elledge, *Milton's "Lycidas,"* 25–26.

61. *Variorum* 651.

62. See Archie Burnett, *Milton's Style: The*

Shorter Poems, Paradise Regained, and "Samson Agonistes" (London: Longman, 1981), 88–90.

63. See *Variorum* 657–58.

64. On the Orpheus passage, see Mayerson, "Orpheus Image," in Patrides, *Milton's* Lycidas, 116–28.

65. Cf. *meditabor ... musam* in *Eclogue* 6.8. In these contexts, the Latin verb can mean "practice," or "work over"; see *Oxford Latin Dictionary*, ed. P. G. W. Glare (Oxford: Clarendon Press, 1982), s.v. *meditor*, 6, 7.

66. Line 71 closely parallels Tacitus, *Hist.* 4.6, though the thought is a classical commonplace; see *Variorum* 663.

67. Cf. Vergil, *Eclogue* 6.3–4.

68. Fish, "Poem Finally Anonymous," in Patrides, *Milton's* Lycidas, 329–30 insists that it is impossible to be sure precisely which lines to assign to Phoebus since Renaissance punctuation does not use quotation marks.

69. Critics differ widely in their interpretations of Apollo's speech. Cf. David Daiches, from *A Study of Literature* (1949), 92–110 (102–3); Tuve, "Theme, Pattern, and Imagery in *Lycidas*," 173; Fish, "Poem Finally Anonymous," 331, all in Patrides, *Milton's* Lycidas; see also Revard, *Milton*, 175.

70. On these rivers in classical literature, see *Variorum* 666–67; Revard, *Milton*, 176 adds Pindar to the list. Allegorical interpretations of the classical myth were developed in late antiquity and circulated in early modern England, though it is impossible to know whether Milton intended his readers to bring such associations to the rivers here.

71. The rhyme *showers/flowers* (140–41) is not feminine since the words have the value of monosyllables (in old spelling they are printed *showres/flowres*).

72. Cf. Stephen M. Fallon, *Milton's Peculiar Grace: Self-Representation and Authority* (Ithaca: Cornell University Press, 2007), 65.

73. The bark has been interpreted as an allegory for the human body, cursed to mortality since the Fall (see *Variorum* 670), an allegorical reading accepted by Lewalski, *Life of Milton*, 84.

74. *OED*, s.v. *perfidious*: "characterized by perfidy, guilty of breaking faith or violating confidence; deliberately faithless; treacherous."

75. See Ovid, *Metamorphoses* 10.174–219. The hyacinth appears in Theocritus 10, the "Lament for Bion," and numerous Renaissance pastorals; see *Variorum* 672.

76. The *Variorum* comments that "Milton had not yet developed his antipathy to episcopacy as such" (680–81).

77. Carey and Fowler, *Poems*, 248; they note that *creep* echoes Spenser, *Shep. Cal.* May, line 126: "There crept in Wolves."

78. Tuve, "Theme, Pattern, and Imagery," in Patrides, *Milton's Lycidas*, 176.

79. *Variorum* 683 paraphrases line 122: "What do they care? [...] What are they in need of? They have got what they wanted (literally, are brought to the condition desired)." The Victorian critic John Ruskin (1865) famously glossed the striking phrase *blind mouths* (an example of catachresis or what he describes as "a broken metaphor") thus: "A 'Bishop' means 'a person who sees.' A 'Pastor' means one who feeds. The most unbishoply character a man can have is therefore to be Blind. The most unpastoral is, instead of feeding, to want to be fed,—to be a Mouth" (quoted by Carey and Fowler, *Poems*, 248).

80. See Patrides, *Milton's Lycidas*, 356–57; *Variorum* 686–706.

81. To the best of my knowledge, no critic has previously connected "Lycidas" with the Longinean sublime, though it was a commonplace in the eighteenth century to describe *Paradise Lost* in such terms. See Charles Martindale, "Milton's Classicism," in *The Oxford History of Classical Reception in England Literature*, vol. 3: *1660-1790*, ed. David Hopkins and Charles Martindale (Oxford: Oxford University Press, 2012), 53–90. I do not claim that Milton was influenced by *On the Sublime* when he composed "Lycidas," though he lists "Longinus" as an authority on rhetoric in his treatise *Of Education* (1644); see John Milton, *Complete Poems and Major Prose*, ed. Merritt Y. Hughes (Indianapolis: Bobbs-Merrill, 1957), 630–39 (636).

82. In southern speech by this time, *r* was probably vocalized (assimilated to a vowel) before consonants and in final position, so it was probably not sounded in *their*; see E. J. Dobson, *English Pronunciation, 1500–1700*, 2nd ed. (Oxford: Clarendon Press, 1968), vol. 2, 945–46, 992.

83. Nitchie (1966), cited *Variorum* 684.

84. On the conflict between Puritans and the Laudian church in 1637, see Elledge, *Milton's "Lycidas,"* 179–224.

85. Tuve, "Theme, Pattern, and Imagery," in Patrides *Milton's* Lycidas, 180 and n. 6 appeals to "the universality, more than the historicity, of Milton's massive indictment." However, we may follow Gadamer's lead and recognize the historicity of both Milton's and our own horizons and thus the historical nature of all acts of understanding.

86. The "swart star" in line 128 is Sirius (the Dog-star), believed to begin the hottest days of summer. The word *amaranthus* (149) may represent either a common ornamental plant or an immortal flower that never fades; the latter appears in *Paradise Lost* 3.353–61 (*Variorum* 716).

87. For details, see *Variorum* 711–12.

88. See Hans Ulrich Gumbrecht, *The Production of Presence: What Meaning Cannot Convey* (Stanford: Stanford University Press, 2003).

89. Elledge, *Milton's "Lycidas,"* 24; cf. the passage from Vergil's fifth eclogue quoted above. See *Variorum* 708 on the pastoral convention of "decking the dead body." On the specific flowers included in Milton's catalogue, see *Variorum* 711–14.

90. See Jack Goody, *The Culture of Flowers* (Cambridge: Cambridge University Press, 1993); *Encyclopedia of Death and Dying*, ed. Glennys Howarth and Oliver Leaman (New York: Routledge, 2001), 270–73.

91. Sacks, *English Elegy*, 112. Cf. William Waters, *Poetry's Touch: On Lyric Address* (Ithaca: Cornell University Press, 2003), 43 on lyrics addressed to the dead.

92. T. S. Eliot, "Milton I," in *On Poetry and Poets* (London: Faber, 1957), 138–45 (144–45).

93. See Immanuel Kant, *Critique of Judgment*, §§25–26.

94. Elledge, *Milton's "Lycidas,"* 307.

95. Most critics agree that Milton alludes to Arion, though other identities have been proposed; see *Variorum* 723–24.

96. Some critics have argued that a new voice intercedes at line 165; see responses by Fish in Patrides, *Milton's* Lycidas, 332, 337 and Alpers, "*Lycidas* and Modern Criticism," 487–88.

97. The scansion of line 165 was debated between two early editors; see Elledge, *Milton's "Lycidas,"* 310.

98. On this symbolism in patristic writings, see *Variorum* 725–26. From the time of the earliest Old English poetry, the similarity of the words *sun* and *son* in English has delighted poets (see "Now goth sonne under wode" in Chapter 3 above).

99. Warton first pointed out that the miraculous walking on water "bears an immediate reference to the subject of the poem" (Elledge, *Milton's "Lycidas,"* 312).

100. See *Variorum* 728–29.

101. Cf. Alpers, *What Is Pastoral*, 111; *Variorum* 730 cites the biblical allusion without commenting on the change.

102. Dr. Johnson condemned Milton's mingling of "trifling [pagan] fictions" with "the most awful and sacred truths, such as ought never to be polluted with such irreverent combinations," though he did not mention this example (a *genius* is a minor pagan deity); for Johnson, see Elledge, *Milton's "Lycidas,"* 230. For the views of nineteenth-century critics on the "genius," see Elledge, *Milton's "Lycidas,"* 314.

103. Carey and Fowler, *Poems*, 253.

104. See Barbara Herrnstein Smith, *Poetic Closure* (Chicago: University of Chicago Press, 1968), 192–94.

Coda

1. Maxwell S. Luria and Richard L. Hoffman, ed., *The Norton Anthology of Middle English Lyrics* (New York: Norton, 1974), no. 143; cf. Rossell Hope Robbins, ed., *Secular Lyrics of the XIVth and XVth Centuries*, 2nd ed. (Oxford: Clarendon Press, 1955), no. 15. Like many scholars, John Scattergood, "The Love Lyric before Chaucer," in *A Companion to the Middle English Lyric*, ed. Thomas G. Duncan (Cambridge: D. S. Brewer, 2005), 39–67 suspects that this is the burden and first stanza of a longer dance song (48).

2. Although most Middle English carols are religious, secular carols also survive; see Karl Reichl, "The Middle English Carol," in Duncan, *Companion to Middle English Lyric*, 150–70.

3. Robbins, *Secular Lyrics*, 233; two of the other poems are among the most famous Middle English secular lyrics: "All Night by the Rose I Lay" and "The Maiden of the Moor" (not all scholars agree these poems are secular).

4. William Butler Yeats, "'I Am of Ireland,'" in *The Collected Poems of W. B. Yeats* (New York: Macmillan, 1956), 262–63.

5. Elaine Scarry, *On Beauty and Being Just* (Princeton: Princeton University Press, 1999), 3–8.

6. Ibid., 25.

7. Ibid., 7.

Appendix

1. Derek Attridge, *The Rhythms of English Poetry* (New York: Longman, 1984), 164–72.

2. Attridge, *Rhythms of English Poetry*, 98; 172–75.

3. Cf. Attridge, *Rhythms of English Poetry*, 361–62; Derek Attridge, *Moving Words: Forms of English Poetry* (Oxford: Oxford University Press, 2013), 223. I have rejected the following symbols from *Moving Words*, which seem less logical or transparent:

-o- double offbeat
-o= double offbeat with demotion of second syllable
=o- double offbeat with demotion of first syllable
~o~ triple offbeat

4. See Attridge, *Rhythms of English Poetry*, 361; he describes stress pattern as "a simplification of the linguistically determined *stress contour* brought about by the perception of a regular rhythm." For our purposes it is unnecessary to go into the linguistics of stress.

Bibliography

Abrams, M. H. "Five Types of *Lycidas*." 1962. Rpt. in Patrides, ed., *Milton's* Lycidas. 216–35.
———. *The Mirror and the Lamp: Romantic Theory and the Critical Tradition*. 1953. New York: Norton, 1958.
———. "Postscript." In Patrides, ed., *Milton's* Lycidas. 341–45.
———. "Structure and Style in the Greater Romantic Lyric." *From Sensibility to Romanticism*. Ed. Frederick W. Hilles and Harold Bloom. New York: Oxford University Press, 1965. 527–60.
Abrams, M. H., and Geoffrey Galt Harpham. *A Glossary of Literary Terms*. 9th ed. Boston: Wadsworth, 2009.
Adams, Richard P. "The Archetypal Pattern of Death and Rebirth in *Lycidas*." *PMLA* 64.1 (1949): 183–88. Rpt. in Patrides, ed., *Milton's* Lycidas. 111–15.
Akehurst, F. R. P., and Judith M. Davis, eds. *A Handbook of the Troubadours*. Berkeley: University of California Press, 1995.
Alexander, Gavin, ed. *Sidney's "The Defense of Poesy" and Selected Renaissance Literary Criticism*. London: Penguin, 2004.
———, ed. William Scott. *The Model of Poesy*. Cambridge: Cambridge University Press, 2013.
———. *The Divine Comedy*. Charles Singleton. Trans. with commentary. 6 vols. Princeton: Princeton University Press, 1977.
Alpers, Paul. "Apostrophe and the Rhetoric of Renaissance Lyric." *Representations* 122.1 (2013): 1–22.
———. "*Lycidas* and Modern Criticism." *English Literary History* 49 (1982): 468–96.
———. *What Is Pastoral?* Chicago: University of Chicago Press, 1996.
Aristotle. *On Rhetoric: A Theory of Civic Discourse*. Trans. George A. Kennedy. New York: Oxford University Press, 1991.
Attridge, Derek. *Moving Words: Forms of English Poetry*. Oxford: Oxford University Press, 2013.

———. *The Rhythms of English Poetry*. New York: Longman, 1982.
———. *Well-Weighed Syllables: Elizabethan Verse in Classical Metres*. Cambridge: Cambridge University Press, 1974.
Barker, Arthur. "The Pattern of Milton's Nativity Ode." *University of Toronto Quarterly* 10 (1941): 167–81.
Bates, Catherine. *Masculinity and the Hunt: Wyatt to Spenser*. Oxford: Oxford University Press, 2013.
———. "Wyatt, Surrey, and the Henrician Court." *Early Modern English Poetry: A Critical Companion*. Ed. Patrick Cheney et al. New York: Oxford University Press, 2007. 38–47.
Bennett, J. A. W. *Poetry of the Passion: Studies in Twelve Centuries of English Verse*. Oxford: Clarendon Press, 1982.
Benveniste, Émile. *Problems in General Linguistics*. Trans. Mary Elizabeth Meek. Coral Gables: University of Miami Press, 1971.
Boccaccio, Giovanni. *Boccaccio on Poetry, Being the Preface and the Fourteenth and Fifteenth Books of Boccaccio's Genealogia Deorum Gentilium*. Ed. and trans. Charles G. Osgood. 2nd ed. Indianapolis: Bobbs-Merrill, 1956.
Boffey, Julia. *Manuscripts of English Courtly Love Lyrics in the Later Middle Ages*. Woodbridge, Suffolk: D. S. Brewer, 1985.
Bolgar, R. R. *The Classical Heritage and Its Beneficiaries*. Cambridge: Cambridge University Press, 1954.
Booth, Stephen. *Shakespeare's Sonnets: Edited with Analytic Commentary*. New Haven: Yale University Press, 1978.
Brewster, Scott. *Lyric*. London: Routledge, 2009.
Brigden, Susan. *Thomas Wyatt: The Heart's Forest*. London: Faber, 2012.
British Library Additional MS 37049. Available at www.bl.uk/manuscripts/FullDisplay.aspx?ref=Add_MS_37049.
Brooks, Cleanth, and John Edward Hardy. "Es-

says in Analysis: *Lycidas*." 1951. Rpt. in Patrides, ed., *Milton's* Lycidas. 140–56.
Brown, Carleton, ed. *English Lyrics of the XVth Century*. Oxford: Clarendon Press, 1939.
———, ed. *English Lyrics of the XIIIth Century*. Oxford: Clarendon Press, 1932.
———, ed. *Religious Lyrics of the XIVth Century*. 2nd rev. ed. Ed. G. V. Smithers Oxford: Clarendon Press, 1965.
Bruni, Leonardo. *The Life of Dante. The Earliest Lives of Dante: Giovanni Boccaccio and Leonardo Bruni Aretino*. Intro. Francesco Basetti-Sani. Trans. James Robinson Smith. New York: Frederick Unger, 1963. 80–95.
Burnett, Archie. *Milton's Style: The Shorter Poems, Paradise Regained, and "Samson Agonistes."* London: Longman, 1981.
Burrow, Colin, ed. William Shakespeare. *The Complete Sonnets and Poems*. Oxford: Oxford University Press, 2003.
Butterfield, Ardis. *The Familiar Enemy: Chaucer, Language and Nation in the Hundred Years' War*. Oxford: Oxford University Press, 2009.
———. "Lyric." *The Cambridge Companion to Medieval English Literature*. Ed. Larry Scanlon. Cambridge: Cambridge University Press, 2009. 95–109.
Campbell, Gordon. "King, Edward (1611/12–1637)." *Oxford Dictionary of National Biography*. Oxford University Press, 2004. Online edn. Oct 2007. 9 June 2013.
Campion, Thomas. *The Works of Thomas Campion*. Ed. Walter R. Davis. New York: Norton, 1970.
Carey, John, and Alastair Fowler, eds. *The Poems of John Milton*. London: Longmans, 1968.
Carruthers, Mary J. *The Book of Memory: A Study of Memory in Medieval Culture*. Cambridge: Cambridge University Press, 1990.
———. *The Craft of Thought: Meditation, Rhetoric, and the Making of Images, 400–1200*. Cambridge: Cambridge University Press, 1998.
Chaucer, Geoffrey. *The Minor Poems, Part One, The Variorum Edition of the Works of Geoffrey Chaucer*. Vol. 5. Ed. George B. Pace and Alfred David. Norman: University of Oklahoma Press, 1982.
———. *The Riverside Chaucer*. Gen. ed. Larry D. Benson. 3rd ed. Boston: Houghton Mifflin, 1987.
Cheney, Patrick et al., *Early Modern English Poetry: A Critical Companion*. New York: Oxford University Press, 2007.
Cheney, Patrick, ed. *The Cambridge Companion to Shakespeare's Poetry*. Cambridge: Cambridge University Press, 2007.
Cousins, A. D., and Peter Howarth, eds. *The Cambridge Companion to the Sonnet*. Cambridge: Cambridge University Press, 2011.

Cubeta, Paul M. "A Jonsonian Ideal: 'To Penshurst.'" *Philological Quarterly* 42 (1963): 14–24.
Culler, Jonathan. "Apostrophe." *The Pursuit of Signs: Semiotics, Literature, Deconstruction*. Ithaca: Cornell University Press, 1981. 135–54.
———. "Changes in the Study of the Lyric." Hošek and Parker, eds. *Lyric Poetry*. 38–54.
———. *Theory of the Lyric*. Cambridge, MA: Harvard University Press, 2015.
———. "Why Lyric?" *PMLA* 123 (2008): 201–206.
Curtius, Ernst Robert. *European Literature and the Latin Middle Ages*. 1948. Trans. Willard R. Trask. Princeton: Princeton University Press, 1953.
Daiches, David. *A Study of Literature*. 1949. Excerpt rpt. in Patrides, ed., *Milton's Lycidas*. 92–110.
Daniel, Samuel. *Poems and A Defence of Ryme*. Ed. Arthur Colby Sprague. 1930. Chicago: University Chicago Press, 1965. 126–58.
Dante Alighieri. *De vulgari eloquentia*. Ed. and trans. Steven Botterill. Cambridge: Cambridge University Press, 1996.
Davies, R. T., ed. *Medieval English Lyrics: A Critical Anthology*. Evanston: Northwestern University Press, 1964.
Daly, Peter M. et al. *The English Emblem Tradition (Index emblematicus)*. Vol. 1. Jan van der Noot, *A Theatre for Worldlings*; Paolo Giovio, *The Worthy Tract of Paulus Jovius*; Lodovico Domenichi, *Certain Noble Devises both Militarie and Amorous*; Geffrey Whitney, *A Choice of Emblemes*. Toronto: University Toronto Press, 1988. 79–337.
De Grazia, Margreta. "The Scandal of Shakespeare's Sonnets." *Shakespeare Survey* 46 (1994): 35–49. Rpt. in Schiffer, ed., *Shakespeare's Sonnets*. 89–112.
De Man, Paul. "Lyric and Modernity." *Blindness and Insight: Essays in the Rhetoric of Contemporary Criticism*. 2nd rev. ed. Minneapolis: University Minnesota Press, 1983. 166–86.
———. "Lyrical Voice in Contemporary Theory: Riffaterre and Jauss." Hošek and Parker, eds., *Lyric Poetry*. 55–72
Derrida, Jacques. *Of Grammatology*. Trans. Gayatri Chakravorty Spivak. 1967. Baltimore: Johns Hopkins University Press, 1976.
The Devonshire Manuscript: A Women's Book of Courtly Poetry. Lady Margaret Douglas and Others. Ed. Elizabeth Heale. Toronto: Centre for Reformation and Renaissance Studies, 2012.
Dobson, E. J. *English Pronunciation, 1500–1700*. 2nd ed. 2 vols. Oxford: Clarendon Press, 1968.
Donaldson, Ian, ed. *Ben Jonson*. Oxford: Oxford University Press, 1985.
———. *Ben Jonson: A Life*. Oxford: Oxford University Press, 2011.
Donne, John. *The Complete Poetry of John*

Donne. Ed. John T. Shawcross. Garden City, NJ: Anchor, 1967.

Donow, Herbert S. *A Concordance to the Sonnet Sequences of Daniel, Drayton, Shakespeare, Sidney, and Spenser.* Carbondale: Southern Illinois University Press, 1969.

Dronke, Peter. *The Medieval Lyric.* New York: Harper, 1969.

Dubrow, Heather. *The Challenges of Orpheus: Lyric Poetry and Early Modern England.* Baltimore: Johns Hopkins University Press, 2008.

_____. "The Country-House Poem: A Study of Generic Development." *Genre* 12 (1979): 153–79.

_____. "'Dressing Old Words New'? Reevaluating the 'Delian Structure.'" Schoenfeldt, ed., *Companion.* 90–103.

_____. *Echoes of Desire: English Petrarchism and Its Counterdiscourses.* Ithaca: Cornell University Press, 1995.

_____. "'Incertainties Now Crown Themselves Assur'd': The Politics of Plotting Shakespeare's Sonnets. *Shakespeare Quarterly* 47.3 (Fall 1996): 291–305. Rpt. Schiffer, ed., *Shakespeare's Sonnets.* 113–33.

Duffell, Martin J. *A New History of English Metre.* London: Modern Humanities Research Associates and Maney Publishing, 2008.

Duncan, Thomas G. *A Companion to the Middle English Lyric.* Cambridge: D. S. Brewer, 2005.

Duncan-Jones, Katherine, ed. *Shakespeare's Sonnets.* Arden. London: Nelson, 1997.

_____. "Sidney, Stella, and Lady Rich." *Sir Philip Sidney: 1586 and the Creation of a Legend.* Ed. Jan van Dorsten, Dominic Baker-Smith, and Arthur F. Kinney. Leiden: Brill/Leiden University Press, 1986. 170–92.

_____. *Sir Philip Sidney: Courtier Poet.* New Haven: Yale University Press, 1991.

_____, ed. *Sir Philip Sidney.* Oxford: Oxford University Press, 1994.

Eliot, T. S. "Milton I." *On Poetry and Poets.* London: Faber, 1957. 138–45.

_____. *The Sacred Wood: Essays on Poetry and Criticism.* 2nd ed. London: Methuen, 1928.

_____. "Tradition and the Individual Talent." *Selected Essays.* 1932. New York: Harcourt, 1964. 3–11.

Elledge, Scott, ed. *Milton's "Lycidas," Edited to Serve as an Introduction to Criticism.* New York: Harper & Row, 1966.

Empson, William. *Seven Types of Ambiguity,* 3rd ed. New York: New Directions, 1947.

_____. *Some Versions of Pastoral.* New York: New Directions, 1974.

Engle, Lars. "William Empson and the Sonnets." Schoenfeldt, ed., *Companion.* 163–82.

Evans, G. Blakemore, gen. ed. *The Riverside Shakespeare.* Boston: Houghton, 1974.

Fallon, Stephen M. *Milton's Peculiar Grace: Self-Representation and Authority.* Ithaca: Cornell University Press, 2007.

Favorite Poem Project. Boston: Boston University. Available at http://www.favoritepoem.org.

Ferguson, Margaret W. *Trials of Desire: Renaissance Defenses of Poetry.* New Haven: Yale University Press, 1983.

Ferrari, G. R. F. "Plato and Poetry." Kennedy, ed., *CHLC* 1:92–148.

Ferry, Anne. *All in War with Time: Love Poetry of Shakespeare, Donne, Jonson, Marvell.* Cambridge: Harvard University Press, 1975.

_____. *By Design: Intention in Poetry.* Stanford: Stanford University Press, 2008.

_____. *The "Inward" Language: Sonnets of Wyatt, Sidney, Shakespeare, Donne.* Chicago: University Chicago Press, 1983.

_____. *Tradition and the Individual Poem: An Inquiry into Anthologies.* Stanford: Stanford University Press, 2001.

Fineman, Joel. *Shakespeare's Perjured Eye: The Invention of Poetic Subjectivity in the Sonnets.* Berkeley: University California Press, 1986.

Fish, Stanley E. "*Lycidas*: A Poem Finally Anonymous." *Glyph* 8 (1981): 1–18. Rpt. in Patrides, ed., *Milton's Lycidas.* 319–40.

Fletcher, Alan J. "The Lyric in the Sermon." Duncan, *A Companion to the Middle English Lyric.* 188–209.

Forshaw, Helen P., S.H.C.J., ed. *Edmund of Abingdon, Speculum Religiosorum and Speculum Ecclesie.* London: pub. for British Academy by Oxford University Press, 1973.

Fowler, Alastair. *Conceitful Thought: The Interpretation of English Renaissance Poems.* Edinburgh: Edinburgh University Press, 1975.

_____. *The Country House Poem: A Cabinet of Seventeenth-Century Estate Poems and Related Items.* Edinburgh: Edinburgh University Press, 1994.

_____. "Country-House Poems: The Politics of a Genre." *Seventeenth Century* 1 (1986): 1–14.

_____. *Kinds of Literature: An Introduction to the Theory of Genres and Modes.* Cambridge, MA: Harvard University Press, 1982.

_____. "The Locality of Jonson's 'To Penshurst.'" Fowler, *Conceitful Thought.* 114–34.

_____. "Obscurity of Sentiment in the Poetry of Wyatt." Fowler, *Conceitful Thought.* 1–20.

_____. "'To Shepherd's Ear': The Form of Milton's *Lycidas.*" Fowler, ed., *Silent Poetry: Essays in Numerological Analysis.* London: Routledge, 1970. 170–84.

_____. *Triumphal Forms: Structural Patterns in Elizabethan Poetry.* Cambridge: Cambridge University Press, 1970.

_____, ed. *The New Oxford Book of Seventeenth-*

Century Verse. Oxford: Oxford University Press, 1991.

French, J. M. "The Digressions in Milton's 'Lycidas.'" *Studies in Philology* 50 (1953): 485–90.

Frye, Northrop. *Anatomy of Criticism: Four Essays*. Princeton: Princeton University Press, 1957.

———. "Approaching the Lyric." Hošek and Parker, eds., *Lyric Poetry*. 31–37.

———. "Literature as Context: Milton's *Lycidas*." 1960. Rpt. in Patrides, ed., *Milton's Lycidas*. 204–15.

Fussell, Paul, Jr. *Poetic Form and Poetic Meter*. New York: Random, 1965.

Gadamer, Hans-Georg. *Truth and Method*. 2nd rev. ed. Trans. Joel Weinsheimer and Donald G. Marshall. 1989. New York: Continuum, 1999.

Gaunt, Simon, and Sarah Kay, eds. *The Troubadours: An Introduction*. Cambridge: Cambridge University Press, 1999.

Gaunt, Simon, and John Marshall. "Occitan Grammars and the Art of Troubadour Poetry." Minnis and Johnson, eds., *CHLC* 2: 472–95.

Genette, Gérard. *The Architexte* (1979). Excerpt rpt. in Jackson and Prins, eds., *The Lyric Theory Reader*, 17–30.

Gillespie, Vincent. "From the Twelfth Century to c. 1450." Minnis and Johnson, eds. *CHLC* 2:145–235.

Goody, Jack. *The Culture of Flowers*. Cambridge: Cambridge University Press, 1993.

Gorak, Jan, ed. *Canon vs. Culture: Reflections on the Current Debate*. New York: Garland, 2001.

———. *The Making of the Modern Canon: Genesis and Crisis of a Literary Idea*. London and Atlantic Highlands, NY: Athlone, 1991.

Graff, Gerald. *Professing Literature: An Institutional History*. Chicago: University Chicago Press, 1987.

Gray, Douglas, ed. *English Medieval Religious Lyrics*. Exeter: University of Exeter Press, 1992.

———. *Themes and Images in Medieval English Religious Lyric*. London: Routledge, 1972.

Greenblatt, Stephen. *Renaissance Self-Fashioning: From More to Shakespeare*. Chicago: University Chicago Press, 1980.

———. *Will in the World: How Shakespeare Became Shakespeare*. New York: Norton, 2004.

Greene, Roland. "The Lyric." Norton, ed., *CHLC* 3: 216–28.

———. *Post-Petrarchism: Origins and Innovations of the Western Lyric Sequence*. Princeton: Princeton University Press, 1991.

———, ed. in chief. *The Princeton Encyclopedia of Poetry and Poetics*. 4th ed. Princeton: Princeton University Press, 2012.

Grossman, Marshall, ed. *Aemilia Lanyer: Gender, Genre, and the Canon*. Lexington: University Press Kentucky, 1998.

Guillory, John. *Cultural Capital: The Problem of Literary Canon Formation*. Chicago: University of Chicago Press, 1993.

Gumbrecht, Hans Ulrich. *The Production of Presence: What Meaning Cannot Convey*. Stanford: Stanford University Press, 2003.

Hadfield, Andrew. *Edmund Spenser: A Life*. Oxford: Oxford University Press, 2012.

Halliwell, Stephen. "Aristotle's Poetics." Kennedy, ed., *CHLC* 1:149–83.

Hanford, James H. "The Pastoral Elegy and Milton's *Lycidas*." *PMLA* 25.3 (1910): 403–47. Rpt. in Patrides, ed., *Milton's Lycidas*. 31–59.

Hanna, Ralph. "Miscellaneity and Vernacularity: Conditions of Literary Production in Late Medieval England." *The Whole Book: Cultural Perspectives on the Medieval Miscellany*. Ed. Stephen G. Nichols and Siegfried Wenzel. Ann Arbor: University of Michigan Press, 1996. 37–51.

Hardison, O. B., Jr. *The Enduring Monument: The Idea of Praise in Renaissance Literary Theory and Practice*. Chapel Hill: University of North Carolina Press, 1962.

———, ed. *English Literary Criticism: The Renaissance*. New York: Appleton, 1963.

Harrier, Richard C. *The Canon of Sir Thomas Wyatt's Poetry*. Cambridge, MA: Harvard University Press, 1975.

Harrison, Thomas Perrin, ed. *The Pastoral Elegy: An Anthology*. Edited with introduction, commentary, and notes by Thomas Perrin Harrison; English translations by Harry Joshua Leon. Austin: University Texas Press, 1938; rpt. New York: Octagon, 1968.

Hay, Millicent V. *The Life of Robert Sidney, Earl of Leicester (1563–1626)*. Cranbury, NJ: Associated University Press, 1984.

Heale, Elizabeth. "Women and Courtly Love Lyric: The Devonshire MS (BL Additional 17492)." *Modern Language Review* 90 (1995): 296–313.

Hegel, G. W. F. *Lectures on Aesthetics (Selections). The Philosophy of Hegel*. Ed. Carl J. Friedrich. New York: Random House, 1954. 333–395.

Helgerson, Richard. *Self-Crowned Laureates: Spenser, Jonson, Milton, and the Literary System*. Berkeley: University California Press, 1983.

Hibbard, G. R. "The Country House Poem of the Seventeenth Century." *Journal of the Warburg and Courtauld Institutes* 19 (1956): 159–74.

Horace. *Satires, Epistles and Ars poetica*. Ed. and trans. H. Rushton Fairclough. Loeb. London: Heinemann, 1926.

Hošek, Chaviva, and Patricia Parker, eds. *Lyric Poetry: Beyond New Criticism*. Ithaca: Cornell University Press, 1985.

Howarth, Glennys, and Oliver Leaman, eds. *Encyclopedia of Death and Dying*. New York: Routledge, 2001.

Hughes, Merritt Y., ed. *John Milton: Complete Poems and Major Prose*. Indianapolis: Odyssey Press, 1957.

"Introduction to Ovid's *Epistles*." *Medieval Literary Theory and Criticism, c. 1100-c.1375: The Commentary Tradition*. Ed. A. J. Minnis and A. B. Scott, with David Wallace. Rev. ed. Oxford: Clarendon Press, 1991. 20–24.

Jackson, Virginia. "Lyric." *The Princeton Encyclopedia of Poetry and Poetics*. 4th ed. Roland Greene, gen. ed. Princeton: Princeton University Press, 2012. 826–34.

Jackson, Virginia, and Yopie Prins. "Lyrical Studies." *Victorian Literature and Culture* 27 (1999): 521–30.

Jackson, Virginia, and Yopie Prins, eds. *The Lyric Theory Reader: A Critical Anthology*. Baltimore: Johns Hopkins University Press, 2014.

Jager, Eric. *The Book of the Heart*. Chicago: University Chicago Press, 2000.

Jakobson, Roman. "Linguistics and Poetics." Thomas A. Sebeok, ed. *Style in Language*. Cambridge, MA: Technology Press of Massachusetts Institute of Technology, 1960. 350–77. Rpt. *Language in Literature*. Ed. Krystyna Pomorska and Stephen Rudy. Cambridge, MA: Harvard University Press, 1987. 62–94. Also *Selected Writings* 3: 18–51.

———. *Selected Writings*. The Hague: Mouton, 1962-1980.

———. "Shifters, Verbal Categories, and the Russian Verb." *Selected Writings* 2: 130–47.

Jauss, Hans Robert. *Toward an Aesthetic of Reception*. Trans. Timothy Bahti. Minneapolis: University Minnesota Press, 1982.

Javitch, Daniel. "The Assimilation of Aristotle's *Poetics* in Sixteenth-century Italy." Norton, ed., *CHLC* 3: 53–65.

Jenkins, Hugh. *Feigned Commonwealths: The Country-House Poem and the Fashioning of the Ideal Community*. Pittsburgh: Duquesne University Press, 1998.

Johnson, W. R. *The Idea of Lyric: Lyric Modes in Ancient and Modern Poetry*. Berkeley: University California Press, 1982.

Jones, Ann Rosalind, and Peter Stallybrass. "The Politics of *Astrophil and Stella*." *Studies in English Literature* 24 (1984): 53–68.

Jonson, Ben. *Ben Jonson*. Ed. Ian Donaldson. Oxford: Oxford University Press, 1985.

Kalstone, David. *Sidney's Poetry: Contexts and Interpretations*. New York: Norton, 1965.

Kaplan, Charles, ed. *Criticism: The Major Statements*. New York: St. Martin's Press, 1975.

Kay, Dennis, ed. *Sir Philip Sidney: An Anthology of Modern Criticism*. Oxford: Clarendon Press, 1987.

Kennedy, George A., ed. *The Cambridge History of Literary Criticism, 1. Classical Criticism*. Cambridge: Cambridge University Press, 1989.

———. *A New History of Classical Rhetoric*. Princeton: Princeton University Press, 1994.

Kennedy, William J. "European Beginnings and Transmissions: Dante, Petrarch and the Sonnet Sequence." *The Cambridge Companion to the Sonnet*. Ed. A. D. Cousins and Peter Howarth. Cambridge: Cambridge University Press, 2011. 84–104.

———. *The Site of Petrarchism: Early Modern National Sentiment in Italy, France, and England*. Baltimore: Johns Hopkins University Press, 2003.

Kermode, Frank. *The Appetite for Poetry*. Cambridge, MA: Harvard University Press, 1989.

Kerrigan, John, ed. *William Shakespeare: The Sonnets and A Lover's Complaint*. Harmondsworth: Penguin, 1986.

Kökeritz, Helge. *Shakespeare's Pronunciation*. New Haven: Yale University Press, 1953.

Kolbas, E. Dean. *Critical Theory and the Literary Canon*. Boulder, CO: Westview, 2001.

Lanham, Richard A. *A Handlist of Rhetorical Terms*. 2nd ed. Berkeley: University California Press, 1991.

Lanyer, Aemilia. *The Poems of Aemilia Lanyer: Salve Deus Rex Judæorum*. Ed. Susanne Woods. New York: Oxford University Press, 1993.

Lawry, Jon S. "'Eager Thought': Dialectic in *Lycidas*." *PMLA* 77.1 (1962): 27–32. Rpt. in Patrides, ed., *Milton's Lycidas*. 236–45.

Lentricchia, Frank. *After the New Criticism*. Chicago: University Chicago Press, 1980.

Lerer, Seth. "Medieval English Literature and the Idea of the Anthology." *PMLA* 118.5 (2003): 1251–67.

Levinson, Marjorie. "What Is New Formalism?" *PMLA* 122.2 (2007): 558–69.

Lewalski, Barbara K. "Imagining Female Community: Aemilia Lanyer's Poems." Lewalski. *Writing Women in Jacobean England*. Cambridge, MA: Harvard University Press, 1993. 213–41, 394–99.

———. "The Lady of the Country-House Poem." *The Fashioning and Functioning of the British Country House*. Ed. Gervase Jackson-Stops et al. Washington, D.C.: National Gallery of Art, 1989. 261–75.

———. *The Life of John Milton: A Critical Biography*. Rev. ed. Malden, MA: Blackwell, 2003.

———. "Of God and Good Women: The Poems of Aemilia Lanyer." *Silent But for the Word: Tudor Women as Patrons, Translators, and*

Writers of Religious Works. Ed. Margaret Patterson Hannay. Kent: Kent State University Press, 1985. 203–24, 283–87.

———. "Rewriting Patriarchy and Patronage: Margaret Clifford, Anne Clifford, and Aemilia Lanyer. *Yearbook of English Studies* 21 (1991): 87–106.

———. "Seizing Discourses and Reinventing Genres." Grossman, ed., *Aemilia Lanyer*. 49–59.

Lindley, David. *Lyric*. London: Metheun, 1985.

Lovejoy, Arthur O. *The Great Chain of Being: A Study of the History of an Idea*. Cambridge, MA: Harvard University Press, 1964.

Luria, Maxwell S., and Richard L. Hoffman, eds. *Middle English Lyrics*. New York: Norton, 1974.

Marotti, Arthur F. "'Love is Not Love': Elizabethan Sonnet Sequences and the Social Order." *English Literary History* 49 (1982): 396–428.

———. *Manuscript, Print, and the English Renaissance Lyric*. Ithaca: Cornell University Press, 1995.

Martindale, Charles. "Milton's Classicism." *The Oxford History of Classical Reception in England Literature*, vol. 3: *1660–1790*. Ed. David Hopkins and Charles Martindale. Oxford: Oxford University Press, 2012. 53–90.

Maslen, R. W., ed. *Sir Philip Sidney. An Apology for Poetry (Or The Defense of Poesy)*. Ed. Geoffrey Shepherd. Rev. 3rd ed. Ed. R. W. Maslen. Manchester: Manchester University Press: 2002.

Matthew of Vendôme. *The Art of Versification*. Trans. Aubrey E. Galyon. Ames: Iowa State University Press, 1980.

Mayerson, Caroline W. "The Orpheus Image in *Lycidas*." *PMLA* 64.1 (1949): 189–207. Rpt. in Patrides, ed., *Milton's* Lycidas. 116–28.

Matz, Robert. *The World of Shakespeare's Sonnets: An Introduction*. Jefferson, NC: McFarland, 2008.

McBride, Kari Boyd. *Country House Discourse in Early Modern England: A Cultural Study of Landscape and Legitimacy*. Aldershot: Ashgate, 2001.

———. "Remembering Orpheus in the Poems of Aemilia Lanyer." *Studies in English Literature 1500–1900* 38 (1998): 87–108.

McClung, William A. *The Country House in English Renaissance Poetry*. Berkeley: University California Press, 1977.

McLaughlin, Martin. "Latin and Vernacular from Dante to the Age of Lorenzo (1321–c.1500)." Minnis and Johnson, eds., *CHLC* 2:612–25.

McNamer, Sarah. *Affective Meditation and the Invention of Medieval Compassion*. Philadelphia: University Pennsylvania Press, 2010.

———. "The Origins of *the Meditationes vitae Christi*." *Speculum* 84.4 (2009): 905–55.

The Electronic Middle English Dictionary. Available at http://quod.lib.umich.edu/m/med/.

Mill, John Stuart. "Thoughts on Poetry and Its Varieties." *Autobiographical and Literary Essays. The Collected Works of John Stuart Mill*. Vol. 1. Toronto: University Toronto Press, 1981. 341–70.

Milton, John. *The Poems of John Milton*. Ed. John Carey and Alastair Fowler. London: Longmans, 1968.

———. *Complete Poems and Major Prose*. Ed. Merritt Y. Hughes. Indianapolis: Odyssey Press, 1957.

Minnis, A. J., and Ian Johnson, eds. *The Cambridge History of Literary Criticism, 2. The Middle Ages*. Cambridge: Cambridge University Press, 2005.

Minnis, A. J., and A. B. Scott, eds. with the assistance of David Wallace. *Medieval Literary Theory and Criticism, c. 1100–c. 1375: The Commentary Tradition*. Rev. ed. Oxford: Clarendon, 1991.

Modern Language Quarterly 61 (2000). (Special issue on New Formalism).

Molesworth, Charles. "Property and Virtue: The Genre of the Country-House Poem in the Seventeenth Century." *Genre* 1 (1968): 141–57.

Morrissey, Lee, ed. *Debating the Canon: A Reader from Addison to Nafisi*. New York: Palgrave, 2005.

Moss, Ann. "Horace in the Sixteenth Century: Commentators into Critics." Norton, ed., *CHLC* 3:66–76.

———. "Humanist Education." Norton, ed., *CHLC* 3: 145–54.

———. "Theories of Poetry: Latin Writers." Norton, ed., *CHLC* 3:98–105.

Mueller, Janel. "The Feminist Poetics of 'Salve Deus Rex Judaeorum.'" Grossman, ed., *Aemilia Lanyer*. 99–127.

Muir, Kenneth. *Life and Letters of Sir Thomas Wyatt*. Liverpool: Liverpool University Press, 1963.

Murphy, James J. "The Arts of Poetry and Prose." Minnis and Johnson, eds., *CHLC* 2:42–67.

———. *Rhetoric in the Middle Ages: A History of Rhetorical Theory from St. Augustine to the Renaissance*. Berkeley: University California Press, 1974.

Nelson, C. E. "A Note on Wyatt and Ovid." *Modern Language Review* 58 (1963): 60–63.

Nelson, Karen. "Annotated Bibliography: Texts and Criticism of Aemilia Bassano Lanyer." Grossman, ed., *Aemilia Lanyer*. 234–54.

Norbrook, David. *Poetry and Politics in the English Renaissance*. 1984. Rev. ed. Oxford: Oxford University Press, 2002.

Norton, Glyn P., ed. *The Cambridge History of Literary Criticism*, 3. *The Renaissance*. Cambridge: Cambridge University Press, 1999.

Ovid. *The Metamorphoses*. Ed. and trans. Frank Justus Miller. 3rd. ed. 2 vols. Loeb. Cambridge, MA: Harvard University Press, 1977.

The Oxford English Dictionary. 2nd ed. Ed. J. A. Simpson and E. S. C. Weiner. Oxford: Clarendon Press, 1989.

Oxford Latin Dictionary. Ed. P. G. W. Glare. Oxford: Clarendon Press, 1982.

Palgrave, Francis Turner. *The Golden Treasury of the Best Songs and Lyrical Poems in the English Language*. Ed. Christopher Ricks. London: Penguin, 1991.

Patrides, C. A., ed. *Milton's Lycidas: The Tradition and the Poem, New and Revised Edition*. Columbia: University of Missouri Press, 1983.

Pearsall, Derek. *The Life of Geoffrey Chaucer: A Critical Biography*. Oxford: Blackwell, 1992.

Peterson, Douglas L. *The English Lyric from Wyatt to Donne: A History of the Plain and Eloquent Styles*. Princeton: Princeton University Press, 1967.

———. "A Probable Source for Shakespeare's Sonnet CXXIX." *Shakespeare Quarterly* 5.4 (1954): 381–84.

Peterson, Richard S. *Imitation and Praise in the Poems of Ben Jonson*. New Haven: Yale University Press, 1981.

Petrarch, Francis. *Petrarch's Lyric Poems: The Rime sparse and Other Lyrics*. Trans. and ed. Robert M. Durling. Cambridge, MA: Harvard University Press, 1976.

Pigman III, G. W. *Grief and English Renaissance Elegy*. Cambridge: Cambridge University Press, 1985.

Phillips, Helen. "'Almighty and al merciable quene': Marian Titles and Marian Lyrics." *Medieval Women: Texts and Contexts in Late Medieval Britain: Essays for Felicity Riddy*. Ed. Jocelyn Wogan-Browne et al. Turnhout: Brepols, 2000. 83–99.

Plato. *The Collected Dialogues of Plato, including the Letters*. Ed. Edith Hamilton and Huntington Cairns. Princeton: Princeton University Press, 1961.

Poe, Edgar Allan. "The Poetic Principle." *Criticism: The Major Statements*. Ed. Charles Kaplan. New York: St. Martin's, 1975. 381–401.

Poe, Elizabeth W. "The *Vidas* and *Razos*." *A Handbook of the Troubadours*. Ed. F. R. P. Akehurst and Judith M. Davis. Berkeley: University of California Press, 1995. 185–97.

Poetry in America: Review of the Findings. Chicago: Poetry Foundation, 2006. Available at http://www.poetryfoundation.org/foundation/PoetryinAmerican_FullReport.pdf.

Powell, Jason. "Marginalia, Authorship, and Editing in the Manuscripts of Thomas Wyatt's Verse." *English Manuscript Studies* 15 (2009): 1–40.

Preminger, Alex, and T. V. F. Brogan, ed. *The New Princeton Encyclopedia of Poetry and Poetics*. Princeton: Princeton University Press, 1993.

Puttenham, George. *The Art of English Poesy: A Critical Edition*. Ed. Frank Whigham and Wayne A. Rebhorn. Ithaca: Cornell University Press, 2007.

Quintilian. *The Institutio Oratoria of Quintilian*. Trans. H. E. Butler. 4 vols. Loeb. Cambridge, MA: Harvard University Press, 1920–22.

Quirk, Randolph, Sidney Greenbaum, Geoffrey Leech, and Jan Svartvik. *A Grammar of Contemporary English*. Harlow, Essex: Longman, 1972.

Ragusa, Isa, and Rosalie B. Green, eds. *Meditations on the Life of Christ: An Illustrated Manuscript of the Fourteenth Century: Paris, Bibliothèque Nationale, MS. Ital. 115*. Princeton: Princeton University Press, 1961.

Ransom, John Crowe. "A Poem Nearly Anonymous." *American Review* 1 (1933): 179–203, 444–467. Rpt. in Patrides, ed., *Milton's Lycidas*. 68–85.

Rathmell, J. C. A. "Jonson, Lord Lisle, and Penshurst." *English Literary Renaissance* 1 (1971): 250–60.

Reichl, Karl. "The Middle English Carol." Duncan, ed., *Companion to Middle English Lyric*. 150–70.

Revard, Stella P. *Milton and the Tangles of Neaera's Hair: The Making of the 1645 Poems*. Columbia: University Missouri Press, 1997.

Riddy, Felicity. "The Provenance of *Quia Amore Langueo*." *Review of English Studies* 18 (1967): 429–33.

Ringler, William, ed. *The Poems of Sir Philip Sidney*. Oxford: Clarendon Press, 1962.

Robbins, Rossell Hope. "The Lyrics." *Companion to Chaucer Studies*, rev. ed. Ed. Beryl Rowland. New York: Oxford University Press, 1979. 380–402

———, ed. *Secular Lyrics of the XIVth and XVth Centuries*. 2nd ed. Oxford: Clarendon Press, 1955.

Robey, David. "Humanist Views on the Study of Italian Poetry in the Early Italian Renaissance." Minnis and Johnson, eds., *CHLC* 2: 626–28.

Roche, Thomas P., Jr. *Petrarch and the English Sonnet Sequences*. New York: AMS, 1989.

Rollins, Hyder Edward, ed. *A New Variorum Edition of William Shakespeare: The Sonnets*. 2 vols. Philadelphia: Lippincott, 1944.

Russell, Donald A. *Criticism in Antiquity*. Berkeley: University California Press, 1981.

Russell, D. A., and M. Winterbottom, eds. *Ancient Literary Criticism: The Principal Texts in New Translations*. Oxford: Clarendon Press, 1972.

Sacks, Peter M. *The English Elegy: Studies in the Genre from Spenser to Years*. Baltimore: Johns Hopkins University Press, 1985.

Saupe, Karen, ed. *Middle English Marian Lyrics*. TEAMS. Kalamazoo, MI: Medieval Institute Publications, 1997. Available at http://d.lib.rochester.edu/teams/publication/saupe-middle-english-marian-lyrics.

Scarry, Elaine. *On Beauty and Being Just*. Princeton: Princeton University Press, 1999.

Scattergood, John. "The Love Lyric before Chaucer." Duncan, ed., *Companion to the Middle English Lyric*. 39–67.

Schiffer, James, ed. *Shakespeare's Sonnets: Critical Essays*. New York: Garland, 1999.

Schnell, Lisa. "'So Great a Difference Is There in Degree': Aemilia Lanyer and the Aims of Feminist Criticism." *Modern Language Quarterly* 57 (1996): 23–35.

Schoenbaum, Samuel. *William Shakespeare: A Compact Documentary Life*. Oxford: Oxford University Press, 1977.

Schoenfeldt, Michael, ed. *A Companion to Shakespeare's Sonnets*. Malden, MA: Blackwell, 2008.

Scodel, Joshua. *The English Poetic Epitaph: Commemoration and Conflict from Jonson to Wordsworth*. Ithaca: Cornell University Press, 1991.

Scott, John A. *Understanding Dante*. Notre Dame: University Notre Dame Press, 2004.

Scott, William. *The Model of Poesy*. Ed. Gavin Alexander. Cambridge: Cambridge University Press, 2013.

Shakespeare, William. *See under* Burrow, Duncan-Jones, Evans, Kerrigan, Rollins.

Shrank, Cathy. "'But I, that knew what harbred in that hed': Sir Thomas Wyatt and His Posthumous 'Interpreters.'" *Proceedings of the British Academy* 154 (2008): 375–401.

Sidney, Sir Philip. *An Apology for Poetry (Or The Defense of Poesy)*. Ed. Geoffrey Shepherd. Rev. 3rd ed. R. W. Maslen. Manchester: Manchester University Press, 2002.

———. *The Old Arcadia*. Ed. Katherine Duncan-Jones. Oxford: Oxford University Press, 1999.

———. *The Poems of Sir Philip Sidney*. Ed. William Ringler. Oxford: Clarendon Press, 1962.

———. Duncan-Jones, Katherine, ed. *Sir Philip Sidney*. Oxford Poetry Library. Oxford: Oxford University Press, 1994.

Smith, Barbara Herrnstein. *On the Margins of Discourse*. Chicago: University of Chicago Press, 1978.

———. *Poetic Closure: A Study of How Poems End*. Chicago: University Chicago Press, 1968.

Smith, G. Gregory, ed. *Elizabethan Critical Essays*. 2 vols. Oxford: Clarendon Press, 1904.

Smith, Jeremy J. *Essentials of Early English: An Introduction to Old, Middle and Early Modern English*. 2nd ed. New York: Routledge, 2005.

Spearing, A. C. *Medieval to Renaissance in English Poetry*. Cambridge: Cambridge University Press, 1985.

———. *Textual Subjectivity: The Encoding of Subjectivity in Medieval Narrative and Lyric*. Oxford: Oxford University Press, 2005.

Spenser, Edmund. *The Yale Edition of the Shorter Poems of Edmund Spenser*. Ed. William A. Oram et al. New Haven: Yale University Press, 1989.

Spiller, Michael R. G. *The Development of the Sonnet: An Introduction*. New York: Routledge, 1992.

Spitzer, Leo. "Note on the Poetic and Empirical 'I' in Medieval Authors." *Traditio* 4 (1946): 414–22.

Stallybrass, Peter. "Editing as Cultural Formation: The Sexing of Shakespeare's Sonnets." *Modern Language Quarterly* 54.1 (March 1993): 91–103. Rpt. in Schiffer, ed., *Shakespeare's Sonnets*. 75–88.

Stamatakis, Chris. *Sir Thomas Wyatt and the Rhetoric of Rewriting: "Turning the Word."* Oxford: Oxford University Press, 2012.

Steffes, Michael. "'As Dewe in Aprylle': 'I Syng of a Mayden' and the Liturgy." *Medium Ævum* 71 (2002): 66–73.

Stewart, Susan. *Poetry and the Fate of the Senses*. Chicago: University Chicago Press, 2002.

Strohm, Paul. *Chaucer's Tale: 1386 and the Road to Canterbury*. New York: Penguin, 2014.

Switten, Margaret. "Versification and Music." *The Troubadours: An Introduction*. Ed. Simon Gaunt and Sarah Kay. Cambridge: Cambridge University Press, 1999. 141–63

Teskey, Gordon. *The Poetry of John Milton*. Cambridge, MA: Harvard University Press, 2015.

Thomson, Patricia. *Sir Thomas Wyatt and His Background*. Stanford: Stanford University Press, 1964.

Tillyard, E. M. W. *Milton*. 1930. Excerpt rpt. in Patrides, ed., *Milton's Lycidas*. 62–67.

Tucker, Herbert F. "Dramatic Monologue and the Overhearing of Lyric." Hošek and Parker, eds., *Lyric Poetry*. 226–46.

Tuve, Rosamund. "Theme, Pattern, and Imagery in *Lycidas*." 1957. Rpt. in Patrides, ed., *Milton's Lycidas*. 171–204.

Quintilian. *The Institutio Oratoria of Quintilian*. 4 vols. Trans. H. E. Butler. Loeb Classical Library. Cambridge, MA: Harvard University Press, 1920–22.

Veeser, H. Aram, ed. *The New Historicism*. New York: Routledge, 1989.

Vendler, Helen. *The Art of Shakespeare's Sonnets*. Cambridge, MA: Harvard University Press, 1997.

———. *The Music of What Happens: Poems, Poets, Critics*. Cambridge, MA: Harvard University Press, 1988.

———. *Poems, Poets, Poetry: An Introduction and Anthology*, 2nd ed. Boston: Bedford/St. Martin's, 2002.

Vickers, Brian. *Classical Rhetoric and English Poetry*. 1970. Carbondale: Southern Illinois University Press, 1989.

———, ed. *English Renaissance Literary Criticism*. Oxford: Clarendon Press, 1999.

Virgil. *Eclogues, Georgics, Aeneid I–VI*. Trans. H. Rushton Fairclough. Loeb. New York: G. P. Putnam's Sons, 1916.

von Hallberg, Robert. *Lyric Powers*. Chicago: University Chicago Press, 2008.

Walker, Jeffrey. *Rhetoric and Poetics in Antiquity*. Oxford: Oxford University Press, 2000.

Wall, Wendy. *The Imprint of Gender: Authorship and Publication in the English Renaissance*. Ithaca: Cornell University Press, 1993.

Waswo, Richard. "The Rise of the Vernaculars." Minnis and Johnson, eds., *CHLC* 3:409–16.

Waters, William. *Poetry's Touch: On Lyric Address*. Ithaca: Cornell University Press, 2003.

Wayne, Don E. *Penshurst: The Semiotics of Place and the Poetics of History*. Madison: University Wisconsin Press, 1984.

Wellek, René. "Genre Theory, the Lyric, and Erlebnis." *Discriminations: Further Concepts of Criticism*. New Haven: Yale University Press, 1970. 225–52. Rpt. *Lyric Theory Reader*. Ed. Jackson and Prins, 40–52.

Wellek, René, and Austin Warren. *Theory of Literature*. 3rd ed. 1942. New York: Harcourt, 1977.

Whitney, Geoffrey. *A Choice of Emblems* (London, 1586). *See under* Daly.

Williams, Raymond. *The Country and the City*. New York: Oxford University Press, 1973.

Williamson, Colin. "Structure and Syntax in *Astrophil and Stella*." Rpt. in Kay, ed., *Philip Sidney*. 227–42.

Wilshere, A. D., ed. *Edmundi Abingdonensis Mirour de Seinte Eglyse*. London: Anglo-Norman Text Society, 1982.

Wilson, Gayle Edward. "Jonson's Use of the Bible and the Great Chain of Being in 'To Penshurst.'" *Studies in English Literature* (Houston) 8 (1968): 77–89.

Wilson, Thomas. *The Arte of Rhetorique*. Ed. G. H. Mair. Oxford: Clarendon Press, 1908.

Wimsatt, James I. *Chaucer and His French Contemporaries: Natural Music in the Fourteenth Century*. Toronto: University Toronto Press, 1991.

Wiseman, Rebecca. "Introspection and Self-Evaluation in *Astrophil and Stella*." *Sidney Journal* 30.1 (2012): 51–77.

Womack, Mark. "On the Value of *Lycidas*." *Studies in English Literature* 37 (1997): 119–36.

Woodhouse, A. S. P., and Douglas Bush, ed. *A Variorum Commentary on The Poems of John Milton, Volume Two, The Minor English Poems, Part Two*. New York: Columbia University Press, 1972.

Woods, Susanne. *Lanyer: A Renaissance Woman Poet*. New York: Oxford University Press, 1999.

———. *Natural Emphasis: English Versification from Chaucer to Dryden* San Marino, CA: Huntington Library, 1984.

———, ed. *The Poems of Aemilia Lanyer: Salve Deus Rex Judaeorum*. New York: Oxford University Press, 1993.

Woolf, Rosemary. *The English Religious Lyric in the Middle Ages*. Oxford: Clarendon, 1968.

Wordsworth, William. "Preface to *Lyrical Ballads* (1800)." *Criticism: The Major Statements*. Ed. Charles Kaplan. New York: St. Martin's Press, 1975. 301–20.

Woudhuysen, H. R. *Sir Philip Sidney and the Circulation of Manuscripts*. Oxford: Oxford University Press, 1996.

Wyatt, Sir Thomas. *Collected Poems of Sir Thomas Wyatt*. Ed. Kenneth Muir and Patricia Thomson. Liverpool: Liverpool University Press, 1969.

———. *Sir Thomas Wyatt: The Complete Poems*. Ed. R. A. Rebholz. New Haven: Yale University Press, 1979.

Zarnowiecki, Matthew. *Fair Copies: Reproducing the English Lyric from Tottel to Shakespeare*. Toronto: University Toronto Press, 2014.

Yeats, William Butler. *The Collected Poems of W. B. Yeats*. New York: Macmillan, 1956.

Zickuhr, Kathryn. "New Reading Data from the NEA's Survey of Public Participation in the Arts." *Pew Internet & American Life Project*. October 3, 2013. Available at http://libraries.pewinternet.org/2013/10/02/new-reading-data-from-the-neas-survey-of-public-participation-in-the-arts/.

Index

"An ABC" 80
Abrams, M. H. 12, 42, 153, 163
"accents" 31–32
Accessus ad auctores 20
address 50, 67, 76, 80, 81, 102, 103, 105, 108, 126, 135, 184
addressee *see* address
"Adonais" 158
Adonis 157
Aeneid 58; *see also* Vergil
"affective piety" 62–63, 69, 193*n*15
"affective triad" 18, 29, 40, 97
"Affliction of Daphnis" 152
"Against Women Unconstant" *see* "Madame, for your newefangelnesse"
"Alas, have I not pain enough, my friend" 98–100
Alberti, Leon Battista 27
Alcaeus 170
Alexander, Gavin 32
Alexandria 42, 61, 156
alexandrine 95
allegory 20, 26, 27, 48, 68, 93, 96, 110, 205*n*70, 205*n*73
alliteration 94, 99, 104, 106, 112, 131, 147, 166, 175, 180
Alliterative Revival 192*n*2
Alpers, Paul 164
Alphonso Lanyer 133
amaranthus 205*n*86
Ambrosian quatrain 21
Amores 85; *see also* Ovid
Amoretti and Epithalamion see Spenser, Edmund
anacoluthon 169
anadiplosis 127
anaphora 147
Anglesey (Wales) 169
Anglican Church *see* Church of England
Anglo-Norman French 62; *see also* French (language)
antifeminism *see* misogyny
antithesis 127
Apocalypticism 114

An Apology for Poetry (*The Defence of Poesy*) 36–38, 94
apostrophe 49, 50, 100, 103, 135, 139, 143, 146, 165, 168, 176, 180, 198*n*43
apposition 121
Arcadian Rhetoric 95
aretē 15; *see also* excellence
Arethusa (river) 157, 172
Arion 179
Aristotle 12, 14–17, 18, 30, 36, 46, 51, 56, 147, 184; absence of lyric theory 188*n*10; *On Length and Shortness of Life* 128; *On the Generation of Animals* 128; *Poetics* 14–16, 18, 37, 42, 56, 118; *Rhetoric* 15, 16–17
ars poetriae 21, 25
Art of English Poesy 38–39
Art of Love 21; *see also* Ovid
Art of Poetry (*Ars poetica*) 17–18
Art of Versification 21
Arte of Rhetorique 29, 162
Ascham, Roger 29–30; *The Scholemaster* 29–30
assonance 106, 131
astrology 133
Astrophil and Stella 94–103
Athanasian Creed 117
Athens 12
Attridge, Derek 4, 5, 7, 8, 32, 33, 34, 62, 85, 86, 87, 131, 185–86, 206*appn*3

Bacon, Francis 128–29
ballade 8, 72, 73, 74, 81, 84; *see also* love complaint; rhyme royal
Barker, Arthur 161, 179
Batteux, Charles: *Principles of Literature* 44
beat 4, 5, 32, 86, 87, 88; *see also* Attridge; meter; offbeat; rhythm; scansion
beauty 16, 17, 29, 37, 39, 65, 110–11, 112, 183, 184
being (ontological): being-towards-death 182; being-with-others 174; being-with-others in the world 184
Bible: Apocalypse (5:9, 14:3) 68; Apocalypse (12:1) 66; Daniel 114; 1 Corinthians (13) 123;

217

218 Index

Isaiah (11:1) 70; John (10:1) 174; John (19:26–27) 62; Luke (1:26–38) 70; Luke (5:30) 174; Matthew (5:28) 126; Matthew (16:19) 174; Revelation (7:17, 14:1–4, 19:6–7) 180; Ruth (1:20) 64; Song of Songs (1:5) 64; Song of Songs (2:5) 66, 100; Song of Songs (5:8) 66; Song of Songs (6:9) 66
"biographical fallacy" 97
Bion: "Lament for Adonis" 157–58, 177
Bishops' War 154
Boccaccio, Giovanni 26–27, 160; *Genealogy of the Pagan Gods (Genealogia deorum)* 26–27
Boethius: *Consolation of Philosophy* 73
Boke named the Governour 29
Boleyn, Anne 92, 197*n*12
Book of Common Prayer 122
Book of Hymns 21
Booth, Stephen 115, 117, 123, 131
Boyle, Elizabeth 102, 106
Brewster, Scott 43
Browning, Robert 44
Bruni, Leonardo: *Lives of Dante and Petrarch* 27
bucolic 156
Burrow, Colin 116

Caesar, Augustus 114, 158
Caesar, Julius 159
caesura 94, 151
Cam (river) 173
Cambridge University 9, 102, 154, 173
Camden, William 141
Campion, Thomas: *Observations in the Art of English Poesy* 39
canon, literary 1, 18, 53, 59–60, 73, 80, 192*n*5; history of 187*intrn*4
canonical hours 62
Canterbury Tales 79; *see also* Chaucer, Geoffrey
canzone 23, 24, 25
Canzoniere 27, 90–91, 95
carol 183, 206*codn*2
carpe diem 2, 76, 183
Carthusians 66, 67
Cary, Henry, Lord Hunsdon 133
Catholicism 62, 63, 178; *see also* "affective piety"; Christianity; Eucharist; monasticism
Catullus 57
Cavalcante, Guido 23
Certayne notes of Instruction 6, 30–36
Charles I 154
Chaucer, Geoffrey 8, 28, 30, 33, 37, 38, 60, 73, 74, 75, 77, 84, 99, 101, 161; "An ABC" 80; *Canterbury Tales* 79; "Complaint of Chaucer to His Purse" 8, 78–81; "Gentilesse" 8; *Legend of Good Women* 77; life 78–79; "Madame, for your newefangelnesse" 8, 74–78; *Squire's Tale* 75, 84; *Troilus and Criseyde* 77

chiasm 101
chiasmus 127
A Choice of Emblemes 115–16
Christianity 18, 19, 21, 105, 111, 114, 116, 122, 123, 136, 138, 150, 162, 172, 174, 175, 179, 180; *see also* Catholicism; Church of England; Protestantism
Christ's College, Cambridge 155
Church of England 173
Cicero 18, 29, 53
Cistercians 63; *see also* "affective piety"; meditation; monasticism
Civil War *see* English Civil War
classicism 30, 39, 141
Clifford, Anne, Countess of Dorset 9, 134, 138, 139, 140
Clifford, George, Earl of Cumberland 134
Clifford, Margaret, Countess of Cumberland 9, 134, 135, 139, 140
climax *see gradatio*
close reading 3, 126
closure, poetic 89, 151, 181
Coleridge, Samuel Taylor 56
colonialism 102, 184
comedy 12
commonplace 104
Compassion of the Virgin 62
complaint *see* love complaint
"Complaint of Chaucer to His Purse" 8, 78–81
Comus 155
conceit, Petrarchan 97; *see also* Petrarchism
Confessions of St. Augustine 20, 198*n*58
consolation 162, 179, 181
consonance 106
Cookham Manor (Berkshire) 134
"copula" 127, 200*n*109
Cornwall 178
corporal punishment 96
"corporality," gendered 198*n*50
cosmology 144
coterie 82, 83, 92, 97, 102, 197*n*19, 197*n*21
country house poem 9, 132–51; label 200*n*1
couplet 36, 88, 92, 99, 103, 113, 122, 126, 141, 143, 151
courtly love 23; 73, 75, 76, 111; *see also fin'amor*
courtly lyric 73, 78, 80
Creeds 116
Cromwell, Oliver 3, 154
Crucifixion 64; *see also* Jesus Christ; Passion
Cubeta, Paul 144
Culler, Jonathan 17, 43–44, 46, 47, 49, 50, 56, 64, 66, 76, 80, 90, 100, 105, 135, 136, 168, 177, 184
Cupid 99

dactylic hexameter 53, 156
dance 183
Daniel, Samuel: *A Defence of Ryme* 39
Dante Alighieri 23–26, 27, 28, 52, 117; *On Ver-*

nacular Eloquence (*De vulgari eloquentia*) 23–26, 38, 52; *Purgatorio* 24; *Vita Nova* 23
death 111, 113, 115, 116, 119, 121, 124, 152, 157, 158, 163, 164, 166, 168, 169, 171, 174, 178
deconstruction 45, 48
decorum 16, 24, 30, 31
Defence of Poesy see An Apology for Poetry
Defense and Illustration of the French Language 28
Defense of Helen see Gorgias of Leontini
deictic 8, 45, 64, 103, 105, 118–19, 137, 165
delight *see* pleasure
de Man, Paul 48; *see also* deconstruction
Demetrius 17; *On Style*, 17
demonstrative rhetoric *see* epideictic
demotion 5, 196*n*41
Derrida, Jacques 48, 191*n*16; *see also* deconstruction
"Description of Cookham" 9, 132, 134–41, 142, 152
Devereux, Penelope 94, 96, 198*n*33, 198*n*34
diction 37, 64–65, 98, 103, 131, 149, 173; *see also* lexis; style
Diodati, Charles 154
Discoveries see Jonson, Ben
dispositio 127
dolce stil nuovo 23
dolnik 62, 66, 193*n*7
Donne, John 3, 128
dramatic monologue 43
Drummond, William 142, 148
Dryden, John 3, 54
du Bellay, Joachim: *Defense and Illustration of the French Language* 28
Dubrow, Heather 43
Dunbar, William 78
Duncan-Jones, Katherine 98, 101, 122, 131
Dyer, Edward 115

Early Modern English 29, 33, 39, 121; pronunciation 88, 198*n*54, 200*n*116, 205*n*82
eclogue 53
Eclogues 156, 158–60, 170, 181, 182; *see also* Vergil
Edinburgh 142
education 90, 101; humanist 28, 29, 102; medieval 20–21; Roman 18–19
Education of the Orator (Institutio oratoria) 18–19
Edward III 78, 79
elegy 9, 137, 152; 156–61, 162
Eliot, T. S. 15, 44–45, 178
Elizabeth I 29, 53, 94, 106, 142
elocutio 127
eloquence 19, 29, 37, 46, 55
Elyot, Thomas 29; *The Boke named the Governour* 29
emblem book 115–16, 147, 202*n*47
emotion 13, 15, 33, 35, 45, 54, 57, 71, 72, 75, 83, 84, 87, 88, 89, 91, 93, 94, 96, 100, 102, 109, 117, 125, 126, 131, 138–39, 140, 141, 144, 151, 153, 160, 162, 163, 167, 171, 174, 178, 182
Empson, William 58, 117, 156
enargia 123
encomium 109, 132, 143
end-stopping 94; *see also* enjambment
energia 123
English (language) 30, 37–38, 114, 200*n*116; *see also* Early Modern English; Middle English; Old English
English Civil War 154, 156, 182
English Revolution *see* English Civil War
enjambment 94, 99, 101, 103, 113, 124, 149, 166, 175
envoy 73, 78, 80
epic 12, 53, 156
epideictic 16–17, 29, 30, 37, 51, 69, 75, 88, 97, 109, 112, 125, 139, 143, 146, 149, 174, 189*n*65, 189*n*66, 199*n*74; ancient topoi and medieval lyric 196*n*2
epideixis 17, 50, 200*n*100; *see also* epideictic
epigram 57, 132, 141, 149; epigrammatic "point" 52, 103, 151
epigraph 57
"Epistle to persuade a young gentleman to marriage" 110
epitaph 120
epizeuxis 166
Erasmus, Desiderius: "Epistle to persuade a young gentleman to marriage" 110
Erlebnis 45, 54
estate poem *see* country house poem
Eucharist 67
excellence 15, 19, 39, 141, 153; *see also* value, poetic
existentialism 164
"Th'expense of spirit in a waste of shame" 125–31
expressive theory 11, 44, 46, 55, 57, 126, 163

fame 116, 170
Favorite Poem Project 6
feign 202*n*33
feminism 201; *see also* "corporality," gendered; misogyny
Ficino, Marsilio 26
fiction 20, 27, 43, 45, 102, 163, 191*n*34
figures of speech 17, 21, 35, 39, 200*n*110
figures of thought 17, 39
fin'amor 23
Fineman, Joel 130
Florence (Italy) 23, 26
flowers 111, 157, 158, 173, 176–77, 206*n*89
formalism 47, 187*ch*1*n*10
formalist theory *see* objective theory
Forman, Simon 133
Forms, theory of 13; *see also* Plato
Fortune 77
fourteeners 115
Fowler, Alastair 51–54, 57, 84

Franciscans 63; *see also Meditations on the Life of Christ*
Fraunce, Abraham: *Arcadian Rhetoric* 95, 197*n*26
Frederick II 23
French (language) 23, 184; *see also* Anglo-Norman French
"From fairest creatures we desire increase" 109–13
frontispiece 141
Frye, Northrop 46–47, 184
funeral 177, 206*n*89
"fusion of horizons" 63, 65, 105, 115, 116, 120, 122, 128, 175

Gadamer, Hans-Georg 63, 105, 205*n*85; *see also* "fusion of horizons"
Gallus, C. Cornelius 159
Gamage, Barbara 142, 148, 149
Gascoigne, George: *Certayne notes of Instruction* 6, 30–36
Gaunt, John of 78, 79
Genealogy of the Pagan Gods (*Genealogia deorum*) 26–27
genre: hierarchy 53, 192*n*54; label 53; modulation 52, 57; repertoire 51, 90, 128, 132; theory of 41–42, 51–54, 126
"Gentilesse" 8, 73
Geoffrey of Monmouth: *History of the Kings of Britain* 81
georgic 53, 132, 145
Georgics 146; *see also* Vergil
German idealism 56
Glossary of Literary Terms 42
Golden Age 132, 145, 146, 202*n*43
Golden Treasury 82
Gorgias of Leontini 14, 47, 124; *see also* sophists
gradatio 95, 103, 197*n*26
grammarians, Roman 31, 188*n*31, 192*n*54
Great Chain of Being 144, 148
Great Vowel Shift 193*n*23
Greek (language) 18, 28, 29, 30, 155, 156
Greene, Roland 43
gripe 198*n*40
Guarino da Verona 27
Guinizelli, Guido 23
Guittone d'Arezzo 23
Gumbrecht, Hans Ulrich 198*n*56

"Happy ye leaves when as those lily hands" 102–4
Hardison, O. B. 30
Harington, John 96
Hathaway, Anne 107
Hazlitt, William 153
heart 96, 197*n*28
Hebrides (Scotland) 178
Hegel, G. W. F.: *Lectures on Aesthetics* 43–44, 190*n*10

Henry, Prince of Wales 148–49
Henry IV 78, 80, 81
Henry VIII 81, 82, 92–93, 121
Herbert, George 2
Heroides 20, 21
Herrick, Robert 57–58
hierarchy 144; generic 192*n*54
Hilarius 21; *Book of Hymns* 21
historicism 7, 49, 50, 60, 91, 133, 187*ch*1*n*10, 191*n*25, 201*n*5
Homer 12, 13, 19, 27, 46, 156, 184
Horace 17–18, 36, 53, 141, 147; *Art of Poetry* (*Ars poetica*) 17–18; *Odes* 113, 116
hospitality 147–48
Hours of the Cross 62
humanism: English 6, 29–30, 36, 102, 141; Italian 6, 26–28, 36; Renaissance 18, 30, 113
hunting 93
hymn 21–22
hyperbaton 168, 171
hyperbole 49, 51, 66, 77, 80, 112, 135, 192*n*43

"I" 44, 64, 72, 82–83, 90, 96, 108, 119, 130, 165, 172
"I sing of a maiden" 69–71
iambic pentameter 8, 30, 31, 33, 34, 77, 85, 86, 87, 88, 89, 99, 141, 143, 161, 165, 169
"Ich am of Irlaunde" 9, 183–84
iconography 66, 67
identity, social 1, 124
Idylls 156–57, 158
Imago pietatis 67
imitation (of models) 19, 29; *see also mimēsis*
immortality, poetic 95, 104, 106, 113–17, 114–15, 141, 199*n*80
"In a tabernacle of a toure" 65–69
Indo-European (language) 118
International Phonetic Alphabet (IPA) 6
inventio 96, 127
invocation 166
Ireland 102, 106, 184
"The Irish Dancer" *see* "Ich am of Irlaunde"
Italian (language) 23

James I 142, 147, 148–49
Jauss, Hans Robert 199*n*82
Jesus Christ 62, 63, 67, 69, 70, 174, 180
Johnson, Saumuel 161, 163, 206*n*102; *Lives of the Poets* 153
Jonson, Ben 9, 132; life 141–42; *Timber, or, Discoveries* 143, 147; "To Penshurst" 9, 132, 141–51, 152; *Workes of Benjamin Jonson* 141
Judaism 114
Judgment Day *see* Last Judgment
Juvenal 145

Kant, Immanuel 48, 56, 178
Keats, John 158; "To Autumn" 145
Kennedy, George 16

Kerrigan, John 108, 125
kharjas 22
kind *see* genre, theory of
King, Edward 9, 163, 167, 169, 170, 182; memorial volume 155, 168

labor 147
"Lak of Stedfastnesse" 73
Lamb, Charles 97, 101
"Lament for Adonis" 157–58, 177
"Lament for Bion" 158, 168, 170
Lancastrian 78; propaganda 81, 195*n*20
Landino, Cristoforo 26, 27
Lanyer, Aemilia 9, 132, 133–41, 142; "Description of Cookham" 9, 132, 134–41, 142, 152; life 133–34; *Salve Deus Rex Judaeorum* 133, 134
Last Judgment 105, 114, 116, 117, 122
Latin 18, 20, 22, 24, 25, 27, 28, 29, 30, 62, 114, 155; classical pronunciation 188*n*30; mispronunciation 189*n*62; Vulgar 21
Laud, William, Archishop of Canterbury 156, 175
laus Marie 69
Lectures on Aesthetics 43–44
Legend of Good Women 77
Lentini, Giacomo da 23
"Let me not to the marriage of true minds" 122–25
lexis 13, 35; *see also* diction
Lindley, David 43
liturgy 66
Lives of Dante and Petrarch 27
Lives of the Poets 153
locus amoenus 137, 145
"logocentrism" 191*n*16
London 78, 79, 102, 141, 147, 153–54; dialect 198*n*59
"Longinus" 175; *On the Sublime* 18, 205*n*81
love complaint 9; 72–89, 100, 106
love sonnet *see* sonnet
A Lover's Complaint 107
"Loving in truth, and fain in verse my love to show" 95–98
lust 129–30
"Lycidas" 9, 152–53, 155, 156, 158, 159, 160–82; external form 161; internal form 161
lyre 42, 166
lyric: brief definition of 1; definitions of 42–43; history and theory of 190*n*2, 190*n*10; lack of theory by Greeks 41; "lyric hyperbole" 192*n*43; "lyric present" 64, 102, 105, 106, 137; "lyric reading" 191*n*25; Marian lyric 7, 61–71, 194*n*31

Machaut, Guillaume de 72, 74–75
Machen, Arthur 153
"Madame, for your newefangelnesse" 74–78
Malone, Edmond 108
Mantuan 160
manuscript 59, 60–61, 65, 66, 67, 71, 74, 80, 82, 83, 92; Arundel-Harington MS 97; Bodleian MS Douce 322 66, 67, 69, 193*n*26; Bodleian MS Rawlinson D.913 183; Bodleian MS Rawlinson poet. 172 198*n*34; British Library MS Add. 17492 (Devonshire Manuscript) 82; British Library MS Add. 37049 66, 194*n*27; British Library MS Egerton 2711 89, 197*n*16; British Library MS Harley 2253 61, 73; Lambeth Palace MS 853 193*n*26; Trinity College, Cambridge MS R.3.4 155, 168, 176, 181, 203*n*11
Maria Misericordia 68
Marian lyric 7, 61–71, 194*n*31; *see also* Virgin Mary
Marot, Clément 203*n*30
marriage 102, 111, 122–23
Martial 145, 150
Marvell, Andrew 2, 3
Marxism 144, 201*n*5, 202*n*32
Mary *see* Virgin Mary
A Maske Presented at Ludlow Castle see Comus
masterpiece 59
Matthew of Vendôme: *Art of Versification* 21
"meaning effect" 176; *see also* "presence effect"
medicine 128–29, 204*n*40
meditation 62, 63, 64, 69
Meditations on the Life of Christ 63; authorship 193*n*16
"melic" 25
melos 46–47
Merchant Taylors' School (London) 102
Meres, Francis 53
Metamorphoses 113, 116, 169
metaphor 112, 118, 120, 121, 122, 123
meter 4, 13, 14, 17, 19, 21, 30, 31, 33, 38, 53, 77, 82, 85, 95, 103, 117, 121, 123–24, 131, 165, 179; accentual-syllabic 6, 31–34, 38, 60; alliterative 60; duple 5, 33; free 32; quantitative 21, 25, 31, 38, 39; triple 5, 33; *see also* prosody; tension, metrical
Middle Ages 20, 73, 90, 183
Middle English 7, 60, 75; pronunciation 65, 193*n*6, 193*n*23, 193*n*25; syllabic final *e* 33
Middle French 72, 73, 74, 75; *see also* French (language)
Middle High German 23
Mill, John Stuart 46, 55
Milton, John 9, 164, 183; "L'Allegro" 153; *Comus* 155; "Epitaphium Damonis" 154; life 153–55; "Lycidas" 9, 152, 155, 156, 158, 159, 160–82; *Of Education* 205*n*81; *Paradise Lost* 153, 155; "Il Penseroso" 153; *Poems of Mr. John Milton* 156, 175; *Samson Agonistes* 153
Milton, John (father of poet) 153
Milton, Sara 154
mimēsis 12–13, 14, 15, 18, 25
mimetic theory 12–13, 14, 15–16, 18, 36–37, 46, 54–55, 125, 126, 163

Index

Mincius (river) 172
Mirour de Seinte Eglyse (*Mirror of Holy Church*) 62, 64
Mirror of the Church (*Speculum Ecclesie*) 62, 63, 64
miscellany (manuscript compilation) 61, 73
misogyny 73, 77, 81, 134
modal auxiliary 121
mode 52
Model of Poesy 39
modernism 55
Molesworth, Charles 146
monasticism 62–64; *see also* Carthusians; Cistercians; Franciscans
monody 162
mood *see* emotion
Moscus: "Lament for Bion" 158, 170
Mt. Helicon 103, 166
Mulcaster, Richard 101
muse 96, 103, 115, 135, 157, 158, 160, 166, 169, 170
musicality 191n32

nature 111, 112, 118, 119, 121, 123, 137, 139, 140, 144, 172, 177; *see also* flowers; pathetic fallacy
Neoplatonism 26, 27, 111
New Arcadia 106
New Criticism 47–48, 49, 50, 56, 97, 107, 161, 163, 174, 191n25, 204n46; *see also* formalism
New Formalism 50; *see also* formalism
New Historicism 50, 187ch1n10
newefangelnesse 75, 84, 195n8
Norbrook, David 142
Norman Conquest 7, 60, 184
"Not marble, nor the gilded monument" 113–17
"Now goth sonne under wode" 61–65

objective theory 14, 56, 164
Obsequies by mourning friends ... for Edward King see King, Edward, memorial volume
Observations in the Art of English Poesy 39
Occitan 22–23
octave 95–96, 99, 101
Octavian *see* Caesar, Augustus
octosyllabic 22
"Of on ic wille singen that is makeles" 194n39
offbeat 4, 32; double 5; implied 113, 140; virtual 179, 198n53; *see also* Attridge; beat; meter; rhythm; scansion
Old Arcadia 199n61
Old English 60, 65, 206n98
On Length and Shortness of Life 128
On Liberal Manners (*De ingenui moribus*) 27
On Style 17
On the Generation of Animals 128
On the Sublime 18, 205n81
On Vernacular Eloquence (*De vulgari eloquentia*) 23–26, 38, 52; *see also* Alighieri, Dante

opsis 46–47
oratory 12, 37, 55, 189n65; *see also* rhetoric
Orpheus 158
otium 167
ottava rima 161, 175, 181
Ovid: *Amores* 85; *Art of Love* 21; *Heroides* 20, 21; *Metamorphoses* 113, 116, 169
Oxford English Dictionary (*OED*) 42, 81, 129–30
oxymoron 112

Palgrave, Francis T.: *Golden Treasury* 82
panegyric 146
parody 58, 90
passion *see* emotion
The Passion 62, 63, 67, 68, 136
pastoral 9, 132, 137, 152, 153, 156–61; names as generic markers 203n20; *see also* elegy
"pathetic fallacy" 100, 137, 139, 157, 168; *see also* emotion; nature
pathos 166
patriarchy 147; *see also* feminism
patronage 73, 83, 135, 142–43, 149
Pattison, Mark 153
Penshurst Place (Kent) 142, 145–46, 147
perception 5, 33, 124
performance 50, 166
persona 43, 44, 95, 98, 163, 164, 174
personification 96, 123, 173
Peterson, Douglas 127
petitionary poem 78
Petrarch, Francis 26, 27, 30, 90–91, 95, 109, 160, 191n34, 199n64; *Rime* 190: 92; *see also* Canzoniere
Petrarchism 90, 91, 96, 112, 130
Phaedrus 14
Phoebus Apollo 163, 171, 172
phonetics 131, 166
Pindar 203n16
Pinsky, Robert 6
Plato 15, 27, 184; *Phaedrus* 14; *Republic* 12–14, 56; *see also* Forms, theory of; Neoplatonism
pleasure 13, 14, 15, 19, 27, 30–31, 35, 55, 136, 147, 173
Poe, Edgar Allan: "The Poetic Principle" 46
Poems of Mr. John Milton, Both English and Latin 156
"Poetic Principle" 46
Poetics 14–16, 18, 37, 42, 118
poetics 14, 37, 40
poetry, decline in reading of 1, 187intrn1; defense of 6, 26, 27–28, 38; handbooks 21, 25; theory of *see* expressive theory; mimetic theory; objective theory; rhetorical theory
Poetry in America 6
poiësis 58
polyptoton 101, 127
Ponsby, William 102
poststructuralism 45, 48
"poulter's measure" 36

Pound, Ezra 44
pragmatic theory *see* rhetorical theory
Preface to *Lyrical Ballads* 44, 127
prescriptivism 37, 42
"presence effect" 45, 105, 119, 165 166, 176, 198n56
present tense 119–20, 165; *see also* "lyric present"
presentation, mode of 12, 42
Prick of Conscience 60
Principles of Literature 44
printing 61, 74, 82, 83, 102, 107, 141, 155, 156, 195n23, 197n19, 198n50
Priscian 188n31
"procreation" sonnets 108, 109, 113, 130
prodigy house 143, 150
promotion 5, 196n44
prosody 30, 31, 82; beat 4; classical system of 4, 20, 21, 25, 30, 31, 39; *see also* Attridge; meter; scansion
prosopopoeia 48
Protestantism 94, 150, 178
Provençal *see* Occitan
proverb 126
pun 65, 70, 131, 198n33, 206n98
punctuation 82, 93–94, 113, 125, 205n68
Puttenham, George 91, 162; *Art of English Poesy* 38–39

quatrain 22, 62, 92, 106, 112, 120, 121, 122, 126
Quintilian 18–19, 36, 143; *Education of the Orator* (*Institutio oratoria*) 18–19

Ransom, John Crowe 153, 161
razos 22; *see also* troubadours
refrain 66, 68, 75, 76, 80
Renaissance 18, 19, 20, 28, 36, 37, 39, 45, 73, 81, 90, 91, 92, 96, 98, 107, 109, 110, 111, 112, 123, 141, 143, 147, 158, 160, 183, 199n64; misunderstanding of Greek theory 41
Republic 12
Restoration 154
Resurrection 67
rhetoric 6, 16–17, 55, 75, 90, 91, 110, 123, 127, 162; classical 11, 18; deliberative 16, 125; epideictic 16–17, 125; forensic 16, 125; *see also* epideictic
Rhetoric 15, 16–17
rhetorical figures *see* figures of speech; figures of thought
rhetorical theory 11, 66, 69, 125, 126, 163
rhubarb 99
rhyme 21, 25–26, 35, 38, 60, 65, 93, 95, 96, 103, 106, 113, 121, 161, 165, 166, 167; feminine 95, 136, 173, 175, 178; link with meaning 204n56
rhyme royal 8, 36, 72, 81, 84, 89, 107, 194n1
rhythm 5, 31, 86, 88, 100, 124, 149; *see also* Attridge
Rich, Penelope *see* Devereux, Penelope
Richard II 79

"riding rhyme" 36
Rime sparse see *Canzoniere*; Petrarch, Francis
Ringler, William 101
Ripa, Cesare 202n47
ritual 50–51, 80, 135, 136, 177, 191n34
rivers, classical myth 205n70; *see also* Arethusa, Mincius
Robbins, R. H. 183
Roet, Philippa 79
Roman Empire 113–14, 116; Republic 158
Romance languages 21
Romanticism 2, 7, 11, 43, 44, 45, 48, 55, 158
Rouse, A. L. 133
Ruskin, John 100, 153, 205n79
Russell, William, of Thornhaugh 134

Sacks, Peter 178
Sackville, Richard, Earl of Dorset 134
St. Ambrose 21–22
St. Augustine: *Confessions* 20, 198n58
St. Bernard of Clairvaux 63
St. Edmund of Abingdon 62, 63, 64, 65; *Mirror of the Church* (*Speculum Ecclesie*) 62, 63
St. Jerome 20
St. Paul 123
St. Paul's School (London) 154
St. Peter 163, 174
Salutati, Coluccio 27
Salve Deus Rex Judaeorum 133, 134
Sannazaro, Jacopo 203n30
Sappho 17, 158, 170
satire 132, 143, 149, 150, 160–61, 174
Scaliger, Julius Caesar 36, 162
scansion 32–33, 34, 77, 85–89, 99–100, 104, 112, 117, 124, 131, 140, 141, 165, 169, 171, 179; symbols 5, 123, 131, 185–86, 206codn3; *see also* meter
Scarry, Elaine 110, 183, 184
Scholemaster 29–30
Scott, William: *Model of Poesy* 39
Servius 158
sestet 95–96; 99, 101
sexuality 108, 128–29, 199n72; heterosexual 109, 123; same-sex 109, 199n72
Shake-speares Sonnets see Shakespeare, William
Shakespeare, William 9, 107–31, 133, 155; life 107, 142; *Love's Labor's Lost* 130; 1609 Quarto (Q) 107–8, 109, 110, 111, 113, 122; Sonnet 1 ("From fairest creatures we desire increase") 109–13; Sonnet 9 130; Sonnet 10 110, 130; Sonnet 18 ("Shall I compare thee to a summer's day?") 109; Sonnet 55 ("Not marble, nor the gilded monument") 113–17; Sonnet 65 115; Sonnet 73 ("That time of year thou mayst in me behold") 118–22; Sonnet 81 115, 116; Sonnet 94 126; Sonnet 116 ("Let me not to the marriage of true minds") 122–25; Sonnet 123 115; Sonnet 129 ("Th'expense of

spirit in a waste of shame") 125–31; Sonnet 130 90; *Sonnets* 107, 108, 114, 117, 125, 126, 127, 129
"Shall I compare thee to a summer's day?" 109
Shelley, Percy Bysshe: "Adonais" 158
"shifters" *see* deictic
Sicilian school 23
Sidney, Henry 142
Sidney, Mary, Countess of Pembroke 3, 94, 150, 197n19
Sidney, Philip 8, 9, 36–38, 53, 94–101, 103, 106, 108, 109, 115, 125, 142, 150, 184; *An Apology for Poetry* (*The Defence of Poesy*) 36–38, 94; *Astrophil and Stella* 94–103, 197n19; *AS* 1 ("Loving in truth, and fain in verse my love to show"): 95–98; *AS* 14 ("Alas, have I not pain enough, my friend"): 98–100; *AS* 31 ("With how sad steps, O moon, thou climb-s't the skies"): 100–1; Certain Sonnets 199n61; life 94, 97–98; *New Arcadia* 106; *Old Arcadia* 199n61
Sidney, Robert 9, 142–43, 145, 146, 148, 149
Sidney, William 142
Skeat, Walter W. 74
Socrates 12
song 45, 46, 58, 74–75, 80, 89, 162, 166
Songes and Sonettes see Tottel's Miscellany
sonnet 9, 23, 36, 52, 90–131; English form 92, 93, 103, 113, 122; Italian form 93, 103, 113; sequences 199n64; Spenserian form 103; *see also* couplet; octave; quatrain; sestet; *volta* (turn)
sophists 12
sovereignty 138
Spain 22, 178
speaker 42–43, 110; *see also* persona
Spenser, Edmund 8, 53, 101–6, 109, 125, 156; *Amoretti—Am* 1 ("Happy ye leaves when as those lily hands") 102–4, *Am* 33 104, *Am* 74 102, 106, *Am* 75 ("One day I wrote her name upon the strand") 104–6; "Astrophel" 204n30; *Epithalamion* 102; *The Faerie Queene* 101; life 101–2; pronunciation 198n54, 198n59
Speroni, Sperone: *Dialogue on Languages (Dialogo delle lingue)* 28
sponte sua 145, 146
Squire's Tale 75
stanza 26, 36
Steevens, George 121
stewardship 146, 149
Stewart, Susan 45
Stowe, John 74
Stratford-upon-Avon 107, 120
stress, linguistic 31–32, 99, 123–24, 186, 206codn4
style 15, 16, 17, 24, 27, 29, 53, 83, 90, 131, 143, 159, 168; courtly 94; plain 65, 94
subgenre 2, 3, 8, 52–53, 58, 78, 128
subjectivity 43–45, 50, 130

sublimity 175, 178
subsequence, "dark lady" 108–9, 125; "fair youth" 108–9, 122
Surrey, Henry Howard, Earl of 92, 115
syllabus 192n5
symbolism 69, 76–77; color 75, 182; number 69, 138, 146; rose 111; sun 180, 206n98; typology 69
synonymia 127
syntax 70, 76, 96, 99, 101, 103, 117, 120, 127, 131, 135, 143–44, 149–50, 151, 168, 170

tekhnē 15
tekhnē psychagōgia 14
tension, metrical 33, 112, 151, 165, 169, 171, 204n54
"That time of year thou mayst in me behold" 118–22
Theocritus 9, 158, 169; *Idylls* 156–57, 158
Theophrastus: *On Style* 17
"They flee from me that sometime did me seek" 8, 84–89, 91
Thorpe, Thomas 107, 108
Tillyard, E. M. W. 163
time 64, 105, 114, 115, 119, 120, 123, 181
"To Autumn" 145
"To Penshurst" 9, 132, 141–51
"To yow, my purse, and to noon other wight" *see* "Complaint of Chaucer to His Purse"
topos see commonplace
Tottel, Richard 82, 87, 88, 196n36, 196n46
Tottel's Miscellany 31, 82, 83, 84, 115, 196n36, 196n46
tragedy 12, 46
translatio imperii 114
triangulation *see* address
Trinity MS *see* manuscript, Trinity College, Cambridge MS R.3.4
trobairitz 22
Troilus and Criseyde 77
troubadour 22, 83
"Truth" 73
"turn" *see volta*
Tuve, Rosamund 162, 174

Valla Lorenzo 28
value, aesthetic *see* value, poetic
value, literary *see* value, poetic
value, poetic 2, 3, 26, 27, 49, 153
Vendler, Helen 54–58, 124–25, 126, 127
Vergerio, Pier Paolo: *On Liberal Manners (De ingenui moribus)* 27
Vergil 9, 19, 20, 27, 53, 58, 145, 156, 158, 170, 172; *Aeneid* 58; *Eclogues* 156, 158–60, 170, 181, 182; *Georgics* 146
vernacular 6, 20, 24, 26, 27, 38, 63
versification *see* prosody
vertutes 19; *see also* excellence
Vickers, Brian 17, 127
vidas 22; *see also* troubadours

Virgin Mary 62–71, 80, 81; cult of 66, 194*n*31; *see also* Compassion of the Virgin
Vita Nova (*The New Life*) 23
vituperation 109
vocation, poetic 170–71
voice 45, 49, 50, 100, 164, 173, 175, 184, 206*n*96
voicing *see* voice
volta 95
Vulgar Latin 21

Warton, Joseph 153, 178
Waters, William 105
Wayne, Don 144, 150
Westminster Abbey (London) 142
Westminster School (London) 141
Whitney, Geoffrey: *A Choice of Emblemes* 115–16
"Whoso list to hunt, I know where is an hind" 92–94
Wife of Bath 99

Wilson, Thomas 29; *Arte of Rhetorique* 29, 127, 162
Wilton House (Wiltshire) 94
Wingfield, Susan Bertie, Countess of Kent 133
"With how sad steps, O moon, thou climbs't the skies": 100–1
women 147; *see also* feminism; misogyny
Words for Music Perhaps 183
Wordsworth, William: Preface to *Lyrical Ballads* 44, 127
Workes of Benjamin Jonson 141
Wyatt, Thomas 8, 31, 81–85, 88, 91–94; life 92, 196*n*7, 196*n*8; references to courtiers 197*n*10; "They flee from me that sometime did me seek" 8; 84–89, 91; "Whoso list to hunt, I know where is an hind" 92–94

Yeats, William Butler: *Words for Music Perhaps* 183

www.ingramcontent.com/pod-product-compliance
Lightning Source LLC
Chambersburg PA
CBHW032050300426
44116CB00007B/681